The Event of the Good

The Event of the Good

Reading Levinas in a Levinasian Way

Edited by

CHRISTOPHER BUCKMAN,
MELISSA BRADLEY, JACK MARSH,
and JAMES McLACHLAN

Cover image: © Tomas Castelazo, www.tomascastelazo.com / Wikimedia Commons / CC BY – SA 4.0.

Published by State University of New York Press, Albany

© 2025 State University of New York

All rights reserved

Printed in the United States of America

No part of this book may be used or reproduced in any manner whatsoever without written permission. No part of this book may be stored in a retrieval system or transmitted in any form or by any means including electronic, electrostatic, magnetic tape, mechanical, photocopying, recording, or otherwise without the prior permission in writing of the publisher.

Links to third-party websites are provided as a convenience and for informational purposes only. They do not constitute an endorsement or an approval of any of the products, services, or opinions of the organization, companies, or individuals. SUNY Press bears no responsibility for the accuracy, legality, or content of a URL, the external website, or for that of subsequent websites.

EU GPSR Authorised Representative:
Logos Europe, 9 rue Nicolas Poussin, 17000, La Rochelle, France
contact@logoseurope.eu

For information, contact State University of New York Press, Albany, NY
www.sunypress.edu

Library of Congress Cataloging-in-Publication Data

Names: Buckman, Christopher, 1978– editor. | Bradley, Melissa (Teacher), editor. | Marsh, Jack (Jack E.), editor. | McLachlan, James, editor.
Title: The event of the good : reading Levinas in a Levinasian way / edited by Christopher Buckman, Melissa Bradley, Jack Marsh, and James McLachlan.
Description: Albany : State University of New York Press, [2025] | Includes bibliographical references and index.
Identifiers: LCCN 2024049497 | ISBN 9798855802689 (hardcover : alk. paper) | ISBN 9798855802696 (ebook) | ISBN 9798855802672 (pbk. : alk. paper)
Subjects: LCSH: Lévinas, Emmanuel—Ethics. | Lévinas, Emmanuel—Criticism and interpretation.
Classification: LCC B2430.L484 E896 2025 | DDC 194—dc23/eng/20250107
LC record available at https://lccn.loc.gov/2024049497

Contents

Introduction. The Event of the Good   1
    James M. McLachlan

Path I. Reading Levinas

1. Reading Levinas in a Levinasian Way   11
    Jean-Michel Salanskis

2. Levinas in North America Today: Richard A. Cohen's Contributions   31
    Jack Marsh and Christopher L. Southland

3. Book Review: *Ethics, Exegesis and Philosophy: Interpretation after Levinas*   47
    Robert Gibbs

4. *Cohenfest*: Did Rich Cohen Eat Al Lingis's Octopus?   53
    Don Ihde

5. Cohen as Philosopher   61
    Marie-Anne Lescourret

6. Book Review: *Elevations*   71
    Edith Wyschogrod

Path II. Ethical Exegesis

7. Post-Levinasian Sketch of Ambivalent Relations: Between
   Art, Criticism, and Ethics — 77
   Rossitsa Varadinova Borkowski

8. Rhythm and Sense in the Philosophy of Levinas — 95
   Masato Goda

9. After the End of Philosophy: Ethical Exegesis and
   Ethical Body — 105
   Irina Poleshchuk

10. Senseless Kindness, the Church, and the Betrayal
    of Mercy in *Don Quixote* — 127
    Steven Shankman

11. Art of the Uncanny: Seeing with Cohen and Levinas — 143
    Jolanta Saldukaitytė

Path III. Ontological Contests

12. Review: Levinas's Reading of Spinoza — 169
    Jacques J. Rozenberg

13. Imagine Freedom — 181
    Brunella Antomarini

14. Sovereignty in Levinas and Hobbes — 201
    Christopher Buckman

15. On Ethics: Levinas and Badiou in the Post-Postmodern
    Condition — 215
    Chung-Hsiung Lai

16. On the Importance of Importance: Emmanuel Levinas on
    the First Challenge to Jewish Thought Today — 237
    Richard Sugarman

17. Levinas and the Ethics of Sacrifice: Reading "Dying
    For . . ." Adverbially   257
    Sandor Goodhart

Path IV. Ethical Religion

18. The Small Goodness Never Wins, But Is Never Defeated:
    On How Emmanuel Levinas Finds Inspirtation in
    Vasily Grossman for His Vision of a Humane Society   271
    Roger Burggraeve

19. Sympathy for the Devil: On Richard Cohen's Levinasian
    Meditations on Sartre and Theology   293
    James M. McLachlan

20. Incarnate Religion   317
    Mark K. Spencer

21. The Ethical Event: A Phenomenology of חסד *Chesed* for
    Asylum-seeking Refugees   337
    Devorah Wainer

Conclusion: Cohen Responds

Response to Contributors   361
    Richard A. Cohen

List of Contributors   381

Index   387

Introduction

The Event of the Good

JAMES M. MCLACHLAN

At the beginning of *Totality and Infinity*, Emmanuel Levinas describes the event of being as the ontological event that casts us into an objective order from which there is no escape. "The ontological event that takes form in this black light is a casting into movement of beings hitherto anchored in their identity, a mobilization of absolutes, by an objective order from which there is no escape" (*Totality and Infinity*, 21). Escape from ontology, from being, is a Levinasian theme stretching back at least to Levinas's first major work *On Escape* (1935), where he declares his intention to escape ontologism. This was still the Levinasian project in 1973. For him, there is the event of being but also the transcendence to the "otherwise than being." The question is: What is being's other? "If transcendence has meaning, it can only signify the fact that the event of being, the *esse*, the essence passes over to what is other than being. But what is Being's other?" (*Otherwise Than Being*, 2).

In 1960, Levinas asked: "Do the particular beings yield their truth in a whole in which their exteriority vanishes? Or, on the contrary, is the ultimate event of being enacted in the outburst of this exteriority? Our initial question now assumes this form" (*TI*, 24). Escape from ontologism is, for him, the ethical event, the affirmation of exteriority: he says it is at the basis of the intention of language. I speak always to another; this is the basis of all generalizations about the world around me. Ontology comes later in the generalizing of the world for thought, and the most general of all things is being, the Totality in *Totality and Infinity*. Language requires exteriority, and this would mean that exteriority is prior to being. Thus, the ethical event is more primordial than the event of being. "The ethical event at the basis of generalization is the underlying intention of language. The relation with the Other does not only stimulate, provoke generalization, does not only supply it with the pretext and the occasion (this no one has ever contested), but is this generalization itself" (*TI*, 173).

It is not the mediation of the sign that forms signification but the primordial event that precedes the ontological event. The primordial event is the ethical event, the face to face, which allows for the emergence of linguistic signification. This is the essence of language and of thought that the other calls to us: this is the good beyond being. "It is the contrary that must be affirmed; it is not the mediation of the sign that forms signification, but signification (whose primordial event is the face to face) that makes the sign function possible. The primordial essence of language is to be sought not in the corporeal operation that discloses it to me and to others and, in the recourse to language, builds up a thought, but in the presentation of meaning" (*TI*, 206).

The event of the good is the foundation of signification and the event of infinity. Infinity doesn't present itself to transcendental thought: it presents itself in the other. It is the other who faces me and puts me in question. The Other demands my response, activates my freedom, in that they call into being my interiority. This is the ethical event of sociality that calls forth an inward discourse. The face is not constituted by consciousness as are other beings. It reveals infinity. For Levinas signification is infinity, the Other whose demand calls me into question but also activates my freedom. Levinas indicates that the condition of possibility of the relation to the other does not entail metaphysical idealism, as in Kant, but rather transcends its boundary. It is the ethical event that commands the inward discourse.

> Signification is the Infinite, but infinity does not present itself to a transcendental thought, nor even to meaningful activity, but presents itself in the Other; the Other faces me and puts me in question and obliges me by his essence qua infinity. . . And the epiphany that is produced as a face is not constituted as are all other beings, precisely because it "reveals" infinity. Signification is infinity, that is, the Other. The intelligible is not a concept, but an intelligence. Signification precedes *Sinngebung*, and rather than justifying idealism, marks its limit. (TI 207)

The social relation is not a relation like any other produced in being: it is the ultimate event. When I put it in words, I bring it into being as the said; I lose the immediacy of the event, the "face to face" relation. And yet the very fact that I tell this truth to another brings it back. Language is founded on sociality. The ethical event is not a mystical event in which all of being is revealed but is an event that repeats in the everyday. The transcendent is an everyday event but not an empirical one. It is metaphysical. The social relation differs from other relations produced in being. It is the event of the good, the ultimate event: "The very utterance by which I state it and whose claim to truth, postulating a total reflection, refutes the unsurpassable character of the face to face relation, nonetheless confirms it by the very fact of stating this truth—of telling it to the Other" (*TI*, 221).

Meaning, cognition, and knowing all begin with the ethical event. In the *Il y a*, the indeterminacy of Being before and against individuation, there is no meaning—only arbitrariness. It is the Other who invests me with freedom and the possibility of meaning.[1] The *Il y a* is of itself arbitrary, which is both what is unfree about it but also its potential. The event of separation itself is arbitrary. "Freedom, the event of separation in arbitrariness which constitutes the I, at the same time maintains the relation with the exteriority that morally resists every appropriation and every totalization in being" (*TI*, 302). Meaning transcends the *Il y a* as the arbitrary and meaningless. The transcendent event of the good breaks with nothingness into meaning through the face to face, the call of the other. This interpretation determines the way Levinas understands the event of creation ex nihilo.

Levinas doesn't see chaos in the same way as, say, Bergson does, who sees it as as a different type of order. It is chaos of the *il y a* that precedes order or refuses order.[2] The metaphysical event, the question of the other coming to me, is what invests me with freedom and creativity. "And if the other can invest me and invest my freedom, of itself arbitrary, this is in the last analysis because I myself can feel myself to be the other of the other" (*TI*, 84). The ethical event makes existing mean more than just continuing in the totality of being. It can go beyond being. Going beyond death is in the pluralist relation, in justice or the goodness of being for the other. Duration itself becomes visible in the relation with the other, as this is where being is surpassed. Levinas criticizes Bergson's notion of duration as the metaphysical intuition of the real, arguing rather that duration is visible in the relation of the other. It is also here that being is surpassed: "The surpassing of being starting from being—the relation with exteriority—is not measured by duration. Duration itself becomes visible in the relation with the Other, where being is surpassed" (TI 301). But notice that just as the intuition of Bergsonian duration was an everyday event, the relation to the Other, the otherwise than being, is also an everyday event.

Richard Cohen has described the ethical event, the break with the arbitrary as the reorientation of the relation of ethics, to epistemology and ontology. In Cohen's view Levinas justifies philosophy as not merely a sense of wonder at being but describes the trace of the face-to-face relation, which places us in first person relation with others: "In this way, taking the 'break' with naivete to be neither a theoretical nor an ontological event but an ethical event, Levinas at once not only reorients the relation of ethics to epistemology and ontology, and not only provides an account of the beginning of philosophy, but, even more importantly, justifies philosophy."[3] For Levinas, subjectivity itself comes to be in the event of ethics. Ontology is based in ethics, as Cohen writes of this: "For Levinas, in contrast, the human psyche—ego, self, subjectivity, soul, I—is from the first not a scientific object, not even a failed or deferred scientific object, but a moral event, an event of sensibility deeper than rationality."[4]

Reading Levinas in a Levinasian Way

As Jean-Michel Salanskis points out in his essay in this volume, Emmanuel Levinas is often "read against himself." Salanskis refers to the many interpretations of Levinas's thought coming from perspectives at odds with Levinas's insistence on the centrality, and asymmetry, of ethics: Heideggerian phenomenology, Derridean deconstruction, or religious traditions not his own. And we fully endorse this practice. The value of a major thinker's contribution can often be measured by the use to which it is put by a wide variety of researchers and schools. By this measure, Levinas's philosophy has proved to be extremely valuable. We also do not mean to suggest that all readers inevitably fall into one of two groups: authentic and inauthentic; loyal and deviant. There is a wide variety of credible Levinasian approaches, and this is gratifying.

But there is also something to be said for seeing a philosopher's work from where he stands. This is what we try to do in this book, and the reason we borrow its subtitle, *Reading Levinas in a Levinasian Way*, from Salanskis's essay. The common theme running through the chapters is just this: the authors attempt to enter into Levinas's thought on his own terms.

In our understanding of the matter, no one has done more to advance the cause of the Levinasian reading than Richard A. Cohen. For this reason, many of the papers we have chosen for this volume reflect and comment on Cohen's contribution. Absent Cohen's labor, the field would not be what it is today. He studied with Alphonso Lingis as an undergraduate at Penn State, and as a graduate student at Stony Brook arranged to study with Levinas at the Sorbonne for the academic year of 1974–1975. This was Levinas's penultimate year as a fulltime professor, and Cohen attended all of Levinas's seminars that year ("Being and Being Given," "Ontology and Transcendence," and others). Levinas and his wife Raissa even cordially received Cohen at their home above the École Normale Israélite Orientale, where they discussed a variety of philosophical questions. Cohen completed his doctoral dissertation in 1980, "Time in the Philosophy of Emmanuel Levinas." Cohen went on to become one of the most important voices in the history of English-language Levinas studies. His subsequent career is detailed in the contribution by Jack Marsh.

The Essays

Section 1: Reading Levinas

In his essay "Reading Levinas in a Levinasian Way," Jean-Michel Salanskis claims that many Levinas scholars read *Otherwise Than Being* as Levinas's reply to Derrida's "Violence and Metaphysics." Such readers may end up reading Levinas against him. But to read Levinas in a Levinasian way would be to read him through *Otherwise Than Being*. This is to understand that this was Levinas's project from at least 1935 with *On Escape* and not a response to Derrida's essay. Jack Marsh charts the English-language reception and application of Levinas's philosophy, paying close attention to Cohen's central role. Robert Gibbs notes Cohen's loyalty to Levinas and says this raises an important question about philosophical thought. Must it stand free of relations to authorities? Or should it invest authority in the great thinkers? Don Ihde describes Cohen's contributions to the philosophy of technology. Marie-Anne Lescourret investigates Cohen's own philosophical contribution. She identifies a particular reading of Levinas; Cohen's thinking emphasizes the centrality of simple kindness in Levinasian ethics. Edith Wyschogrod in her 1996 review of Richard Cohen's *Elevations: The Height of the Good in Rosenzweig and Levinas* (Chicago

1994) calls Cohen an "exacting interpreter" of Levinas who sees that Levinas aims to reorient philosophy toward the good beyond being.

Section 2: Ethical Exegesis

In Section 2: Ethical Exegesis, Rossitsa Varadinova Borkowski enters into Cohen's interpretation of Levinas in art and art criticism. Levinas's essay "Reality and Its Shadow" is an ambiguous look at the role of art in the ethical life and the necessity of taking up aesthetics into criticism. Masato Goda, Japanese translator of *Totality and Infinity* and *Otherwise Than Being*, explores Levinas's writings through the theme of the interruption of rhythm, which he calls the rupture of the continuous sequence of time. Irina Poleshchuk follows Cohen's view that ethical exegesis appeals to the very concrete embodied situation. She argues that ethical exegesis is a necessary step to format an ethical body, as "being responsible for." Steven Shankman is inspired by a transcription of a lecture that Levinas delivered in 1976, in his last set of lectures as professor of philosophy at the Sorbonne, "God and Onto-Theo-logy." Shankman sees the lecture "Don Quixote: Bewitchment and Hunger" as an *ethical* response to the narrowly doctrinal focus of the Counter-Reformation, which began with the Council of Trent. Finally, Jolanta Saldukaityte, "Art of the Uncanny: Seeing with Cohen and Levinas" is interested in questions of the monstrous; what does it look like, how does it function, and, most importantly, how does it challenge our own ideas of the world? The uncanny is not totally alien or "other"; rather, it draws out things buried within us that we may not want to face.

Section 3: Ontological Contests

In "Imagine Freedom," Brunella Antomarini engages Richard Cohen's contrast between Levinas and Spinoza. She maintains that both philosophers, while starting with radically different theoretical positions, end up approaching each other in their respective ethical claims. In Jacques Rozenberg's "Levinas Reading Spinoza," he challenges Cohen's claim that Spinoza offered a form of rationalism that allowed Christianity to be imposed on Jewish thought. He lays out the different ways Levinas and Spinoza look at justice, freedom, and ethics. Christopher Buckman, in "Sovereignty in Levinas and Hobbes," returns to the famous Levinasian question of whether we are duped by morality. He engages with the idea that the political order is founded on war, and aims to make explicit Levinas's critique of Hobbes. The explanation of these connections draws inspiration from Richard A. Cohen's work on the relation between Levinas and Spinoza. Chung-Hsiung Lai, in "On Ethics: Levinas and Badiou" examines Badiou's criticism of Levinas's ethics. Chung-Hsiung responds to the questions of whether Levinas provides an adequate reasoning of the philosophical truth of ethics, whether Levinas's ethics are essentially religious, and what the critical differences are between Levinas and Badiou regarding ethics. In his essay, "On the Importance of Importance: Emmanuel Levinas on the First Challenge to Jewish Thought Today," Richard Sugarman turns to the problem of post-Holocaust theology and theodicy. Sugarman sees Levinas as a philosophical minimalist who remains committed to a phenomenological approach. Ethics is shown to be first philosophy through his careful analysis of the "face to face." In "Levinas and the Ethics of Sacrifice: Reading 'Dying For. . . ' Adverbially," Sandor Goodhart explains that, in Levinas's estimation, Heidegger's greatest contribution was to construe Being as a verb, an event. Goodhart follows Levinas's adverbial modification in discussing the notions of "dying for" in Levinas and "my death" in Heidegger. He shows how the adverbial approach radically subverts Heidegger's analyses.

SECTION 4: ETHICAL RELIGION

Roger Burggraeve's essay "The Little Goodness Never Wins But Is Never Defeated: Or How Emmanuel Levinas Finds Inspiration in Vasily Grossman for his Vision on the Future of a Humane Society" discusses Levinas's frequent references to Vasily Grossman's *Life and Fate*, In particular, the "holy fool," Ikonnikov. Confronted with Stalinism, this "feeble-minded person" has lost his faith in the collectively organized Good and finds salvation only in the small, daily goodness of ordinary people. Levinas integrates the idea of the "little goodness" in his ethical thought on society, politics, and the state. James McLachlan's "Richard Cohen's *Levinasian Meditations* on Sartre and Theology" focuses on Cohen's interpretation of Sartre as Levinas's humanistic ally but also offers Levinasian critiques of Sartre. McLachlan uses this critique to indicate that there is a theological character to much of Sartre's existentialism. From a Levinasian standpoint, this makes perfect sense because much of Western philosophy has been theological in its aim at the ideal of totality. It is to Sartre's credit that he did so much to exhibit the failure of this enterprise. In "Incarnate Religion," Mark Spencer presents Emmanuel Levinas's and Richard Cohen's criteria for a religion being genuine or "adult," as well as criteria for critiquing their conclusions. Both of these are based on their analysis of the body's role in experience. Spencer first presents Levinas and Cohen's version of phenomenological method and then shows how they use their phenomenological method to reveal the role of the body in genuine religion. Finally, he assesses their criteria for genuine religion. In "The Ethical Event: A Phenomenology of חסד chesed for Asylum Seeking Refugees" Devorah Wainer takes an utterly unique approach to interpreting Levinas. Wainer writes this piece as a narrative that explores the characters of the refugees she meets, the philosophical questions Wainer is working through, and what she learns from the refugees themselves. She employs the Jewish concept of chesed—a term that roughly translates to "loving-kindness" and midrash—a form of writing—to engage with Levinas as a Jewish thinker. Her goal, she writes, is to enable readers to "see" the face of the incarcerated and begin to perhaps feel that ethical pull of which Levinas so often speaks.

The book concludes with Richard Cohen's response.

Notes

1. Contra Sartre, existence is not condemned to freedom but invested with it. Investiture liberates freedom from the arbitrary. Existence is not in reality condemned to freedom but is invested as freedom. Freedom is not bare. To philosophize is to trace freedom back to what lies before it, to disclose the investiture that liberates freedom from the arbitrary (TI 84–85).

2. In *Otherwise Than Being* Levinas, who thinks highly of the Bergsonian critique of nothingness, critiques Bergson as falling into the trap that Bergson himself had criticized. Contrary to what is maintained in *Creative Evolution*, all disorder is not another order. The anarchy of the diachronic is not "assembled" into an order, except in the said. Bergson, distrustful as he is of language, is here a victim of the said (OTB 9 n. 6).

3. Richard A. Cohen, *Ethics, Exegesis and Philosophy: Interpretation after Levinas* (Kindle Locations 1106–1108). Kindle Edition.

4. Richard A. Cohen, *Ethics, Exegesis and Philosophy: Interpretation after Levinas* (Kindle Locations 1106–1108). Kindle Edition.

Path I
Reading Levinas

1

Reading Levinas in a Levinasian Way

Jean-Michel Salanskis

The influence of Levinas's philosophy has not been restricted to a small group of devoted scholars. It has won international attention and regard; and it is now frequently evoked and discussed by researchers who do not share much with it. Such recognition did not happen easily and quickly: it started, at least in its current form, around 2006, the year of celebration of "one century with Levinas." Still, it is not difficult to realize that he is most often read against himself, for very deep-rooted and, in a way, legitimate reasons. These readings and reasons we usually explain easily in connection with what we know of the history of Levinas's reception.

Reading Levinas against Him

There has been, perhaps before other receptions, a strong interest in Levinas in Christian circles. Marie-Anne Lescourret describes this interest in a chapter of her excellent biography.[1] Levinas lectured widely—in Italy, Belgium, the Netherlands, etc.—at historically Christian universities and to this day is studied seriously by Christian scholars. But for a Christian, it is difficult to accept Levinas's materialism, his suspicion of theology, his antipathy for the principle of unlimited forgiveness, and things of that nature. In addition, Christians cannot accept the conception of radical asymmetry of ethical plot, advocating rather for reciprocity.

There is also a phenomenological reception, which makes sense if one considers the intellectual trajectory of Levinas and his constant reference to phenomenological texts in his writings. Still, this reception, from what I know, often leads to understanding Levinas's philosophy as a reaction to Heidegger's, and maybe even as an internal consequence or development of it. Scholars reading him in that way criticize Levinas for not understanding the true meaning of Being in Heidegger, neglecting its withdrawing, for underestimating the late Heidegger, for failing to recognize the ethical significance of Heidegger's *Fürsorge*, for imposing without good reason a dreadful picture of *Sein* and so on (reintroducing subjectivity in a founding position being not a minor point in the list).

Many scholars, especially in English-speaking countries, have come to Levinas in the context of Derridean interpretation. This leads scholars to read him from the point of view of a philosophy gravitating around language, finding its most essential and radical orientation in the practice of deconstruction. A deconstructive critic of Levinas would sound approximately like the following: Levinas too easily proposes the notion of an "absolute other." Levinas is wrong to suggest that the other person could count as "pure" alterity and wrong to suggest that the other person could count as pure alterity. Levinas does not understand that we always already live in the "third person" plot, and that in some sense the universal impersonal stakes of justice come first; Levinas does not acknowledge the fact that intentionality remains on the ground level, as enfolded in language, and Levinas has no way of understanding how impersonal wrongs may victimize a group or a category (e.g., women).

But then, there are also readers who come to Levinas from other sites or perspectives, and sometimes, ironically, they reject him as belonging to one of these schools of thought many critics consider him a part of: they reject Levinas as a phenomenologist, as a Heideggerian, as an irrational French Derridean, and so on.

To make my point quantitative, it is quite rare, I think, to find a philosopher genuinely convinced that Levinas has taught us a lot and that there is still much more to learn in his writings. In France, I would say that we have less than ten thinkers in a category like this. I am not a position to say how many one can find in the United States: I may only say that each time I met Richard Cohen, I felt him to be one of these rare genuine "soldiers" of Levinas's cause. And reading some of his writings confirmed that feeling. For example, in Cohen's *Ethics, Exegesis and Philosophy*, he spends some time vindicating Levinas against classical (French) criticism (typically against Ricœur's arguments).[2]

In light of these questions, I want to inquire here: instead of only considering Levinas's location in larger methodological debates, how can or should we read Levinas in a Levinasian way? Is it possible to delineate at the methodological level an alternative reading, where we do not read Levinas's philosophy as accountable for requirements coming from another philosophical agenda, considering Levinas from the outset as committed to it?

I'd like to propose an answer to that question, although it implicitly outlines quite a difficult program: the answer would be that we should read Levinas under the guidance of the most specific, original, and audacious Levinasian notion of "otherwise than being."

Reading Levinas through the Category of "Otherwise than Being"

Immediately after making such a statement, I have to clarify my point against a common misunderstanding. The notion of "otherwise than being" does not only belong to the book *Otherwise than Being or Beyond Essence*. I take the notion to correspond to Levinas's orientation and inspiration from the very beginning (in *On Escape*), and I read it as involved in the true meaning of what is said and elaborated in all of Levinas's subsequent work up to *Of God Who Comes to Mind*.

Many Levinas scholars are blocked from seeing things in that way because of an influential narrative, according to which "otherwise than being" would be Levinas's reply to Derridean criticism in "Violence and Metaphysics." According to this reading, Levinas would have realized that in *Totality and infinity* he was falling into the scope of such criticism, and therefore he would have written the 1974 book, where the notion of "otherwise than being" would emerge for the first time. It is not surprising that a lot of scholars are convinced by that narrative. This is true for at least three reasons:

1. The first and strongest one: they come to Levinas "from" Derrida, thus the narrative makes sense, as far as it describes Levinas as thinking in Derridean terms like our scholars.

> We are always tempted to understand authors as saying what we already know and think.

2. As a matter of fact, Levinas uses the expression "Being" with a capital B in *Totality and Infinity*, seeming not to have abandoned Heidegger's ontological difference and perhaps allowing readers to locate what the book is about in the realm of being.

3. "Otherwise than being" is paradoxical. It does not make sense. Isn't Derrida the master of logical impossibility? So, it is likely that Levinas, using such notions, enters the Derridean field.

Still, this narrative is wrong. Reading *On Escape* is enough to come to that conclusion. As a matter of fact, in this little book (which first was published as a paper in the important journal *Recherches philosophiques*), Levinas openly declares his intention to write a philosophy escaping what he calls "ontologism," and he observes that available philosophical discourses underlining becoming, offering a constantly changing picture of being, do not do the job: to become cannot but mean to reach another state of being—to become cannot but be ontologically motivated. Already in this very early paper Levinas wants us to understand that for us being as such means imprisonment. And he does not hide from us the fact that finding a philosophical way of escaping looks like an impossible challenge. He does not sing proudly, in a Dylanian way, "There must be some way out of there": in some sense, "no way" would be more appropriate.

Such early orientation against "ontologism" does not disappear after this first paper/book. Any cautious reader will find it again and again all along the path.

We have it in a quite emphatic and novel way in *From Existence to Existents*, another early work, possibly the most significant work from the early period. Here Levinas introduces one of the major concepts of his thought, the concept of *il y a* (*there is*): it does the work of staging pure being, being as such, Being, without any being, as we would have to say in Heideggerian language. And it stages being as absurdity: absurdity of self-sufficiency of process as such, forbidding any existent to arise and to count, not leaving room for any lack or for any expressible goal. Self-sufficiency of the pure fact of being was already underlined in *On Escape*. *From Existence to Existents* gives a better picture of the enfolding horror of *Being* as such, and what's more, it posits the narrative of subjectivity as originally tearing itself away from *il y a*. *Hypostasis* is the name of that function, giving rise to a *now*, a *here*, an *I*, a *body*. Original existent is a self-referring presence, ignoring or denying the encompassing, absurd process of being.

If we jump to *Otherwise Than Being Or Beyond Essence*, we know that the leitmotiv of fighting against ontologism is not lost. "Otherwise of being" is the explicit content of the book, and it is shown as implied or expressed by subjectivity in a kind of archaic, impossible, and unlikely figure of it: a subjectivity to which the book gives a lot of names or essential attributes (like proximity or obsession), but of which the basic formula appears to be "one-for-the-other." In the three books we mentioned so far (*On Escape, From Existence to Existent,* and *Otherwise Than Being*), the connection between "otherwise than being" and subjectivity is never lost: in the first, escaping the prison of the pure fact of being appears as the original feeling of humankind; in the second, subjectivity arises as a breakup with absurdity of Being as process; in the third, the mode of otherwise than being is only "reached" or "accomplished" in the paradoxical move of ethical subjectivity as one-for-the-other.

But in between we have *Totality and Infinity*. What should be said of what we cannot avoid but recognize as the "Bible" of Levinas's thought? At the center of the book, Levinas expounds his fundamental thought on the "ethical plot": me facing the other person and not taking them as an item of the world, hearing them rather as call of distress or teaching voice. In such an original plot arises the feeling of duty, and the meaning of morality is originally given. Part of the story is that the other person, as we said, gets subtracted from the world, receiving the paradoxical status of "beyond being." Thus, we also meet in the central book the notion of "otherwise of being," but here it applies rather to the other person in the context of the ethical plot. Still, such intrigue, engaging us in moral obligation, is described by Levinas as a way of "beating the record" of strangeness with respect to being first established by what he calls *separation* in the book, in formulations connecting it with our experience of enjoyment. And if we go back to the beginning of the book, Levinas first presents what he calls "metaphysical desire" and defines it as an aspiration for the absolute other: a notion that cannot be satisfied in the realm of being. Hence the general perspective is still that humankind turns to otherwise than being. It is true that Levinas expressed some regrets about his written expression in the book, as far as he from time to time seems to use the word "being" with its general quasi-logical universal meaning. But, if we read each of these passages carefully, we realize that Levinas, at the same time, makes clear that he really means more than being as a modalizing dimension.³

We should add here some reference to the last synthesis of Levinas's thought, the one we find in *Of God Who Comes to Mind*: in that collection, Levinas speaks of an additional plot, which we could call "plot of the infinite." The meaning of infinite, or of what maybe deserves to be named God (Levinas also calls it *Goodness* or *Illeity*), receives a new phenomenological description and gets articulated and superimposed with the meaning of the demanding other person. No doubt that infinity here once again features the "otherwise than being," explaining its centrality for our most legitimate human life.

So, the Derridean reading of the issue is wrong: not so much because it misconstrues issues it raises but rather because it fails at perceiving the *Leitfaden* of Levinas's thought from the very beginning. Indeed, otherwise than being is a paradoxical and slippery notion, as was stated in point (3) above, but we cannot escape it if we want to understand what Levinas has to say. The strength of Levinas's thought precisely resides in making sense of it.

One of the consequences of seeing this correctly is that we stop interpreting *Totality and Infinity* and *Otherwise Than Being* as conflicting, as related by a characteristic tension. The difference between the books is that "otherwise than being" (as an adverbial category) is not staged the same way in each of them: it is not that "otherwise than being" would arise as a new motive but it is also not that Levinas has broken with his earlier thought. As Richard Cohen argues in *Ethics, Exegesis and Philosophy*, what Levinas does do is show otherwise than being as a sort of "accomplishment" of subjectivity as far as it would (unlikely, against all odds) turn to a subjectivity fitting to ethical call.⁴ In that way, "otherwise than being" is brought back to subjective stance, as it was in early books. Also, "otherwise than being" is now taken as a dimension supporting language (at the level of *Saying*) and destining humankind to science, logic, and philosophy. All this makes the book quite fundamental and rich, adding a number of new themes. But we have no serious reason to interpret a contradiction between it and *Totality and Infinity*.

Although I am not a systematic reader of everything written about Levinas, I have the impression that contemporary scholarship, simply perhaps because it works more and more at reading and understanding internally Levinas's thought, slowly moves toward such an apprehension of his work. Analyses and interpretations remain caught in the biased understanding I have first underlined, only insofar as the first generation of scholars strongly implemented it. Students supervised by them or even meeting them as the most conspicuous secondary literature were influenced by them. There is still much to do, then, in order to bring Levinasian studies into a Levinasian reading of Levinas. But we may have some reasonable hope. Richard Cohen, at least, has been one of the few working in that direction, at least to my knowledge. I would like to jump to a second issue, which is the issue of locating Levinas within French contemporary philosophy. As we will see, this is not totally unrelated to previous issues.

Locating Levinas in the French Landscape

Let us begin by a short comment inspired by the interesting way Frédéric Worms organizes French philosophy of twentieth century.[5] He sees it as having gone through at least three successive "moments."

1) The moment of *mind*. This would correspond more or less to the years 1900 to 1935. In this moment philosophers wonder whether and how mind could be released from a wrong level, or modality, of experience inside which it gets lost. The leading figures of that moment are Bergson and Brunschvicg, and the name of a philosophical attitude epitomizing the moment is *spiritualism*.

2) The moment of *existence*. This roughly encompasses the years 1935 to 1965. In this phase, philosophers question existence as always being the object of an encounter rather than given; they come to discuss whether existence should be understood as contingent or necessary. It is typically the moment of French phenomenology, but Cavaillès, Simone Weil, or Gaston Bachelard may also be considered members of the moment, epitomizing the philosophical attitude of *existentialism*.

3) The moment of *structure*. Years 1965 to 1995, let's say. The central problem is the structure, or, of difference (whether linguistic structure is the general form dominating culture, or whether difference as basic unit of structure requires a new and radical critique). The major thinkers of this period are Deleuze, Derrida, Foucault, Lyotard, Althusser, and so on. The typical philosophical approach is *structuralism*.

Worms thinks that since the end of the nineties we have entered a new moment, dominated by the problem of the living entity (even if dealing with such issues, philosophers also come to consider *justice*). He is tempted to designate Ricœur and Levinas as main thinkers of the new moment (even if they did most of their major work before it). Still, in a discussion some time ago with me, he was ready to admit that Levinas, as a matter of fact, was connected to each of the moments.

Indeed, Levinas was influenced by moment 1, and he never forgets Bergson, with whom he felt he had some filial connection (like his friend Jankélévitch). Due to his birth date though, he belongs to the second moment (we could remember that he discovered phenomenology and visited Germany for that reason in the same years Merleau-Ponty, Aron, and Sartre did, and that he was possibly the first in France to speak about Husserl and Heidegger and to pass on their teaching). His first books radiate a kind of tragic-existential mood (*On Escape* and *Existence and Existents*) characteristic of that generation. But he became famous during the third moment, thanks to Derrida's and Lyotard's reading of his work. Both of them used Levinas as a way to add alterity to poststructuralist discussion. Alterity was understood as a kind of complement to the notion of difference, which had first been at the center of discussion. In that way, Levinas came to be thought of among the ranks of Deleuze, Derrida, Foucault, and Lyotard. I believe that he was especially read in this way in the English-speaking international reception that he got. This reception was less sensitive to the "abysses" between generations and authors that we, bound to our country and its history, were so impressed with. Truth is that Levinas divided our four authors: those on the one side, who read him and took him into account (Derrida and Lyotard), and those on the other who more or less ignored him (Deleuze and Foucault).

In order to read Levinas in a Levinasian way, we also have to understand him in the context of twentieth-century French intellectual life: it is as important to realize how his formulations, interests, and concepts are related to similar gestures or motives among his fellow countrymen (meaning, not only the philosophers), as it is to make explicit how he nevertheless distances himself from them. Doing both is how we read Levinas according to his basic intention, which was as much celebrating a context he felt indebted to, as to promote a kind of radically new discourse and feeling.

I shall take here just one example, which I voluntarily choose from outside philosophy *stricto sensu*: one can be tempted to relate Levinas's thought with radical insights from Bataille or Blanchot, who are rather seen as writers, and who mostly claimed to sustain the cause of literature (although they were strongly concerned by the issues of philosophy). I chose them because I happened to listen to a very enlightening talk Richard Cohen gave about Bataille.

Indeed, one can detect analogies between Levinas's conceptualization and Bataille's intense texts, or Blanchot's rigorous and enigmatic thematization of the space of literature and of the neuter. Connection will be more indirect and partly metaphoric in the first case, while in the second case, we have the basis of the long-standing friendship between Blanchot and Levinas, and their mutual acknowledgment of a shared notion (which is named *il y a* in Levinas and *neuter* in Blanchot). Still, any honest reading of corresponding material will lead to the conclusion that the surrounding landscape and encompassing economy are quite different on both sides: to the effect that the notion, while formally the same at some level, does not mean the same at the end of the day in both works, and does not receive the same axiological accent.[6]

Despite the claim I made above, referring to previous discussions with Frédéric Worms—that Levinas belonged in some sense, sometimes in a tenuous way, to each of the four moments of French contemporary philosophy outlined by Worms—Levinas scholars should not limit their comparative and contextualizing work to French philosophy and French intellectual culture. It also makes sense to confront Levinas with German thinkers who like him tried, although in different ways, to cross the stakes and teachings of philosophy and of Jewish tradition: thinkers like Herman Cohen, Franz Rosenzweig, Martin Buber, or Gershom Scholem.[7] And we certainly should also read Levinas from the perspective of the long history of intellectual attempts to conjugate Greek philosophy and Jewish tradition, taking into account the major figures of Spanish medieval period (as Maïmonides or Yehudah Halevy).

To honor an author does not mean to read him or her only in the context of what seems to be—in any possible way—similar to said author. It also means using confrontation with authors who do not share his views or axioms, in order to make salient the price of thinking like Levinas and not at all like Levinas at the same time. I have begun this chapter by arguing, implicitly, that usual reception of Levinas did not help in understanding his own project because that reception originally submits his thought and his notions to external norms, like "being-to-the world phenomenology," Christianity, or deconstruction. To understand something indeed always means first to understand it as it asks to be understood. This means welcoming the new and specific perspective, the set of priorities, feeling, and norms the message brings. If we are not able to do that, we simply learn nothing. But then, we have also to confront, translate, and assess the teaching of the new voice by letting external disagreements and rejections have their say against it. This means that we may now use framework of post-Heideggerian phenomenology, Christian theology, or of Derridean deconstruction as playing that part: only after having understood Levinas internally, in a Levinasian way. From what I've read, I believe Richard Cohen has been working on Levinas in that kind of spirit. I would like to end this brief and rather programmatic chapter by raising an issue that is probably the most problematic in Levinasian studies nowadays.

Levinas and Our World

We know all very well that there is strong criticism against Levinas happening in philosophical circles and that goes more or less in following way: Levinas's picture is beautiful and touching. One wishes the world was like the one he describes. We do not face the other person as the absolutely demanding face; we also do not experience any original peace "under" Hobbesian generalized war. We need, therefore, justice as a set of rules limiting the predators we are. Or we cannot hope any improvement of the world outside of a critical fight emanating from people diminished by the system. Freedom is a fundamental value, simply because human beings cannot live any genuine human life without freedom: and we do not wish freedom as a value to come after a sacrificial principle (as, it is claimed, Levinas puts it).

On the whole, and even if objections we formulated differ from one another and do not attack Levinas's construction in exactly the same way, the kind of resistance we set forth could be called a *realist* one. Levinas's discourse is challenged because it is grounded upon a false picture of human reality, on the basis of which it sells impossible values.

Here, a reading of Levinas in the line of post-Heideggerian phenomenology of "being-to-the-world" may play an important part. Such phenomenology, as a matter of fact, has always claimed to be a true description of our (fundamental) situation. Beneath the idealized construction of physics and of science, there is a first *strata* of the world that phenomenology of "being-to-the-world" claims to have captured, unraveled, and described.

We can then explain the difference between Levinasian and non-Levinasian people inside the community of "phenomenologists of being-to-the-world": the former think that Levinas has added a missing component to available descriptions, by giving the other person its right and corrected place in such phenomenology; the latter think that phenomenological status of the other person is better staged in Heidegger or in Merleau-Ponty. Still, both camps agree that Levinas's philosophy should first be read as a true description of our (phenomenologically or ontologico-phenomenologically) fundamental world. Here we encounter the main issue I pinpointed in second section of this chapter. We have to decide whether everything Levinas wrote has to be understood in the light of the modality of *otherwise than being* or not.

If we do so, then Levinas's philosophy should not be read as a true description of the world. It sounds very strange to say that because we know from the experience of reading him that what he writes often seems closer to our lives than anything else, or at least anything philosophical. How could he manage that without dealing with the actual world?

Still, that's exactly the point I think we have to understand better. As I attempted to show in some dedicated books (my series, *Levinas vivant*)[8], Emmanuel Levinas has taken up the method of phenomenology but applied it to meanings rather than to objects. This was a brand new path, because, for him, meanings are not the presentation mode of objects: they are rather commanding contents that we share, more or less. Hence in Levinas, we come to understand a meaning when we are made aware of the original scene or intrigue through which we access this meaning in question. Understanding goes through experience; we grasp what is at stake by going across canonical experiences determining our original relation to concerned contents. But what we access is not an object but a meaning: which entails that corresponding experience cannot be understood as participating the machinery of unraveling of being.

The basic and crucial example of that is ethical intrigue or plot. Levinas scholars rightly insist that in our "encounter" with the face, the other person does not shine as phenomenological manifestation, that the category of the face is precisely introduced in order to block such reading. As far as we are speaking of the other person as an object and of their status, it has to be said that ethical intrigue is only deceptive. The face is the dismantling of phenomenon in its typical ontological reading.

Still at the same time, and for the same reason, ethical intrigue determines our correct and normative access to the meaning of ethics. We originally learn the meaning of ethics while failing to access phenomenologically the other person as an objective content, motivating an objective category. Within that intrigue, we learn the command, the infinite, the giving, and so on. Ethics cannot be rationally grounded, but we may recover our original connection to it, which amounts to this strange experiential stuff, kind of mythical, that Levinas offers in his books as a kind of new "description." Not a description of the canonical conditions of manifestation for a type of objects, but the description of the fundamental intrigue through which we relate to some meaning and understand it as it asks to be.

As much has to be said of the meaning of *subject*, or of the meaning of *justice*. The first one gets disclosed in many books. It seems that Levinas had to work again and again on it. The picture offered in *On Escape* is not quite the same as the one given in *Existence and Existents* (they are close to each other). Things change again in *Totality and Infinity*, and then another strata is added in *Otherwise than being*, where we learn the meaning of "ethical subjectivity." I would claim that in *On God Who Comes to Mind*, Levinas again modifies his conception, or at least introduces new modulations.

The meaning of justice is the subject matter of the end of *Otherwise Than Being*. Accessing this new and fundamental meaning, we also come to better understand logic, language, science, and philosophy. In justice, Levinas finds the phenomenological key to the whole realm of *logos* or *theoria*. The ultimate picture is that as long as we keep on practicing classical ontological philosophy we won't properly understand the meaning of theoria or science. They are dissimulated, as it were, by their functional relation with being. Understanding theoria as the unraveling of being is not understanding it in the deepest and most loving way. Such is the troubling and revolutionary lesson of *Otherwise Than Being*.

I cannot do better than evoking all that material in a very quick and insufficient way. I have tried to do the job better in other writings. However, I think more is still to be done and in a stronger and more convincing way. In conclusion, I would like to give an idea of how my personal philosophy—etho-analysis—is derived from such a reading of Levinas.

Etho-analysis

Another way of making the preceding point is by saying that Levinas does not provide an anthropology. That's not an easy issue because there is a strong habit of presenting anything ethical or political on the basis of a prior anthropological picture. Such a habit has been prevalent in French philosophy, probably under Marxist influence: it was taken for granted that no non-situated insight about what had to be done could be seriously considered. On the one hand, such insight was likely to be inefficient, lacking any leverage for modifying reality. On the other hand, its own way of speaking from nowhere was interpreted to betray its ideological character (the fact that it secretly expressed the interests of upper classes). Contemporary analytic moral and political philosophy is sometimes described as having reinstated classical nonsituated moral and political theory: John Rawls's philosophy is often attacked in that way. On the other hand, analytic spirit very much values reality and realist attitudes. Therefore, the analytic motivation may also lead us to look for an anthropological basis for any moral or political assertion. We could say that corresponding issue is about the connection between ethics and *ethos* (deciding to speak Greek for the occasion). Usually, the word *ethos* names the regularity of human behavior, likely to be grasped and diagnosed in some historical and social context. While ethics, although deriving from the same Greek root, rather refers to the norms supposed to govern such located behavior: even someone who believes in absolute ethics is tempted to think and say that ethical norms legitimately govern any collective human life, whatever the culture or the period.

How should we place Levinas's thought with respect to such implicit debate? Clearly, by definition, he stands on the side of absolute ethics: ethical meaning gets originally approached, for him, at the level of a break with ontological perspective. Ethical demand bears on us in spite of ontological war or of the prevailing economic life of humankind. Ethical demand means such a break: until we welcome such disruption, we are not properly dealing with ethics. As another revealing feature of that posture, we could simply mention the fact that Levinas considers that we should not read the biblical message as dated and overcome, from the certainty of our distance and our historical superiority.

Still, being haunted by ethical call is part of human strata as Levinas understands it. Ethics is not supported by our anthropological structure but rather by the whole story of ethics. It is about taking advantage of such structure, and tentatively turning it into its orientation. Enjoyment does not coincide with our biological-cognitive machinery, our fundamental metabolism, but rather corresponds to our using that structure as a pretext for us to self-wrap in our satisfaction, regardless of any worldly finality. In the same way later in Levinas's construction, the one-for-the-other in *Otherwise than Being* consists in diverting enjoyment onto the other person. "Otherwise-than-being" the ethical move means hijacking ontological structure twice, or on two levels: turning it into solipsist enjoyment and then turning that enjoyment itself into ethical giving, when I offer the Other *my* bread.

More generally, Levinas sees humankind as the place where an ethical "otherwise-than-being" order overdetermines ontological logic. This sounds paradoxical, as it seems to say that we are not what we are: we are objects of a kind of sublime alienation, turning us into the impossible "otherwise-than-being" (which cannot though be equated with any actual entity). I have tried to make that paradox systematic, and to use it as an inspiration for a new type of description and philosophical inquiry.

As a matter of fact, I see our shared cultural, social, and historical world as haunted by a plurality of calls that come to us through some specific words—which I name *solicitators*—and bring among us the stakes of answering to such calls. A solicitator, then, is an *ideality word* rather than and extensional term. It does not do the basic job of gathering in reality items covered by its conceptual meaning (as the word *cat* does), or it has another function: that of pointing to specific stakes, that of calling us to such stakes (a function going beyond any empirical content then). My best example was for a long time the word *love*, which, I think, we hardly ever hear used as collecting a class of "love-objects" or of "love-episodes." We rather use *love* in order to express that "love is in the air" (as the song says). But in my second book about etho-analysis, I have maintained that the word *truth* had to be heard in that way and that philosophical tradition had known it for a long time (even if sometimes reluctantly).

Each time a solicitator is given, we may access a collectivity of people hearing the call as such and engaging themselves in answering the call and satisfying what we are asked to: that collectivity I call the *ethos* around the solicitator. It should not be seen only as a "geographical" group when such an ethos takes place. Its followers also try to transmit the call to ulterior generation, allowing the ethos to persist along history. Therefore, any ethos appears as a contingent tradition: because it holds only as long as we remember what is asked from us. Thus, the ethos may disappear in a very simple and nonviolent way: by being forgotten. People who care for the stakes of romantic love often feel such precariousness, that "love could die" (I could quote some popular songs here, again). There is even a novel that was built on such an assumption: *Brave New World* by Aldous Huxley, whose dystopia may be described as that of a world where the very meaning of love has been forgotten.

As a matter of fact, my perspective is that to any ethos corresponds a "sense region." An ethos is that through which a sense is shared and collectively understood. If we follow Levinas's fundamental insight, indeed, sense should be understood not as the presentation mode of an entity, like in Frege,[9] but rather at the level of being addressed by a message, and working at relaunching it as it asks to be understood. Therefore, sense entirely rests on our ability to feel demands, on our access to the asking structure. As our faculty of relating to demands is rooted in our hearing the ethical demand of the other person, semantic ability depends on ethical "competence." One could say: we cannot make sense of the semantic responsibility of relaunching speeches and texts as they ask to be—if we do not hear demand in general, if we never accepted the ethical responsibility. This does not mean we have behaved righteously, but we have not done violence in restating the demand of the Other. Still, semantic responsibility is quite different from ethical responsibility: being answerable to the first does not make one quit the second. To put it bluntly, one may be a respectable intellectual without being a good person. Even if for being a respectable intellectual one has to take up something from ethical intrigue, one cannot be purely deaf with respect to it, as regularly as one may avoid its call.

What etho-analysis does more precisely is to unfold the call of the solicitator into a list of explicit prescriptions: together they build what is called the *sensance* of the ethos, constituting, so to speak, the tables of the law of concerned ethos. They are rules that we should follow if we want to stand at the level of the call of the solicitator. Usually we don't really observe them, but as long as the ethos lives, we never forget that we should. Each follower of the ethos would agree that prescriptions of the *sensance* have to be obeyed, and that each time they are not, something of the splendor of the solicitator is lost. Referring to such list of prescriptions is how we share the sense of the call, thus it is through its *sensance* that the ethos makes sense as a sense region.

I have offered an etho-analysis, so far, of eight 'sense regions' connected to corresponding solicitators: *politics*, *love* and *subject* in *Territoires du sens* (Vrin, 2007), *truth*, *dialog*, *body*, *death* and *philosophy* in *Partages du sens* (Presses Universitaires de Paris Nanterre, 2014). Some solicitators in my mind are good cases (their working as an ideality word is perhaps more salient than their functioning as an extensional word), others are not (usually they are heard extensionally; that would be the case of *subject*, to begin with).

Etho-analysis results in describing human kind as perplexed in two ways:

1. Most of the time we are called at the same moment in the same situation by several solicitators, to the effect that we have to choose between behaving as, for example, a lover or as a scientist.

2. More radically, any ethos has a tendency to give itself as the only moral, 'screening' so to say fundamental ethical demand; hence we have to balance to what extent we are authorized, in the perspective of what we ethically owe to the face and to justice, to follow the prescriptions of our preferred ethos.

Such perplexity, though, is not the same as the one described by contemporary "critical anthropology," as French philosophers of the sixties and the seventies developed it. They rather claimed, indeed, that any apparent command in our culture had to be relativized by suited genealogy. That we were nothing but conditioned agency, that our destiny as such was changing and moving, turning into difference and renewal of our determined situation and being. We are perplexed in the sense that we don't know what is us, and what demands us, in the sense that we discover the best possible us, and best possible world only inside agency. Etho-analysis sees human person as perplexed because they are too richly obliged. Critical anthropology sees human person as perplexed because they lack any obligation and any identity.

On the whole, etho-analysis offers a strange anthropology, which is not really anthropological, as far as it stands "beyond ontology." Our human world appears as what it is (the ontological level) and at the same time as haunted by demands (the anontological level). This second level is only felt. It has only phenomenological support. But it is typical of the human way that we never strictly inhabit ontological level, we take every piece of it as concerned by sense horizons referring to prescriptions of ethoses.

Discourse of etho-analysis, therefore, could be taken as illustrating the strange assertions of Levinas, according to which the human level is the level where being turns to "otherwise than being." So much can be said not only because we engage ethics, or at least are concerned by it as far as we welcome our humanity, but also because, on the basis of such ethical commitment—declined or accepted, at least felt—we are able to play the game of ethoses and adding the perspective of corresponding stakes to our factual life. This is so much human habit that in our concrete experience, it is sometimes very difficult to come back to actual processes and things, subtracting, so to speak, the strata of stakes. A difficulty which perhaps accounts partly for classical methodological debate in human and social sciences.

Conclusion

Levinas scholars differ quite a bit from one another, which is good news. Each of them has their way not only to hear Levinas's teaching, but also build a personal path out of it. I have only tried to enumerate some aspects of what I call a "Levinasian reading of Levinas," more or less shared by researchers whom I feel belong to the close circle of the truthful ones, among whom I count Richard Cohen. Clearly the path of etho-analysis is only mine, even if for me, it does nothing else than formulating the "general philosophy" implicit in Levinas. It is quite interesting to know whether, in the future, interpretations of Levinas such as the Derrridean and the Heideggerian readings will remain prominent, or whether a closer connection to Levinas's own conceptual tools will be considered a prerequisite for Levinasian studies. In this paper, I have clearly indicated, I hope, the kind of future I am working at promoting.

Notes

1. Marie Anne Lescourret, *Emmanuel Levinas* (Paris: Flammarion, 1994, 2006), 268–87.
2. Richard Cohen, *Ethics, Exegesis and Philosophy* (Cambridge: Cambridge University Press, 2001), 283–25.
3. We could take here the example of page 247 of original edition, which is only about being. Levinas says that with fecundity, being overcomes the impersonal threatening figure of the sacred, appears as multiple and divided into Same and Other. And he then introduces transcendence as time going toward the other person; and also as addressed speech reaching the I. And even, later on, he mentions Goodness and Goodness of Goodness as the deeper relation

behind the "for the other person." The whole conceptualization of otherwise of being, as other books will make it explicit, is thus already there under the heading of being.

Goodness as the deeper relation behind the "for the other person." The whole conceptualization of otherwise of being, as other books will make it explicit, is thus already there under the heading of being.

4. That's what I understand as the teaching of chapter "Maternal body/maternal psyche" in *Ethics, Exegesis and Philosophy*, at least (pp. 180–215).

5. Frédéric Worms, *La Philosophie en France au XXe siècle: Moments* (Paris: Gallimard, 2008).

6. In the same vein, it is of much interest to reflect on correspondences between Lacan (another propagandist of alterity) and Levinas. But not in the perspective of recovering any king of homology between their conceptions: rather as a preparatory work in order to actually grasp what each of them meant and wanted us to understand, and which was not the same.

7. To that list for sure other names should be added. Sophie Nordmann in France has studied many of these authors, and Robert Gibbs and Uli Goetschel in Toronto have constituted a group dealing systematically with this "German/Jewish" heritage, which I understand had been brought to the Canadian city by Emil Fackenheim.

8. Jean-Michel Salanskis, *L'Emotion Ethique—Levinas Vivant I* (Paris, Klincksieck, 2011); *L'Humanité de l'Homme—Levinas Vivant II* (Paris: Klincksieck, 2011); *Le Concret et l'Idéal—Levinas Vivant III* (Paris: Klincksieck, 2015).

9. Or, as "intended object as such" as in Husserl.

Bibliography

Cohen, Richard A. *Ethics, Exegesis and Philosophy: Interpretation after Levinas.* Cambridge: Cambridge University Press, 2007.

Kearney, Richard. *The God Who May Be: A Hermeneutics of Religion.* Bloomington: Indiana University Press, 2002.

Levinas, Emmanuel. *Existence and Existents.* Translated by Alfonzo Lingus. Pittsburgh: Duquesne University Press, 2001.

Levinas, Emmanuel. *Of God Who Comes to Mind.* Translated by Bettina Bergo. Stanford: Stanford University Press, 1998.

Levinas, Emmanuel. *On Escape.* Translated by Bettina Bergo. Stanford: Stanford University Press, 2003.

Levinas, Emmanuel. *Otherwise than Being or Beyond Essence.* Translated by Alfonzo Lingus. Pittsburgh: Duquesne University Press, 1969.

Levinas, Emmanuel. *Totality and Infinity: An Essay in Exteriority.* Translated by Alfonzo Lingus. Pittsburgh: Duquesne University Press, 1969.
Salanskis, Jean Michel. *Territoires du sens.* Paris: J.Vrin, 2007.
Salanskis, Jean Michel. *Partages du sens.* Paris: Presses Universitaires de Paris-Nanterre, 2014.

2

Levinas in North America Today
Richard A. Cohen's Contributions

JACK MARSH AND CHRISTOPHER L. SOUTHLAND

Richard A. Cohen is one of the most important voices in English language Levinas studies. Indeed, absent Cohen's labor the field would not be what it is today. In honor of his enduring contributions, we will sketch here a brief history of English-language Levinas study and Cohen's irreplaceable role in it. The general shape of English-language Levinas scholarship is largely determined by its history. Hence, we must tell a brief story of the origin and development of Levinas studies before turning to its present situation. This story refers to a larger one, and hence we must also say something about the North American philosophical scene. The problematic nature of such narratives is very familiar to all of us, so we simply note it at the outset. Next, and more obviously, it remains simply impossible to know every craggy nook in the landscape of Levinas's North American dissemination. Inevitably, and in spite of our best efforts, we will leave out a name, a paper, or a book that in the last analysis warrants mention. For this we offer our regrets at the outset. Finally, the most formidable problem that confronts us lies in the fact that Levinas's North American "story" has, from the beginning, not been *properly North American*. The story of Levinas scholarship in the United States is inevitably an international one, as the story we tell will reflect.

The North American Philosophical Scene

As most of us already know, Levinas's work has achieved something of a canonical status in the US, at least within scholarly circles sometimes associated with continental philosophy. The meaning of the term "continental philosophy" emerged in the 1970s with a minority of philosophers and theorists who drew stylistic inspiration from such diverse sources as existential phenomenology, German critical theory, and a then-emerging structuralism and poststructuralism. The postwar philosophical scene in the United States was dominated by a tedious and highly specialized form of language analysis we now call "analytic philosophy." Analytic philosophy was the hegemonic philosophical style in the US, a style oriented by overly austere ideals of scientificity, logicality, and semantic minimalism inherited from the logical positivist movement. In this context, "continental philosophy" came to name a rebellion, a dissent, *an engagement*. Names like Kierkegaard, Nietzsche, Marx, and Heidegger represented thinkers *engaged with life* or with what *really and ultimately matters*. Whether the horizon of meaning specified was faith, art, politics, revolution, or being as such, what ultimately set them and others apart from the aridity of analytic philosophy was their *engagement* with the *lived situations* through and in which philosophy gets itself done. For these minority philosophers and the generation of students they taught, "continental" vs. "analytic" philosophy named a distinction between *authentic* and *inauthentic* or *living* and *dead* philosophy.[1] To this day, analytic philosophy remains the predominant philosophical style in North America. Though thanks to thinkers like Rawls, Rorty, and Cavell, and important new traditions in feminist philosophy and pragmatism, the situation is substantially different. Indeed, one must now interpose "so-called" when referring to "continental philosophy," because the term no longer signifies the way it did twenty or thirty years ago.[2] Though still a minority, so-called continental philosophy occupies a privileged place in numerous reputable faculties across the United States.[3] And beyond philosophy proper, it still names a hodgepodge of divergent methods and positions—existential phenomenology, Marxism, hermeneutics, psychoanalysis, and poststructuralism—deployed and treated across virtually every department in the humanities and social sciences.

Cohen himself came to his philosophical calling studying at two of the best-known trailblazing departments that came to be associated with so-called continental philosophy. He studied with Alphonso Lingis as an undergraduate at Penn State, and as a graduate student worked under Don Idhe at Stony Brook. At the completion of his coursework, Cohen arranged to study with Levinas at the Sorbonne for the academic year of 1974–75. This was Levinas's second to last year as a fulltime professor. On his arrival in Paris, Richard was understandably quite eager to meet *l'maître*, he recalls: "Though I knew full well that the Sorbonne doesn't assign books, I phoned Levinas and asked to meet with him about it. He graciously agreed." The first of two meetings took place on September 14, 1974, at the Levinas's apartment above ENIO: "Raïssa welcomed me, and showed me into Levinas's study. The apartment was lovely though modest, and his study was peppered with stacks of books and scattered papers. After a few moments, Levinas himself entered. We shook hands as he welcomed me kindly." Richard asked him about the assigned texts for the class, and afterward Levinas inquired about his school (he had not yet heard of Stony Brook). At the time Richard nursed a grad school interest in Foucault, and asked Levinas a question about their proximity. "My thinking is very different from Foucault," Levinas rejoined. Over the next half hour, they discussed a variety of topics, from Hegel to Judaism: "Hegel is an example of the same," Levinas insisted. "Being Jewish is a state of alertness." They enjoyed such a pleasant meeting, that Levinas invited him back the next week. Richard recalls, "Raïssa served little cakes and Cointreau, and over small talk Levinas even asked my opinion about titles he was considering for a working essay on Blanchot. I cherish the brief time I was able to spend with him. I mean, here was one of the most important philosophers of the century, willing to share his time and kindness with me: a lowly American grad student! He was not only a great philosopher, but also a superlative human being." Throughout the rest of the academic year, Richard attended each of Levinas's seminars, including "Being and Being Given," "Ontology and Transcendence," and "General Philosophy." Ever the plucky American, he even once transgressed Sorbonne convention by daring to ask an in-class question, to Levinas's surprise and the giggles of his classmates. Levinas, with intentional care and kindness, answered Richard in detail and at length, as if to model for the entire class what *welcome to the stranger* means in the humdrum of everyday university life.

Cohen went on to complete his doctoral dissertation in 1980, "Time in the Philosophy of Emmanuel Levinas." Cohen started his career back at Penn State, and began developing his distinctive interpretation of Levinas and the translation work for which he is well known. He introduced

Lingis's English translation of *Otherwise than Being or Beyond Essence* in 1981, and followed up with his own translations of *Ethics and Infinity* (1985) and *Time and the Other* (1987). In 1986 he published one of the most important collection of essays on Levinas's work in print, *Face to Face with Levinas*, with contributions by Blanchot, Lyotard, de Boer, Irigaray, Bernasconi, and Levinas himself, among others. Cohen's early work played an important role in the ongoing reception of Levinas's philosophy in English-language scholarship.

The Origins and Development of North American Levinas Studies

Levinas studies in the US proceeded in two distinct phases, or what we will call, following Atterton and Calarco, "two waves."[4] The first wave can be marked chronologically by the 1969 publication of *Totality and Infinity* (hereafter TI) in English translation. The second wave emerged primarily as a result of critical exchanges between Levinas and Derrida, which began to register in the scholarship by the late 1980s and began to receive intense treatment by the mid-90s. Hence, each wave of Levinas scholarship very roughly corresponds to what Richard Cohen has called "two schools"[5] of Levinas studies. If the phrase "two waves" signifies two distinct temporal periods of scholarship, the phrase "two schools" signifies two distinct ways of reading Levinas.[6] As we will see more concretely below, these "two schools" remain living traditions in contemporary Levinas scholarship. The names associated with the first wave didn't all of a sudden stop writing with the emergence of the second. The second wave was inaugurated precisely by putting *new questions* to Levinas's work. We will now turn to describe these two waves and two schools in more detail.

The first wave of English language Levinas studies properly begins with Alphonso Lingis's English translation of TI, published by Duquesne University Press in 1969. As Atterton & Calarco underline, this phase involved a considerable amount of commentary and exposition, or in getting a handle on precisely what Levinas was saying in its broad significance. The publication of TI was quickly followed by the first three English language dissertations dedicated solely to Levinas' work: Edith Wyschogrod's beautiful treatment eventually published as *Emmanuel Levinas: The Problem of Ethical Metaphysics* (1970); Phillip Lawton's *Emmanuel Levinas's Theory of Language* (1973), and Richard Cohen's *Time in the Philosophy of Emmanuel Levinas* (1980). As far as I've been able to ascertain, some of the first published papers treating Levinas's work in English were Luk Bouckaert's "Ontology and Ethics: Reflections on Levinas' Critique of Heidegger," (1970) and Adriaan Peperzak's "Freedom" (1971).[7] The first wave of Levinas studies is attended by such well-known and important names as Cohen, Wyschogrod, and Peperzak, and by other noteworthy names, for example, Theodore de Boer.

Throughout the 1970s and 1980s Levinas was primarily read as a phenomenologist, and his philosophical proposals were treated and evaluated within the pale of the phenomenological method and the fundamental questions it poses. Of course, these questions were not (and still are not) "dead": not merely specialist or scholastic discussions, they included Levinas's placement in and contributions to existential phenomenology as a living philosophy erupting on the American philosophical scene. The debates to which Levinas's work contributed and in which it intervened involved such *still live* questions as the proper place of theory in the fundamental meaning phenomenology opens up, the relation of Husserl, Heidegger, and Levinas's respective visions of phenomenology, the "meaning" of the *limits* of meaning, or the proper character of phenomenology's involvement with its "others." Levinas broke upon and was treated within a living philosophical milieu; a milieu Levinas and his American readers helped to shape. The work done on Levinas at this time wasn't simply "anatomical" or uncritical, but reflects the passions and signatures of those philosophers who read him, clarified him, questioned him, criticized him, or, in other words, affirmed or rejected his philosophy as approaching, or as failing to approach, what we usually call "truth."

With the slow emergence of the second wave of scholarship in the late 1980s, the *questions put to* Levinas changed. With the second wave enters Derrida and his disciples. Derrida's justly acclaimed reading of TI—"Violence and Metaphysics"—and subsequent critical exchanges between Levinas and Derrida provoked a whole new set of questions.[8] This is one reason our two-wave description is somewhat artificial, but still remains relatively apt in designating the trajectory of the scholarship. Derrida's essay first appeared in English translation in 1964.[9] Though Derrida's reading of TI remained a reference during the US reception of Levinas in the 1970s and early 1980s, it was not until Levinas's *Otherwise than Being or Beyond Essence* appeared in English (1981)—and perhaps not until Derrida's own "ethics crisis"[10]—that the questions begin to change in the scholarship. The questions that emerge in the second wave of US Levinas studies are no longer simply intra-phenomenological, or the question of living versus dead philosophy by which existential phenomenology defined itself in its North American philosophical context. Intra-phenomenological questions became questions about the very (im)possibility of phenomenology; authentic versus inauthentic philosophy becomes the question of the *possibility of philosophy itself*. In other words, all the questions asked, and variously answered in the first wave get *put into question* in the second wave. Levinas the phenomenologist becomes Levinas the poststructuralist. Though its initial currents can be felt as early as the mid-1980s, the second wave of Levinas scholarship in the US doesn't decisively break until the early 1990s.[11] There are two names that are central in turning the tide: Robert Bernasconi and Simon Critchley. Bernasconi is without a doubt the single most important force for deconstructive interpretations of Levinas's work in the US. He began an in-depth exploration of Levinas and Derrida's relationship almost a decade prior to the rest of the scholarship. Along with Cohen, Wyschogrod, and Peperzak, Bernasconi has indelibly and unalterably marked US Levinas scholarship. Simon Critchley, too, and his very important *Ethics of Deconstruction*, deserves special mention here.[12] In this book, Critchley diagnoses the ethical lacuna in deconstruction precisely by summoning Levinas. Levinas's late work is brought to bear to rectify what was then perceived as deconstruction's ethical deficits. Levinas no longer only spoke to the unique situation of minority methods on the American philosophical scene, no longer was simply one live option among others within existential phenomenology and critical theory: with Critchley's *Ethics*, Levinas comes to have meaning for deconstruction's own self-identity. The question Levinas posed and poses to deconstruction becomes *deconstruction's own questions*, and as such "redeems" whatever deficits or deficiencies it was previously thought to harbor. To their credit, Bernasconi and Critchley, each on their own way, raised these questions and redeemed deconstruction in the very midst of Derrida's own appropriation of Levinas. Theirs and others' signatures are felt in Derrida's own so-called ethical turn.[13] The basic movement that specifies the character of our so-called second wave is this: Levinas is *Aufgehoben* in Derrida.

Of course, there are those who appear to simply defy our two-school description. Bettina Bergo, for example, is a properly autonomous interpreter of Levinas in her own right.[14] She notes but never yields to deconstructive appropriations of Levinas and ultimately reads him in fidelity with his properly phenomenological philosophical pedigree. For this very reason, Bergo can be placed in "school 1," or as one who reads Levinas's work as properly phenomenological in character. Many other names warrant mention here, but each one can ultimately be included in one of the two schools outlined above. Why? My two-school description remains valid to the extent that those who do not fit neatly within either side must necessarily refer to one Levinas or another in enlisting him in their own projects. For instance, Robert Gibbs accepts the complication of classical phenomenology Levinas performs, but does so not in Derrida's name but as a Jewish philosopher that presents Levinas's contributions as the contributions of Jewish philosophy to our contemporary situation.[15] This is an eminently valid and noble project, but one that ultimately involves the position one takes with respect to Levinas's relatedness to phenomenology and deconstruction. Even when a specific reading simply refuses to validate its claims through reference to phenomenology or deconstruction, one can surmise the position in question through a review of the actual arguments and evidences presented. For instance, Gibbs praises the complicated way Levinas comes to relate philosophy and Judaism, but does so precisely by underlining his *phenomenological descriptions*.[16] This contrasts, for example, to Critchley's plainly structural interpretation in explicitly Derridean terms.[17] Gibbs's Levinas may ultimately be "deconstructive," but if he is, he is only by virtue of the *concrete sense* or *orientation* that is opened in Levinas's actual phenomenological descriptions. In just this way, every reader of Levinas can be classed according to whether she or he reads him *first as a phenomenologist*, or *first as deconstructionist*. With respect to our two-school description, it matters little what particular aspect or theme a reading treats. If the character of the reading is *oriented* by a sense yielded in Levinas's phenomenological descriptions, it can be said to belong to "school 1" or the *phenomenological school* of Levinas scholarship. If the character of its reading is *governed by* the protocols of "double reading" that defines deconstruction, it can be said to belong to "school 2" or the *deconstructive school* of Levinas scholarship. These two schools aren't always mutually exclusive in practice, but they are ultimately distinguished by this: the analyses of the former can ultimately be traced back to an *appeal* or a *showing*, to phenomenological evidence and the transcendental or ontological conditions it involves; whereas the latter tends to proceed as an apparently pure criticism, though a criticism ultimately *premised* on a specific account of the conditions for meaning in general.

As our own partisan description betrays, the two schools that characterize the questions posed to Levinas's work are living traditions in the scholarship. These schools are fundamentally distinguished by those who

(a) read Levinas *first* as a phenomenologist and (b) those who read Levinas *first* as a poststructuralist. Of course, partisans of the Derridean school will contest this distinction because they have already *decided for* a specific interpretation and problematization of phenomenology, already *decided for* a *specific account* of phenomenology's basic problems and possibilities, an account that remains contested in every quarter of phenomenological research. As we will see below, the only readings of Levinas that ultimately defies my "two school" description has been conducted, unsurprisingly, by those in different methodological traditions.

Cohen himself carried out a distinctive interpretation of Levinas over the course of the 1990s, and never yielded to the "Levinas/Derrida" amalgam that became scholarly common sense for a time. He moreover continued contributing not only to the philosophical debates of the era but also contributed creatively and institutionally to North American Jewish studies. In 1989 Cohen founded the first Judaic studies program at University of Alabama, Tuscaloosa. Beyond his new administrative tasks, he began research eventually published as his first monograph: *Elevations: The Height of the Good in Rosenzweig and Levinas* (1994). The work was received to universal acclaim. Wyschogrod judged it "profound and original," and Drabinski called the book "impressive," and "arguably some of the most important philosophical essays from recent years on Emmanuel Lévinas and Franz Rosenzweig."[18] In 1994 he was appointed Isaac Swift Distinguished Professor of Judaic Studies and Professor of Religious Studies at the University of North Carolina at Charlotte, where he founded their first Judaic studies minor. He wrote the preface to the second edition of Orianne's translation of *The Theory of Intuition in Husserl's Phenomenology* (1998), co-translated Levinas's *Discovering Existence with Husserl* (1998), and published his own translation of *New Talmudic Readings* (1999).

Finally, no description of the history of Levinas scholarship in the US would be complete without mentioning his wider reception by and treatment within North American Jewish studies.[19] In the first wave of Levinas's US reception, and the importance of Levinas's Judaism for his philosophy, was always underlined and, by in large, celebrated. The first wave tended to read Levinas as he himself wanted to be read: as a phenomenologist who drew inspiration from his heritage. All Levinas's most important American readers read him in this way. Levinas's Judaism and its relation to his philosophy did not begin to receive explicit treatment until the late 1980s, with wider debate only emerging in the mid-1990s.[20]

Cohen and Wyschogrod again warrant special mention here: as early as 1988, they began publishing on Levinas's relation to modern Jewish thought and the religious dimensions of his work.[21] Their respective readings of Levinas informed and helped to shape subsequent discussion that emerged on Levinas and Judaism in the 1990s, to which, of course, they also contributed.

In the mid-1990s, discussion and debate of Levinas and his Judaism began in vigor across the scholarship. This period of Levinas's Jewish reception can be characterized as claiming Levinas as a properly Jewish thinker. Robert Gibbs is of decisive importance here. Gibbs's work substantially treats Levinas next to other giants in modern Jewish thought, and presents Levinas's ethics as a religious and specifically Jewish challenge to the philosophical hubris of modernity. Other noteworthy contributors to this discussion were Annette Aronowicz and Jill Robbins.[22] The debates and discussions of this period eventually opened upon a new discussion by a younger generation of scholars. With the turn of the millennium, new voices raised questions about the viability of separating Levinas's Judaism and his philosophy. Some important voices variously weighing in on this continuing discussion include Claire Elise Katz, Michael Fagenblat, Martin Kavka, and Michael Morgan.[23]

How do Jewish readings of Levinas stand with respect to our two-school description above? We have to confess that we are not as familiar with the discussions in Jewish studies as we ought to be. What is clear is that the scholarship does reflect this two-school character, with the exception of voices that simply ignore more abstract philosophical considerations for singularly thematic reasons. There are those who read him as a phenomenologist and a Jewish thinker (i.e., as reflecting differences of style depending on the community he is addressing and the particular questions being considered). Of course, those who read Levinas phenomenologically accept the legitimacy of his heterodox contributions to phenomenology, contributions that have been questioned from Husserlian and Heideggerian quarters.[24] This amounts to an intra-phenomenological debate, however, and partisans of this camp don't simply cede Levinas to the poststructuralists. There are those who accept and read Levinas as a poststructuralist and Jewish thinker, and hence barely detect a difference between Levinas and Derrida's respective projects. Much of the way Levinas is read with respect to Derrida depends on a specific scholar's estimation of Derrida's own work and the complicated question of the Jewish "credentials" of his thought. It remains possible to class specific readings as we suggested above, but we must underline that much of the scholarship circulates within the two-school composition of US Levinas studies without specifically or explicitly locating itself. What does remain clear is that, from the North American perspective, Levinas has justly joined the ranks of Hermann Cohen, Martin Buber, and Franz Rosenzweig in the pantheon of modern Jewish thought.

Contemporary Levinas Studies

As we hinted above, the phenomenological and deconstructive schools of Levinas studies constitute the current shape of Levinas scholarship in the US. Much of the latest research finds its home in one of these schools. The noteworthy exception to this involves readers of Levinas's work from different methodological traditions. These readers, we suggest, are inaugurating what we might call a "third wave" of North American Levinas studies: what we will call *cross-methodological exchange*.

First, let us reiterate that throughout the entire history of the scholarship, Levinas has been read, interpreted, and applied across disciplinary boundaries. This has not ceased. Recently published titles disclose Levinas's influence in virtually every corner of the academy: political theory,[25] Jewish studies,[26] intellectual history,[27] postcolonial studies,[28] theology,[29] film studies,[30] education,[31] cultural studies,[32] literary theory,[33] and even organizational management.[34] If anything, contemporary scholarship suggests that Levinas's influence is vibrantly expanding. Perhaps Levinas's treatment in management theory and other empirically guided theoretical disciplines is not surprising to our new generation of scholars. But twenty or even ten years ago such a thing was scarcely thinkable. Levinas's interdisciplinary treatment is not a distinctively or starkly new development, but the swath of these interdisciplinary treatments is expanding to new and novel domains.

What is genuinely new in recent philosophical scholarship is Levinas's treatment alongside methods and figures traditionally associated with "analytic style," or specifically American traditions of philosophy. Even this must be qualified, however, since as early as 2002, Levinas was subject to comment by such well-known American philosophers as Hillary Putnam and Richard J. Bernstein.[35] Nevertheless, the past few years have witnessed the emergence of a series of substantial studies setting Levinas into conversation with specifically American philosophies and philosophical traditions. For example, in his most excellent book *Discovering Levinas*,[36] Michael Morgan conducts a series of interesting comparative analyses of Levinas next to, for example, Stanley Cavell, Christine Korsgaard, and (Canadian) Charles Taylor, among others. To my knowledge, Morgan is the first to enact a dialogue of this sort between Levinas and the Anglo-American tradition. Next, Michael Barber published a very interesting comparative study on Levinas and Darwall, and their respective accounts of the significance of the "second person" perspective for ethics and ethical theory.[37] Finally, the past few years have witnessed two book-length treatments of Levinas next to the founders of American pragmatism: Richard Steven's *Burning for the Other: Levinas, Pierce, and an Ethical Aesthetics* and Megan Craig's *Levinas and James: Toward a Pragmatic Phenomenology*.[38] Such cross-methodological exploration, exchange, and cross-fertilization between our "continental" Levinas and Indigenous North American philosophy signal a genuinely new development in US Levinas studies. Perhaps it's a bit too early to call this trend a "wave" in its own right, but it does signal a genuinely new development.

The turn of the millennium moreover saw no hiatus in Cohen's prolific scholarly activity. He edited and introduced Rosenzweig's *Ninety-five Poems and Hymns by Judah Halevi* (2000), and published his second monograph *Ethics, Exegesis and Philosophy: Interpretation after Levinas* (2001). Coterminous with these efforts, he edited *Ricoeur As Another: The Ethics of Subjectivity* (2002) with James L. Marsh and *In Proximity: Emmanuel Levinas and the Eighteenth Century* (2001) with Melvyn New and Robert Bernasconi; and continued on introducing new Levinas texts as translations came available. Cohen's tireless efforts as a scholar of Levinas played a significant role, as one of a cohort of first and second-generation scholars, in calling forth the community of readers that resulted in new institutional realities: the first English language journal dedicated to Levinas's work, *Levinas Studies*, founded in 2005 by Jeffrey Bloechl, and the North American Levinas Society, founded in 2006 by Michael Paradiso-Michau and Sol Neely. In 2008, he again founded and directed a new Judaic studies center: the Department of Jewish Thought and Institute for Jewish Thought and Heritage at SUNY Buffalo, and soon after published his third monograph *Levinasian Meditations: Ethics, Philosophy and Religion* (2010).

Beyond Cohen's institutional service and research activity, he taught and lectured widely at home and internationally, at Berkeley School of Law, John Cabot University, Jewish Theological Seminary, Tel Aviv

University, Meiji University, and Hebrew University of Jerusalem, and became the founding director of the Levinas Summer Seminar. His most recent monograph, *Out of Control: Confrontations between Spinoza and Levinas* (2016), was received to rave reviews.

Conclusion

If what we have described above is accurate, it is safe to describe the present situation of North American Levinas scholarship as *vibrant* and *thriving*, thanks in part to the irreplaceable contributions of Richard A. Cohen. The sheer swath of disciplines and concrete issues Levinas is summoned to address is a testament to the power and continuing relevance of his thought. What surprises could there be in store? Could our proposed "third wave" of Levinas studies described above come to disturb and transform its present two-school composition? Or will some other, unforeseeable text or movement break upon us? We will have to wait and see.

Notes

1. This description is, of course, oversimplified. To our knowledge, the "analytic/continental" distinction doesn't actually show up until the 1980s. Nevertheless, a review of the literature of the period reflects the defiance this distinction came to name.

2. The "analytic/continental" divide has been subject to numerous explicit treatments and debunkings in the literature. For example, see Babette E. Babich. "On the Analytic-Continental Divide in Philosophy: Nietzsche's Lying Truth, Heidegger's Speaking Language, and Philosophy," in *A House Divided: Comparing Analytic and Continental Philosophy*, ed. C. G. Prado (Amherst: Prometheus, 2003), 63–103.

3. For instance, New School University, Boston College, SUNY Stony Brook, DePaul University, etc.

4. We gratefully borrow this phrase from Peter Atterton and Matthew Calarco, eds., *Radicalizing Levinas* (Albany: State University of New York Press, 2010), x [hereafter cited as *RL*]. For those not aware of the specificities of US critical theory, the figure of the wave is often employed to characterize development in a specific critical or methodological tradition. For example, feminist philosophy in the US is often described as having proceeded in three waves, with each wave

being described as exhibiting a unique set of identifiable traits within the overall arc of feminist theory in its living movement.

5. We are gratefully indebted to Richard Cohen's brief account of the history of Levinas's US reception. See Richard Cohen, *Levinasian Meditations: Ethics, Philosophy, and Religion* (Pittsburgh, PA: Duquesne University Press, 2010), 169–71 [hereafter cited as *LM*].

6. As Cohen succinctly notes, "There are those . . . who came to Levinas through Levinas. And there are those . . . who came to Levinas through Derrida . . . The result, not surprisingly, is two quite different readings of Levinas" (*LM*, 171).

7. Luk Bouckaert's "Ontology and Ethics: Reflections on Levinas' Critique of Heidegger," *International Philosophical Quarterly* 10 (September 1970): 402–19; Adriaan Peperzak. "Freedom," *International Philosophical Quarterly* 11 (September 1971): 341–61.

8. Jacques Derrida, *Writing and Difference*, Alan Bass, trans. (Chicago: University of Chicago Press, 1980), 79–153.

9. Robert Bernasconi and Simon Critchley, eds., *The Cambridge Companion to Levinas* (Cambridge: Cambridge University Press, 2002), xxiv.

10. We do not mean this as a cheap shot at Derrida and his apostolate. In all sincerity, the only thing more annoying than reflexive critics of Derrida is Derrida's (and his helpers') own responses to these critics. In any case, it was not mere chance that talk of "the ethics of deconstruction" happened to emerge in the late 1980s. The de Man affair and the English publication of *De l'esprit* roused considerable controversy, and gave the impression that Derrida was soft on fascism; or at the very least, excused his friends and influences that flirted with it. Right in the midst of this controversy Derrida authored and presented the text that some consider to mark or inaugurate his so-called ethical turn (*Force of Law*). On the controversy, see John Brenkman and Jules David Law, "Resetting the Agenda," *Critical Inquiry* 15, no. 4 (Summer 1989): 804–11; Thomas Sheehan. "Normal Nazi," in *The New York Review of Books*. XL, 1–2 (January 14, 1993): 30–35; Jacques Derrida, *Of Spirit: of Heidegger and the Question*, trans. Bennington and Bowlby (Chicago: University of Chicago Press, 1989); and "Like the Sound of the Sea Deep within the Shell: Paul de Man's War," *Critical Inquiry* 14 (Spring 1988): 590–652.

11. For an early treatment of Levinas and the "ethics of deconstruction," see Stephan Watson's "Levinas, the Ethics of Deconstruction, and the Remainder of the Sublime," *Man and World* 21 (January 1988): 35–64.

12. Simon Critchley, *The Ethics of Deconstruction: Levinas and Derrida* (London: Blackwell, 1992).

13. Derrida's texts that are said to compose the so-called turn are: Jacques Derrida, "Force of Law," in *Deconstruction and the Possibility of Justice*, ed. Cornell, Rosenfeld, and Carlson (New York: Routledge, 1992), 3–67; *Specters of Marx*, trans.

Peggy Kamuf (New York: Routledge, 1994); *The Politics of Friendship*, trans. G. Collins (London: Verso, 1997); *Adieu to Emmanuel Levinas*, ed. Naas and Brault (Stanford, CA: Stanford University Press, 1999); *Of Hospitality* (Stanford: Stanford University Press, 2000).

14. See Bettina Bergo. *Levinas Between Ethics and Politics* (Pittsburgh, PA: Duquesne University Press, 1999).

15. Robert Gibbs. "Jewish Dimensions of Radical Ethics," in *Ethics as First Philosophy*, ed. Adriaan T. Peperzak (New York: Routledge, 1995), 13–23.

16. Gibs, 13–23.

17. We are not necessarily criticizing Critchley's move. Indeed, we welcome it within the context of deconstructive method. But what motivates Critchley's project is the *structural determinations* that *result* from, and will subsequently be said to mediate, Levinas's actual phenomenological descriptions, and not those descriptions themselves. See Critchley, *The Ethics of Deconstruction*, 26–29.

18. John Drabinski, "Review of Elevations: The Height of the Good in Rosenzweig and Levinas," *Shofar* 16, no. 1 (Fall 1997): 157–60. Edith Wyschogrod, "Review of Elevations: The Height of the Good in Rosenzweig and Levinas," *International Studies in Philosophy* 28, no. 4 (1996): 108–9.

19. We are not as familiar with the work done on Levinas in Jewish studies as we perhaps should be. As such, we heartily thank Richard A. Cohen and Martin Kavka for offering us their perspective on this matter.

20. This, again, is a bit oversimplified. Wyschogrod published on the "religious" dimensions of Levinas's work very early on. See "Emmanuel Levinas and the Problem of Religious Language," *The Thomist* 26, no. 1 (1972), 38; and "Emmanuel Levinas," in *Encyclopedia Judaica* (New York: Macmillan, 1971), II: 114.

21. See Edith Wyschogrod, "From the Disaster to the Other: Tracing the Name of God in Levinas," in *Phenomenology and the Numinous: The Fifth Annual Symposium of the Simon Silverman Phenomenology Center* (Pittsburgh: Duquesne University Press, 1988), 67–86. Richard Cohen, "Levinas, Rosenzweig, and the Phenomenologies of Husserl and Heidegger," in *Philosophy Today* (Summer 1988), 165–78.

22. Robert Gibbs, *Correlations in Rosenzweig and Levinas* (Princeton, NJ: Princeton University Press, 1994); "Levinas and Jewish Thought," *Jewish Book Annual* 51 (1993–1994), 112, 124; "Blowing on the Embers: Two Jewish Works of Emmanuel Levinas," *Modern Judaism* 14, no. 1 (1994): 99–113; "Jewish Dimensions of Radical Ethics," in *Ethics as First Philosophy*, ed. Adriaan Peperzak (New York: Routledge, 1995), 13–23; Annette Aronowicz, "Emmanuel Levinas's Talmudic Commentaries: The Relation of the Jewish Tradition to the Non-Jewish World," from Dorff and Newman, eds., *Contemporary Jewish Ethics and Morality. A Reader* (Oxford: Oxford University Press, 1995); Jill Robbins, *Prodigal Son/Elder Brother: Interpretation and Alterity in Augustine, Petrarch, Kafka, Levinas* (Chicago: University of Chicago Press, 1991); *Altered Reading: Levinas and Literature* (Chicago: University of Chicago Press, 1999).

23. Michael Fagenblat, *A Covenant of Creatures: Levinas's Philosophy of Judaism* (Stanford: Stanford University Press, 2009); Claire Elise Katz, *Levinas, Judaism, and the Feminine: The Silent Footsteps of Rebecca* (Bloomington: Indiana University Press, 2003); Martin Kavka, *Jewish Messianism and the History of Philosophy* (Cambridge: Cambridge University Press, 2004); Michael L. Morgan, *Discovering Levinas* (Cambridge: Cambridge University Press, 2007); *The Cambridge Introduction to Emmanuel Levinas* (Cambridge, Cambridge University Press, 2011).

24. Steven Galt Crowell, "Authentic Thinking and the Phenomenological Method," in *Husserl's Logical Investigations in the New Century: Western and Chinese Perspectives*, ed. John Drummond and K.-Y. Lau (New York: Springer, 2007), 119–33; and Dominique Janicaud, ed., *Phenomenology and the 'Theological Turn': The French Debate* (New York: Fordham University Press, 2000).

25. Ernst Wolff, *Political Responsibility for a Globalised World: After Levinas' Humanism* (Bielefeld, Transcript Verlag, 2011).

26. Michael Fagenblat, *A Covenant of Creatures: Levinas's Philosophy of Judaism* (Stanford: Stanford University Press, 2009).

27. Linda Bolton, *Facing the Other: Ethical Disruption and the American Mind* (Baton Rouge: Louisiana State University Press, 2010).

28. John E. Drabinski, *Levinas and the Postcolonial: Race, Nation, Other* (Edinburgh: Edinburgh University Press, 2011).

29. Alain Mayama, *Emmanuel Levinas' Conceptual Affinities with Liberation Theology* (New York, Peter Lang Publishing, 2011).

30. Sam Girgus, *Levinas and the Cinema of Redemption: Time, Ethics, and the Feminine* (New York: Columbia University Press, 2010).

31. Denise Egta-Kuehne, *Levinas and Education: At the Intersection of Faith and Reason* (London: Routledge, 2011).

32. Steven Shankman, *Other Others: Levinas, Literature, Transcultural Studies* (Albany: State University of New York Press, 2010).

33. Colin Davis, *Critical Excess: Overreading in Derrida, Deleuze, Levinas, Zizek, and Cavell* (Stanford: Stanford University Press, 2010).

34. Naud van der Ven, *The Shame of Reason in Organizational Change: A Levinasian Perspective* (Dordrecht, Springer, 2010).

35. See Hilary Putnam. *Ethics Without Ontology* (Cambridge, MA: Harvard University Press, 2004), 15–32; and "Levinas and Judaism," in *Cambridge Companion to Levinas*, ed. Robert Bernasconi and Simon Critchley (Cambridge: Cambridge University Press, 2002), 33–62; Richard J. Bernstein. *Radical Evil: An Interrogation* (Cambridge: Polity, 2002), 166–179; and "Evil and the Temptation of Theodicy," in *Cambridge Companion to Levinas*, ed. Robert Bernasconi and Simon Critchley (Cambridge: Cambridge University Press, 2002), 252–67.

36. Michael L. Morgan, *Discovering Levinas* (Cambridge: Cambridge University Press, 2007).

37. Michael Barber, "Autonomy, Reciprocity, and Responsibility: Darwall and Levinas on the Second Person," *International Journal of Philosophical Studies* 16, no. 5 (2008): 629–44.

38. Megan Craig, *Levinas and James: Toward a Pragmatic Phenomenology* (Bloomington: Indiana University Press, 2010); and Richard Stevens, *Burning for the Other: Levinas, Peirce, and an Ethical Aesthetics* (Saarbrücken: VDM Verlag, 2009).

Bibliography

Atterton, Peter, and Matthew Calarco. *Radicalizing Levinas.* Albany: SUNY Press, 2010.

Cohen, Richard. Elevations, *The Height of the Good in Rosenzweig and Levinas.* Chicago: University of Chicago Press, 1994.

Cohen, Richard A. *Levinasian Meditations: Ethics, Philosophy, and Religion.* Pittsburgh, PA: Duquesne University Press, 2010.

Critchley, Simon, and Robert Bernasconi. *The Cambridge Companion to Levinas.* Cambridge: Cambridge University Press, 2008.

Critchley, Simon. *The Ethics of Deconstruction: Derrida and Levinas.* Edinburgh: Edinburgh University Press, 2014.

3

Book Review

Ethics, Exegesis and Philosophy: Interpretation after Levinas

ROBERT GIBBS

Cohen, Richard A., *Ethics, Exegesis and Philosophy: Interpretation after Levinas*, Cambridge University Press, 2001, 370 pp.

> Joshua ben Perahyah said: "Provide yourself with a teacher; acquire for yourself a companion; judge each person inclined toward merit."
>
> —*Sayings of the Fathers*

Richard Cohen is a great student of Emmanuel Levinas. This quality is displayed in many of Cohen's writings, but nowhere more clearly and cogently than in this current book. Cohen is not a simple thinker, nor a docile student. His writings are complex and at the same time forthright, even moral. He argues that Levinas's thought responds to a basic and important suspicion of morality. Cohen writes both in a technical philosophical idiom, and more significantly, in a general and accessible voice about things that matter. That voice and, indeed, Cohen's loyalty to Levinas, raise important questions about the task and style of philosophical thinking. Often there is a presumption that a philosopher must stand free of relations to teachers and to authorities—that thought is self-governed and independent. Others are willing to invest authority in great thinkers (Plato, or Thomas Aquinas, or Kant, or in our time in Heidegger or Freud, Derrida, etc.) but are unwilling to recognize Levinas as an authority. Whom shall I make my teacher?

At the heart of this book, and of this review, is the meaning of exegesis—the process of offering an interpretation of texts. Cohen offers us insight on several levels into the significance of exegesis—and I will briefly outline the main tasks in his book, but I urge you to reflect further with me, on how those tasks are self-reflexive: that is, they are not only described but also performed. The central insight is that Levinas provides a way to make ethics first philosophy in order to show the intellectual elite "that morality is a matter for adults, intelligent adults included." (1)

The first part of the book ("Exceeding Phenomenology") locates Levinas in a context of twentieth-century Continental philosophy. Cohen makes a strong claim for the importance of Bergson as the turning point that led to a postmodern harmony of revelation and reason. He tells the story of phenomenology, from Husserl to the students (Merleau-Ponty, Heidegger, Sartre, Levinas, Schutz, and others) in a counterpoint with Bergson. He examines the relation between Heidegger and Levinas and maintains a constant critical distance from Derrida, who becomes the leading French student of Heidegger. These relations are explored with careful technical treatments of important themes in phenomenology. But there is a second level of interpretation here: for Cohen frames the agenda in a much more general idiom. The central questions are the relation of reason and revelation and the status of science and its reason. Bergson, even more than Husserl, represents a critical view of modern science but one that also preserves the achievements of modern rationality.

But against this backdrop, of a crisis of science and a new rapprochement with revelation, there is a much more serious conflict that defines Levinas's context for Cohen; a division and antagonism between an elevation of aesthetics to first philosophy and an elevation of ethics. This oppositional polarity provides a scale for the contemporary Continental philosophical scene (including the North American outposts). For many who are further toward the aesthetic pole (which seems in Cohen to often be a military camp), ethics seems trivial, secondary, even a matter for the not-so-smart scholars. Levinas and his students, then, represent one of the few alternatives. While the ethics crowd (represented almost exclusively by Levinas) stands for the priority of the other person and of responsibility, for Cohen the aesthetics crowd consists of followers of both Nietzsche and, particularly, Heidegger. They understand themselves as beyond good and evil, exploring the appearing and concealing of what is. The primacy of ontology is purchased at the expense of a concern for serious ethics.

The heuristic value of Cohen's further polarizing of what is indeed a polar tendency in Continental thought is clear and strong. It forces us to ask which questions are the most important, which intellectual tasks are most pressing. It has a tendency to force specific thinkers into one camp or the other (Derrida is repeatedly driven toward Heidegger and away from Levinas, for instance). It raises other questions as well. First, is the Kantian tradition of ethical reflection (represented most recently by, say, Rawls or Korsgaard) simply irrelevant to this polarizing schema? That is, if we include what people who are *not* Continental philosophers are thinking about, does this opposition still hold? This drives us back to the critique of modern reason that both sides of this Continental polarity share—that the models of formalist ethics and autonomy are somehow inadequate for raising the most important questions. But we might then ask again, this time about the Frankfurt School. Of course, Cohen might push Adorno, along with Benjamin to the aesthetic side of the scale—but with some difficulty, and then return with Habermas and his followers on the ethical side? Surely the Frankfurters share a profound critique of modern reason, but they do divide up so easily?

Cohen, however, is legitimately addressing the intellectual context in which Levinas studied and wrote. Aside from one essay on Ernst Bloch, Levinas has almost no direct engagement with the Frankfurt School. Levinas studied and wrote about Kant's ethics but had almost no word even about Hermann Cohen much less later neo-Kantian ethics. This limitation of Levinas's claim about ethics as first philosophy is often encountered when Levinas scholars talk with others in philosophy—because it depends on a specific genealogy of thought. There is, simply put, no way to Levinas except through Husserl and especially Heidegger.

When we turn then to the second part ("Good and evil"), Cohen offers important readings of Levinas's thought that is more on its own terms. Although there is also a long engagement with Paul Ricouer, with Charles Blondel (another of Levinas's teachers), and with Derrida again. The primacy of ethics is defended here in terms of the key themes of Levinas: the election for responsibility, the passivity of this assignment, the suffering for-the-other as the base of consciousness itself. In addition, the key chapter of this part (Chapter 7: Humanism and the Rights of Exegesis), explores the way that Jewish traditional texts can provide resources for philosophical thought. This chapter provides a simply magnificent treatment of the way that Levinas appropriates Jewish traditions of exegesis for the sake of a truly humanistic ethics. My own interpretations of Levinas confirm Cohen's claim that the "source" of Levinas's way of thinking ethics is a response and continuation of the interpretative tradition of the rabbinic Sages of the Talmud. Ethics becomes here an exegetical task, and exegesis becomes intrinsically ethics. Cohen shows how this way of thinking is in marked opposition and contrast with first Spinoza and then with Nietzsche (and his followers). As impressive and important as the treatment of complex matters in phenomenology was, this relation to a thinking that is in no sense dogmatic or parochial offers great insight not only into Levinas's thought but also into the task of ethics.

This second part also includes an important discussion of the "uselessness" of the Holocaust. Drawing on two important essays by Levinas ("Useless Suffering," and "To Love the Torah More Than God"), Cohen assembles a clear and forceful argument about why ethics must be pursued in response to an evil that admits of no "good" interpretation. Levinas insists that theodicy is impossible in relation to these evils, that such suffering is truly useless, and that only my own suffering undergone for another is capable of meaning. Given Levinas's relentless, even infinite, view of ethical responsibility, the "problem of evil" seems to be a huge hurdle—until one notices that the refusal to justify another's suffering is the fulcrum upon which Levinas's ethics moves. Cohen offers this reading in a particularly clear and trenchant way.

The salient quality of Cohen's interpretations, however, is his loyalty and discipline following Levinas. That is, Cohen argues and explicates the philosophical claims of Levinas, claims about ethics, about thinking, about exegesis, and so forth. The project has a further twist—for there is a clear translation, a transatlantic adaptation of Levinas. Levinas had developed a rich and demanding style that suited (and disrupted) the French intellectual scene of the 1960s and 1970s. Cohen writes in a voice that is frankly American—and so it often shocks us with its directness and its unwillingness to make things subtle, or even oversubtle. Some of the essays are rich in complex technical philosophical writing, but the point, again and again, is about the importance of being good, and not just thinking about being. This moral style is self-conscious and is obvious. And it dares us to ask ourselves why this more blunt and moral tone is almost embarrassing for philosophers.

And then we can turn to the issues I raised at the beginning of this review: (1) should a philosopher serve the work of another thinker? and (2) is Levinas a suitable authority? To interpret another thinker, to be a loyal student, is to recognize the authority of the other, of my teacher. Perhaps one of Levinas's greatest insights is that another person can teach me new things, such as a new way of responding. Learning not only content but also to question myself and to respond for the other, even to suffer for the other, my teacher. The self-confidence of a philosopher, to *not* have any teacher, is a betrayal of the ethics of thinking, a betrayal of the others whom I encounter, and that includes those whom I read and study. Thus Cohen not only reports this lesson about exegesis and responsibility; he also performs it in his adherence to Levinas and more importantly to Levinas's thought.

As great as this ethical claim upon thinking is, it occurs in a long-practiced (if unrecognized) structure of authority in philosophy. Most contemporary Continental philosophers adhere to some figures and strive to give as a rich and sympathetic reading of their works as possible. For Cohen, Derrida, for example, is a disciple of Heidegger and always tries to save Heidegger's thought, to think it further and to make it address us again. Cohen, like Levinas, does not conclude that exegesis is simply repetition or uncritical defense. On the contrary, precisely on the issues that concern us most, we are required to criticize, to explore what lies undeveloped, to think with and at times even against the text we study (see 232). Yet Cohen, as capable as he is of strong and blunt criticism of some (Heidegger, Derrida, Nietzsche), is completely won over by Levinas. And there is a great benefit in reading a book so wholeheartedly devoted.

Some would object, in relation to the second question, that Heidegger, Derrida, or Plato, for example, are more worthy of such intellectual loyalty. But Cohen mounts a series of arguments about what makes a life good, about what is the highest aspect of our humanity, about the primacy of ethics that shows a strong justification of Levinas's viewpoint. If one makes Levinas one's teacher, then one should learn the primacy of ethics and the value of biblical humanism. And one has, as Cohen fulfills, obligations to justify the aspects of Levinas that seem limited or faulty.

Two questions, however, remain: (1) whether such a moral and loyal reading is the best reading of Levinas, and (2) whether the moral questions are the most important for philosophical reflection. My own reservations with Cohen's work lie less in his relation to Levinas than in his relations to others. His choice of polarizing the range of current questions, while more clear than my own efforts and those of most Levinas scholars, also reduces the complexity of Levinas's own response to those thinkers with whom he disagrees. To hear the moral dimension of others' questioning, even when they themselves were less than righteous and less interested in that very dimension, is still to learn ethics from many others. Cohen shows proper scholarly respect for the Levinas secondary literature, citing and negotiating with much of it in the footnotes. But he is also quite sure that some questions, positions, and viewpoints are wrong. Levinas himself wrote with great rhetorical force, attacking many positions, but also listening to the ethical searching in the thinking. One has only to see his reading of Descartes to see this rehabilitation of a truly ethical aspect in a thinker who has so often been identified as the origin of what is wrong in modernity. The moral tone of Cohen's work is content to label some ways of thinking as bad, even evil. Is this the best translation of Levinas's own moral authority into an American idiom?

We learn here, then, one way to be a student of Levinas—and the book serves as a great introduction to Levinas, quite possibly the best we now have. If it judges and criticizes others bluntly, then it may be that its force is that of moral thinking, but it may also be a tactical gesture and as such one that we must suspect and engage with great care. For the proper companions are the others with whom I do not agree and who are still other. To acquire a companion requires patience, even passivity, and a listening—to learn even from those who refuse to recognize the primacy of ethics. By offering a bold presentation of the priority of ethics, Cohen teaches us one way to become a student.

4

Cohenfest

Did Rich Cohen Eat Al Lingis's Octopus?

Don Ihde

I begin with a provocative title referring to a Stony Brook (SBU) urban legend because the first third of my contribution to this volume will be biographical, recounting earlier days of SBU's philosophy program. Then, as a philosopher of technology, I will comment on Richard Cohen's three published articles in that field.

Everyone knows that today's SBU PhD program in philosophy was designed by Patrick Heelan, a Fordham University philosopher of science, hired as a new chair; Patrick Hill, the instigator of both Heelan's and my appointments to SBU; and by me, its first director, 1971–1974. We deliberately designed the program to be pluralistic, interdisciplinary, and strongly "Continental," a minoritarian contrast to the 1970s' American Analytic dominance. There were lots of ironies in both the timing and design. First, an earlier version of the program had been turned down by SUNY Central for being too much like the then-dominant Analytic-plus-tokenism design of many programs. SUNY Central demanded something new. Our design was quickly accepted in 1971. We knew it would attract large numbers of graduate students interested in Continental philosophies simply given the paucity of strong programs available. That, indeed, drew Rich Cohen from Penn State to us. Penn State's program was also more Continental than most.

At Penn State Cohen knew and worked with Alphonso Lingis, who also taught David Allison, a Penn State PhD and Lingis admirer already on our faculty when Rich arrived (David is sadly now deceased). Al was always known as a bit of a "wild man." I had known him even before our PhD program began, when he spent virtually all his summers in Paris. I soon detected his romantic streak—he was quite convinced that France, especially Paris, was superior to the US. But after a number of years even Al tired of Francophilia and started to spend summers and leaves in other countries, including Scandinavian countries—each of which became for the time occupied "better" than "us." I am sure I am not the only one who began to recognize that even his costume and bodily appearance took on an "aura" of whatever his latest romantic identification was. I can illustrate this by his appearance at presentations I witnessed, sometimes at SPEP, the fast-growing, now second-largest special interest philosophy organization in the USA, or sometimes at papers given at SBU. Here is a sample:

- Subject: Death. Skin sallow and anemic (due to diet of solely cheesecake). Dressed all in black.
- Subject: Savages (after his adoration of Leni Riefenstahl's *The Last of the Nuba,* 1974). Tanned/dressed in open flowered shirt, seated cross-kneed on a table, undergraduate audience members flirting actively while listening.
- I will not comment much upon his short-term marriage to an Indian outcaste, whose pictures I still have . . .

During a question session I once asked Al why others are always better than we are, pointing out his changes of appearance.

But now Rich Cohen and our urban legend. Many of us would annually attend SPEP, and, if near enough, either take a university van or drive in carpools. Rich sometimes would stop over and stay a night at Al Lingis's house in State College. On one of these occasions—as legend has it—he took Al's pet octopus, cooked it, and ate it.

I will neither confirm nor deny the legend here; it is only one of numerous tales of Rich's wild acts in his early graduate years at SBU. Then came Levinas. I do not recall, possibly do not even know, how and why Rich became attracted to Levinas, but his work would become Rich's dissertation topic. I do remember that I, as advisor, and our committee decided in advance we would really grill Rich at the defense—which lasted a full three hours. And I remember how the Levinasian influence began to temper Rich's wilder behaviors. Those who know him today see him with a short haircut, usually a tie, and quite Orthodox in religion. In short, Levinas seemed to "tame" Rich, who today is widely recognized as a major Levinas scholar.

I am now ready to turn more philosophical and respond to the three published entries Rich authored on philosophy of technology. I shall look at all three chapter-article length publications in chronological order. The earliest, "Ethics and Cybernetics: Levinasian Reflections," was presented first as a lecture at the London School of Economics in 1998.[1] The second to appear, "Technology: The Good, the Bad, and the Ugly," was in my Festschrift, edited by Evan Selinger.[2] The third was presented at SPEP in 2009.[3] In all three publications, Levinas plays at least a background role.

The first article I will characterize as "pre-phil-tech" for two reasons: as the editor points out, "Richard Cohen uses the word 'cybernetics' to refer to all forms of information and communication technology."[4] This is anachronistic in two senses. First, early thinkers, including Heidegger, and later writers like Andrew Pickering chose Norbert Wiener's system of cybernetics—a program for directing antiaircraft fire—as symbolic for an AI-related "systems" approach; these early thinkers, like Cohen, used the term as a catchall for information and communication technologies. Second, virtually all more recent philosophers of technology agree that technologies are "non-neutral," if my coined term is used, or at least not neutral. I offer key examples noted in *American Philosophy of Technology*, edited by Hans Achterhuis:[5]

- Ihde: Example: Dentist's probe instrument, "explorer." A steel probe used to examine tooth surfaces; its sharp point "amplifies" cracks, fissures, cavities, but, compared to one's finger, dampens moisture, temperature, and other gross textures. Or, erasure end of pencil, no dampness, but also no detection of cracks, fissures, or cavities. Each variant yields an experiential difference and displays a different "magnification/reduction" of felt affects, i.e., the material technology *non-neutrally transforms experience.*[6]

- Borgmann: "Focal activities" versus "design paradigm." In the first, the subject is highly involved, as in preparing wood for a wood burning stove—chopping, stacking, filling, experiencing a sort of "earned" warmth. Compare to an automatic stove, requiring little or no pre-activity to "earn" the warmth gained.[7]

- Winner: Artifacts have politics. In his often-cited example, Robert Moses deliberately designed parkways with low bridges to keep buses and other public transport for lower classes from Long Island beaches. Later, during the Eisenhower cold war, interstates were designed with high bridges to allow intercontinental missiles to go under—confirming non-neutral selectivities of material design.[8]

These three examples of technological nonneutrality are sufficient to show a consensus among twentieth-century philosophers of technology. All were detailed looks at particular technologies; none were taken as typical of technology überhaupt.

The example Cohen deals with—admittedly an early look at virtuality in information and communications technology (ICT)—regards diametrically opposed accounts of how distance virtuality changes, for better or worse, human experiences of the other. On one side is Sherry Turkle, who sees distance virtuality positively since it allows the experience of multiple "selves," thus "freeing" the user from stable, single selves; on the other, Lucas Introna, who, drawing from Levinas, sees the same technologies as threatening face-to-face relational contact. Turkle thus accepts a quasi-embodiment at a distance; Introna does not. Cohen rejects—to my mind rightly—typical utopian/dystopian first responses to new technologies but reverts to a very old and pre-phil-tech position I will call an "engineer's instrumental-functionalism": technologies are "neutral" and can be used for both good and bad ends. Such a stance, to my mind, is totally outdated in relation to phil-tech's deeper understanding of non-neutrality, revealed through the "empirical turn" to specific technologies.[9]

Cohen's next publication is in my first Festschrift. Cohen reverts to a muted version of "engineering instrumental functionalism": "Technology is 'good' or 'evil' as the human hand or foot are good or evil, or rather as human action . . . is good or evil."[10] He then deals with utopias and dystopias, which are always wrong regarding technologies, depicting them as exaggerated and distorted. He clearly situates Heidegger as an extreme dystopian regarding technology. "Obviously Heidegger takes a strong dystopian view of technology . . . it contextualizes and demonizes technology within a vast philosophy of historical revelation."[11] In a transition, Cohen reviews the growing tension between science and what he calls "romanticism." Often linking scientism with utopianism, it ends up being antireligious: "If a god can no longer save us from science, science can save us from God."[12] Finally, once scientistic rationality is opposed to romanticism, Cohen, as in all his philosophy of technology writings, turns to his own answer—Levinasian *ethics*. "I think the proper term Ihde is seeking, or the term which lies beneath the term 'politics' that he has chosen, the term that directs us to the genuine root of politics, is the *ethical*."[13]

Levinas is unique in the spectrum of phenomenological thinkers. As Cohen often points out, ethics takes precedence over both epistemology and ontology in Levinas's thought. Levinas holds that ethics—phenomenologically climaxed in a *face-to-face* meeting of the self and an Other—is for phenomenology an "'ethical metaphysics' that ultimately undergirds and ruptures the phenomenological method in its search to understand the meaning of the human."[14] Cohen turns then to two biblical vignettes: the Tower of Babel and the secret invisibility cloak of Nimrod, great-grandson of Noah. Cohen draws his interpretation from the Jewish interpretation traditions, the Talmud and multiple Midrash, showing theological roots which clearly predate any scientific tradition (anthropology, archeology, etc.). The rabbis interpret the tower tale as one of hubris. The tower, made of bricks instead of stones, is designed to reach heaven and involves three forms of hubris: "(1) those who wanted to ascend to heaven to dwell there, (2) those who wanted to ascend to heaven to erect idols there, and (3) those who wanted to ascend to Heaven to wage war against God."[15]

The building was stopped, and the builders punished by God by the confounding of languages. Cohen also discusses Nimrod, an evil king who obtained heavenly garments given to Adam, which allowed the wearer to see but not be seen while hunting animals.[16] Cohen's riff includes the "technologies" of bricks and cloaks. Bricks, the "artificial" stones that are the materials of the tower, are forbidden, along with iron, for use in constructing altars. One would think this tradition negatively values technologies. Yet Cohen concludes, "a technology is in itself neither good nor evil . . . "[17], thus returning to his pre-phil-tech neutrality.

The third article, one might have thought, might deal primarily with Levinas—but instead it deals primarily with Heidegger. Cohen compares the early Heideggerian thought in *Being and Time* with the later *Question of Technology*. Cohen sees Heidegger as continuing what he takes as the modern tradition of philosophy favoring epistemological and ontological traditions, which take *representation* in knowledge as primary. Heidegger's rejection replaces "philosophy" with *thinking*, taking his famous "Being" question as the forgotten theme of thinking. Cohen notes that Heidegger recognizes three periods of philosophical thought: Greek, medieval, and modern, each with distinct themes, with the modern era having *technology* as its theme, the most negative and *dangerous*. At this point I will not delve more deeply into Cohen's early and late Heidegger interpretation and critique except to say I find it well done and properly critical. Instead, I will underline what Heidegger did to (a) invert the usual valuation of science to technology, and (b) to show how this relates to subsequent generations of philosophers of technology.[18] Early Heidegger, in his *Being and Time* discussion also noted by Cohen, differentiates between "readiness to hand" and "presence at hand," effectively inverting the usual implications for technology and science. "Readiness to hand" recognizes what I will call "use experience" of technologies—also termed "tacit knowledge" by Polanyi, and often described by Merleau-Ponty. This is *praxis* over theory. The "tacit knowledge" needed to ride a bicycle, or Heidegger's "hammer use," is the learned skill needed to bodily perform as bicycle rider or hammer user, a nontheoretical performance skill that is also central for postphenomenology. (It was a skill only indirectly referenced in the later Husserl.) "Presence at hand" is theoretical, "Cartesian," and third person object-oriented, and according to Heidegger comes from broken, absent, or nonworking technologies—his famous "break-down" move from praxis-knowledge into scientific knowledge. Most post-Heideggerian philosophers of technology accept some version of this inversion.[19] Paul Forman recognized Heidegger's inversion in his well-known article, "The Primacy of Science in Modernity, of Technology in Postmodernity, and the Ideology in the History of Technology."[20] Forman, however, regards the Heideggerian inversion a mistake.

This leaves us with what I regard as an incompleteness in Cohen's three philosophy of technology articles. He owes us, as it were, one more article, directly dealing with how and why we should consider Levinas's importance for the philosophy of technology. If Levinas's argument is that ethics should take precedence, this claim relates well to the dominant public belief that philosophers should be first of all ethicists, and Cohen is well positioned to answer that call.

Notes

1. Richard Cohen, "Ethics and Cybernetics: Levinasian Reflections," *Ethics and Information Technology* 2 (2000): 27–35.

2. Richard Cohen, "Technology: The Good, the Bad, and the Ugly," in Evan Selinger, *Postphenomenology: Critical Companion to Ihde* (Albany: State University of New York Press, 2006), 145–60.

3. Richard Cohen, "Heidegger's Dasein-Analytic of Instrumentality in *Being and Time* and the Thinking of the 'Extreme Danger' of the Question of Technology, and Frederick Tonnies' *Community and Society*," in *Philosophy Today* 54 (2010): 91–100.

4. Cohen, "Ethics and Cybernetics," 27, fn. 1.

5. Hans Achterhuis, ed., *American Philosophy of Technology: The Empirical Turn* (Bloomington: Indiana University Press, 2001).

6. Peter-Paul Verbeek, "Don Ihde: The Technological Lifeworld," in *American Philosophy of Technology*, 127.

7. Peter Tijmes, "Albert Borgmann: Technology and the Character of Everyday Life," in *American Philosophy of Technology*, 23–25.

8. Martijntje Smits, "Langdon Winner: Technology as a Shadow Constitution," in *American Philosophy of Technology*, 160–63.

9. Should the reader like to see my own extended work on this, see Don Ihde, *Bodies in Technology* (Minneapolis: University of Minnesota Press, 2001) and *Embodied Technics* (Copenhagen: Automatic Press/VIP, 2010).

10. Cohen, "Technology: The Good, the Bad, and the Ugly," 146.

11. Cohen, "Technology," 148.

12. Cohen, "Technology," 150.

13. Cohen, "Technology," 153. I disagree with Cohen on this point. All ethics is social and with most Continental authors, such as Habermas, etc., I think politics is wider and deeper than ethics.

14. Cohen, "Technology," 154.

15. Cohen, "Technology," 158. The rabbinic commentary cited by Cohen is precritical, a commentary launched in the late nineteenth century, which includes "demythologization" or recognition that the largely Babylonian cosmology of a tiny, three-story cosmology, cannot hold for modern cosmology. The Tower of Babel, designed to reach heaven, did not envision the 240,000-mile distance to the Moon, beyond which Heaven would be located. No building on earth was conceivably 240,000 miles high.

16. Cohen, "Technology," 158.

17. Cohen, "Technology," 159.

18. Cohen, "Heidegger's Dasein-Analytic of Instrumentality," 91–100. See also my reprinted chapters 1 and 2 covering similar territory in *Heidegger's Technologies* (New York: Fordham University Press, 2010).

19. Peter Galison, Paul Forman, and others note the Heidegger "break down" theory as well.

20. Paul Forman, "The Primacy of Science in Modernity, of Technology in Postmodernity, and of Ideology in the History of Technology," in *History and Technology*, 2007, 23, nos. 1–2, 1–152.

Bibliography

Cohen, Richard. "Ethics and Cybernetics: Levinasian Reflections." *Ethics and Information Technology* 2 (2000): 27–35.
Cohen, Richard. "Heidegger's Dasein-Analytic of Instrumentality in *Being and Time* and the Thinking of the 'Extreme Danger' of the Question of Technology, and Frederick Tonnies' *Community and Society*." *Philosophy Today* 54 (2010): 91–100.
Cohen, Richard. "Technology: The Good, the Bad, and the Ugly," in *Postphenomenology: Critical Companion to Ihde*, edited by Evan Selinger, 145–60. Albany: State University of New York Press, 2006.
Forman, Paul. "The Primacy of Science in Modernity, of Technology in Postmodernity, and of Ideology in the History of Technology" *History and Technology* 23, nos. 1–2 (2007): 1–152.
Ihde, Don. *Bodies in Technology*. Minneapolis: University of Minnesota Press, 2001.
Ihde, Don. *Embodied Technics*. Copenhagen: Automatic Press/VIP, 2010.
Ihde, Don. *Heidegger's Technologies: Postphenomenological Perspectives*. New York: Fordham University Press, 2010.
Smits, Martijntje. "Langdon Winner: Technology as a Shadow Constitution," in *American Philosophy of Technology: The Empirical Turn*, edited by Hans Achterhuis, 147–69. Bloomington: Indiana University Press, 2001.
Tijmes, Pieter. "Albert Borgmann: Technology and the Character of Everyday Life," in *American Philosophy of Technology: The Empirical Turn*, edited by Hans Achterhuis, 11–36. Bloomington: Indiana University Press, 2001.
Verbeek, Peter-Paul. "Don Ihde: The Technological Lifeworld," in *American Philosophy of Technology: The Empirical Turn*, edited by Hans Achterhuis, 119–46. Bloomington: Indiana University Press, 2001.

5

Cohen as Philosopher

Marie-Anne Lescourret

It is difficult to find a title in Richard Cohen's impressive bibliography that does not mention Emmanuel Levinas. As if Cohen not only had devoted his work to a task of commentary, which actually is the case for most practitioners of philosophy nowadays, but also had concentrated this commentary on one and the same thinker, namely the Lithuanian-born Jewish philosopher Emmanuel Levinas. Rare, indeed, are the specialists of the conceptual corpus who can flatter themselves with the discovery of a concept, of a new way of thinking, an insight, such as the Heideggerian rejection of rationality, the Husserlian return to the things as such, or the Wittgensteinian focus on linguistic use and grammar. The great majority of scholars who engage in philosophical studies are doomed, as it were, to comment, explain, and discuss the milestones of tradition since Parmenides, together with their forerunning commentaries, explanations, and discussions—a kind of everlasting exercise that yearly enriches the already abundant Cartesian studies (for instance) field with thousands of pages. Sometimes, this sticking to the classical sources responds to the pedagogical exigency of basic or fundamental knowledge: learn the alphabet before pretending to invent words and worlds. Sometimes, scholars are committed to providing an enlightening approach to a most familiar work: hence the everlasting tradition of Platonic or Hegelian research. After all, Emmanuel Levinas died relatively recently (1906–1995). He really entered the philosophical scope only in the second half of the former century, later still in the United States where one had to await the translations. He is a newcomer, and as such certainly in need of presentation and clarification, therefore widely justifying, even demanding, Richard Cohen's undertaking.

But is the election of one thinker among others purely objective? Does one fulfill a strict epistemological duty in ploughing a specific philosophical field, and does this happen without any personal involvement? Or does the encounter obey a sympathy, something shared between the philosopher and his commentator? Actually, Cohen is very clear about his choice. He states it unambiguously in the preface of one of his great books: "What I remember distinctly to this day is the impression Levinas made on me: 'This is *true*' I thought, in contrast to all the philosophers and philosophies which are *fascinating* or *provocative*."[1] Lucky man who does meet truth, while by profession as it were, he is supposed to track it, fortunate enough if he happens to be on the right path. But according to his words (and my own conviction),[2] far from innocent or self-detached, the choice of a philosopher for commentary reveals the commentator as a philosopher, denotes what he considers philosophy to be. Studying Cohen's writings should therefore lead us to his definition of philosophy, and perhaps, speaks to the man himself.

From the start, the interesting point is that Cohen does not contrast "true" with "false"—its usual contrary—but with "fascinating" and "provocative." He uses a vocabulary of seduction, of appeal, as if philosophy was a matter of passion (of rhetoric), his notion of "truth" pertaining to persuasion and sincerity rather than to dialectical argumentation, as Plato taught us. In this spontaneous confession of his immediate adhesion to Levinas's thought, Cohen implicitly reckons that philosophy for him amounts neither to the contemplation of eternal ideas nor to the knowledge of the external world, and that its "truth" does not rely on the correspondence of its propositions with empirical data. We therefore expect him to show us what this "truth" consists in and perhaps to convince us of his certitudes.

Cohen can't but be aware of the presumption of his inaugural assertion. Who indeed—even beyond the rigors of the correspondence theory of truth, or after the Kantian critical approach of knowledge has been generally admitted—would dare claim to know what truth is and to have found it?[3] Such an immediate and overwhelming experiment in truth evokes the aesthetic experience in Wittgensteinian terms: the beautiful is the piece of art that silences my interpretation.[4] I feel well, at home, "natural," in the painting I am admiring, and I rest in it. Cohen felt "natural" in Levinas's work. But since his job is not sheer contemplation and enjoyment, he then endeavours to spread this truth, transmit this understanding of life and the world. He does it in a very broad and dedicated way.

As we saw, Levinas's work is "young" enough first not to have (yet) given rise to an enormous set of "secondary literature," and second to reserve lots of "virgin" areas still to be discovered. Cohen could have made a philosophical career just with a kind of internal explanation of Levinas, happy with the identification of the problematics, concepts, and notions that belong specifically to the philosopher of his choice. But what makes his work unique and somehow out of reach is that Cohen does not content himself merely with drilling specific Levinasian notions, such as "enjoyment," "separation," "said," or "alterity." More than that: he aims at showing the relevance of Levinas's work for the philosophical tradition by questioning each of its problematics from the perspective of the Western philosophical tradition. Cohen studied in the United States and in Europe. He therefore is able to magnify his "hero's" thought by confronting it with the usual representative of phenomenology, the trend Levinas is supposed to belong to (since he introduced it to France) but also with those of German idealism, with the tenants of the linguistic turn, and with those of the classical rationalism, and—what seems reserved to initiated people—with the Jewish tradition, be it the Talmudic corpus or the Jewish philosophers themselves. Each confrontation reinforces Cohen's convictions about Levinas's excellence and allows him to assert, if not the truth of Levinas's work, at least what philosophy means for him as a scholar. Understanding Levinas helped him understand himself as a philosopher. "I conceive this book as such an introduction [. . .]—to the reorientation of thinking, but also to myself, to Levinas, to yourself and to life."[5]

In my view, Cohen identifies two major types of philosophers: the rationalists who mistrust all transcendence and the aesthetes who glorify the visible and stick to it. Each type refuses in its own way a "world behind the scenes": be it the realm of the true ideas for the Nietzschean aesthete or the "hypothesis" of an almighty God for the supporters of reason who wonder how a violent and unjust world can be the creation of a perfect being. Both positions arise from the same puzzlement: the opposition between reason and revelation, also understood as the opposition between Athens and Jerusalem, between the Greeks and the Bible; as if traditionally, all religious belief was incompatible with any provable knowledge. When Cohen regrets that those major currents of Western philosophy lead either to violence (of the rationality of the real, in Hegelian words), or to Nietzschean dance, Cohen's response neither succumbs to the sirens of irrationality, nor to the Romantic assertion of an omnipotent subject, nor to the postmodern rejection of argumentative deduction. In Cohen's work, epistemology—the examination of the conditions of possibility of the knowledge of the world, relying either on the structure of understanding or on grammar—is not the primary problem, and does not for Cohen constitute initial access to philosophy. He is not seeking that kind of truth. There seems to be an inaugural evidence to him—comparable to Levinas's prephilosophical experiences. Aren't indeed the usual philosophical incentives the questions of the existence of the world and of the meaning of life?

Levinas regularly mentions Russian literature and the reading of the Bible as his introduction to philosophy, hence obviously as existential and ethical questioning. From Dostoyevsky and his colleagues, he drew interrogations about the meaning of life and about what had to be done, as well as the famous motto that runs through his writings: "We are guilty, and I more than the others." From the start for him, philosophy is a matter of morality, inspired by the Judaic tradition: not so much the scientific tradition of the famous Gaon of Vilna but rather the admonishment to responsibility uttered by the rabbi and kabbalist Voloziner, an admonishment also displayed in the biblical injunction: "Remember that you were slaves in Egypt" (Duet. 24:18).[6] The classical problem of the confrontation between reason and revelation alternatively makes the first handmaiden of the second, or by contrast dissolves the problem by understanding ethics as first philosophy. Forgetting the alternative between the God of Abraham, Isaac and Jacob versus the God of the philosophers, there remains the conviction of an exteriority, something outside the empirical world that calls one into being as passivity, response, and debt. Levinas then refined his understanding of being as second in the readings of the German phenomenologists, namely Husserl on intersubjectivity in the *Cartesian Meditations*, and Heidegger in *Being and Time*, and more specifically §26 on *Mitsein*. Briefly, self-consciousness is not a personal, individual matter.

Of course, Levinas always took care to entrust his "confessional" texts to one publisher, and the "philosophical" ones to others.[7] But as Cohen wisely notices, Levinas's philosophy is one: "for my part, the only difference between these two sorts of writings is not in what Levinas says, but in who he says it to."[8] He specifies: "We cannot indulge in the misleading notion that Levinas interprets monotheism *ethically* in his philosophical works alone."[9] Interestingly, as to the reconcilement between reason and revelation, Cohen refers to Henri Bergson. Beyond his subtle treatment of the debate between being and becoming, Bergson appears to him as a major turning point in the history of philosophy, since "he claims to intuit a deeper reality beneath both rational constructions and revelatory declarations. And in this deeper reality, furthermore, Bergson discovers the source point or the meeting point, or the primal origin of both reason and revelation."[10] Could that be a reappearing of the intellectual intuition, this shibboleth of German romantic philosophy? Actually, the original encounter with Bergson sounds as a logical echo to Levinas's first phenomenological concerns, that integrate at the beginning a religious dimension, specifically understood in its existential and practical bearing. There arises the question: Would his philosophy be the same without its Jewish core, listening and responding? And would Cohen have reacted the same way to this work if he had not been trained in Judaic studies? Is it not as a Jewish philosopher that Cohen experiences Levinas's philosophy as true, claiming in our atheistic times the breaking of immanence, and the harmony between earth and heavens by means of moral conduct?

By his clear statements, Richard Cohen admits the autobiographical dimension to philosophy, encouraged by Levinas's mention of the tragic events of his own life and the famous dedication of *Otherwise Than Being*.[11] But Cohen nevertheless does not indulge in a kind of personal "wisdom." He indeed does not subscribe to the usual conception of philosophy as knowledge of the external world based either on a critique of pure reason or of language, or any immediate access to the absolute. He falls at first sight for the only ethical philosophy of the twentieth century, Levinas's deep conception of alterity, which resolves the fashionable question of the subject—free or irresponsible—in the ironic formula: "I am subject to affection by the other." For Levinas questions before the beginning of the quest for knowledge, before the definition of man as master and owner of nature, and wonders what it is that brings us to existence before the amazement caused by the world. For him, there is a step prior to the thinking that understands God as first cause of the world: precisely the step that Bergson identifies or perceives in intuition, or the one that is testified to by Judaism for which every being is, but second, as a response to an otherwise than being. The Bible begins with the second letter of the alphabet, and the Talmud has no first page.

I won't repeat Cohen's philosophical itinerary and his successive displays of Levinasian truth against Spinoza, Kant, Hegel, Heidegger, Nietzsche, etc., be it to confirm or to dismiss them. But I would like to salute the clarity of his accounts, when, in Wittgensteinian terms, the difficulty comes from the depth of thought rather than from sophistication or obscurity of the vocabulary. Summarizing the lesson drawn from Levinas's work, Cohen writes very assertively (without the question mark underlined by Levinas himself): I am my brother's keeper. As if responding to the call of transcendence turned me into a kind of compassionate neighbor.

Of course, one cannot help being seduced by this understanding of human destiny as morality, care for the other, according to the biblical commands to, for example, feed the hungry, clothe the naked, and so on. Except for the supporters of the totalitarian ideology identified by Hannah Arendt, which rests on terror and isolation, those compassionate tenets are more than convincing. They are as old as the Book of Books, though they do not satisfy the human moral need: except for some interruptions, ethics has always been part of philosophy. As if those simple commands could not be fulfilled and were in constant need of specification, thus nearly turning ethics into a kind of battlefield.

Since we proceed in the mode of the autobiographical confession, allow me two avowals. First, after having come to philosophy out of moral need and questioning, and having been disappointed by the "answers" provided by the tradition, I turned to aesthetics, to the hermeneutics of the visible (and the audible).[12] I took my method from Wittgenstein and applied his "philosophical grammar" to the understanding of the work of art, music, fine arts, and literature. But of course, this questioning had not left me. When I first met Levinas in order to present my project as his biographer, I told him how moved I was to deal with a philosopher who specialized in ethics, my first philosophical love, since, I said, I always wondered what my duty was. With his usual quiet irony, he replied that he did not have to ask philosophy what to do, being happy enough with halachic commands. He was thereby pointing to the aim and content of his ethics. As if ethics as first philosophy did not belong to the old tradition of moral philosophy, from the *Theaetetus* to the will to power, via the categorical imperative.

Levinas's challenge goes deeper than creating or repeating rules of life in accordance with the exigencies of morality. He does not wonder whether one has to know what goodness is in order to accomplish it, or what is the motto of the right action, or whether morality is just a concern for weak people. The split consciousness, the certitude of an otherwise than being that renders impossible any conception of a unique and closed self or world, has a bearing that exceeds what has to be done in this or that circumstance, and actually governs any behavior. Stating that any being comes second, be it the mundane totality crossed by transcendence, or the human person indebted to intersubjective recognition, Levinas undermines the ontological grounding of Western philosophy. Being and persisting in being cannot be the first preoccupation of the philosopher, be it in the knowledge of what there is or of what has to be done in order to keep on being. The first reality is that of passivity and response to that which exceeds me and actually calls me to being. "No one does the good voluntarily," states Levinas, inverting Plato's saying.

One could of course read a kind of humbling determination of manhood in this fundamental subordination to a transcendent instance to whom man owes his being as response (or guilt), that pushes him away from his Cartesian pedestal as "master and owner of nature." But, in that very respect, and taking for granted my full admiration for Cohen's knowledge and understanding of Levinas, I hereby confess that I have been puzzled by the many occurrences of the formula "love–mercy" in his account of the Levinasian ethics.

Levinas's lesson does not in my eyes amount to a compassionate and loving wisdom. I'd rather consider him a necessary and helpful thinker of conflict, of opposition. Recognizing the otherness of the other and feeling indebted to that which, in its difference, brings my own difference into the fore, is not a matter of compassion, nor mercy, nor love. Of course, as Cohen writes, "The 'West' is a will to truth, the quest for universal knowledge of the real, reason: this determination is what unites being totality and essence . . . Above the will to truth, Emmanuel Levinas discerns the call to goodness."[13] Actually, goodness is not a familiar word in Levinas's work. He seems to value above all Ikonikov's "little goodness," this day-by-day care for the other, in Vassily Grossman's *Life and Destiny*. His ethics sounds at first like a radical critique of the Western onto-theological approach to truth, which sets being as its very concern and indeed value, and therefore totality as its realization, contradiction being overcome in the Hegelian synthesis. Beyond the unity of being and thought rings in his ears what exceeds knowledge, naming, and perception: precisely what calls me to being as answer—response and responsibility—and definitely the self to debt. Ethics is not so much a matter of positively doing good than of a gratitude toward the otherwise than being. It is not a matter of care or compassion, but a face-to-face relationship with the inexorable other that settles each of us in need of the other one in an unending dialogue. Contrary to the usual seeking for unity and understanding, which gives not only the Western definition of the beautiful but also the rationality of the whole as a totality (scientific and political), which excludes or condemns all disturbance in shape or argument, Levinas underlines and encourages the consideration of otherness as such: that which strikes or breaks order. Ethics, moral conduct, and consideration of the other happen on a background if not of hostility, at least of irreducible difference, a difference maintained as the condition of survival of each partner of the intercourse, even sexual.[14] Any "last word" convincing or silencing one of them would signify his/her death. Being as debt is the way to peace since it integrates negativity as such, grounded not on kindness but just on a sheer and universal desire for survival that relies not on the one-sided *perseveration sui* but on the acknowledgment of the other as such. As obliged to you (the other) for calling me into being, my duty is to feed and clothe you. Perhaps because he had an early experience of the hatred of racism and of the threat of extermination, Levinas proves anthropologically if not pessimistic at least devoid of any outrageous hopes. His ethics, his moral philosophy, does not arise by virtue of kind feelings, close to the Christian love for the neighbor, or charity. Once again, he enjoys inverting the usual order of a formula: "philosophy," etymologically love of wisdom, becomes in his words "wisdom of love," but "love" isn't anything but the infinite in me, something that I cannot master (no one does the good voluntarily), and that determines my being by listening to the Other, my being second as affected by otherness. Therefore, it seems to me that, according to Levinas, my first ethical, conscious feeling toward the other, far from being an altruist first move of compassion, is a passion, a feeling of debt, and then (hopefully) of gratitude. Before being a positive, kind benefactor, I am a debtor. But this reading relies perhaps on the fact that I am not as kind and understanding as Richard Cohen.

Notes

1. Richard Cohen, *Elevations, The Height of the Good in Rosenzweig and Levinas* (Chicago: University of Chicago Press, 1994), xi.

2. I once heard from a famous French philosopher (but in a private talk) that all philosophy is "autobiographical."

3. Perhaps not by Jonathan Bennett.

4. "What happens is not that this symbol cannot be further interpreted, but: I do no interpreting. I do not interpret because I feel natural in the present picture." Ludwig Wittgenstein, *Philosophical Grammar*, trans. A. Kenny (Oxford: Basil Blackwell, 1974), 147.

5. Richard Cohen, *Ethics, Exegesis and Philosophy: Interpretation after Levinas* (New York: Cambridge University Press, 2001), 24.

6. Although Levinas was proud to belong to the rationalist Lithuanian trend of Judaism, as opposed to the sentimental Hassidism. As Scholem used to say, he is more Litvak than he wants to reckon.

7. Mainly *Les Éditions de Minuit* that edited the overwhelming Talmudic lessons.

8. Richard Cohen, "Emmanuel Levinas," in *Modern Jewish Philosophy*, ed. M. L. Morgan and P. Gordon (New York: Cambridge University Press, 2007), 246.

9. Cohen, 246.

10. Cohen, 242.

11. To the victims not only of the Shoah but also to all those who suffered from the hatred of the other.

12. A tradition in which Levinas was not yet involved in those years.

13. Cohen, *Elevations*, 122, 123.

14. Male and female remain and do not merge.

Bibliography

Cohen, Richard. *Elevations, The Height of the Good in Rosenzweig and Levinas*. Chicago: University of Chicago Press, 1994.

Cohen, Richard. "Emmanuel Levinas." In *Modern Jewish Philosophy*, edited by M. L. Morgan and P. Gordon. New York: Cambridge University Press, 2007.

Cohen, Richard. *Ethics, Exegesis and Philosophy, Interpretation after Levinas*. New York: Cambridge University Press, 2001.

Wittgenstein, Ludwig. *Philosophical Grammar*. Trans. A. Kenny. Oxford: Basil Blackwell, 1974.

Wyschogrod, Edith. *International Studies in Philosophy* 28, no. 4:108–9 (1996).

6

Book Review

Elevations

Edith Wyschogrod

Elevations: The Height of the Good in Rosenzweig and Levinas. Chicago: The University of Chicago Press, 1994. Xxi + 342pp.

Richard A. Cohen is an original and exacting interpreter of both Levinas and Rosenzweig, whom Levinas identifies as such a profound influence upon his thought that no work of commentary by him about Rosenzweig is required.[1] Levinas's aim is not to abandon philosophy but to reorient philosophical thinking by displaying the primacy of the good that is beyond being. Because a language geared to ontological disclosure is inadequate to this good, Levinas creates a new often complex. aphilosophical or postphilosophical idiom.

How is the interpreter to alert the reader to this extra-discursive good? Cohen skillfully avoids the neologisms and syntactical twists of Levinas's own language by taking to heart one of Levinas's conceptions, exposure, and transposing it into a new stylistic imperative. ("Exposure" is an ethical term signifying the manner in which the I places itself at the disposal of the Other.) In this context, exhortation, solicitation and command are prior to descriptive language but must be conveyed indirectly. Cohen has evolved a register and tone that convey urgency without sacrificing scholarly rigor.

The work is divided into three parts. Part I, "Rosenzweig," concerns Rosenzweig's own thought and his relation to Buber and Nietzsche; Part I explicates themes in Levinas including his view of gender; Part III brings together both thinkers as well as Levinas's relation to Husserl, Heidegger, Buber, and Derrida. The artfully interwoven essays in each part exhibit the connection of ethics in Levinas's sense to philosophy. Ethics cannot be a subset of philosophical reason because reason cannot account for the relation of one and the Other. With this claim as his focus, Cohen examines the conceptual nexus in which both Levinas and Rosenzweig are imbricated: God, creation, the face, the self and Other, revelation, election. He also explores the relation of the two to Nietzsche, Husserl, Heidegger, Buber, and Sartre among others.

Central to Cohen's treatment of Rosenzweig and Levinas is their use of Jewish themes. Unlike commentators who perceive a split between Levinas's philosophical and Jewish writings, Cohen sees the use of religious motifs as fearless invocations that question and fissure philosophical reason. Thus, Cohen does not restrict Jewish themes to Levinas's explicitly Jewish writings.

Two essays convey some sense for both the substance and manner of this work. In "Rosenzweig versus Nietzsche" Cohen shows how Rosenzweig plays off the love of neighbor against the Nietzschean new man. Rosenzweig appreciates Nietzsche as one who has escaped from Hegelianism and who sees that "the flight into philosophy is a flight into deathlessness." By recognizing that death inevitably prevails over philosophy's wrongheadedness, Nietzsche steps out of philosophy so that, as Cohen writes, "The mind experiences adventures rather than inductions, deductions or dialectical developments. "Yet Nietzsche fails to understand the power of love which, for Rosenzweig, has the authority of an event, makes Biblical revelation possible and undergirds what Rosenzweig calls "the new thinking." Cohen has broken a path through Rosenzweig's *Star* that begins with Nietzsche as individual, the one who overcomes philosophy, and ends with Nietzsche as image, the one who gazes into the future.

The other essay "The Face of Truth and Jewish Mysticism," is a wonderful piece in which Cohen links Levinas's and Rosenzweig's conceptions of the face to the Jewish mystical tradition. He distinguishes Levinas's elaborate accounts of the face from the brief but pregnant description of the face in Rosenzweig. Cohen provides a diagram of this face linking its starlike form to the title of Rosenzweig's work. "Thankfully Rosenzweig does not belabor their geometrical aspect but turns the reader to real human faces," Cohen writes. He then considers corporeal symbolism in Jewish mysticism noting that the later medieval period grafts onto the contemplative mystical tradition "the positivity and sociality of Jewish ethics." Finally, Rabbi Chaim of Volozhin, a nineteenth-century favorite of Levinas, claims boldly that the divine depends upon human ethical behavior. Both agree that the Other's face appears as though it were God's face and thus commands unequivocally.

Many of Cohen's other essays are equally suggestive. He shows the deepening of the Other's impact upon time as Levinas continually rethinks the enigma of the Other, depicts Derrida as a Heideggerian adversary of Levinasian alterity and situates Levinas topographically between Rosenzweig and Husserl. Readings of Levinas and Rosenzweig proliferate. This one is profound and original.

Note

1. This review was originally published in *International Studies in Philosophy* 28, no. 4 (1996): 108–9.

Path II

Ethical Exegesis

7

Post-Levinasian Sketch of Ambivalent Relations

Between Art, Criticism, and Ethics

ROSSITSA VARADINOVA BORKOWSKI

It is not enough to say that the work of Richard A. Cohen has always been a systematic exegesis of Emmanuel Levinas's metaphysical ethics. It is, to use Cohen's own term, "ethical exegesis." His mission to preserve and spread Levinas's thought includes tireless translation and interpretation of Levinas's texts and ideas, corrections of their numerous misinterpretations and misunderstandings, and placement of them on the map of Western thought, thus forwarding them to the next generation of philosophers as they were originally conceived.[1] As Cohen rightly points out, "Getting Levinas right . . . is the first step to serious criticism or to acceptance."[2] In other words, I regard Cohen's philosophical mission as an ethic-durational (heterogeneous) endeavor rather than an onto-dialectical (homogeneous) one.

In this contribution, I would like to enter into dialogue with Levinas's thoughts on art, criticism, and ethics through Richard Cohen's interpretations. The discussion revolves around Levinas's article "Reality and Its Shadow," but is not limited to it. I agree with Cohen that the most obvious and productive approach to analyzing Levinas's theory of art is to "contextualize" it "within his ethical metaphysics,"[3] and would like to try this approach. This chapter sets as its main task to demonstrate how Cohen's exegeses serve as fruitful ground for sketching the ambivalent relations between (a) art and criticism, (b) aestheticism and philosophical criticism, and (c) art, criticism, and Levinas's ethics.

In *The Levinas Reader*, the article "Reality and Its Shadow" appears in the section "Aesthetics."[4] The short explanatory text preceding the article also gives the impression that Levinas treats the topics of art, literature, and aesthetics. This arrangement is understandable given the complexity of the editor's task to compile texts that represent Levinas's complex thought in the most adequate fashion. However, it is also partly misleading because the article "Reality and Its Shadow" is not primarily about art and aesthetics. At the end of the introductory part of the article, "Art and Criticism," after explaining his vision of the relation between art and criticism, Levinas specifies that the discussion of art is subordinated to the more general question of the "non-truth of being." The explicit goal that he sets before himself is to demonstrate that there is a dimension of nontruth that does not form a dialectical pair with truth. The communication with this "independent ontological event" cannot be reduced to or explained by the categories of cognition.[5] Levinas's primary concern is not to analyze art as part of an aesthetic theory but, as Cohen correctly explains, explore the relation between art and science as part of Levinas's ethical theory.[6] Moreover, at the very end of the article, Levinas hints that telling the truth of being requires introducing "the perspective of the relation with the other without which being could not be told in its reality; that is, in its time."[7] We know that Levinas's entire philosophical career was devoted precisely to this greater mission. Therefore, "Reality and Its Shadow" is a multifaceted text with three distinct levels: art, the relation between art and science, and ethics. The latter requires the article to be read in the context of Levinas's metaphysical ethics.[8] This approach would help us to recognize Levinas's concern with distinguishing senses in art from senses in ethics via the relation between philosophical criticism, aestheticism, and art. I would like to examine Levinas's view of these relations through the prism of Cohen's productive exegeses of Levinas's thoughts on art, science, philosophy, and ethics.

The present text is organized into four parts. The first presents Cohen's terminological framework based on his article "Levinas on Art and Aestheticism," in which he adopts the approach of *explication de texte* through the argument that Levinas regards art as disengaged (irresponsible) and engaged (responsible) at the same time. Also, by claiming that Levinas perceives criticism as an integral part of art, Cohen elaborates a fruitful distinction between two types of criticism: aestheticism and philosophical criticism. This interpretative framework and terminology are adequate to what Levinas explicitly sets as the purpose of "Reality and Its Shadow," to reveal the nondialectical "un-truth of being," and allow Cohen to demonstrate how the relation between science (philosophical criticism) and art, or what I correspondingly call "reason" and "senses in art," is submissive to the first without being hostile to the latter.

Relying on Cohen's terminology, in the second part I explore the tension between art and criticism (science) through the concept of interruption. I advance the position that the section "For Philosophical Criticism" in "Reality and Its Shadow," by analogy with Plato's dialogue Timaeus, where Plato discusses the relation between seers and interpreters,[9] reveals a paradoxical compatibility between Cohen's claim that philosophical criticism is an integral part of art (when regarded from the perspective of bridging art to the larger world) and the necessity to think of philosophical criticism as being separate from art (when regarded from the perspective of protecting reason from dissolving into nonsense).

The third part focuses on the relation between aestheticism and philosophical criticism. I regard the necessity of separating philosophical criticism from art as complementary to what Cohen (in his article "Some Reflections on Levinas and Shakespeare"[10]) recognizes as the underlying meaning of Levinas's article "Reality and Its Shadow": namely, the danger of aestheticism. I believe that it is also in line with Cohen's analysis of the relations between aesthetics, science, philosophy, and ethics, developed in the introduction of his book *Ethics, Exegesis and Philosophy: Interpretation after Levinas* (2001).[11] I will show that Levinas's first book, *De l'existance à existent* (1947), where he discusses the relation between art and the anonymous dimension of being (*il y a*),[12] justifies Cohen's distinction between aestheticism and philosophical criticism, as well as the above claim concerning the necessity of keeping philosophical criticism exterior to art.

Finally, the last part discusses the senses as a common ground of art, criticism (broadly science), and ethics. Richard Cohen's ethical exegeses of Levinas's vision of the relation between ethics, philosophy, science, and aesthetics helps us to situate "Reality and Its Shadow" within the context of Levinas's overall philosophy and answer the question as to why in this article Levinas needed to touch the minor question of nontruth of being qua art. Read together with Levinas's articles "The Philosophical Determination of the Idea of Culture" and "Signification and Sense," I identify three relations: (a) between reason and senses in art, (b) between reason and ethics (senses in ethics), and (c) between senses in art and senses in ethics. I believe that the distinction between these three ambivalent relations adds to our understanding of Levinas's strategy throughout his overall project. While in the first relation Levinas "brackets" the senses in art in favor of reason, in the second he marginalizes reason and favors the senses in ethics. It seems to me that the third relation (between senses in art and senses in ethics) remains underexplored in the literature and thus is open for further research.

Framework and Terminology

In his recent article "Levinas on Art and Aestheticism," Cohen rightly points out that in "Reality and Its Shadow," Levinas focuses on the relation between art and science.[13] He elaborates a productive terminological framework helpful for situating this relation within Levinas's metaphysical ethics. The framework allows us to navigate better between various perspectives and follow the shift in meaning of art, science, and their interrelationships with regard to the larger world as the milieu of ethics.

Traditionally, the term "art" assumes three aspects: art creation, artwork, and perception of an artwork. Obviously, criticism falls within the latter, or as Levinas puts it, "It has its source in the mind of the listener, spectator, or reader; criticism exists as a public mode of comportment."[14] He sees the immediate perception of an artwork as mind being absorbed by aesthetic enjoyment, or what Levinas denotes by using Lévy Bruhl's term: *participation*.[15] Furthermore, under the rubric "perception of artwork," we customarily recognize two types, criticism and a general audience. Although after perceiving the artwork they both respond to it, criticism formulates evaluative positions by means of science (reason) while the general audience shares opinions predominantly based on emotion. If I am to extend Levinas's analysis, I would say that the critics' attitudes emerge from the general perception of an artwork, but through reason they are able, to a greater degree, to detach themselves from the immediate perception of the artwork. In other words, while the general public responds to the artwork from within or on the borderline of the artwork, critics comment on it from outside. The outside of the artwork is "being in the world," or reality, where knowledge, language (i.e., truth) operates, or what Cohen calls the "larger social-political-economic world."[16] Therefore, if the line that separates art from the larger world is not drawn, then the existence of criticism would not be justified because art tends to equalize (thus totalize) the artistic with the larger world.[17]

Cohen also accurately insists on Levinas's distinction between two types of criticism: aestheticism (Cohen's term) and philosophical criticism. He defines aestheticism as focusing on, and totalizing, what he identifies as centripetal (enclosing in itself or detaching from the larger world) movements in art, which mark art as essentially disengaged. On the other hand, philosophical criticism concentrates on the centrifugal (opening to the larger world) tendencies in art, which characterize art as inherently engaged.

Cohen's terminological apparatus adequately serves as a basis to explain Levinas's specific intention in "Reality and Its Shadow" to reveal art as an independent ontological event irreducible to cognition, as well as Levinas's general task of underlining the ability of philosophical criticism to remain related to the larger world by the means of reason. I find the term "aestheticism" especially relevant. It represents what Levinas identifies as a dimension of criticism (scientific thinking) where reason through the channel of rhythm "enters into the artist's game" of sensuous images and denudes the subject of conscious self-awareness. In other words, aestheticism reveals the possibility of reason's abdication of its essential role in assembling interiority by scattering light and clarity; in aestheticism reason participates in that it allows itself to enter in "commerce with the obscure."

In brief, art is detached from the larger world and can be described in its three distinct aspects: art creation, artwork, and art perception. Criticism is a form of art perception driven by reason rather than senses. There are two types of criticism: aestheticism and philosophical criticism. Aestheticism is a type of criticism that operates from within art where the aesthetic enjoyment (senses) dominate; it remains attached to art and thus represents the possibility of reason (science, knowledge, truth) being dragged into the whirling centripetal movements of art down to the anonymous dimension of being (shadow or *il y a*)—or where reason loses its power. In other words, in aestheticism reason is dissolved into nonsense. Philosophical criticism, on the other hand, operates outside of the event of art. Although this criticism also emerges as a response to the artwork (i.e., a form of art perception), it remains rooted in the larger world and operates from and with regard to it. Philosophical criticism then does not "enter into the artist's game"; it does not subordinate reason to the senses, and reason keeps the relation to truth and meaning alive.

Disjunction: Interruption of Mind in Art and "the Muscles of Mind" in Science

On the axis of the relation between aestheticism and philosophical criticism lies the tension between art and science, or what I correspondingly term "senses in art" and "reason." The analysis of this relation revolves around the concept of interruption. It is based on analogy between the section "For Philosophical Criticism" in "Reality and Its Shadow"[18] and Plato's dialogue *Timaeus*, in the part on the relation between seers and interpreters.[19] The analogy points to a paradoxical compatibility between Cohen's claim that philosophical criticism is an integral part of art and the necessity to think of philosophical criticism as being separate from art. The paradox finds its explanation through a shift of perspective. When regarded from the point of view of bridging art to the larger world, philosophical criticism appears inseparable from art. However, when regarded from the perspective of protecting reason from dissolving into nonsense, art and philosophical criticism must be kept as separate ontological events.

Generally, the dialogue *Timaeus* represents Plato's cosmology. I want to focus on the part where Plato's philosophical character Timaeus, a Pythagorean astronomer, explains through the concept of divination the work of Reason and Necessity, and more specifically the relation between body and soul in human beings. The background of Timaeus's explanation is that one divine Creator (Demiurge) brings into existence the living universe and perfect immortal beings (gods). These gods create human beings with two parts that are distinct and remote from each other: lower—mortal bodies and mortal soul, and higher—the immortal soul (reason or nous), which has direct access to truth. It is significant that Plato depicts the relation between the lower and higher parts as boldly disjunctive. The understanding between the two runs only from the higher to the lower, but not vice versa: "The gods knew that this [lower] part of the soul would never understand reason." If we translate this situation in Levinas's and Cohen's vocabulary, the relation between art and science in terms of understanding seems to be a one-way flow, from science to art. This fits with Levinas's suggestion that it is philosophical criticism (reason or nous) that can understand (and thus elevate) art, but not the other way around. Furthermore, the mortal body and soul function through images rather than concepts: "They [the gods] knew that it [the lower part] would much more readily be bewitched by images and phantasms, whether they appeared at night or in the daytime."[20] This seems to correspond to Levinas's vision of art working through images while criticism operates with concepts. However, Cohen correctly distinguishes between the concept of image in Plato and Levinas. While in Plato "image" is understood as a copy of an object of an idea (concept) and thus, although twice removed from the real, still belonging to the process of knowing and illumination,[21] in Levinas, Cohen argues, the image is an alternate reality,[22] an "independent ontological event."[23]

It might be significant to pursue the analogy on another line, namely the concept of interruption. Timaeus further explains that to bridge the lower and higher parts, the gods provide humans with a liver. It serves two purposes, to mirror rational thoughts, thus controlling the lower part, and also to receive visions (phantasmata) from the immortal soul.[24] The lower part also has access to truth, which comes from reason (nous), but indirectly through the liver. Not all human beings have visions. Those who have are seers, or fortunetellers. They are given the power to receive messages from elsewhere to "compensate for human stupidity."[25] Plato describes a seer's mind as an interrupted or "altered state of consciousness." While receiving images, a seer is possessed by them, and the seer's intellect is weakened. Even though the seers go back to their normal state of consciousness and are able to recall, retell, and reflect on what was sent to them, they are not able to interpret their visions; that is, to transmit their true meaning. Why? Because, Timaeus explains, "It is not the job of someone who has been out of his mind and remains so to assess by himself the visions and the voices; no, it is an old, true saying that only a man of sound mind possesses the ability to do what pertains to himself, and to know himself."[26] This is the task of the interpreters (*prophetai*). They assess and translate the "riddling sayings and seeings, and should properly be thought of not as diviners, but as interpreters of omens."[27]

Poets (and by extension artists) have always been regarded as a type of seer who receive images coming from elsewhere. We can find similarity between them and Plato's description of seers, who have visions coming from the immortal soul. Both Plato and Levinas regard this kind of person as unable to communicate the meaning of the visions. Levinas writes, "The most lucid writer finds himself in the world bewitched by its images. He speaks in enigmas, by allusions, by suggestion, in equivocations." In the role of Plato's *prophetai*, we can identify Levinas's philosophical critics, who speak "in full self-possession, frankly, through concepts, which are like the muscles of the mind." [28] Behind Plato's requirement of a "sound mind" we recognize Levinas's "muscles of the mind." Both philosophers point to the uninterrupted mind of interpreters/philosophical critics as a condition of the ability and right to judge images. Both refer to a disjunctive, either-or situation, where two states of human mind are separated by an unbridgeable gap: either images (art senses), or wits (reason).

The centrifugal movements in art (those related to the larger world) that Cohen recognizes are not movements immanent in art but come from philosophical criticism of art. They cannot be initiated from within the artistic experience; thus, if we refer to Plato, they must come from outside, or above—from the immortal soul, reason, or nous, which has direct access to truth. Aestheticism denotes the movement of reason going down to the lower, obscure part of the mortal soul but entrapping itself there instead of elevating the lower to the higher part (immortal soul). Aestheticism then is to be regarded as the work of reason involved in irrational activity, attempting to make sense out of non-sense within the terrain of the nonsensical, and thus presenting the latter as if it were intelligible. If the artists' and general audience's irrationality is understandable and justifiable, for they are driven by sensual powers, then aestheticism's irrationality represents a hazardous reverse. The next part sketches the danger of aestheticism from the perspective of non-sense, or *il y a*.

The Danger of Art and Aestheticism

According to Levinas, art is dangerous if it is considered as being capable of telling truths about the world, or if it attempts to say something about reality by its own means. Aestheticism is dangerous because it allows reason to be "dragged down" to a realm outside of its own expertise where it acts as if this realm were rational. In both cases, the two distinct regions, art and science, merge to produce ambiguity. There would be nothing wrong with it if it did not threaten the subject's ability to hear the suffering of another human being. In his article "Some Reflections on Levinas and Shakespeare," Cohen points out that another aspect of Levinas's article "Reality and Its Shadow" is "recognition of the dangers of aestheticism." He analyzes this danger from the perspective of ethics, claiming that, according to Levinas, aestheticism celebrates art's essential detachment, thus leaving out interpretations of art's (dis)engagements, that is, ethical exegeses. The combination between art's mythic power of participation by means of rhythm and aestheticism's position of "art for art's sake," can dangerously (and easily) lead the mind perceiving an artwork to become indifferent to both good and evil.[29]

But what of the danger itself, if we are to paraphrase Levinas's question in *De l'existence à existent*, with which he opens a phenomenological description of the nonsensical and anonymous dimension of being?[30] On one hand, as we have seen, Levinas assumes that aestheticism has the potential to involve reason "into the artist's game," to live a "parasitic life" and thus substitute itself for art.[31] This assumption equalizes art and aestheticism. On the other hand, if we compare Levinas's explanation in *De l'existence à existent* of the anonymous aspect of being (*il y a*) with his description of art as "a depth of reality inaccessible to conceptual intelligence," we may infer that the term "shadow" denotes the concept of *il y a*. Therefore, the inability of the aesthete's mind to stay connected with reality leads to what Levinas (borrowing Jean Wahl's term) calls "transdescendence," or going down to the realm of the shadow. This inference is confirmed by Cohen's association of the horror of Hitlerism with art[32] and Levinas's depiction of *il y a* as horror. I propose further exploration of the danger of aestheticism by zooming in on the mechanism of reason's degradation back to non-sense (*il y a*).

In Levinas's first book, *De l'existence à existent* (part 3, "Existence without a World," section "Exoticism"), he claims that art is essentially exotic, what Cohen describes as a "detachment from the larger world." Levinas identifies two major aspects of human interiority that art distorts. The first concerns the mutual dependence of world and man. Levinas postulates that, on one hand, direct perception of the forms of worldly objects constitutes human interiority, either as objects of knowledge or use; on the other hand, objects (exteriority) function meaningfully as such, as far as they are represented through sensation, perception, and understanding in (human) inwardness. This twofold structure of reciprocal reliance is analogical to Kant's well-known reconciliation of empiricism with rationalism by tying up in a seamless unity the sense perceptions with reason: "Thoughts without content are empty, intuitions without concepts are blind."[33] The distortion of the relation between man and world, according to Levinas, comes from the fact that art cuts the joint of object/inwardness by slipping an image between them. The cutting consists of taking the worldly form away from the object and replacing it with an artistic image. Although the image might be "realistic," it nevertheless prevents consciousness from communicating directly with the object, and this "modifies the contemplation itself."[34] The original twofold structure is now threefold: object (world), artwork (image), and inwardness (man); the first two are represented in the latter,[35] a deformalization in terms of a "coexistence of worlds that are mutually alien and impenetrable."[36]

The artistic experience (perceiving art) troubles the way we perceive the world. Both the perceived object (phenomenon) and perceiving subject represented in the inwardness are not such anymore, because they cannot relate directly. Moreover, going against the traditional view, Levinas believes that artistic forms uncover "things in themselves" and that thus "reality remains foreign to the world inasmuch as it is given."[37] The dichotomy "things-in-themselves" and "things as they appear to our senses" might tempt us to refer to the Kantian relation between noumena and phenomena; we might gladly say that in art, we are left with blind or bare intuitions or sensations that cannot connect to understanding. However, Levinas clarifies that Kant's analysis envisions the sensation before its interior transmutation. The Kantian "blindness" of sensation is indifferent to sensation's objectivity or subjectivity, because understanding does not have access to noumena. Therefore, "the movement of art consists in leaving the level of perception so as to reinstate sensation, in detaching the quality from its object of reference. Instead of arriving at the object, the intention gets lost in the sensation itself, and it is this wandering about in sensation, in aesthesis, that produces the esthetic effect."[38] In other words, according to Levinas, the chaotic sensation in art happens after the interiority achieves certain objective meaning; it is a chaos after order, not before as it is in Kant, and therefore distorts both the objective and subjective dimensions of the perceived object.

Levinas examines another aspect of distortion of human interiority from the viewpoint of art's production. As we have seen, he claims that artwork prevents consciousness from being able to relate to the object through either knowledge or practical use. This is not a simple fragmentation that the mind recognizes as detached from the whole. The detachment is more substantial and gives the fragment a being of its own. In cinema, Levinas explains, the close-up details and the camera's various playful perspectives "stop the action in which a particular is bound up with a whole."[39] The image is artistic inasmuch as it exposes things stripped of their forms, as they are in themselves, and not as they appear to our inwardness (phenomena). Sensations are captured in the image with no connection to the "natural" direct perception of the object and its interior understanding. This means, according to Levinas, that the artwork acquires its own personality: "A still life, a landscape, and, a fortiori, a portrait have their own inner life which their material covering expresses. A landscape is, as we say, a state of mind."[40]

Both distortions are ethically dangerous. The first, chaos after order, denudes the subject from any capability of conscious or even unconscious action; the subject is turned into a living automaton. It is precisely this state of the human mind's numbness, neither dead nor alive, that both Levinas and Cohen recognize as being indifferently open to both evil and good. Aestheticism celebrates it and thus reinforces art's immanent irresponsibility. The second distortion, artwork acquiring its own personality, allows for a substitution of the otherness of another living person for an artwork.

The Ambivalence of Senses in the Relation between Art, Science, and Ethics

As I have sketched, building on Cohen's exegeses, in "Reality and Its Shadow" Levinas privileges science over art by following a negative and positive strategy (broadly speaking). The negative strategy outlines art's major deficiencies: (a) exoticism or detachment from reality (the larger world) and truth, (b) distortion of the direct subject-object relation and stripping the subject of its subjectivity, (c) interruption of reason, (d) obscurity and descending back to the nonsensical horror of *il y a*, and (e) moral disengagement or indifference to good and evil. The positive strategy underlines science's strong points: (a) retaining an engagement with the larger world and truth, (b) maintaining a stable, sound, and uninterrupted mind, (c) enlightenment and clarity.[41] Although aestheticism is a form of criticism (like science) and as such is supposed to judge art from the perspective of the larger world, it gets involved with the artistic sensation and thus threatens to dissolve sense into nonsense.[42] Therefore, philosophical criticism qua science and knowledge, not aestheticism, should be considered capable of bridging art to the larger world.[43]

Seen from the broader perspective of Levinas's metaphysical ethics, however, "Reality and Its Shadow" is more than that. It is well known that his entire project aims at marginalizing the power of reason in favor of the senses, the completeness of the self interrupted by the shock of encountering the Other. Cohen also rightly points out that science lacks the capacity to recognize importance and priority and for this reason tends to reduce everything to itself.⁴⁴ Levinas not only separates ethics from knowledge but, more importantly, places it before knowledge. This means that philosophical criticism of art, qua enlightening and truth, is not sufficient; before being evaluated in terms of poiesis and the relation to truth, art is to be judged with reference to the ethical.⁴⁵ This new (and higher, more important) requirement before science and reason raises the question: if art and ethics are both driven by sensitivity, why then would Levinas "bracket" aestheticism and art as incapable of being affected directly by the ethical? Besides the above pointed danger of dissolving meaning into non-sense, it seems to me that the answer lies in a distinction Levinas makes between two kinds of sensitivity: that coming from beneath, from the anonymous dimension of being, and that awakened by the ethical. The relation between reason and senses in both cases differs. In the first, senses in art are separated from reason and can have meaning in terms of truth and ethics only with its help: the meaning is bestowed, added. In the second case, reason is dethroned and follows the senses: the meaning qua ethics emerges from the face-to-face relation and ordains reason, which is then entitled to judge art.

Therefore, with "Reality and Its Shadow" Levinas resolves the problem of the senses in art and focuses on the relation between science (reason) and ethics (senses in ethics). The justification of this claim comes from the fact that Levinas's concept of art as exoticism does not change throughout his philosophical career. In *Otherwise Than Being*, over two decades after *De l'existance à existent* and "Reality and Its Shadow," Levinas re-states his vision that art is essentially exotic (this time through the lens of the dichotomy "saying-said").⁴⁶ The usage of the same term "exotic" suggests that all accompanying ideas stated previously also remain unchanged. The collection of essays, *Proper Names*, assembled in 1975 and devoted to writers and thinkers "whose saying signifies a face,"⁴⁷ also confirms this conclusion; it is an example of the philosophical criticism Levinas had in mind in his early articles. This means that Levinas considers the problem of the relation between the senses in art and senses in ethics resolved through reason.

In the article "Philosophical Determination of Culture" (1983, 1986), however, Levinas approaches the question of the meaning of human existence—a question that preoccupies him throughout his entire career—through the concept of culture, and develops the idea that art, science, and ethics are all embodied (i.e., rooted in the senses) and that all three are tangled in the "Gordian knot of the body."[48] He first defines knowledge and art as two dimensions of the "culture of immanence" as opposed to "culture as responsibility for the Other." What does this mean? The culture of immanence revolves around the relation between the human subject (interiority) and the otherness of nature (exteriority, or being that is given in presence), characterized by two major movements: internalization and exteriorization. The first one is the essence of knowledge, defined as a process, in which the knowing subject internalizes what lies outside and is otherwise than the subject itself. Levinas defines the act of internalization as accessing the otherness of an external object through the senses and reducing it to the contents of the subject's mind by means of the universal categories of understanding; the Kantian "transcendental apperception is the gathering of the sensed into knowledge." He advances the idea that since knowledge begins with experience and practice, thought is originally embodied and knowledge turns out to be insufficient to fulfill its own purpose. He argues that the human body is part of the physical world and as such seems to represent the otherness of Nature within the knowing subject, "the Other in the Same." In other words, the otherness from outside meets with the otherness inside and the ultimate goal of acquiring meaning through learning something new fails; the knowable object turns out to be already part of the knowing subject. Levinas concludes that the human body is more primordial and always ahead of the act of grasping and understanding. Therefore, on the one hand, nothing essentially new is learned, while on the other hand the body as an element of the process of acquiring knowledge remains unknowable. Through the body, via the senses, the otherness of nature remains irreducible to the immanence of knowledge.

The other dimension of the culture of immanence is art, which is also corporeal. Just as the body is an instrument for learning through experience and practice, so it is also a mode of manifestation of the enveloped otherness of nature. If knowledge is a process of internalization, art is the process of externalization, or an expression of the subject's unknowable interiority. Levinas defines this expression as an act of driving the internal content out into the exteriority. Poetry and art represent the non-thematizing wisdom of the flesh and could be regarded as another way of acquiring meaning. However, like the culture of knowledge, which reduces the otherness of Nature to the oneness of universal wisdom, the culture of expression celebrates the oneness of being qua the Beautiful. Thus, both dimensions of the culture of immanence revolve around human interiority and are devoted to the Neoplatonic ideal of the One.[49] The breach of this circling [50] comes from the absolute otherness of another human being.

Levinas's analysis of art, knowledge, and ethics as entangled in the body provokes further questions. Can art relate directly to the ethical, or is it always mediated by reason and science? If both science and art are marked by centripetal movement and tend toward disengagement, what qualifies science as a translator of art? Is reason the major, sufficient condition for constituting human interiority? To ask metaphorically, what is the difference between blindness when looking at the sun and when inhabiting complete darkness? If philosophical criticism can be ethical exegesis, why is it that art cannot be ethical in its production or immediate perception? Can ethical philosophical criticism find something ethical in an unethically conceived artwork? These questions are also provoked by Cohen's analysis of the relation between art and science on the one hand in terms of parallelism[51] and the primacy of science on the other. The concreteness of art (especially literature) seems to stay closer than conceptual abstract thinking to the concreteness of the larger world.[52] However, science measures, compares, and works with concepts that do not distort the subject-object unit (as I have described). I believe that although Levinas is clear about the primacy of ethics compared to both science and art (while elaborating in great detail the relation between ethics and science), the relation between art and ethics within his key ideas remains a fruitful area of further exploration.

To sum up, Cohen's distinction between aestheticism and philosophical criticism adequately explains Levinas's nonpejorative subordinating of art to science. This distinction is an example of exegeses that is both inventive and ethical. It is ethical for two reasons. First, it faithfully sticks to the purpose of "Reality and Its Shadow," to reveal the beyond-dialectical relation between the truth of being qua knowledge and the un-truth of being qua art. Second, it is inventive and ethical because it allows us to explore on a deeper level the article's specific purpose with regard to Levinas's ethical project. The term "aestheticism," paired with the concept of the interruption of reason in art, enables us to approach the concept of philosophical criticism from two simultaneous perspectives and to reveal it as being both an integral part of art and separate from it. The latter is necessitated by the dangerous possibility of dissolving reason into nonsense and/or presenting the nonsensical as reasonable. When situated in the context of Levinas's overall philosophy, the term "aestheticism," along with Levinas's concept of the culture of immanence, helps to identify the ambivalence of the relation between art, science, and ethics as rooted in their corporeality. Owing to Cohen's interpretations, the relation between senses in art and senses in ethics opens further research. On a general account, his brilliant, inspiring work points Levinasian scholars toward sober and ethical interpretations of Levinas's work. Translating and deepening the thought of one of the most prominent and original philosophers of the twentieth century, Cohen teaches us that ethical exegesis is the first method of doing philosophy.

Notes

1. I experienced the effectiveness of Richard Cohen's method of academic rigor when I participated in the close reading of Levinas's *Totality and Infinity* during the annual Levinas Philosophy Summer Seminar "Eros and Ethics," organized by Richard Cohen, James McLachlan, and Jolanta Saldukaityté (Rome, 2015).

2. Richard A. Cohen, "Levinas on Art and Aestheticism: Getting 'Reality and Its Shadow Right,'" *Levinas Studies* 11 (2017): 158.

3. Cohen, "Levinas on Art and Aestheticism," 160.

4. Emmanuel Levinas, *The Levinas Reader*, edited by Seán Hand (Cambridge, MA: Blackwell, 1989).

5. *The Levinas Reader*, 131–32.

6. Cohen, "Levinas on Art and Aestheticism," 162.

7. *The Levinas Reader*, 143.

8. Cohen, "Levinas on Art and Aestheticism," 160.

9. Plato, *Timaeus and Critias*, trans. Robin Waterfield, introduction and notes by Andrew Gregory (Oxford: Oxford University Press, 2008), ebook, 72 a-b, 71–72.

10. Richard A. Cohen, "Some Reflections on Levinas and Shakespeare," in *Levinasian Meditations: ethics, philosophy, and religion* (Pittsburgh: Duquesne University Press, 2010), 150–168.

11. Richard A. Cohen, *Ethics, Exegesis and Philosophy: Interpretation after Levinas* (Cambridge University Press, 2004) ebook, 12.

12. Emmanuel Levinas, *Existence and Existents*, trans. A. Lingis (Pittsburgh: Duquesne University Press, 2001).

13. Cohen, "Levinas on Art and Aestheticism," 160.

14. *The Levinas Reader*, 130.

15. Levinas consistently associates his appropriation of the term "participation" in the sense of Lévy-Bruhl's analysis of the primitive mind with the term *il y a*, the anonymous nonsensical dimension of being. He carefully distinguishes it from Plato's concept of participation in the ideas and Heidegger's term being-in-the-

world. See *De l'existence à existent* (1947), chapter 3 "Existence without a World," section 2 "Existence without Existent," "Reality and Its Shadow," in *The Levinas Reader*, p. 133, and "Lévy-Bruhl and Contemporary Philosophy" (1957) in *Entre Nous: Thinking-of-the-Other*, Columbia University Press, 1998. In the third part of my contribution, I show how through the term "participation" Levinas bridges art and *il y a*, thus warning against what Richard Cohen recognizes as a danger of dragging reason back to the non-sense of *il y a* by the means of aestheticism.

16. Cohen, "Levinas on Art and Aestheticism," 162.

17. Cohen, "Levinas on Art and Aestheticism," 162. Cohen parallels art and science in their teleological totalizing tendencies. On the other hand, in the introduction to Levinas's *The Theory of Intuition in Husserl's Phenomenology* (1930), he regards Levinas's use of the Husserlian concept of *regions* as Levinas's persistent distinction of "a variety of levels of meaning in a variety of ways, without reducing one to another." See Emmanuel Levinas, *The Theory of Intuition in Husserl's Phenomenology*, trans. André Orianne, foreword to the second edition by Richard A. Cohen (Evanston, IL: Northwestern University Press, 1995), xxv. With regard to our discussion in the fourth part, it is worth noticing that Levinas differentiates the intuition of sensible objects from categorical and eidetic intuition. This means that it is justifiable to think (in line with Levinas) of senses in art, reason, and senses in ethics as different categories irreducible to each other.

18. *The Levinas Reader*, 141–43.

19. Plato, *Timaeus*, 72 a–b, 71–72.

20. Plato, *Timaeus*, 71 b, 70.

21. Cohen, "Levinas on Art and Aestheticism," 174.

22. Cohen, "Levinas on Art and Aestheticism," 176.

23. *The Levinas Reader*, 132.

24. Plato, *Timaeus*, 71 b, 70.

25. Plato, *Timaeus*, 72 a, 71.

26. Plato, *Timaeus*, 72 b, 71–72.

27. Ibid.

28. *The Levinas Reader*, 143.

29. Cohen, *Levinasian Meditations*, 153.

30. Levinas, *Existence and Existents*, 51. After inviting the reader to imagine "all beings reverting to nothingness," Levinas asks, "But what of this nothingness itself?"

31. *The Levinas Reader*, 130.

32. Cohen, *Levinasian Meditations*, 158.

33. Immanuel Kant, *Critique of Pure Reason*, trans. Paul Guyer and Allen W. Wood (New York: Cambridge University Press, 1998), A 51/B 75.

34. Levinas, *Existence and Existents*, 46.

35. In "Reality and Its Shadow," Levinas further clarifies how the artistic image functions. He disagrees with Jean-Paul Sartre ("The theory of image"), who

claims that the image is transparent and insists on the image's opaqueness, the "thought stops on the image itself; it consequently supposes a certain opacity of the image." See *The Levinas Reader*, 133. Therefore, the essence of art's exoticism is the "coexistence of worlds that are mutually alien and impenetrable." For a detailed analysis of Levinas's vision on artistic image, see Cohen, "Levinas on Art and Aestheticism," 173–76.

36. Levinas, *Existence and Existents*, 48.
37. Levinas, *Existence and Existents*, 46.
38. Levinas, *Existence and Existents*, 47 (italics added).
39. Levinas, *Existence and Existents*, 49.
40. Levinas, *Existence and Existents*, 49.
41. Outside of the article falls the role of reason *qua* light and thus knowledge in the emerging of existent's interiority out of the anonymity of *il y a* and constituting the human ego. See *Ethics and Infinity*, trans. Richard A. Cohen (Pittsburgh: Duquesne University Press, 1985), 51; *Time and the Other*, trans. Richard A. Cohen (Pittsburgh: Duquesne University Press, 1987), 64; *Totality and Infinity*, section "Sensibility and the Face," 187–94. Also in "Signification and Sense," Levinas argues that the "*consciousness* of philosophy is essentially reflective," and the ethical requirement "without reflection" is not simply pre-reflective naïve spontaneous consciousness; it is not pre-critical [*Humanism of the Other*, trans. Nidra Poller, introduction by Richard A. Cohen (University of Illinois Press, 2005), 35], but apparently postreflective; otherwise the challenge coming from the Other would not be realized.
42. In his second treatise *Otherwise than Being*, Levinas sustains the vision of *il y a* as the nonsense to which the essence of being returns, "The rumbling of the *there is* [*il y a*] is the nonsense in which essence turns, and in which thus turns the justice issued out of signification. There is ambiguity of sense and non-sense in being, sense turning into non-sense. It cannot be taken lightly." See *Otherwise Than Being*, 163.
43. Cohen, *Ethics, Exegesis and Philosophy*, "Introduction: Philosophy as Ethical Exegesis," 12–16.
44. Cohen, *Ethics, Exegesis and Philosophy*, "Introduction: Philosophy as Ethical Exegesis," 5.
45. According to Cohen, the ethical themes are what Levinas values in Shakespeare. The greatness of literature (and art in general) is not to be measured only by the means of knowledge and ontology, but also and in first place ethics. See *Levinasian Meditations*, 158. A perfect example of ethical exegeses is Levinas's book *Proper Names* (1976). There he analyzes the work of various thinkers and writers from the perspective of ethics. He evaluates the aesthetic and philosophical suggestions with regard to their ethical implications understood in terms of ethics detached from knowledge and truth, as a separate realm coming to the mind rather being absorbed by it.

46. Emmanuel Levinas, *Otherwise than Being or Beyond Essence*, trans. A. Lingis, foreword by Richard A. Cohen (Pittsburgh: Duquesne University Press, 1998), 41.

47. Emmanuel Levinas, *Proper Names*, trans. Michael B. Smith (Stanford: Stanford University Press, 1996), 4.

48. Levinas, *Otherwise than Being*, 77.

49. Levinas, *Entre Nous*, 184.

50. Levinas refers to the etymological meaning of the term "culture" as a dwelling. The term has also the meaning of circling; *kwel-*, Proto-Indo-European root meaning "revolve, move around; sojourn, dwell." (https://www.etymonline.com/word/*kwel-)

51. Cohen, "Levinas on Art and Aestheticism," 168.

52. Cohen, "Levinas and Shakespeare," 152.

Bibliography

Cohen, Richard A. "Levinas on Art and Aestheticism: Getting 'Reality and Its Shadow Right.'" *Levinas Studies* 11. Pittsburgh: Duquesne University Press, 2016.

Cohen, Richard A. "Some Reflections on Levinas and Shakespeare." In *Levinasian Meditations: Ethics, Philosophy, and Religion*, 150–68. Pittsburgh: Duquesne University Press, 2010.

Cohen, Richard A. *Ethics, Exegesis and Philosophy: Interpretation after Levinas*. Cambridge: Cambridge University Press, 2004.

Kant, Immanuel. *Critique of Pure Reason*. Translated by Paul Guyer and Allen W. Wood. New York: Cambridge University Press, 1998.

Levinas, Emmanuel. *Existence and Existents*. Translated by Alphonso Lingis. Pittsburgh: Duquesne University Press, 2001.

Levinas, Emmanuel. *Otherwise than Being or Beyond Essence*. Translated by Alphonso Lingis, foreword by Richard A. Cohen. Pittsburgh: Duquesne University Press, 1998.

Levinas, Emmanuel. *Proper Names*. Translated by Michael B. Smith. Stanford University Press, 1996.

Levinas, Emmanuel. *The Levinas Reader*. Edited by Seán Hand. Cambridge, MA: Blackwell, 1989.

Plato. *Timaeus and Critias*. Translated by Robin Waterfield, introduction and notes by Andrew Gregory. Oxford University Press, 2008.

8

Rhythm and Sense in the Philosophy of Levinas

MASATO GODA

It has been more than thirty years since I discovered the texts of Emmanuel Levinas. Before publishing the Japanese translations of *Totality and Infinity* and *Otherwise Than Being*, I published an anthology of Levinas's work that included texts such as "Il y a," "Reality and Its Shadow," and so on.[1] When I translated these texts, I noticed the importance Levinas accorded to the notion of "breaking of rhythm," as well as to that of "rhythm" itself; for example, when he compared "il y a" to a prose poem by Edgar Allan Poe or when he stressed the musicality of the image in "Reality and Its Shadow." In Levinas's writings we find several very significant fragments on rhythm.

What is rhythm or breaking of rhythm for Levinas? For the latter, we find a decisive passage in *Otherwise Than Being*: "Proximity is nothing but difference—non-coincidence, arrhythmia in time, diachrony refractory to the thematization, refractory to the reminiscence which synchronizes phases of a past. Impossible to narrate—other losing his face in the narration."[2] As far as I know, Levinas did not use the term "arrhythmia" (*arythmie*) in any other text; nevertheless, there is a relationship between "breaking of rhythm" in the essay "Il y a" and "arrhythmia" used in *Otherwise Than Being*; a link running through thirty years of his authorship. And it is not an exaggeration to affirm that Levinas's philosophy is nothing but philosophy of arrhythmia. This is what I want to suggest in this essay.

∼

In his book *Levinas: The Life and the Trace*, Salomon Malka wonders why he began to read *Totality and Infinity* at the seashore near Montpellier. He recalls how he spent his summer vacations reading *Totality and Infinity* and he also remembers the sensation of being shaken by the waves. He says it was as if the tide of the phrases by Levinas had kept on crashing against the shore. Before Malka, Jacques Derrida wrote about the style of *Totality and Infinity* as follows: "In *Totality and Infinity*, the development of the themes isn't purely descriptive or purely deductive. It unrolls itself with infinite insistence of the waters against the shore: return and repetition forever of the same wave against the same shore, in which all, in summing up itself each time, renews itself infinitely and enhances itself."[3] In this way, Levinas's style of writing is compared to the movement of waves in the littoral zone. Levinas was himself very sensitive to the styles of writers such as Céline, Proust, and Poe. He was one of the first to appreciate Céline's *Journey to the End of the Night*, describing its style in *Carnets de captivité*: "Style of Céline—the verb took refuge in the interjection. The obscene word adds to this character of interjection. The phrase in crisis. The phrases without verb which give static appearance can also have this kind of exclamation." [4] This remark on the verb relates closely to Levinas's own philosophical reflection. In fact, Levinas's words in *Carnets de captivité* anticipate the position he takes in *Otherwise Than Being*: "Be(ing) isn't only a verb—but the Verb. (. . .) Be(ing) equals verb. Isn't the essence of the word the verb? Hence the link between word and verb be(ing)."[5] Furthermore, we find there a very interesting phrase: "The verb to be—dilatation, contraction of being." Just like the heart, just like respiration, the "to be" or being has its own rhythm of repetition. Levinas also uses the word "vibration." I will come back to this point later.

What Levinas says about Proust also has something to do with the problematics of rhythm, included in the realm of sensation or of sensibility: "In Proust there is something unique that isn't his style or his theory of time or his fineness and precision of psychological analysis. It's the aristocratic character of his sensations. Proust comes to understand the interior life as something unique, as an inimitable thrill."[6] But, regarding the question of literature (or the literary) in Levinas's writing, we must mention the case of Edgar Allan Poe above all. Levinas quotes a long passage from the deleted part of Poe's "Loss of Breath." I'd like to quote it in French:

> "Ceci donc, méditait mon esprit, cette obscurité qui est palpable et opprime d'un sentiment de suffocation—ceci—ceci—est véritablement la mort. Ceci est la mort—la terrible mort—la

sainte mort. (. . .) La raison est folie, la Philosophie un mensonge. Nul ne connaîtra mes sensations, mon épouvante—mon désespoir. Et pourtant les hommes continuent à raisonner, à philosopher, à faire les imbéciles. Il n'y a, je le vois bien, point de ci-après que ceci. Ceci—ceci—ceci—est la seule Eternité !—et quelle, ô Belzébuth !—quelle éternité—être étendu dans ce vaste—ce redoutable vide—à l'état de hideuse, de vague, d'insignifiante anomalie—sans mouvement, mais désireux de me mouvoir—sans puissance, mais avide d'être puissant—pour jamais, pour jamais, pour jamais !⁷

It looks as if paratactic repetition of "*ceci*" swallowed the verb "*être*," and Levinas comments on this passage as follows: "It is worth noticing that repetitions here give a rhythm of the situation rather than the contents." In the essay mentioned above, "Il y a," Levinas spoke about "breaking of rhythm" (*rupture du rythme*). I have come to think it is one of the most important concepts in Levinas's philosophy. You might know that Levinas defines "alterity" as "unpredictability." Is not unpredictability a type of breaking of rhythm?

Furthermore, the title of this prose poem, "Loss of Breath," became a keyword associated with Levinas, that is, "*essoufflement*." Levinas wrote in *Otherwise Than Being* that "The Good supposes the breathlessness of spirit or the spirit stopping breath—where the beyond the essence passes itself, says itself, since Plato. One must from now on wonder if this breathlessness or this halt isn't the extreme possibility of the Spirit which carries a sense of the beyond the Essence."⁸

∽

It was Merleau-Ponty who asked Levinas to write something about art for *Les Temps Modernes*; and it was also Merleau-Ponty who wrote the preface for Levinas's text. In this preface, Merleau-Ponty compared Levinas with Sartre. In fact, Levinas stresses "disengagement" (*dégagement*) whereas Sartre professes the "commitment" (*engagement*) of the writer. Instead of committing himself into the world of light, the artist escapes from the world into the obscure region of untruth. This Hadean descent is made possible only by the fact that things as well as persons have no absolute identity and do not resemble themselves. Each of them has its own double, its own image, its own shadow of itself. Levinas calls this "allegory." Caricatures fix and exaggerate it. But what is important here is an involuntary movement of distraction from oneself. We no longer have our shadow; we are dragged down into shadow and lose our personality.

It is precisely in this process or recess that rhythm and musicality play their essential roles. Rhythm signifies precisely the hold images have upon us. It is a kind of enchantment; on this point Levinas draws his inspiration from the anthropological research of Lucien Lévy-Bruhl. The terms Levinas uses, such as "resemblance," "double," and "shadow," come from Lévy-Bruhl's *The Primitive Soul* (*L'âme primitive*), published in 1927. As in the case of participant-observation conducted by Lévy-Bruhl, we lose our individuality in rhythm and find that we belong to a collectivity as an anonymous being. Levinas writes: "Rhythm represents the situation where we cannot speak of consent or of assumption, or of initiative, or of liberty, because the subject is seized, taken away by rhythm. (. . .) In the rhythm, there isn't self (*soi*) anymore, but something like passage from self to anonymity. It is the charm or incantation of the poesy or of music."[9] If this is the case, *Totality and Infinity*, as a defense of subjectivity, should necessarily oppose rhythm. Indeed, we read there this passage:

> To the language in which influences appear without our knowing it from conscious activity for enveloping it and lull it as rhythm, where the action is carried by the work it created, and where the artist becomes an artistic work in Dionysian manner—according to the expression by Nietzsche—language is opposed to language which breaks all the time the charm of rhythm and prevents an initiative from becoming a simple role. The discourse is breaking and beginning, breaking of rhythm which ravishes and takes away the interlocutor—that is prose.[10]

I've already said that "breaking of rhythm" is characteristic of the Other; but it is precisely this passage that once stopped me from continuing research on the problematics of rhythm in *Totality and Infinity*. But now, I think I was wrong to stop. Even if Levinas himself wasn't conscious of this fact at all, a kind of underground dialogue, or rather polylogue, around this problematic transpires in *Totality and Infinity*. The early Nietzsche, at the epoch of *The Birth of Tragedy*, planned a Philosophy of Rhythm; in its draft he writes that "rhythm is an attempt at individuation. With the existence of rhythm, multiplicity and becoming must exist."[11] For Nietzsche, rhythm is an Apollonian principle of individuation, whereas for Levinas it is Dionysian principle of dis-individuation.

What strikes me most in this respect is that a change, or a total reversal, happened in the trajectory from *Totality and Infinity* to *Otherwise Than Being*. Levinas, who rejected Nietzsche's poesy or Dionysian rhythm, came to praise the poetical writing of Nietzsche: "So-called placing into brackets—is it enough to execute the transcendental reduction? No, it isn't. To achieve it, we must reach the nihilism of Nietzsche's poetical writing, nihilism which reverses the irreversible time into vortex. We must reach laughter which refuses speech."[12] Before getting into the details of this shift, I'd like to point out a few things. These two passages suggest that *Totality and Infinity* is to *Otherwise Than Being* what prose is to poesy. I know very well that the term "poesy" might cause misunderstanding. But Levinas himself acknowledges that *Totality and Infinity* still used ontological language that he later tried to escape. In fact, Levinas came to situate the birthplace of ontology in the Said (*le Dit*) and speaks about Saying without Said (*Dire sans Dit*) in his own style of exaggeration. The Said is propositional, which Levinas called apophansis, that is, "S is P," whereas the Saying cannot be integrated or gathered into the proposition, and therefore is called "delirium" (*délire*). Needless to say, delirium can relate to the perpetual tearing of the Dionysian. That is why Levinas came to praise Nietzsche's poetical writing.

In *Totality and Infinity*, Levinas connects Nietzsche's poetical writing with nihilism, with vortex. Nihilism is an overcoming of European metaphysics, and the term "vortex" suggests Nietzsche's idea of "*ewige Wiederkunft des Gleichen*," eternal return of the same. This chain of Nietzsche's ideas—poetical writing, Dionyisian rhythm, nihilism, eternal return of the same—also exerts influence on *Otherwise Than Being*.

The notion of "otherwise than being" itself can be conceived as breaking the regular rhythm of breathing on the ground of ontology. Only this breaking of rhythm makes possible a "sense." In a word, the philosophy of Levinas is a philosophy of "sense." It takes "sense" for "bottomless being;" it refuses to take "being" for the "bottom of sense." On this point, I dare to assert that "otherwise than being" is another name of being. We know Levinas qualifies "il y a" as "absurd," that is, "non-sense." Therefore, we can now complement our previous definition: the philosophy of Levinas is philosophy of the birth of "sense" based on "non-sense." For Levinas, the impossibility of this birth of "sense" is nothing but the inevitability of ethics and of philosophy.

Regarding what is called "sense," we find several impressive descriptions in the *Carnets*, his notebooks written in captivity during World War II. In particular, in fragments about the battle of Alençon, a town in

Normandy: "The wall-hangings which fall in my scene in Alençon concern also the things. The things decompose themselves, lose their sense. (. . .) But I don't want to speak simply about the end of illusions, it is rather the end of sense."[13] As the end of the philosophy is for Levinas the beginning of the time when all things become philosophical, the end of sense turns itself into the rebirth of sense. It corresponds with the breaking of rhythm and with breathlessness. Breathlessness here signifies the excluded third term within the pairing of inspiration and expiration. The same would be true of other key concepts presented in *Otherwise Than Being*, such as Saying-Said. With the third notion of "Unsaying," Levinas stressed amphibological alternant rhythm of the correlation Saying-Said. As for the rebirth of sense, he employs the word "twinkling" (*clignotement*), which must remind us of rhythm. Let's read another passage, including the word "modulate": "The trace draws itself and erases itself in the face as equivocality of Saying; it modulates thus the modality of the Transcendent."[14] It is true the modulation isn't rhythm itself; but rhythm as well as modulation might belong to what the Jewish interpretative tradition calls *Taam*, meaning flavor or taste.

To this I must add that in chapter 5 of *Otherwise Than Being*, Levinas came to speak about the sense of "Il y a," which he originally defined as "breaking of rhythm," as "non-sense." Obsessive repetition deranging our rhythm as subject or as citizen is necessary for the advent of sense itself and prevents both "justice" and "charity" (love) from institutionalizing themselves. In this sense, it is very interesting to find passages that relate both "justice" and "good" with the notion of rhythm:

> Justice is a relation that exists between parts and whole, where parts are neither absorbed in the whole, nor annihilated by the whole, and parts do not absorb the whole. Speech consists in breaking this rhythm—and justice consists in my presence in the whole and against whole, in the manner according to which a speaker coexists with another speaker.[15]

And

> The essence of time is rhythm, which liberates the instants from their tragic character of stance. Thus, we get the first vision about the Idea of the Good. The Good isn't Being; it comes

from the rhythm of time itself. It is precisely the rhythm of time. (. . .) It signifies the fact that Being isn't accomplished all of a sudden. The Good isn't an accomplishment—because an accomplishment consists in having been already accomplished forever. Whereas the Good is the fact that what has been accomplished is decomposed. We can thus understand why the Good is beyond Being.[16]

∽

Levinas said about his experience as a prisoner that "there was a new rhythm of life."[17] How then should we read Levinas's *Notebooks During Captivity*? Naturally each reader will have his or her own way. Nothing can forbid it. As for me, I have been wondering why Levinas started the text by mentioning Maimonides, Bahiya, and their notions of allegory. For me, it wasn't fortuitous.

You may know that at this time, Levinas was much interested in Proust's novel *In Search of Lost Time*, in particular its fifth and sixth volumes, titled *The Prisoner* (*La prisonnière*) and *The Fugitive* (*Albertine disparue*). Albertine, both prisoner and fugitive, represents for Levinas the alterity of the Other. As Levinas writes, "What is Albertine unless an evanescence of the other? Her reality is made with her nothingness, her presence with absence, the struggle against the elusive."[18] But that is not all. The word "prisoner" (*prisonnière*) has often been used, by Ibn Gabirol, for example, to designate the state of the Jewish diaspora. As for Maimonides, he was obliged to live in the Islamic world. According to Abraham Heschel, Maimonides recalled that he had "known affliction since childhood, since the womb."[19] At that time of persecution, diasporic Jews faced the alternative of apostasy or martyrdom. In this situation, Maimonides opened the third way, even within verbal apostasy. I think this fact prepared the Marrano's way of existence, which, through its essential ambiguity, could disclose the inanity of the martyrdom of logical radicalism.

As a prisoner of war, Levinas was clearly conscious of this historical fact, and like Maimonides he tried to create a new rhythm of life in the prisoner camp to escape the false alternatives of apostasy or martyrdom. The expression "*Kiddush Hashem*" in the following passage testifies to the fact that Levinas situated himself in the rabbinic tradition.

As I said above, it is no accident that Levinas began his notebooks with the mention of Maimonides. He writes, "For the people deported to the concentration camps, martyrdom was imminent, whereas the prisoners of war had enough time to prepare themselves for it. There was an interval where one could take certain attitudes toward suffering before it captured and tore them. (. . .) The people deported to the concentration camps experienced it as torture, death, *Kiddush Hashem* (sanctification of the name [of God])."[20] Levinas seldom uses the word "martyrdom," but we can find a very important passage that includes this term in his second magnum opus, *Otherwise Than Being*, as well as in one of his books on Judaism, *Beyond the Verse*. I would like to quote two passages, one from each of these books:

> Signification as witness or martyrdom—intelligibility preceding the light, preceding the present of initiative by which signification of logos signifies being in its present or its synchrony.[21]

And

> Crudeness of the world, of which Judaism isn't only the conscience but also the witness, that is martyrdom. Cruelty where the burns of my suffering and the anguish of my death can transform themselves into dread and into worry about the other man.[22]

Therefore we can say that for Levinas, "martyrdom" constitutes precisely the essence of Judaism; nevertheless the second passage suggests that here "martyrdom" doesn't consist of dying, even if it were for God; rather, it takes place in my concern for the other person. The etymological sense of martyrdom is to bear witness. Therefore, "witness" is another name for this kind of concern. For Levinas, to witness is "Saying," but "Saying" isn't simple saying. It is not an action based on my initiative. On the contrary, I have always been obliged to "Saying" an "Unsayable;" in other words, to send excessively and gratuitously my Being-for-the-Other. Levinas would say I am obliged to expose myself "beyond my death." That is what Levinas calls "infinite responsibility" for the Other. But it should be evident here that the Other isn't God at all, and that in the philosophy of Levinas, the responsibility for another man prevails over the responsibility for God. Such an extraordinary plot of ethics is in all respects a breaking of rhythm.

Notes

1. This text reproduces my lecture given at the Levinas Summer Seminar organized by Dr. Richard Cohen at Berkeley on July 23 in 2016. The translations are mine except where noted.
2. Emmanuel Levinas, *Autrement qu'être ou au-delà de l'essence* (Leiden: Martinus Nijhoff, 1974), 258.
3. Jacques Derrida, *Ecriture et Différence* (Paris: Minuit, 1968), 124.
4. Emmanuel Levinas, *Œuvres completes*, tome I (Paris: Grasset, 2009), 127.
5. Ibid., 167.
6. Ibid., 179.
7. Ibid., 67; "This then," my mind pondered, "this darkness which is palpable and oppresses with a feeling of suffocation—this—this—is truly death. This is death—terrible death—holy death. (. . .) Reason is madness, Philosophy a lie. No one will know my feelings, my Terror—my despair. And yet men continue to reason, to philosophize, to be foolish. There is, I see clearly, no hereafter other than this. This—this—this—is the only Eternity!—and what, O Beelzebub!—what an eternity—to be lying in this vast—this dreadful void—as a hideous, vague, insignificant anomaly—without movement, but eager to move—without power, but lusting to be powerful—forever, forever, forever!"
8. Levinas, *AQE*, 16.
9. Emmanuel Levinas, *Les impévues de l'histoire* (Montpellier: Fata Morgana, 1999), 111.
10. Emmanuel Levinas, *Totalité et Infini* (Leiden: Martinus Nijhoff, 1961), 222.
11. Friedrich Nietzsche, "Rhythmische Untersuchungen," *Kritische Gesamtausgabe* II 3 (New York: Walter de Gruyter, 1967).
12. *Levinas, AQE*, 10.
13. Levinas, *ŒC*, tome I, 132.
14. Levinas, *AQE*, 27.
15. Ibid., 534.
16. Levinas, *ŒC*, tome III, 203.
17. Levinas, *ŒC*, tome I, 203.
18. Ibid., 72.
19. Abraham Heschel, *Maimonides: A Biography*, trans. Joachim Neugroschel (New York: Farrar, Straus and Giroux, 1982), 39.
20. Ibid., 246.
21. Levinas, *AQE*, 124.
22. Emmanuel Levinas, *L'au-delà du verset* (Paris: Miuit, 1982), 18.

Bibliography

Derrida, Jacques. *Ecriture et Différence*. Paris: Minuit, 1968.

Heschel, Abraham. *Maimonides: A Biography*. Translated by Joachim Neugroschel. New York: Farrar, Straus and Giroux, 1982.
Levinas, Emmanuel. *Autrement qu'être ou au-delà de l'essence*, Leiden: Martinus Nijhoff, 1974.
Levinas, Emmanuel. *Les impévues de l'histoire*. Montpellier: Fata Morgana, 1999.
Levinas, Emmanuel. *Œuvres completes*, tome I. Paris: Grasset, 2009.
Levinas, Emmanuel. *Œuvres completes*, tome III. Paris: Grasset, 2013.
Levinas, Emmanuel. *Totalité et Infini*. Leiden: Martinus Nijhoff, 1961.
Levinas, Emmanuel. *L'au-delà du verset*. Paris: Minuit, 1982.
Lévy-Bruhl, Lucien. *L'âme primitive*. Paris: Librairie Félix Alcan, 1927.
Malka, Salomon. *Emmanuel Lévinas : la vie et la trace*. Paris: Albin Michel, 2005.
Nietzsche, Friedrich, "Rhythmische Untersuchungen," Kritische Gesamtausgabe II 3. New York: Walter de Gruyter, 1967.

9

After the End of Philosophy
Ethical Exegesis and Ethical Body

Irina Poleshchuk

Being the birthplace and home for all reasoning and deliberate thinking, philosophy gave rise to ethics, aesthetics, and science. At first glance, Levinas reads the history of philosophy as a source of concepts and inspirations for humanities, especially ethics. His approach to the history of philosophy is an ambiguous one. Constantly not only addressing the heritage or history of philosophy in his texts but also building up his sense of ethics pertaining to this heritage, he does not have in mind a very hallowed and highly respected discipline with impressive compendiums of texts. Rather, he discloses it as a great potentiality for understanding the very essence of humanism. However, it also seems that Levinas reads the history of philosophy in a very critical way, as being a rigid construction seeking out the truth and being obsessed by the eternal appearance of "the real things," and where quaint phenomena, such as challenges of radical responsibility and radical otherness, were constantly dismissed. For Levinas, the truly philosophical discourse oriented toward the human and toward the other does not derive from rationality, from complex and well-balanced imperative structures and meanings. Over and over in his works Levinas continuously interprets the history of philosophy as a history of ontology, where the primacy of ontology tends to encompass the diversity of all phenomena within comprehension and to reduce plurality to the unity.

In *Totality and Infinity*, Levinas elaborates his famous thesis: "ethics is first philosophy." The exposition of this thesis does not reveal the philosophical content of ethics but intends to tune attention to ethics such that it would occupy the privileged position within philosophical discourse. Levinas insists that one should question the status and hierarchy of knowledge in the long run of Western philosophy's history: it was always a constant struggle for the truth and an attempt to bring into presence the triumph of science. It is well known that being restricted to imperative, ethics has occupied the second or even third place after science. As knowledge of science and truth, philosophical reflection was always the first practice, and ethics begins only after.

The thesis "ethics is first philosophy" does not sound radically new in the history of philosophical thought. Famously Kant affirms the primacy of ethics: "the primacy of practical reason." However, his ethics was always unfolding as the ethics of rationality in that it discusses morality conforming and subordinated to the standards of science. Levinas indeed addresses Kant in his works; however, he moves from the Kantian realm and proposes an ambiguous project: to conceive ethics ethically. He attacks the hegemony exercised by the circling play of truth and knowledge and widely accepted rules of an epistemologically oriented philosophy, that is, philosophy contributing to fields of science. The shift Levinas makes is articulated around the statement that ethics is not just grounded on the power of reason but on the surplus of morality. The simplicity of this idea has a hidden difficulty that does not directly concern philosophical practice and method but the acts of morality. In *Otherwise Than Being*, Levinas's cutting-edge comment is that "No one is good voluntarily."[1] Indeed, care and responsibility for the other before oneself interrupts the vitality of one's own life, energies, actions, and enjoyment. To some extent, the care for the other also leads to a restriction of freedom of the self, as it restrains speech, possibly limits resources and breaks through widely accepted standards of our knowledge. Thus, Levinas's thesis "to see ethics as first philosophy" is no longer to perform philosophical questioning in the first place; rather, it would lead to the questioning of philosophical discourse itself and philosophical practice.

During many centuries, European philosophical tradition emphasized knowledge where meanings and significances were always transparent. It aimed to expose everything with the light of wisdom but also to reduce and to constrain. Aside from this, language seemed to provide a different type of engagement where what is read and addressed is not the same as that which is grasped in a written form. Language is similar to experience, which in many cases does not function on a rational basis. The imminence of the address of the other person avoids the totalizing power of consciousness that would reduce one unique experience to the universality of commonly accepted experiences. Levinas more and more appeals to the correlation between language and vulnerability of the animated body. These two concepts are strengthening a phenomenological insight on the connection between sensory experience and meaning. In "Meaning and Sense," Levinas suggests a deeper problem when he says that "experience is a reading, the understanding of meaning an exegesis, a hermeneutics."[2] In other words, any comparison of the relationship with the other person to the reading of a text would eventually lead to the reduction of experience.

Certainly, Levinas sees a search for the truth not just as a function of pure mind conversing silently, transparently, and simultaneously with itself. Neither is the truth extracted from logics of causality of the material world. Rather, it is constantly and desperately referring to the human. Starting with ethics and the ethics of communication, Levinas reveals sensibility and responsiveness of one singular embodied human being in each exegetical practice, where the face of the other breaks the sophisticated quest of the history of philosophy, its historical and linguistic connotations. In *The Time of the Nations*, Levinas writes: "This is an ascent within words, be they the most recent ones, to I know not what antiquity that is already to be translated, already to be deciphered. A dead language to be resuscitated, in order that its innumerable intentions may be reawakened! The latent birth of Scripture, of the book, of literature, and an appeal to interpretation, to exegesis, an appeal to the sages who solicit texts. A solicitation of solicitation—Revelation."[3] The first world of any philosophical discussion is not spoken or written but, as Levinas would put it, an address and the signification of sensibility. It is an embodied word prior to all words but which would also be the cause of all other words and speech. Prior to anything said, including the proposition of scientific knowledge with all its methodology and formulas, at the very possibility of meaningfulness, we are faced by what is said by one person to another. In other words, before the formation of any knowledge there is embodied sensibility of listening.

To some extent exegesis becomes a phenomenological technique: always standing for the meaning, being methodology, practice and philosophy of interpretation, it goes beyond any general theory of the text, and, what is important, it addresses itself to the lingual conditions, that is, to the Sprachlichkeit of all (embodied) experiences. As Richard Cohen accentuates in his work *Ethics, Exegesis, and Philosophy* Levinas's project of philosophical writing introduces an ethico-exegetical practice questioning the validity of the concept of reasoning. Cohen's extensive commentary locates Levinas's exegetical approach into a broader ethical but also metaphysical project that distinguishes Levinas's contribution to contemporary philosophical thought. While giving tribute to the authority of Levinas's philosophy, Richard Cohen refrains from exegetical praxis of reading by drawing out ethical conditions of being-for. In this sense, the performative act of ethical exegesis consists not only in being transformed by the text but where the text, entering as living substance, is tuned to preserve proximity with the other and with the interlocutor.

There are a number of questions and ideas that I would like to address in this paper. I believe that Levinas's thesis "ethics as first philosophy" implies a more complex approach that could be grasped in terms of "ethical exegesis" developed by Richard Cohen in *Levinasian Meditation* and in *Ethics, Exegesis and Philosophy*. I will show that ethical exegesis derives from Levinas's account of language and discloses sensibility and proximity in the form of the saying. My main argument is that Levinas does not only revise the work of language, but he also finds another approach to dialogue, response and listening by introducing two means or two "effective" solutions—ethical exegesis and ethical body as maternity, in other words ethical sensibility that can shed light on the philosophical practice.

Ethical Exegesis, Language, and Proximity

Before I give an extended analysis of the role of ethical exegesis I shall elucidate the theme of language in Levinas's ethics. Outside any discursive formulation, the relation with the other person opens itself in the language which is revealed through the notion of the said and the saying. The issue of language becomes more fully orchestrated in *Otherwise Than Being or Beyond the Essence*. I will briefly describe the key features of Levinas's understanding of language.

The structure of any linguistic act is regulated by two intertwined concepts: the said and the saying. In Levinas's interpretation, the said (*le dit*) belongs to an objectifying sphere. It can also be described as an originality of the I experience, that is, the ability to state "I am this." The saying (*le dire*) is recalled to tear the totality of the subject's being as it is expressed in the said. It demolishes the limits of language as a settled and logically organized structure.

To represent alterity and to catch it in the experience of consciousness means to find a certain meaning or to signify. "To present oneself as signifying is to speak. This presence, affirmed in the presence of the image as the focus of the gaze that is fixed on you, is said."[4] According to Levinas, what is expressed is also united with what speaks, the speech of the other is always presented in the form of imperative. Levinas introduces the idea of language as an event of the immediate relation with the other. This language is different from the objectifying language of things and the world; it gives access to the other: "the relationship of language implies transcendence, radical separation, the strangeness of the interlocutors, the revelation of the other to me."[5] It is only in responding to the other that language is born as an intersubjective system. To put it differently, objectifying language becomes posterior and is subordinated to ethical language that is primordially described as an encounter with the other. As Levinas states, "Discourse is thus the experience of something absolutely foreign, a pure "knowledge" or "experience," a traumatism of astonishment."[6]

It seems to be insufficient to explain language as a ground for dialogue and for the transformation of an individual. Language is the saying in relation to the other and for the other, preceding thematization in which different qualities of the phenomenon are gathered to a sort of unity. Levinas suggests that "the poem is situated at the moment of pure touching, pure contact, grasping, squeezing—which is perhaps a way of giving, right up to and including the hand that gives. A language of proximity . . . older than the truth of being . . . by its for-the-other, the whole marvel of giving."[7] The saying offers a possibility for approaching the infinite; it is a liberation from my own subjectivity. In the saying I can offer myself to the other and find my being as a being-for-the-other. This offering is a space where responsibility is supposed to be born. In Heidegger's interpretation, language articulates itself, and the concept of language does not place subjectivity in question within the appearance and appeal of the other.[8]

Critchley points out that one significant achievement of Levinas's work *Otherwise Than Being* or *Beyond the Essence* is the structure of the saying and the said, that is, how the ethical could signify within ontological language.[9] The saying is a pure sensibility and openness toward the other; it is affectivity, and it is my inability to refuse the other's approach. It is thought of as a performative stating or expression that describes myself facing the other. The said is disclosed as a judgment about which the truth or falsity can be ascertained. Critchley specifies that Levinas's whole project unfolds around one question: How can the saying, my exposure to the other, be said or described in philosophical exposition without finally betraying this saying?

The saying is not the permanent Husserlian *epoché* of the said; rather, the reduction is the exposure of the saying by way of a continual contestation of the said. The task is to pass beneath or beyond the said to the dimension of experience that transcends the realm of the said toward the other person in its infinite unspeakability. Then, the reduction should take a place within the said by interrupting it. Critchley notices that reduction could never be complete: it uses the language of the said and, at the same time, tries to avoid it. The crucial moment of this process is that this reduced said contains a residue of the unsaid said within the saying: "The saying has to be reached in its existence antecedent to the said, or else the said has to be reduced to it."[10] Thus, the philosophical discourse moves in a spiral between two orders of discourse: between the saying and the said, whereby the ethical signifies or shines through the alternation of these orders.

This thesis can also be illustrated by the quote where Levinas addresses Plato: "Plato maintains the difference between the objective order of truth, that which doubtlessly is established in writings, impersonally, and reason *in* a living being, "a living and animated discourse," a discourse thus "capable of" defending itself, and which knows those to whom it should be addressed and before whom it should be silent" (Phaedrus, 276a). This discourse is therefore not the unfolding of a prefabricated internal logic, but the constitution of truth in a struggle between thinkers, with all the risks of freedom. The relationship of language implies the transcendence, the radical separation, the strangeness of interlocutors, the revelation of the other to me. In other words, language is spoken where a community between the terms of the relationship is wanting, where a common plane is wanting or is yet to be constituted. It takes place in this transcendence."[11]

However, the question remains how to maintain the transcendence in relation with language. I believe that one of the promising solutions Levinas gradually develops is the notion of exegesis that also leads him to focus on the ethics of exegetic practice. At the first glance, a very common reading of exegesis explains it as a response to the text. In the theological context, the term "exegesis" stands together with "hermeneutics"; however, being an interpretation of the biblical script, exegesis is applied practice of interpretation, while hermeneutics works with articulation of concrete rules of interpretation. For Levinas the ethical exegesis is not just a notion he refers to in *Totality and Infinity* but also a method that expresses and aims at the "saying" of the "said." In other words, it deepens ethical conditions, whether they are explicitly acknowledged or not, of the text and speech. The notion of ethical exegesis was also emphasized and elaborated by Richard A. Cohen in his outstanding book *Levinasian Meditations*. Following Levinas's path of reading, he articulates four interrelated dimensions of ethical exegesis among which "pluralism of persons and readings" and "virtue, or existential self-transformative wisdom" are of special interest in the current discussion.[12] Continuing along the same line, phenomenology also accentuates that phenomena bring into visibility something forgotten or hidden and give birth to new meanings. Without being restrained by theoretical concepts, phenomenology engages in what is given in immediate experience. Richard Cohen mentions that exegetical practice has a dimension of relevant hermeneutics. It is indeed concerned with the understanding of texts but also with deep engagement with text, aiming to create rich account of phenomena through intuition, not only focusing on uncovering meanings but rather on dynamic interplay, investigating experience as it is lived by use of rich descriptive language. Exegesis, as it is read within phenomenological context, is also, according to S.J. Smith, a "research methodology aimed at producing rich textual descriptions of the experiencing of selected phenomena in the life world of individuals that are able to connect with the experience of all of us collectively."[13] The phenomenological emphasis here is that in the process of recognition of the experience of phenomena, a deeper awareness of the meaning of that experience is sought.

The existential self-transformative path, revealed in the practice of ethical exegesis, is bound, according to Cohen's interpretation, to "relevant hermeneutics." This is a movement of a sympathetic entering into texts together with an inner understanding that apply to the vivacity of life and to the sensibility of experience, and not only to the intellectual engagement of the reader. The dominating critical attitude in reading often lacks this sympathetic sensibility and sacrifices it to the objectivity of knowledge and to the purity of methodology of reading. Alternatively, exegesis is about showing how the ethical signifies within ontological language. To put it differently, exegesis is also a model of the saying and the said that explains an experience of being transformed by the text and within which the reader can unfold its sensible self: "Exegesis made the text speak; while critical philosophy speaks of the text. The one takes the text to be a source of teaching, the other treats it as a thing."[14] Broadly stated, the ethical exegesis does not neglect a critical approach to the text but tends to emphasize the teaching wrapped in texts. In this compact sentence, Richard Cohen finds a residue of an absolute transcendence of dialogue. And this is exactly what Levinas's objective is—to establish a proximity of two speakers who remain separate yet united and who are able of retaining their individuality. Thus, the ethical exegesis would be a move that forms relations within the text and where "the transcendence is proper to the discourse from out of which the relative transcendence of true knowledge is discovered."[15]

In a more detailed exposition, the ethical exegesis aims to preserve the saying of the said and to create the ethical conditions for the search of truth. These ethical conditions address first of all the sensible embodied person to whom, following Levinas's line of reflection, the Western philosophical tradition was blind. "Truth arises where a being separated from the other is not engulfed in him, but speaks to him. Language, which does not touch the other, even tangentially, reaches the other by calling upon him or by commanding him or by obeying him, with all the straightforwardness of these relations."[16] Now, coming back to the aforementioned Levinas quote referring to Plato's Phaedrus. In the history of philosophy, Plato's dialogues stand as a wonderful example of how exegesis works. Levinas believes that the skills, the art and spirit that Plato employs in his dialogues preserve the unity in difference and a relation of a non-indifference of one person to another; or, in other words, preserve responsibility of one interlocutor for the other.

Thus, ethical exegesis turns to be not only a praxis of interpreting but also an interaction of encounters and their inspiring ideas, utopias. It is also a proximity of embodied individuals expressed in the interplay of the saying and the said. The way Levinas approaches Plato's text as if Plato adopts a similar strategy to the one used in the interpretation of Talmud. Cohen notices that a distinctive feature of Plato's is not the dialogical form itself, but our commentary which is activated and living at the very moment when we are engaging ourselves, "when we 'take it to the heart', because are able of distancing of academic jargon."[17] In *Totality and Infinity*, Levinas writes: "It belongs to the very essence of language, which consists in continually undoing its phrase by the foreword or the exegesis, in unsaying the said, in attempting to restate without ceremonies what has already been ill understood in the inevitable ceremonial in which the said delights."[18]

In the first moment of reading, the textual voice or surface seeks for an embodied person. The intriguing answer Cohen gives in *Levinasian Meditations* is that "no interlocutor too important to be challenged or too insignificant to be ignored, because it is a text driven by a moral desire, or more precisely, by a holy compassion for others, to alleviate the suffering of others, and to in this way come close to God, to bring God's will to earth and to raise human will to God."[19]

One of the further possible ways of exploring this theme would to be to address Critchley's account of language. In *The Ethics of Deconstruction*, Critchley proposes "clôtural" reading as a critical step toward the history of philosophy. "Clôtural reading" comprises a double structure involved in reading the text. Critchley explains it as the following: to preserve the question of ethics, the text is analyzed "in terms of how it is divided against itself in both belonging to logocentric conceptuality and achieving the breakthrough beyond that conceptuality."[20] The interesting point Critchley makes is that conceptual insight of the "clôtural reading" is grounded on deconstructive reading. On the one side "clôtural reading" is adjusted to a logocentric epoch that is closed, and on the other side, as Critchley explains it, it also requires a deconstructive reading that is constantly disturbing this closure and is disrupting the flow of the philosophical discourse in order to allow the appearance of alterity. This incoming movement of alterity interrupts "any unity of logocentric textuality and epochality." Thus, the notion of "clôtural reading" opens up a possibility of questioning the ethics but also stands close to what Levinas articulates as the ethical exegesis. It is clear that Critchley also views "clôtural" reading to be a method of reading the history of philosophy seen from the standpoint of the others, of alterity, of embodied interlocutors, and of the victims of that history; the idea of "clôtural" reading is to speak out the *ethical* history that corresponds to the practice of ethical exegesis. Critchley writes that 'clôtural' reading articulates the ethical interruption of ontological closure, thereby disrupting the text's claim to comprehensive unity and self-understanding."[21] The purpose of this reading as well as of ethical exegesis is to reveal a diversity of insights, interruptions, or alterities hidden in the text and that are the moments of ethical transcendence. In this way, within the practice of reading, the language of ethics would be an event where the saying shines through the ontological exposition of the said.

John Llewelyn provides another inspiring reading of exegesis in Levinas's ethics. To perform ethical exegesis is to hear and to listen (écouter, *entendre*). Listening is not just an active engagement but, to some extent, a traumatic passivity where the embodied self is turned out and is forced to obey. Llewelyn goes on to articulate that the trope "by which the inner ear turns to Autrui, is the turning of my skin inside out, it is the turning of the ego into itself, a self whose responding to the other is its obedience, an obedience prior to the knowledge of what it is commanded."[22] Llewelyn adopts a similar argument with respect to Levinas's idea of exegesis; however, he radicalizes it by articulating the inescapability of response and obedience. These are the tropes found in exegetic practice and in "clôtural" reading, and they are already before any layer of information comes into play. Llewelyn's understanding of the concept of language and interpretation in Levinas's ethics are also challenging. He points to an important moment that the discourse of communication is the one-way communication of the self to the other where the performed saying is not the saying of the said of the message. Moreover, to express it in French, the saying is *se dire* and '*se*' indicates the accusative form of the self; the accused me and my saying signifies a gesture of giving of myself to the other. In Llewelyn's terms, it is a radicalization of ethical exegesis, but the opening up initiated by the exegetical method leads to being disquieted by the other.

On the first opening page of *Otherwise Than Being or Beyond Essence*, Levinas quotes Rachi, the medieval commentator of the Talmud: "The sages have said, Do not read 'begin at my sanctuary', but 'begin with those that sanctify me' . . . as teaches the Talmudic Treatise, *Sabbath*, 55a" (Ezekiel 9:6). The reason why Levinas refers to Rachi is to show, in an indirect way, that the whole text of *Otherwise Than Being* is formed as an exegetical response, an attempt to maintain silence and responsibility in writing for. I suggest that already this short passage points to the practice of ethical.

Before I move to the idea of ethical body, there is still one more important point to add to the discussion. Involving interlocutors of flesh and blood, in all the vivacity of their life, ethical exegesis also concerns sensibility, sensation and proximity, which in their turn condition the ethical body. The speaker, or the other delivering a message, is unreachable for thematizing consciousness. However, Levinas affirms it can be accessible in proximity.²³ He discloses that verbal discourse is not only an additional component to a knowledge that can be recognized. Verbal discourse arises from the proximity preceding the pronunciation; that is, he reserves a privileged place for non-verbal communication. In *Totality and Infinity* Levinas writes that "the eyes break through the mask—the language of the eyes, impossible to dissemble. The eye does not shine; it speaks."²⁴ Most appropriately, the ethical relation to the other interlocutor should not be brought back only to speech, but it can signify ethically by nonverbal indicative signs. However, the notion of proximity as nonverbal communication differs from the perception of the visual. Let us remind ourselves of Husserl's account of sensible intuition, which is actually based on the perception of a visual image; it is the primacy of vision upon senses. In Levinas's view, the real meaning of sensation is hidden not in the process of receiving information that happens as a result of our proximity to objects. If sensation is read as a fulfilment of intention, then this understanding of intention is totally wrong since the real intuition can never be accomplished; it is unsatisfied. Also, Levinas points out that a particular feature of sensation is that it *happens*. It is a meaningful event that happens between the feeling and the felt. Not only was the notion of sensation transformed in our contemporary culture. Touch was also reconsidered as a way of receiving information. Touch in Levinas's phenomenology is a certain concentration of knowledge on the surface of an object. This means that a new notion that can reflect and conceptualize the idea of feeling (visual and tactile) is needed, and it partly explains Levinas's invention of proximity. The notion of proximity reconsiders the visual and tactile sensation; they are no more subjected to language as the said.

Why does Levinas accentuate the notion of proximity and sensibility within the ethical explanation of language structure? Proximity, as a mode of describing the saying, does not presuppose a spatial location. Levinas writes: "Proximity is a relationship with a singularity, without the mediation of any principle or ideality. In the concrete, it describes my relationship with the neighbor, a relationship whose signifyingness is prior to the celebrated 'sense bestowing.'"²⁵ Proximity becomes a newborn intentionality for Levinas. In other words, I cannot escape proximity to the Other, since before I cognize something, I discover myself being appealed to by the Other; proximity is a structural component of consciousness. In fact, such an approach to the other excludes any thematization or possession. The singularity of this ethical proximity excludes mediation through universal notions that belong to language. Language is thought to be an "inter" space that indicates the appeal of the Other. Levinas underlines this statement in a very poetical way: "The precise point at which this mutation of the intentional into the ethical occurs, and occurs continually, as the approach breaks through consciousness, is the human skin and face. Contact is tenderness and responsibility."[26] This special foundation of language is caused by Levinas's desire to free language from logical discourse. So long as thought is the functional model governing any uses of language, it must remain embedded in the ideality it acquires from the basic intentional structure. It is for this reason that Levinas discusses the nature of the sensible in terms of intuition and the metaphysical desire. The sensible, according to Levinas, can be the only approach to the other, and it cannot be known. The sensible does not offer to consciousness something that may not be integrated into the structure of the world. It establishes a unique access to the truth. The original proximity whereby the self is related to the Other is achieved in nonverbal sensibility. "The relation of proximity . . . is the original language, language without words or propositions, pure communication."[27] Language is originally wordless approach and tactile contact. To formulate it differently, it is nudity of skin and silence.

At the end of this discussion, it is important to accentuate that in "Meaning and Sense," Levinas traces possible failures of phenomenology when he offers intuitive support for demonstrating that there is a consistency between the way language, revealed in interplay of the said and the saying, breaks the totality and the way any sensible experience transcends understanding. In sum, I would like to stress that Levinas's project of ethical exegesis is to retrace the passage to transcendence where commentary, reading, and dialogue would be aiming at the ethical saying within the said of the philosophical discourse. The ethical exegesis is not purely a practice of a contemplative mind but rather an articulation of sensible embodied self, manifesting in proximity of two interlocutors. My main claim is that ethical exegesis does not stand alone but is tightly bound to the ethical body found at the core of subjectivity.

Ethical Body, Maternity, and Sensibility

When we enter text, we always immerse ourselves in the intimacy of the text. But the dangerous side of it is that the text is also slippery and intangible. It is imposing its power over the reader, grasping the reader, controlling its present and its past, invading temporality of the interpreter. However, language itself is already conditioned by expressibility of experience. Experience as embodiment and as vulnerability can be said, and it demands to be said, articulated, and developed. The birth of meaning is directly bound to the exegetical practice performed.

My guiding line in examining the ethical body is the title of Levinas's second major book, *Otherwise Than Being or Beyond Essence*. Here I specifically draw attention to the statement "otherwise than being." Mention of "otherwise" might provide the clue to Levinas's answer why one should bring into discussion embodied subjectivity. During the entire history of Western thought the body was understood in terms of being, but for Levinas the meaning of human embodiment is revealed "otherwise than being." He claims that at the very origin of being for the other person there is already embodied ethical expression. In the same spirit, in *Levinasian Meditations*, Richard Cohen writes that each moral action and ethical becoming exceed being.[28] And obviously the human body is the moral body that goes beyond conceptualization of being. The development of our civilization was always based on our capacity to provide a preservation of life and of the self and of the body in the first place. One could see that there is indeed a certain ambiguity within different modalities embodied subjectivity: it is not just self-providing and satisfaction of needs of life, but in doing this one goes beyond animality and eventually is building up the ethical realm of the human.

In its origin, our embodiment is enjoyment, satisfaction of needs; it is aging and suffering; it is exposure, welcome, gift, and vulnerability. And therefore, only the vulnerable, mortal, embodied being is capable of encountering an ethical demand: "a shudder of incarnation though which giving takes on meaning, as the primordial dative of the *for another*, in which a subject becomes a heart, a sensibility, and hands that give."[29]

Thus, Levinas proposes a kind of reverse reading of any theoretical discourse. He believes that the starting point for the philosophy is not a divergence of mind, mental constructions together with embodied being; the history of philosophy and the science should be understood as theory and practice grounded in concrete situation, incarnated in language and time, expressed in varieties of embodied subjectivity, which he also describes as maternity. Certainly, this attitude was not totally ignored in the history of Western thought. Levinas mentions that there are two traditions intertwined that could shed light on the concept of ethical embodiment. During ancient times (and here Levinas mostly refers to Parmenides), being and time are thought within the realm of rationality—and where the body occupies a lower level—and is often "sacrificed to eternity."[30] Starting from Bergson, there was an important breakthrough, which assigned the body the first place. From this moment, the body was thought as a constitutive but also as transcendental principle, because it embraces the very possibility of experience. In his commentary on Levinas's view of embodiment, Cohen describes two promising lines of contemporary thinking. The first, represented by Bergson and Heidegger, is revealing body as an aesthetic body. The second, and here one could refer also to Merleau-Ponty, is conceiving body as the ethical body.

Levinas indeed develops a concept of ethical embodiment in a very detailed way. As I discussed in the previous part, the ethical essence of language, from which the experience of obligation derives, originates in the sensibility of the skin of the other's face and in proximity. The meaningful relation to the other is maintained by a nonverbal language of skin. The ethical self is an embodied being of flesh and blood, a being who is capable of hunger, who eats and enjoys eating: "only a being that eats can be for the Other."[31] Even though we tend to build up our existence on rational consideration, we are ridden with all possible inclinations and aversions, desires for pleasure, fame, prestige, power, and love that format our sensibility. This sensibility is not only a desire for happiness but also neither manifestation of pure rationality nor pure materiality. In describing the ethical body, Levinas insists on the priority of moral responsibility specified in terms of temporalizing unfolding body manifesting as maternal subjectivity.

This is not to deny that contrary to Bergson, Heidegger, and Merleau-Ponty, Levinas sees embodiment as unfolding temporal flow, as mortality and as historicity with imprint of alterity and as being marked by humanity of the other person. Levinas articulates that "corporeity describes the ontological regime of a primary self-alienation."[32] The body is, at the same time, my body, my concrete embodiment, and a thing in the world with and for others. He writes: "The body exceeds the categories of a thing, but does not coincide with the role of 'lived body' ('corps propre') which I dispose of in my voluntary action and by which I can. The ambiguity of corporeal resistance that turns into a means and from means turns into a resistance does not account for its ontological *hybris*. The body in its very activity, in its for itself, inverts into a thing to be treated as a thing."[33] Here the accent is on the embodiment emerging as mortality but also as justice. This is a phenomenological description of the formation of the self that reveals how the sensible self is built and how the embodied self is transformed while accepting the call coming from the other person.

Now I will turn to the idea of embodied maternal sensibility, and I will shortly touch upon connection between ethical exegesis and maternity. Not the easiest concept to read, maternity stands as a radical metaphor for unfolding the meaning of the-one-for-the-other. We do not really see the term of the maternal subjectivity in Levinas's other texts; however, in *Otherwise Than Being of Beyond the Essence*, he speaks about maternity as an ethical formation of sensibility found within subjectivity. There is a complicated algorithm of reading immanence and transcendence manifested as the other within subjectivity revealed as maternity: "It is being torn up from oneself, being less than nothing, a rejection into negative, behind nothingness; it is maternity, gestation of the other in the same."[34] In other words, starting from discussion of the erotic relation, where auto-affective sensibility can still hold its strong positions, in *Otherwise Than Being*, Levinas moves to ethical modality of maternal subjectivity. To pursue this program, he explains that "sensibility is being affected by a non-phenomenon, a being put in question by the alterity of the other, before the intervention of a cause, before the appearing of the other."[35] He is concerned with power of the immediacy of body sensation, which exposes one to the signifying of the other as the-other-in-the-same. Or, to put it another way, Levinas's idea is simply that the saying is emerging into the said on the level of ethical embodiment. The-other-in-the-same means that "the subject is affected without the source of the affection becoming a theme of representation."[36] He confines the role of maternity to serving as a bridge between being and transcendence that expresses a being affected by the other without having a source, and a being also structured as the-other-in-the-same. Let me elaborate on this argument.

In maternity, subjectivity acquires its interpretation as a disrupted temporalizing body and discovers a preontological past: because the birth of a child and an appeal of a child break temporal continuity of subjectivity and affect subjectivity before it is aware of being responsible. "The subjectivity of flesh and blood in matter—the signifyingness of the sensible, the-one-for-the-other itself—is the preoriginal signifyingness that gives sense because it gives. Not because, as preoriginal, it would be more original than the origin, but because the diachrony of sensibility, which cannot be assembled in a representational present, refers to an irrecuperable pre-ontological past, that is of maternity."[37] Here, Levinas provides sophisticated justifications for the rule of a meaning as the one-for-the-other born only in maternity: subjectivity is deposing itself, which, according to Levinas, is the very possibility of giving. This giving could be described as a gift of my body, my food, and clothes to the other before I have been born as a sensible subject, even before my free will and without the possibility of being together since the other has already marked me inside.

This general structure of the experience of maternity is built on a tension arising between auto-affectivity, self-awareness, and disrupted temporal continuity grasped in enjoyment of life and being in the world, in memories and projections, theories and linguistic concepts. Levinas accentuates the diachronical structure of maternity, which is similar to the interplay of the said and the saying happening in the structure of language. He writes:

> Indeed in the transcendence of intentionality diachrony is reflected, that is, psych itself, in which the inspiration of the same by the other is articulated as a responsibility for another, in proximity. Sensibility is in this way situated back in the human exception. But one has to go back from this reflection to the diachrony itself, which is the-one-for-the-other in proximity. It is then not a particular signification. The one-for-the-other in proximity. It is the not a particular signification. The one-for-another has the form of sensibility or vulnerability, pure passivity or susceptibility, passive to the point of becoming an inspiration, that is, alterity in the same, the trope of the body animated by the soul, psyche in the form of a hand that gives even the bread taken from its own mouth. Here the psyche is the maternal body[38]

This tension can be expressed in language emphasizing eventually a meaning of ethical becoming of subjectivity. Maternity thus seems to bring subjectivity to the very limits of rationality, language, and self-consciousness. In *Otherwise Than Being*, Levinas continuously highlights a theme of maternity and language: maternity becomes appropriate for the signifying of the sense: "bearing par excellence."[39] Here I find a remarkable change in the reading of sensibility—it is revealed as the signifying par excellence of alterity, of subjectivity, and of the saying. Describing maternity as the-other-in-the-same, Levinas discovers the ethical saying in the core of the said: "But the saying extended toward the said received this tension from the other, who forces me to speak before appearing to me. The saying extended towards the said is a being obsessed by the other, a sensibility which the other by vocation calls upon and where no escaping is possible."[40] Before the other appeals to me, I am already forced to answer, because in maternity subjectivity is disclosed as being obsessed by the other and being a hostage of the other. This is a crucial point where an ethical exegetical practice is grasped in modality of sensibility and maternity.

Giving, welcoming, and deposing oneself are manifestations of the saying within the said. Let me also add that maternity as subjectivity in absolute exposedness to the other is described by Levinas as speaking to and for. In his interpretation of maternity, Cohen goes even further. In the residue of maternal sensibility, he reveals the psyche playing an important role: questioning the very foundation of intentional consciousness and, consequently, the validity of philosophical discourse. He goes on to assert: "The other morally encountered is 'in-me' as if the other were literally in my body, the other's pain my pain, the other's suffering my suffering. The psyche is born in this introjection. To go beneath or farther than reflection, beneath or father than 'thematising consciousness,' beneath or farther than Husserlian intentionality altogether, to find the genuine concreteness of the psyche is to see the psyche as *responsiveness* to moral exigency, to moral imperative."[41] In relation to the above, it is worth pointing out that the formation of ethical body in terms of maternity becomes an originative component of ethical exegesis: within the confines of exegetical practice one finds sensibility expressed in a radicality of ethical embodiment. Perhaps only the promise of responsibility born together with ethical body silently speaks within philosophical tradition. Ethical embodiment turns into a particular mode of poetic being; it is productivity and creativity, but also in being creative one is exposed to all dangers and violence. To be embodied is to be wounded with an essentially ambiguous existence: one is for oneself and also eventually for others. Considering the body and will, we enter into the public sphere. In maternity, one is exposed to others without one's voluntary will. The subjectivity finds itself already bounded to others and to all these spheres of embodied existence, which mark human realm as opposed to purely natural dimension of being. Therefore, as Levinas makes clear, one has to start with embodiment revealed as the ethical one: "Responsibility for another is not an accident that happens to a subject, but precedes essence in it, has not awaited freedom in which a commitment to another would have been made. I have not done anything and I have always been under accusation—persecuted."[42]

I want to conclude by delineating the contours of ethical exegesis. Interpreting text, reading, being engaged with a message do not declare the correct and fixed meaning of text. To interpret is to bathe in the never-ending transformative process of stumbling into sometimes slippery meanings but also going beyond oneself. Exegesis does not lead to definitive interpretations but to specific forms of disrupted and discontinuous temporality and to a time-before-time. Interpretations will be forever rooted in the temporal flow of the said. However, our reading, construction of meaning, nuances, and traces should aspire for what is beyond the verse. This is a way to intrude the said and to move toward ethical exegesis. Cohen summarizes the way Levinas moves this sense of exegesis into ethics: "The time structure of exegesis is thus the very temporality of ethics, of the encounter of one with another, 'I,' and 'you.' It involves a notion Levinas early in his career called 'trace,' and later calls 'diachrony.' Just as the ethical imperative embedded in the disturbing alterity of the other opens up an unanticipated future more future than the projections of the self, so too it bores more deeply into the self than the self's synthesis, however passive; it fissures the self with responsibilities deeper than its recuperative powers of synthesis."[43] Once again, the innovative reading proposed by Cohen is to conceive exegetical practice as diachronical in its essence. Across exegesis, Levinas's philosophical writings demonstrate a sophisticated fusion of reason and sensibility, neither of which is reducible to one another; each are already inhabited by the other, where consciousness is thought as incarnate and incarnate as an ethical one.

Finally, I should add that in the context of Levinas's ethics the idea of the "end of philosophy" is often employed to mean the transition from philosophical theory to ethics. This means to address the subject of flesh and blood who cannot escape an intersubjective signification, that is, cannot escape "interhumanity." As Levinas elegantly puts it: "The self is a *sub-jectum*; it is under the weight of the universe, responsible for everything."[44] The reason why Levinas talks about the end of the philosophy is that the whole discourse of the Western philosophy was mostly developed as the said ignoring alterity and the other. Henceforth he denotes basic philosophical inquiry and moves to "ethics as first philosophy." This is indeed simple but yet different ethics: to perform unsaying of the said by outlining the importance of the approach to the other interlocutor that is articulated as ethical exegesis and originated in ethical body and sensibility. Behind any interplay of knowledge, myth, or narrative there is a layer of interpretation involving ethical engagement and radicality of vulnerable embodiment. I would like to finish in the same spirit with Richard Cohen: "Levinas does not fight myth with myth, superstition with superstition. Rather, in what seems like myth, in what could be misunderstood as myth, he understands the human by means of exegesis. It is a great difference."[45]

Notes

1. Emmanuel Levinas, *Otherwise Than Being or Beyond Essence*, trans. Alphonso Lingis (Pittsburgh: Duquesne University Press, 2006), 11.

2. Emmanuel Levinas. *Basic Philosophical Writings*, edited by Adrian Peperzak, Simon Critchley, and Robert Bernasconi (Bloomington: Indiana University Press, 1996), 38.

3. Emmanuel Levinas. *In the Time of the Nations*, trans. Michael B. Smith (Bloomington: Indiana University Press, 1994), 110.

4. *Totality and Infinity*, 66.

5. *Totality and Infinity*, 66.

6. *Totality and Infinity*, 66.

7. Emmanuel Levinas, *Proper Names*, trans. Michael B. Smith (Stanford: Stanford University Press, 1976), 41.

8. *Otherwise Than Being*, 47.

9. Simon Critchley, *The Ethics of Deconstruction. Derrida and Levinas* (West Lafayette: Purdue University Press, 1999), 164.

10. *Otherwise Than Being*, 46.

11. *Totality and Infinity*, 73.

12. Richard A. Cohen, *Ethics, Exegesis and Philosophy. Interpretation after Levinas* (New York: Cambridge University Press, 2001), 94.

13. S. J. Smith, "The Phenomenology of Educating Physically," in *Phenomenology and Educational Discourse*, ed. D. Vandenburg (Durban: Heinemann, 1997), 80.

14. Emmanuel Levinas, *Levinas Reader*, ed. Sean Hand (Oxford: Basil Blackwell, 1989), 263.

15. Richard, A. Cohen, *Levinasian Meditations. Ethics, Philosophy, and Religion* (Pittsburgh: Duquesne University Press, 2010), 103.

16. *Totality and Infinity*, 62.

17. *Levinasian Meditations*, 105.

18. *Totality and Infinity*, 30.

19. *Levinasian Meditations*, 104.
20. *The Ethics of Deconstruction*, 30.
21. *The Ethics of Deconstruction*, 30.
22. John Llewelyn, *Emmanuel Levinas. The Genealogy of Ethics* (London and New York: Routledge, 1995), 184.
23. *Otherwise Than Being*, 88.
24. *Totality and Infinity*, 66.
25. *Otherwise Than Being*, 100.
26. Emmanuel Levinas, *Collected Philosophical Papers*, trans. Alphonso Lingis (The Hague: Martinus Nijhoff, 1987), 116.
27. *Collected Philosophical Papers*, 119.
28. *Levinasian Meditations*, 37.
29. *Levinas Reader*, 182.
30. *Levinasian Meditations*, 38.
31. *Otherwise Than Being*, 74.
32. *Totality and Infinity*, 226.
33. *Totality and Infinity*, 229.
34. *Otherwise Than Being*, 75.
35. *Otherwise Than Being*, 75.
36. *Otherwise Than Being*, 75.
37. *Otherwise Than Being*, 78.
38. *Otherwise Than Being*, 67.
39. *Otherwise Than Being*, 75.
40. *Otherwise Than Being*, 77.
41. *Ethics, Exegesis, and Philosophy*, 188.
42. *Otherwise Than Being*, 114.
43. *Ethics, Exegesis, and Philosophy*, 259.
44. *Otherwise Than Being*, 116.
45. *Ethics, Exegesis, and Philosophy*, 231.

Bibliography

Cohen, Richard, A. *Levinasian Meditations. Ethics, Philosophy, and Religion*. Pittsburgh: Duquesne University Press, 2010.

Cohen, Richard, A. *Ethics, Exegesis and Philosophy. Interpretation after Levinas*. New York: Cambridge University Press, 2001.

Critchley, Simon. *The Ethics of Deconstruction. Derrida and Levinas*. West Lafayette: Purdue University Press, 1999.

Levinas, Emmanuel. *Otherwise Than Being or Beyond Essence*, trans. Alphonso Lingis. Pittsburgh: Duquesne University Press, 2006.

Levinas, Emmanuel. *Totality and Infinity: An Essay on Exteriority*, trans. Alphonso Lingis. Pittsburgh: Duquesne University Press, 2004.
Levinas, Emmanuel. *Basic Philosophical Writings*, edited by Adrian Peperzak, Simon Critchley, and Robert Bernasconi. Bloomington: Indiana University Press, 1996.
Levinas, Emmanuel. *In the Time of the Nations*, trans. Michael B. Smith. Bloomington: Indiana University Press, 1994.
Levinas, Emmanuel. *Levinas Reader,* edited by Sean Hand. Oxford: Basil Blackwell, 1989.
Levinas, Emmanuel. *Collected Philosophical Papers*, trans. Alphonso Lingis. The Hague: Martinus Nijhoff, 1987.
Levinas, Emmanuel. *Proper Name,* trans. Michael B. Smith. Stanford: Stanford University Press, 1976.
Levinas, E. 2007. *Totality and Infinity: An Essay on Exteriority*, trans. Alphonso Lingis, Pittsburgh, Duquesne University Press.
Llewelyn, John. *Emmanuel Levinas. The Genealogy of Ethics*. London and New York: Routledge, 1995.
Smith, S. J. "The Phenomenology of Educating Physically," edited by D. Vandenburg in *Phenomenology and Educational Discourse*, Durban: Heinemann, 119–144.

10

Senseless Kindness, the Church, and the Betrayal of Mercy in *Don Quixote*

STEVEN SHANKMAN

My subject is senseless kindness in *Don Quixote*, and how Cervantes often finds this senseless kindness, called mercy (*misericordia*) or charity (*caritas*) in the Christian tradition, betrayed by confessing Catholics during a particularly xenophobic moment in Spanish history. It is a moment that bears an unfortunately uncanny resemblance to our own such perilous time in Europe and the United States. In 1492, the Jews were exiled from Spain. After 1492, a Spanish Jew could remain in Spain only if he renounced his Judaism and became a convert—a Converso—to Catholicism. A Muslim would have to convert as well, becoming a Morisco. Between the publication of Part I (1605) and Part II (1615) of Don Quixote, the Spanish state took its Muslim ban to a new level of intolerance. On April 9, 1609, King Philip III expelled the Moriscos from Spain. These expulsions continued through 1614. Cervantes's critique of the Church is epitomized in a brief sentence that appears in the ninth chapter of Part II of the novel. The senselessly kind—indeed delusional—knight errant Don Quixote and his squire, Sancho Panza, are off on a quest to find Quixote's beloved Dulcinea of Toboso. The two charge ahead toward what Quixote imagines is the palace of the Dulcinea, but that, as they rapidly approach this looming structure, turns out to be the main cathedral in the town of Toboso. "Con la iglesia hemos dado, Sancho, [We have come to the church, Sancho]," Quixote tells his feckless squire.[1] This is a straightforward statement at first glance, but the words have been understood as an iconic reference to the novel's pervasive critique of the institution of the Catholic Church in Spain. Cervantes's twenty-first-century translator Edith Grossman glosses this sentence as follows: "This statement is one of the best known in the novel, for it has been interpreted as meaning that Don Quixote and Sancho have 'run into' the church in the sense of coming into dangerous conflict with the institution. The sentence is sometimes cited using another verb to underscore that meaning: topar [the verb, meaning 'to bump into' or 'to run into a problem with,' used by Sancho just a few lines down] rather than dar."[2]

Before turning to Cervantes's masterpiece and its critique of how the Catholicism of his day often betrays mercy, let us begin our discussion of senseless kindness with its precise articulation in the text that so preoccupied Emmanuel Levinas: Vasily Grossman's extraordinary novel *Life and Fate*. In an interview with Myriam Anissimov included in the volume *Is It Righteous to Be?*, Levinas, in commenting on Grossman's novel, writes that "the mercy of God occurs through the particular man—not at all because he is organized in a certain way or because he belongs to a society or an institution. There are acts of stupid, senseless goodness. Grossman shows us this throughout the whole book."[3]

In the introduction to his recently published book *Out of Control: Confrontations between Spinoza and Levinas*, Richard Cohen points us to the locus classicus for the phrase "senseless kindness," which can be found in the scribblings of the holy fool Ikonnikov in Grossman's *Life and Fate*. There Grossman, through Ikonnikov, speaks of the private kindness of one individual to another, a kindness without witness, small, senseless [без мыслы/bez mysly]. We might call it "senseless kindness" [бессмысленной добротой/bessmyslennoy dobrotoy]. The kindness of people outside of religious and social notions of the good. In the Russian language, we should note, there is a difference between the good [Добро/Dobro], on the one hand, and goodness or kindness [доброта/dobrota], on the other.

The precise phrase "senseless kindness" [бессмысленная доброта/bessmyslennaya dobrota] appears in the narrative proper of *Life and Fate* for the first time in chapter 39 of Part 2 of Grossman's wonderful text.[4] We are in a Nazi prisoner of war camp in German-occupied Belarus. The Communist prisoners are planning an insurrection within the camp. We are witnessing a conversation between two of these committed Communists, Osipov and Mostovskoy. At issue is how the resistance of the pris-

Senseless Kindness, the Church, and the Betrayal of Mercy | 129

oners to their Nazi captors will proceed. What separates the responses of Osipov and Mostovskoy is Mostovskoy's sensing of an ethical responsibility that transcends institutions and politics. Osipov reports to Mostovskoy, to the latter's moral horror, that in order to assert the "iron discipline" of party rule, the Communists have schemed to send a remarkably sympathetic comrade, a Czech named Yershov, to Buchenwald, a notorious death camp. Mostovskoy's sensing of an ethical responsibility beyond politics is the result of two related experiences. First, his response to the face of Ikonnikov, who rejected politics and the demands of an abstract idea of the Good in favor of senseless kindness. And second, his conversation with the Nazi officer Liss, who in a moment of absolute frankness, had confessed to Mostovskoy that, in their rejection of ethics in favor of the absolute demands of the state, the totalitarian regimes of both Hitler and Stalin were, paradoxically, mirror images of each other rather than radically opposed ideologies.

Next, after insisting that the betrayal of their comrade Yershov was "the unanimous decision of all the Communists," Grossman writes, Osipov

> stood in front of Mostovskoy in his miserable clothes, holding a rag in one hand—stern, unshakeable, certain of his rectitude, of his terrible, more than divine, right to make the case he served into the supreme arbiter of a man's fate. And the naked skinny old man, one of the founders of a great Party, sat there in silence, his shoulders hunched and his head bowed.
>
> It was night and he was back in Liss's office. He was overwhelmed by terror. What if Liss hadn't been lying . . . ? What if he had simply wanted to talk to another human being?
>
> He drew himself up to his full height. Then—just as ten years before during the period of collectivization, just as during the political trials when the comrades of his youth had been condemned to the scaffold—he said:
>
> "I submit to this decision; I accept it as a member of the Party."
>
> He took his jacket from the bench and removed several scraps of paper from the lining. They were the texts he had drawn up for leaflets.
>
> Suddenly, in his mind's eye, he saw Ikonnikov's face and large cow-like eyes. If only he could listen once again to the voice of the preacher of senseless kindness [проповедника

бессмысленной доброты/propovednika bessmyslennoy dobroty].

"I wanted to ask about Ikonnikov," he said. "Did the Czech slip his card in too?

"The holy fool? The man you used to call the blancmange [a particularly sweet dessert made with gelatin]? He was executed. He refused to work on the construction of an extermination camp. Keyze was ordered to shoot him."

That night Mostovskoy's leaflets about the battle of Stalingrad were stuck up on the walls of the barrack-huts.[5]

One of the most moving passages in Grossman's novel depicts "the holy fool" Ikonnikov, a prisoner in the camp, recognizing that he has it in his power to resist—even at the expense of his life—the Nazis' command that he dig the foundations of an extermination camp. Mostovskoy feels the full force of Ikonnikov's example here, seeing in his mind's eye the face of Ikonnikov, with his "large cow-like eyes." Mostovskoy betrays the call to responsibility conveyed by the face of Ikonnikov, the call to rise to the dignity of a uniquely responsible subject for a unique and irreplaceable other. Mostovskoy betrays what Richard Cohen, in commenting on Levinas's *Totality and Infinity*, calls "the singularizing of the self as responsibility . . . for the other."[6] Mostovskoy opts for allegiance to politics, to the institution of the Communist Party, to an anonymous totality of which he—the shadow of a true self—is a mere part. Note a particularly revealing grammatical construction, in this regard, in the last sentence of the passage under discussion. The main historical subject of Grossman's novel is the battle of Stalingrad. Mostovskoy had written texts for leaflets that would keep hopes for a Soviet victory alive in a battle, at first favoring the Germans, that would ultimately decide the fate of the world. This last sentence does not state that Mostovskoy or his comrades placed these leaflets on the walls of the barrack-huts. Grossman rather uses a passive verbal construction: these leaflets—as if through some anonymous process—"were stuck up (были раскпеены/byli raskpeyeny) on the walls of the barrack-huts."

~

The arrogant Osipov sarcastically refers to Ikonnikov as an old "holy fool" (юродивы/yurodivy). The most famous of holy fools in Russian literature is Prince Lev Nikolaevich Myshkin, the protagonist of Dostoevsky's novel *The Idiot*. The model for Myshkin is, of course, none other than the senselessly kind Don Quixote, who drew Levinas's attention in the last set of lectures (on *God and Onto-theo-logy*) he gave as professor of philosophy at the Sorbonne in 1976. In one lecture in this course, delivered on Friday, February 13, 1976, and titled "Don Quixote: Bewitchment and Hunger," Levinas reflects on Quixote's understanding of his alleged imprisonment in a cage as an enchantment by hostile forces, an enchantment that makes it impossible for him, at the moment, to respond to the command that he serve those in need, that he respond to those in need with senseless kindness.

We mentioned how, before he affirms his allegiance to the dicta—no matter how cruel—of the Communist Party, Mostovskoy is haunted by "the face of Ikonnikov [лицо Иконникова/litso Ikonnikova] and his large, cow-like eyes." Before, to his shame, he is about to betray the creed of senseless kindness preached by Ikonnikov, Mostovskoy expresses the wish, as if this might prevent that imminent betrayal, to hear the preacher's voice once again. In Mostovskoy's haunting recollection of the face of Ikonnikov, I am reminded of the peculiar power of the face of Don Quixote in Cervantes's novel, a face that, according to Sancho, cannot help but evoke mercy or senseless kindness in those who encounter it. In chapter 19 of the first part of the novel, Sancho dubs Quixote "The Knight of the Sorrowful Face," as translated by Edith Grossman, but that, translated literally, is "The Knight of the Sorrowful Figure" [el Caballero de la Triste Figura].[7] Every knight in Quixote's beloved romances has a clearly identifying moniker, with a corresponding image that appears on the knight's shield. Quixote is so impressed with Sancho's suggestion that he is now determined to assume that name and to have the associated image painted on his shield. There is no reason to paint the image on his shield, Sancho remarks, as Quixote's gauntness and clearly missing teeth will of themselves evoke immediate compassion in those who behold Quixote's face: "There's no reason to waste time and money making that face," said Sancho. "What your grace should do instead is to uncover yours and show it to those who are looking at you, and right away, without any images or shields, they'll call you The Knight of the Sorrowful Face; believe me, I'm telling you the truth, because I promise your grace, Señor, . . . that hunger and your missing teeth give you such a sorry-looking face that, as I've said, you can easily do without the sorrowful picture."[8]

This important passage on the derivation of Don Quixote's famous moniker as a knight errant interrupts a narrative passage that exemplifies the theme of our essay on senseless kindness, the Catholic Church, and the betrayal of mercy in Cervantes's novel. That passage occurs toward the beginning of chapter 19. A group of seminary students studying for the priesthood is carrying a dead body from Segovia for burial, though we do not learn who these men are or what they are doing until the end of the chapter. It is night. Quixote and Sancho are apprehensive when they see coming toward them "a great multitude of lights that looked like nothing so much as moving stars."[9] As the lights approach, it becomes clear that these lights are "burning torches" being held in the hands of "some twenty shirted men" and "behind them came a litter covered in mourning, followed by another six mounted men draped in mourning."[10] Quixote, in his delusional state, imagines that "the litter was a bier carrying a gravely wounded or dead knight, and that it was reserved for him alone to take revenge."[11] Firmly but courteously, Quixote tells the shirted men of his concern, asserting that he is prepared to avenge any wrong done to them, or to stop them if they are responsible for the death of the person whose lifeless body they are carrying.

While Quixote is courteous, the man—a seminary student, as it turns out—to whom he addresses his question is not. It is clear that this seminary student preparing for the priesthood does not see the face of Quixote, the face of the knight errant who, only moments later, will be dubbed by Sancho "The Knight of the Sorrowful Face." He does not see Quixote's sorrowful face because anyone who truly encounters the face of Quixote, according to Sancho, cannot helped but be moved to compassion by its gauntness and its missing teeth. The response of the priest-in-training is unfeeling and abrupt: "We're in a hurry [Vamos de priesa]," he tells Quixote, "and the inn is far and we can't stop to give the accounting you ask for."[12] Quixote is offended by this lack of courtesy and charges the group with his lance. The seminarians imagine that Quixote is "a devil from hell who had come to take the dead body they were carrying on the litter."[13] One of the seminarians is thrown by his mule and suffers what appears to be a broken leg. From him Quixote learns that these men are, in fact, seminary students, and that they are accompanying a dead body to its burial in Segovia. Sancho, on orders from his master, helps the man get back up on his mule (but only after raiding the provisions in the mule's pack!) and apologizes, on behalf of his master, for any harm his master may unwittingly have done to him and to his companions.

It is certainly understandable that Quixote's actions frightened the group of seminarians and caused them to fear for their lives. Quixote is certainly not guiltless in this episode, though one could argue that he is, in fact, guiltless on account of his insanity, his fixed delusion that he is a knight errant devoted to righting wrongs and his subsequent misperception of the actions of those around him. But Cervantes's insertion, in the middle of this passage, of the derivation of Quixote's being dubbed "The Knight of the Sorrowful Face" by Sancho, serves as a critique of the actions of the group of young seminarians, suggesting that, for all their devotion to a religion that places the responsibility to practice acts of mercy as its core, they betray that call to mercy here in failing to see the sorrowful face of Don Quixote. It is the failure to see Quixote's sorrowful face on the part of the seminarian who responds to Quixote with the unsympathetic words "We're in a hurry" that initiates the conflict. Quixote quickly escalates the conflict as a result of his delusion that these men have likely killed the man whose body they are transporting. Quixote threatens, in response to what he perceives as a gross injustice, to kill one of these seminarians, a man named Alonso López, who says he is a "licentiate." But this seminarian, as described by Cervantes, is hardly a model of Christian humility and compassion. He is, for one thing, a braggart and a liar. He introduces himself to Quixote as a lofty "licentiate" when in fact he is "only a bachelor," as he later confesses.[14]

The bachelor shows his true colors when, just after the passage in which Cervantes describes the derivation of Quixote's having been dubbed "The Knight of the Sorrowful Face," by Sancho, he returns and tells Quixote: "I forgot to say that your grace should be advised that you have been excommunicated for having laid violent hands on something sacred, juxta illud: Si quis suadente diabolo [according to the saying: If anyone, persuaded by the devil . . .], etc."[15]

As Edith Grossman informs the readers of her translation, the Latin words here are "part of a phrase established by the Council of Trent for excommunicating those who committed violence against a member of the clergy."[16] The rigidity of the Catholic Counter-Reformation, with its strict rules protecting the clergy and its determination to excommunicate those suspected of failing to follow this rule, here trumps any sense that it is the obligation of this clergy, first of all, to practice charity, to see the sorrowful face—gaunt and toothless—of the other.

We see a similarly hypocritical failure, on the part of confessing Catholics allegedly devoted to the principle of loving-kindness, to respond to the sad and vulnerable face of Don Quixote in chapter 52, toward the end of Part I of the novel. A group of penitents is praying for rain during a drought, "asking God to open the hands of his mercy [misericordia] and allow it to rain."[17] Seeking the mercy of God, the penitents are carrying on a platform "the holy image of the Blessed Virgin," that is, of the Virgin Mary, the very embodiment of compassion.[18] Quixote is convinced that the image is a real lady whom the penitents have captured against her will, and as he begins to gallop after them, Sancho asks Quixote, "What demons in your heart incite you to attack our Catholic faith [nuestra fe católica]?"[19] When Quixote tells the penitents to release this allegedly captive lady, rather than respond to the face of Quixote with the compassion one might expect from penitents devoted to the Blessed Virgin, they instead respond, as did the seminary students in the passage we just discussed, with laughter. The penitents "began to laugh very heartily and this laughter was like gunpowder thrown into the flames of Don Quixote's wrath."[20] Quixote charges the penitents. One of them strikes Quixote with a pole that this penitent used to support the platform on which the image of the Virgin Mary stood when the platform was at rest. The pole that is used to support the very image of compassion par excellence is here being used, paradoxically, to beat a poor madman! Sancho shouts at the penitents to inform them that Quixote is truly "a poor enchanted knight who had never harmed anyone in all the days of his life."[21] What stops the penitent from continuing to beat Quixote is, however, hardly a sense of repentance inspired by Sancho's compassionate words but rather "believing that he had killed" Quixote, the penitent's apparent fear of the legal consequences of being held responsible for Quixote's death.[22] Suddenly aware of the fact that Quixote "lay without moving hand or foot," he "quickly tucked his penitent's robe up into his belt and fled across the countryside like a deer."[23] The penitents devoted to the Virgin Mary, like the seminary students in the earlier episode, thus hypocritically fail to demonstrate mercy, or senseless kindness, to a poor madman.

It is ironic that only two chapters before the one that reveals the hypocrisy of the young seminarians, one of the most unlikely of the novel's cast of many characters, the serving maid and prostitute Maritornes, exhibits precisely the quality of senseless kindness glaringly absent in the souls of the seminarians. Maritornes works at the inn at which Don Quixote and Sancho Panza have been staying before they set out on their adventure with the seminarians. Cervantes goes out of his way to paint an unflattering portrait of Maritornes's physical features. She is described as short, overweight, and unattractive, in stark contrast to the astoundingly beautiful, idealized, shepherdess Marcela of the preceding chapters. Just before Quixote and Sancho leave the inn, Sancho is tossed high in the air in a blanket, again and again, by some rowdy and cruel guests. Having had their fun, Sancho's tormentors finally cease and place the manhandled and exhausted Sancho back on his donkey and drape his overcoat over him. The compassionate Maritornes [la compasiva de Maritornes] then brings water from a cool well for Sancho, who says he prefers wine to water. Maritornes obliges Sancho's request for wine, doing so "very willingly and paid for it with her own money, because it can truly be said of her that though she followed the trade that she did, she bore a remote resemblance to a Christian woman [tenía unas sombras y lejos de cristiana]."[24] True charity! Senseless kindness! The reader is reminded here of the first miracle Jesus performs in the Gospel of John (2:1–11). Jesus, his mother Mary, and Jesus's disciplines are invited to a wedding. The wine runs out, the people are poor, and Jesus miraculously turns water into wine. Maritornes, the disfigured prostitute, thus evokes the generosity and senseless kindness of Jesus. We must not fail to note the irony implicit in the phrase "she bore a remote resemblance to a Christian woman [cristiana]." The irony here cuts in at least two ways. The narrative persona here is—and this persona, like so much in the novel, often shifts with circumstances—prudish, and conventionally and complacently Catholic-Christian. On one reading of the phrase, the narrator can be viewed as judgmental and disapproving of Maritornes's profession, despite Jesus's own empathy for the plight of prostitutes, including Mary Magdalene, whose first name—along with the name of that of the iconically merciful mother (of Jesus), Mary—is contained in the first two syllables of the name "Maritornes." Another reading of the phrase would imply that Christian women in the Spain of Cervantes's time are rarely truly charitable and that therefore Maritornes's truly Christian gesture of compassion hardly resembles the disappointing reality of this less than charitable norm. Maritornes's act of true charity, of senseless kindness, would thus, in its moral excellence, be seen—according to this second reading—as bearing only the faintest resemblance to the sorry norm exhibited by the typical "Christian woman" [cristiana] living in Spain in the early seventeenth century, during the time of the Inquisition.

The final passage we shall discuss appears in the famous "captive's tale" toward the end of Part I of the novel. I have been arguing so far that Cervantes, in *Don Quixote*, often calls into question the triumphalist view of Christianity associated with the Catholic Church at a time when the nation-state sought to cleanse Spain of Jews and Muslims, and even of the converts to Catholicism from Judaism and Islam: the Conversos and Moriscos. Of course, Cervantes had to be very careful about being too openly subversive concerning the Catholic Church and the increasingly absolutist Spanish state. Cervantes, as narrator, often presents himself as a patriotic Catholic, a fact that has led readers to assume that Cervantes's text reflects the conservative ideological certainties of the so-called Golden Age of Spain. As Americo Castro has argued, however, Spain of the seventeenth century should more accurately be referred to as "La Edad conflictiva, 'the Conflictive Age.'" As William P. Childers has recently argued, "The captive's tale is structured as a conversion narrative with many autobiographical details [relevant to Cervantes's life]; thus the tendency has long prevailed of reading it at face value as a triumphalist presentation of the ascendancy of Christianity over its rival faith [Islam] in the Mediterranean."[25] Increasingly, scholars of Cervantes's great text are calling into question its allegedly triumphalist view of Christianity. I shall conclude this essay with a reading of the famous "captive's tale" that, in our view, depicts the betrayal, on the part of recently converted Christian, of Christian mercy—that depicts, that is, the betrayal of senseless kindness.

The captive [el cautivo], after arriving at an inn accompanied by a beautiful woman in Moorish dress named Zoriaida, tells his tale in the presence of Quixote, Sancho, and some other guests. Drawing on Cervantes's own personal experience, the captive describes his captivity in a bagnio, a house in which Turks held Christians as prisoners, and his rescue through the guile of Zoraida, who arranged their elaborate escape from captivity. The captive, when asked by one of the guests at the inn the name of the Moorish woman in his company, replies, "Lela Zoraida," meaning "Señora" or "Lady" Zoraida. Zoraida herself, whose native tongue is Arabic and who barely speaks Spanish, then immediately interjects with "great emotion" and insists otherwise: "No! No Zoraida! María, María."[26] I am not Zoraida, Zoraida insists, but I am Mary, the compassionate mother of Jesus.

Zoraida feels compelled to convert from Islam to Christianity because of her devotion to the Virgin Mary, whom she refers to as "Lela Marién." Mary is the very embodiment of compassion, of pietà. Cervantes, in the captive's tale, presents Zoraida's father Agi Morato, with whom Zoraida lives, as overbearing, in a manner that recalls Shakespeare's portrait of Shylock, the domineering father of Jessica in Shakespeare's *Merchant of Venice*, printed in 1600, just five years before the publication of Part I of Don Quixote. Jessica, like Zoraida, leaves her father to marry a Christian husband and to convert to Christianity. Shakespeare's Shylock is a harsh man with whom it is difficult to sympathize, but Jessica's abandoning of her father for Lorenzo manages to elicit considerable sympathy for him when Shylock discovers that Jessica has absconded with the ring given to him by Leah, Jessica's mother and Shylock's now deceased, beloved wife. Shylock is told that Jessica pawned the ring in order to buy a monkey, a fashionable pet for members of the wealthy aristocratic set that Jessica, through her conversion and marriage to Lorenzo, has now joined. When Shylock hears from his fellow Jew Tubal that his ring has been pawned, he famously remarks: "I had it of Leah when I was a bachelor. I would not have given it for a wilderness of monkeys."[27]

There is no indication in Shakespeare's play that Jessica wishes to convert to Christianity for any reason other than to elope with Lorenzo and, thereby, to abandon Judaism in order to assimilate into upper-class Christian society and to enjoy the material fruits of that assimilation. Zoraida's aspirations appear to be loftier, but her treatment of her father during her escape calls into question her devotion to the pietà, to the senseless kindness, embodied by Lela Marién, or the Virgin Mary. Nor is Zoraida's father, despite his domineering attitude toward his daughter, devoid of compassion himself. When the renegade who facilitates Zoraida's escape scopes out the scene in preparation for his rescue of Zoraida, "he would go to Zoraida's house and ask for fruit, and her father gave it to him."[28] As a good Muslim, Zoraida's father gives alms to the poor, as required by zakat (or charity), which is one of the seven pillars of Islam.

The plan to rescue Zoraida goes forward. The plan is for a group of freed Christian prisoners from the bagnio to remove Zoraida from her house and to take her, by boat, to Christian territory, along with the money she will have stolen from her father. It becomes necessary for those rescuing Zoraida, in the course of their risky endeavor, to capture her father as well. The father is told of his daughter's conversion, and Zoraida confirms this by telling her father, face-to-face, "It is true that I am a Christian" and that she has converted "to do good for myself."[29] When her father asks her precisely what good she has done herself, she tells him to "ask Lela Marién."³⁰ Ask the Virgin Mary, Zoraida tells her father. But what if he doesn't believe in the Virgin Mary? What is he now to do? In despair—how can he, a strict Muslim monotheist, address a deity he does not believe in? He throws himself from the ship and tries to drown himself. He is rescued. Zoraida claims she is motivated by her devotion to Lela Marién, or to the Virgin Mary. Zoraida's father doubts her motivations. As he then tells his Christian captors, in words that have a striking contemporary resonance, that he is convinced his daughter wishes "to change her religion" not "because she believes yours is superior to ours, but only because she knows that in your country there is more lewd behavior than in ours."³¹

Zoraida's father is inconsolable. The renegade feels he must put him ashore and journey onward without him. The group abandons the father on a bleak coast, and as the ship speeds ahead, the men and Zoraida hear him cursing them, praying to Mohammed to ask Allah to destroy them. But then his address turns sorrowful and plaintive: "He pulled at his beard and tore out his hair and threw himself on the ground, and once, when he called as loud as he could, we heard him cry: 'Come back, my beloved daughter, come ashore, I forgive everything! Give those men the money, it is already theirs, and come and console your grieving father, who will die on this desolate strand if you leave him?'"³² Again, there is an echo here of Shakespeare's *Merchant of Venice*, specifically of the doctrinal self-righteousness and obliviousness to religious difference that mars, in our judgment, Portia's famous speech on "the quality of mercy," a Christian sermon that Portia delivers to the Jewish Shylock just after his legal defeat and humiliation in the famous trial scene in the fourth act of Shakespeare's play. You must abandon your narrow, Jewish views of strict justice, she tells Shylock, and instead practice mercy, which "seasons justice. Therefore, Jew," Portia (disguised as the judge Balthasar) continues: "Though justice be thy plea, consider this:/That in the course of justice, none of us/Should see salvation."³³

Who is "us," and what does Portia understand by "salvation"? "Us" appears to mean "us Christians," and salvation appears to mean salvation specifically through the intervention of Christ—salvation, that is, in the Christian sense. But Portia is addressing a Jew! It is no coincidence that, within minutes, Shylock will be forced to convert to Christianity, as demanded by his enemy and tormentor the merchant Antonio, if he wishes to save his life.

Zoraida hears her father's plaintive words. She is not deaf to his entreaties, but she abandons him nonetheless: "Pray to Allah, dear father, that Lela Marién, who is the reason I am a Christian, may console you in your sorrow. Allah knows I could not help doing what I did, and these Christians owe me nothing for my decision, for even if I had chosen not to go with them and to remain in my own house, it would have been impossible for me to do so, given the burning desire in my soul to do this deed that seems as virtuous to me, my beloved father, as it appears wicked to you."[34] What consolation does Zoraida offer her grieving father? That he pray to God that the Virgin Mary will console him in his sorrow. But Zoraida's father, a devout Muslim, may well not believe in the Virgin Mary. Zoraida says she converted to Christianity because of her devotion to Lela Marién, that is, to the Virgin Mary, to the very embodiment of mercy. Her abandonment of her father, however, and her parting words that he seek consolation from a religious figure he may not believe in, betray the very quality of mercy to which she claims she is devoted and for the sake of which, she insists, she felt the irresistible urge to convert to Christianity in the first place. But how pure were Zoraida's motivations? Is there, perhaps, in the Morisca Zoraida, more than a trace of the opportunism, of the desire to assimilate to the dominant religion in order to rise in the nation's social hierarchy, that characterizes the crudely opportunistic Jessica of Shakespeare's *Merchant of Venice*? Both Shakespeare and Cervantes, two of the world's greatest writers who, astoundingly, died on the very same date (April 23, 1616), would then both be critiquing, at the same historical moment, the betrayal of senseless kindness in the name of institutional religion.

Notes

1. Miguel de Cervantes, *Don Quixote*, trans. Edith Grossman (New York: Ecco, 2003), 510.

2. Edith Grossman, *Don Quixote* by Miguel de Cervantes, 510n2.

3. Emmanuel Levinas and Myriam Annisimov, "Interview with Myriam Annisimov (1985)," in *Is It Righteous To Be? Interviews with Emmanuel Levinas*, ed. Jill Robbins (Stanford, CA: Stanford University Press, 2001), 84–92, 89.

4. Vasily Grossman, *Life and Fate*, trans. Robert Chandler (New York: New York Review Books, 2006), 530.

5. Grossman, *Life and Fate*, 530–31.

6. Richard Cohen, "Defending Levinas: Interview with Chung-Hsiung (Raymond) Lai," in *Levinasian Meditations: Ethics, Philosophy, and Religion* (Pittsburgh: Duquesne University Press, 2010), 177.
7. Cervantes, *Don Quixote*, 139.
8. Cervantes, 139.
9. Cervantes, *Don Quixote*, 134.
10. Cervantes, *Don Quixote*, 135.
11. Cervantes, 135.
12. Cervantes, 135.
13. Cervantes, *Don Quixote*, 137.
14. Cervantes, 137.
15. Cervantes, *Don Quixote*, 139–40.
16. Grossman, *Don Quixote* by Cervantes, 140n2.
17. Cervantes, *Don Quixote*, 440.
18. Cervantes, 440.
19. Cervantes, *Don Quixote*, 441.
20. Cervantes, 441.
21. Cervantes, *Don Quixote*, 442.
22. Cervantes, 442.
23. Cervantes, 442.
24. Cervantes, *Don Quixote*, 123.
25. William P. Childers, "Miguel De Cervantes Saavedra," in *Christian-Muslim Relations: A Bibliographical History*, ed. David Thomas and John Cheswick (Leiden: Brill, 2017), 163–272, 233.
26. Cervantes, *Don Quixote*, 321.
27. William Shakespeare, *The Merchant of Venice*, eds. Barbara A. Mowat and Paul Werstine (New York: The Folger Shakespeare Library, 2010), 3.1.120–22.
28. Cervantes, *Don Quixote*, 352.
29. Cervantes, *Don Quixote*, 361.
30. Cervantes, *Don Quixote*, 362.
31. Cervantes, *Don Quixote*, 363.
32. Cervantes, 363.
33. Shakespeare, *The Merchant of Venice*, 4.1.196–99.
34. Cervantes, *Don Quixote*, 363.

Bibliography

Cervantes, Miguel de. *Don Quixote*. Translated by Edith Grossman. New York: Ecco, 2003.
Childers, William P. "Miguel De Cervantes Saavedra." Essay. In *Christian-Muslim Relations: A Bibliographical History*, edited by David Thomas and John Cheswick, 163–272. Leiden: Brill, 2017.

Grossman, Vasily, and Robert Chandler. *Life and Fate*. New York: New York Review Books, 2006.
Levinas, Emmanuel, and Myriam Annisimov. "Interview with Myriam Annisimov (1985). Translated by Thomas Loebel and Jill Robbins. In *Is It Righteous To Be? Interviews with Emmanuel Levinas*, edited by Jill Robbins, 84–92. Stanford, CA: Stanford University Press, 2001.
Shakespeare, William. *The Merchant of Venice*. Edited by Barbara A. Mowat and Paul Werstine. The Folger Shakespeare Library. New York: Simon & Schuster, 2010.

11

Art of the Uncanny

Seeing with Cohen and Levinas

JOLANTA SALDUKAITYTĖ

A year or so ago my friend gave me a very special gift: a handmade ceramic vase. The vase was really lovely, decorated with some Greek ornaments; on one side was a stylized ship of Odysseus, and on the other a realistic-looking face. Because of the depiction of the face, it has some resemblance to the famous Sicilian ceramic head vases. The latter are usually kept outside, both female and male heads. They can be empty, but more likely there will be a plant growing in them. According to a local folk tale, a story going back to the Arab period in Sicily, a Saracen merchant from Palermo fell in love with a local girl. The girl was smitten as well. The love story was unfolding beautifully until the girl found out that the Saracen was married and had a wife and a few children in his homeland. In this version of the story, the girl cut the merchant's head off when he was sleeping, so that he would stay with her forever. She used his head as a pot for a basil plant. Pretty macabre. Another version, probably even more famous, is the story of Isabella, sometimes known as the *Pot of Basil* story. This story takes place in Messina. It was written up by Boccaccio in his Decameron (IV, 5) and later, with some changes, it was narrated by John Keats (1818). Isabella (Lisabetta) fell in love with Lorenzo, even though her marriage with a wealthy nobleman had already been arranged.

Isabella's brothers were not happy when they found out about the affair. Trying to avoid family shame, they secretly killed Lorenzo and buried his body in the woods. Later Lorenzo's ghost came to Isabella in visions. She exhumed his body, took the head from the grave and buried it in a basil pot: Salerno basil, to be precise. Not only Keats, but Pre-Raphaelite artists also became interested in the story and several versions of it were painted: William Holman Hunt (*Isabella and the Pot of Basil*, 1867/8), John William Waterhouse (*Isabella and the Pot of Basil*, 1907), John Everett Millais (*Isabella*, 1849), Joseph Severn (*Isabella*, 1877), Arthur Nowell (*Isabella and the Pot of Basil*, 1904), George Henry Grenville Manton (*Isabella and the Pot of Basil*, 1855), and Edward Reginald Frampton (*Isabella and the Pot of Basil*, 1872), among others.

Of course, the vase I was given had nothing to do with all these stories. The gift was a sincere act of friendship. And, what is even more special, the face depicted on the vase is my own! It is done quite beautifully, and quite accurately as well. But despite that—or maybe because of it—there is something truly uncanny about it. Unlike the basil pot, my vase has no macabre story behind it, but it is still somehow monstrous. No doubt we can find plenty of art that *creates* monsters (i.e., visualizes them): centaurs, gorgons, devils, demons, or Friedrich Wilhelm Murnau's Nosferatu, Bram Stoker's Dracula, Mary Shelley's Frankenstein's monster, Francisco Goya *Saturn Devouring His Son*, the Basilisk described by Pliny the Elder (23–79AD), and later continuing its existence in the cellars of Vilnius, Hieronymus Bosch monsters in the *Garden of Earthly Delights*, depictions of various medieval tortures and monstrosity in The Vic Episcopal Museum (Museu Episcopal de Vic - MEV) in Catalonia. The list could go on and on.[1] Although monstrosity is described in terms of physical characteristics—impossible, unnatural, mixes of features and abilities—monsters are usually (sometimes falsely) connected with ugliness and evil.[2] Another way to talk about monstrosity would be to raise the question of the human monster. In the latter case, this usually refers not only to some jarring physical features but to pure evil, to the sort of act or intent that cannot be understood or justified in any way. We encounter such characters in Greek myth: Antigone, for example, does not belong in a "normal" way to that polis, is weird and even monstrous for being her brother's daughter, her father's sister, and her mother's granddaughter. She is cursed by birth. She also bears radical otherness in not obeying the rules, the law, and exposing herself to the likelihood of death. For Martin

Heidegger she was the uncanny character par excellence.³ Moral monsters, for example, indicated by Michel Foucault's studies on abnormalities, bend all the rules and abuse morality. Unlike the monsters mentioned above, they might not have any monstrous perceivable features and from all externals be rather "banal."⁴

All these depictions of monsters try to represent what in its essence is not representable. In other words, they try to understand and to show—*to demonstrate*—what is essentially hidden, what lies at the bottom of our fears, anxieties, insecurity, and yet remains elusive.⁵ In this essay I am going to ask if and why art can be monstrous or uncanny even if it *does not* depict any evident signs of such, without monstrous animals or people, and even without a macabre backstory.

Uncanniness has been addressed by many thinkers within different contexts: in psychology by Ernst Jentsch and Sigmund Freud; in mythology by F.W.J. Schelling; in philosophy by Martin Heidegger; in literature revealed by Edgar Allan Poe or Howard Phillips Lovecraft, among others; and of course, in various movies.⁶ Sigmund Freud, in his famous essay "The Uncanny" (1919), writes that "the uncanny is that class of the frightening which leads back to what is known of old and long familiar."⁷ In other words, he suggests that in some circumstances the familiar becomes strange, uncanny, and frightening. For Freud, unlike for Jentsche, being novel and unfamiliar is not enough to be uncanny. It concerns not the new or foreign as such, but something familiar and old that has become estranged. Freud agrees with Schelling that "everything is *unheimlich* that ought to have remained secret and hidden but has come to light."⁸ In this sense, art could be understood as the process of turning the strange into the familiar and the familiar into the strange, at once something hiding and something revealing. But the *defamiliarization* or estrangement of art does not necessarily only create and bring out various monsters and anxieties. Rather, art as such might be seen as a locus of the uncanny, or monstrous, as having "an aura" of uncanny.

Even though at first sight Emmanuel Levinas may not look like the best interlocutor for these questions, he several times in his texts mentions that art has something exotic, something monstrous and inhuman in it. The question of the uncanny also naturally leads to the question of alterity and strangeness. With this in mind, I will address the question of the uncanniness of art in Levinas's philosophy, and more specifically, Levinas seen through the texts and explanations of Richard A. Cohen.

Passageway to Art

Although Levinas is above all a thinker of ethics and did not propose his philosophy as an aesthetic theory as such, he nonetheless refers to or uses examples of art quite often. Various references to painting, sculpture, literature, and music appear in all Levinas books but probably are nowhere treated in more detail and depth than in the articles "Reality and its Shadow" (1948), "The Transcendence of Words: On Michel Leiris's Biffure" (1949), "On Maurice Blanchot" (1975), and in the collection of articles *Proper Names* (1976). Levinas's approach to art has been discussed extensively in the secondary literature.[9] In most cases, it has been concluded that Levinas is hostile to art and that art is idolatrous and brings us further from ethical responsibility. It has no ethical dimension, or if so, then only evil, and it therefore has no real or positive meaning in Levinas's ethical metaphysics. Plato criticized artists for creating images of images, mere shadows, suggesting therefore that they should be expelled from the Republic, geared as the latter is meant to be by truth and justice. Levinas, it is said, finds art to hide or even substitute images for the face of the other. Cohen has radically challenged this approach, most recently in his essay "Levinas on Art and Aestheticism: Getting 'Reality and Its Shadow' Right" (2016).

Cohen is known to be one of the most devoted scholars of Levinas. In many of his writings and teaching Cohen opposes the "postmodern" approach and its striving for originality and creativity by claiming that he himself has nothing original to say but only restates what has already been said by Levinas. Paradoxically—indeed, this position makes Cohen original nonetheless—this recalls Socrates, perhaps more arrogant than humble. In opposing a so-called Derridean Levinas reading, Cohen argues that there is continuity to Levinas's writings and that despite certain changes there is no essential rupture, for instance, between Levinas's major works *Totality and Infinity* and *Otherwise Than Being or Beyond Essence*. Even more, Cohen claims that there is no rupture between Levinas's philosophical writings and his so-called confessional or Talmudic lectures.[10] It seems to me that the latter claim, especially, allows us to see Levinas as a universal thinker and genuine philosopher, avoiding parochialism.

Cohen argues throughout his oeuvre that while remaining a phenomenologist, Levinas also shows how and why phenomenology is not enough. For Levinas ethics is primarily philosophy, which means not only that ontology needs ethics but also that phenomenology needs ethics as well. Cohen strongly argues for the position that Levinas first and above all is an ethical and political thinker: "The *ultimum verbum* belongs not to aesthetics but to moral responsibility and the quest for justice.[11] In other words, meaning can come, and can only come—originally—from the encounter with the Other, which is to say, for Levinas, from ethics. So art, too, cannot justify itself by itself. To have meaning, it must have its place in the ethical, in relation to the face of the Other. According to Cohen, Levinas shows the limitations of aestheticism, in contrast to art, and therefore does not deny the meaningfulness of art. By claiming that Levinas is one of the greatest, or perhaps the most important, phenomenologist of the twentieth century,[12] Cohen underlines not only Levinasian faithful expositions of phenomenology but also the depth and novelty of his own proper phenomenological investigations. Much of the article "Reality and Its Shadow" in Cohen's reading is presented as a phenomenological study of art: "Uncovering its essence, in the phenomenological sense. . . Levinas's question is not simply 'What is art (or science)?' because such a question, so obvious to the epistemologically oriented, is already too narrow, too prejudiced. Rather, his question is 'What is art (or science) and what is its value?' or 'What is art (or science) and what is its significance?' "[13] Cohen tries to convey that this is the right way to read Levinas's article on art and that it would be a mistake to claim that Levinas simply condemns or denies art. As Levinas himself richly incorporates references to art in all his writings and here as well, Cohen suggests, we would be turning him into some sort of Jekyll and Hyde figure, unaware of what he himself is doing. What Levinas does warn us about regarding art, is not art, but taking art for art's sake and considering the art world as somehow separate and sufficient in itself: in a word, anesthetizing it by aestheticizing it, ignoring its ethical debts. So, Cohen holds the position that "Levinas is neither hostile to art nor has he misconstrued its nature, nor, in view of his actual theory and valuation, is his own use of art inconsistent or self-contradictory."[14] Cohen indicates that this ambiguity—in art and the interpretation of art—occurs because art is always liable to both disengagement and engagement but not only one of these alone: "Art is not only disengaged from life, set up in its own artificial world, but also always and essentially engaged in and part of the larger world."[15] Disengagement is as essential to art as engagement is. It is here, it seems to me, that we should search for the fundamental uncanniness and monstrosity of art.

Enjoyment and Exoticism

On this interpretation of Levinas, in art there is always the possibility of the turn toward the impersonal, anonymous darkness of *il y a*. This is possible for two reasons: the affinity of art to enjoyment, and its tendency toward self-enclosure. Art, first of all, functions at the level of enjoyment. Enjoyment for Levinas is a necessary but not a sufficient condition for the ethical relation. The subject arises enjoying the world at the elemental level of sensing. It emerges first not as a rational subject but, if we follow the terms of traditional opposition, as empirical, or better, as material, as is explicated in *Existence and Existents* and in the Second Section of *Totality and Infinity*. However, owing to the instability of its emergent sensing, it dwells, labors, represents, and otherwise finds itself engaged in the greater solidity of worldly life. The originary nonintentional structure of sensibility as "enjoyment" entails the irreducibility of corporality and material needs for subjectivity in its worldliness. So Levinas argues that before *knowing* or *using* the world, I *enjoy* the world. Things do not only refer to their way of use, their interconnection, or the structure of the environment and the world. Before that, they are sensed, felt, touched, heard, warm, cold, and so on. I find myself in the world "bathing" in its sensual qualities and taking care of my own body—eating, drinking, dressing, looking for shelter or rest and so on. Enjoyment is naïve and innocent, "carefree," as Levinas suggests in *Totality and Infinity*. But despite the positive side of enjoyment, this kind of material existence, at the level of intersubjectivity, appears as indifference and exploitation of the other. For hedonistic "moralities" there is nothing beyond self-satisfaction. What matters is the satisfaction itself.[16] So art, insofar as it functions at this level of enjoyment and play with sensation, becomes dangerous. It might and can lead to the other, but it also has the capacity to lock up at the level of elemental sensualism, of *il y a*, Levinas writes,

> In enjoyment the things revert to their elemental qualities < . . . >. The aesthetic orientation man gives to the whole of his world represents a return to enjoyment and to the elemental on a higher plane. The world of things calls for art, in which intellectual accession to being moves into enjoyment, in which the Infinity of the idea is idolized in the finite, but sufficient, image. All art is plastic. Tools and implements, which themselves presuppose enjoyment, offer themselves to enjoyment

in their turn. They are playthings [*jouets*]: the fine cigarette lighter, the fine car. They are adorned by the decorative arts; they are immersed in the beautiful, where every going beyond enjoyment reverts to enjoyment.[17]

As Cohen points out, "Art opens up a dimension of evasion, of escape, yes, into the rhythms, lights, and colors, sounds and spectacle, the 'special effects' of movies, of its own fancy, including a Disneyland, all that Levinas will call image and myth."[18] Instead of facing the Other and taking responsibility, we look for ways to escape, and art offers that—it tantalizes us. Levinas wonders, how can we enjoy art and not feel guilty? "There is something wicked and egoist and cowardly in artistic enjoyment. There are times when one can be ashamed of it, as of feasting during a plague."[19] The temptation of the mythical, elemental dimension of art lies in its ability to enable us to be lost in it, to forget not only the Other but oneself as well. Art as escape. Variations of this can be found not only in the entertainment industry of visual and/or sonic pleasures but as well in images of horror and suffering, which, instead of making us responsible, do the opposite: they lead to desensitization and moral anesthesia. In art lies fundamental passivity, and it brings this passivity into our lives.[20] "Instead of arriving at the object, the intention gets lost in the sensation itself, and it is this wandering about in sensation, in *aisthesis*, that produces the aesthetic effect," says Levinas and continues that it is "the way which in art the sensible qualities which constitute an object do not lead to an object and are in themselves as the very event of sensation qua sensation, the esthetic event."[21] The aesthetic as such, or art for art's sake, is thus seen by Levinas (and Cohen) as the disengagement—the disengaging tendency—of art per se.

Contemporary society in many cases takes its cue and hovers here, in hedonistic morality, moving from one pleasure to another like a moveable feast. Enjoyment of the world turns into an eagerness to try to experience everything. How, asks Levinas, might we not be fascinated by Ulysses's life, which "despite its misfortunes, seems to us marvelous, and that of Don Juan enviable, despite its tragic end."[22] Levinas quotes Alexander Pushkin, or more precisely, Prince Peter Viazemsky's poem "First Snow" as an epigraph for Eugenie Onegin "*in a hurry to live. Impatient to feel.*" He calls this the "temptation of temptation," which becomes one of the definitions of the irresponsible modern human being. Everything is always possible; nothing holds us. This temptation of temptation includes but is not limited to the enjoyment or materiality that leads to an aesthetic life. Art deals with various sensations and "in art, sensation figures as a new element. On better, it returns to the impersonality of *elements*."[23] So it is, using the image proposed by Sandor Goodhart, wrapped around itself, inside without real outside, like a Möbius strip.[24]

Art, by dealing with such sensing, tempting to enjoyment alone, is capable of separating itself from life and creating the "world of art." In this light, art remains self-enclosed, disengaged, and irresponsible. Because of its seductive self-enclosure, it is more exotic than anything else in the world, in an exoticism coming from no-place. For Levinas, as we recall, there is alterity not only of human beings, the other person, but of the *il y a*, and of time, language, God. Cohen, as Derrida, using the image of waves, sees in this not a rapture but the several regions of signification and radicalization of alterity.[25] Art, too, can be seen revealing the "other side," a fracture/crack or shadow of the world. It is a disturbance in the familiar: it reveals what is strange and alien. For Levinas, the ultimate sense of alterity, in whatever register, always touches base with the alterity of the other person. This alterity, as we know, cannot be reduced to any features and is absolute, not relative. Art, by contrast, can open the experience of the uncanny, the alterity of abyss; but its alterity, as Levinas mentions in *Existence and Existents,* and later in *Otherwise Than Being or Beyond Essence*, remains only an exotic alterity. "The forms and colors of a painting do not cover over but uncover the things in themselves, precisely because they preserve the exteriority of those things. Reality remains foreign to the world inasmuch as it is given. In this sense an artwork both imitates nature and diverges from it as far as possible."[26] Art's exoticism comes not from its ability to create bizarre, weird, imaginary objects but because the objects it creates primarily intend to belong to the enclosed world of art, and secondly, they do not have the human interiority we try to attribute to them: "What is called the disinterestedness of art does not only refer to the neutralization of the possibilities of action. Exoticism modifies the contemplation itself. The 'objects' are outside, but this outside does not relate to an 'interior;' they are not already naturally 'possessed.' A painting, a statue, a book are objects of our world, but through them the things represented are extracted from our world."[27]

So, in this sense, art is moving away from reality to an imaginary alterity. Since Plato it is common to take the image as the shadow of the world. But the role of image, as accurately pointed out by Richard Kearney, is a parody, because "image ceases to refer to some *original* event—in the world or consciousness—and becomes instead a simulacrum: an image of an image of an image."²⁸ In other words, it is pure ephemera. In the image, then, especially if it is the image of yourself, you might encounter the deathmask-like image. Image is always "too late," it never was alive but pretends to refer to the past moment that never occurred! Art might look more real than real as it can make objects that can stand out of the world—but that is indeed a possibility of existence without an existent, *il y a*. Levinas writes, "Even the most realistic art gives this character of alterity to the objects represented which are nonetheless part of our world. It presents them to us in their nakedness, that real nakedness which is not absence of clothing, but we might say the absence of forms, that is, the nontransmutation of our exteriority into inwardness, which forms realize."²⁹ Artwork, as much as it leans toward isolation and closure, "is in this sense exotic, without a world, essence in dissemination."³⁰ Its world cannot exist outside this world but pretends as if it can. Similarly, in "Eye and Mind," Maurice Merleau-Ponty notices that "the painter's world is a visible world, nothing but visible: a world almost mad, because it is complete though only partial. Painting awakens and carries to its highest pitch a delirium which is vision itself."³¹ The alterity in art (even if it refers to transcendence) bounces back. Art is capable of referring to alterity, showing what is strange in the familiar, but it would be a mistake to confuse the alterity of art with real alterity. As Edith Wyschogrod aptly writes, "Art and ethics in Levinas's sense can be thought of as fields in which disclosures of formlessness occur: in art, the amorphous power of being; in ethics, the other who calls me to responsibility. Each—possession in the case of art and revelation in the case of ethics—grips the individual, in the one instance dissolving, in the other singularizing individuality by positing the other in her uniqueness."³² The "amorphous power of being" does not exhaust the entire nature of art, but it is essential to it.

Impossibility of the Face

Another ambiguity of art appears in its relation to the face. In his early article "Is Ontology Fundamental" (1951) and later in *Difficult Freedom* (1963), Levinas wonders if things have faces. The importance of the face, the human face, in Levinas's thought does not need repeating.³³ In the secondary literature, interpretations vary from trying to describe the face as concrete or as abstract. Levinas himself makes clear that face is not a plastic form, that the face exceeds its perceptible manifestation: "It is not the mere assemblage of a nose, a forehead, eyes."[34] Face reduced to its plastic form turns a person into an object, puts upon the face a mask, permits classification and therefore discrimination and uniformity. Face as expression exceeds the form of the face and in this sense is abstract. "In the concreteness of the world, the face is abstract," says Levinas.[35] It breaks from any context. But it would be a mistake as well to consider that because the face is abstract, it is no one's face and cannot be distinguished or recognized as a particular person's distinctive face. Despite being abstract, the face for Levinas is also concrete. That might seem to be a puzzling idea, but we have to keep in mind the importance of valence of body, of vulnerability, and above all of suffering. The face is concrete not only as a particular object, an object that can be destroyed, but as a particular vulnerability, his/her suffering, the singularized expression "do not kill." In other words, even though the face is not a plastic image and radical alterity cannot be reduced to the materiality of things, the materiality of a face—the vulnerability of the other—requires us to meet them as belonging to some race, some gender, of same age, and so on. In the materiality of the face and body are inscribed particular social-cultural significations, though alterity can never be reduced to such significations. So, while the face of the Other is abstract, it is, at the same time, the most concrete, the most particular. And the face-to-face encounter "is not some idealistic or ethereal revelation. It is in no way abstract, and indeed there is nothing more concrete."[36] When Levinas says that the idea of infinity is encountered in the face of the other, this does not indicate that face is an *eidos*, purified from all concreteness, materiality, and corporality. The face of the other surpasses the plastic image, is better, demands more.

Art, on the other hand, gives image to the face, freezes it in plastic form in a picture, portrait, vase, etc., and by this means turns it inevitably into a caricature. Thus, the face lies between holiness and caricature, abstract and concrete, is singular and calls forth my singularity. Art, however, imprisons the face.[37] Art's plastic form is apparition and "is always already deserted, betrayed, by the being it reveals, such as marble from which the gods it manifests already absent themselves."[38] The face, by contrast, is expression, mobile, alive. The alterity of the other is encountered in the face, the vulnerable and naked face that breaks its form. Art, sculpture, on the other hand, however mysterious, cannot retain the interiority of the face. Art objects hide in their own world or behind the form: "Beauty, perfect form, is form *par excellence*; the statues of antiquity are never really naked."[39]

Meaning comes from transcendence, from irreducible otherness of the other, but only and always as deriving from concrete situations. The other is "abstract" in breaking from its context but at the same time absolutely singular and hence absolutely concrete. The other person is the one who faces, in flesh and blood, this face: you. We must underscore, then, that the otherness of the other, while concrete and singular, is not a function of weirdness, peculiarity, a tic, a pimple, skin color, and the like. "The orphan, the widow, the stranger" might be a metaphor, but it is not just a metaphor. It refers as well to the concrete flesh and blood of the wandering stranger who is likely to be more in need than my neighbor who is at home. The alterity that exerts its pressure, what matters is the *other's vulnerability and need for help*. "Face as the very mortality of the other man."[40] What singularizes both the other and myself is *moral exigency*: the other person as concrete materiality, vulnerable body, and I, and I alone, am the one who must provide. So the face, while being concrete, this or that face, is "abstract" inasmuch as it is more, a surplus over its own genus and species, its relative differences.

Things, on the other hand, have no faces: "They are beings without a face" (Levinas 1990, 8).[41] But they have no face not because they are not abstract enough but because they are not concrete enough. The materiality of the things lies "in the primacy of the Neuter" (Levinas 2007, 298) but not in sensibility and vulnerability. In other words, things are interchangeable, regardless of their particularity, as monetization shows; they do not have singularity; their alterity refers to dissolution in the elemental. A thing, Levinas says, "can never be presented personally and ultimately has no identity." In *Levinasian Meditations*, Cohen underscores that face-to-face encounter is an encounter of two singular beings. He writes, "First, the singularity of the other person who as a mortal being of flesh and blood suffers and commands aid" and "second, the singularity of the mortal subject who responds in a responsibility beholden to the face of the other."[42] Singularity of the face and particularity or uniqueness of art, or thing, are not the same. "The singularity or face of the other person, unlike that of the thing, far from being a unique node within a differential system is rather an explosion of context, an excessive "nudity.""[43] The Face demands meeting the Other personally while such an encounter with things is impossible:

> Through the face, the being is not only enclosed in its form and offered to the hand, it is also open, establishing itself in depth and, in this opening, presenting itself somehow in a personal way. The face is an irreducible mode in which being can present itself in its identity. A thing can never be presented personally and ultimately has no identity. Violence is applied to the thing, it seizes and disposes of the thing. Things give, they do not offer a face.[44]

From considerations such as these, it looks obvious that things do not and cannot have faces: they do not suffer, die, or ask for help.

> The face has no form added to it, but does not present itself as the formless, as matter that lacks and calls for form. Things have a form, are seen in the light—silhouettes or profiles; the face signifies itself. As silhouette and profile a thing owes its nature to a perspective, remains relative to a point of view; a thing's situation thus constitutes its being. Strictly speaking it has no identity; convertible into another thing, it can become money. Things have no face; convertible, "realizable," they have a price. They represent money because they are of elemental nature, are wealth. Their rootedness in the elemental, their accessibility to physics, and their signification as tools are thus confirmed.[45]

The question of the face in Levinasian philosophy is unavoidably attended by further questions about other living entities. For example, does a dog have a face? Or a tree? Or a stone? Does the *I* have a face? Levinas himself wonders if things can "get faces" from art. Art, he suggests, might be "an activity that lends faces to things," it "seeks to give a face to things, and in this its greatness and its deceit simultaneously reside."[46] The face art seeks to give to things, of course, is not only the plastic/visual face. It is expression, the real, the concrete. And an artistic movement is "another way than that of knowledge to give meaning to being."[47] Levinas continues,

> In the still technical gesture applied to attain a proposed goal, skill and elegance are already delineated; in the voice, already the delineation of a signifying language and the possibilities

of song and poem. Legs that can walk will already be able to dance; hands that touch and hold, will be able to feel, paint, sculpt, and play a piano in the surprise of conforming to an ideal never seen previously. A precocious or original embodiment of thought, a birth, in all its diversity, of an artistic culture, in which the meaningful does not refer to the noetic/noematic structure of the transcendental constitution in knowing, nor to any common rule; but in which harmonies and disharmonies in the human occur without recourse or reduction to the universal, and remain in the extreme exoticism of that variety.[48]

To have a face, to encounter the face, means to be in the realm of ethics. On one hand, we are in the network of various relationships, and through enjoyment, labor, and science, we connect with others. Therefore, things are not only things, but things that belong to somebody, give us pleasure or comfort, help us to help others, and so on. Things can "get" faces through enjoyment or labor and are not limited to being present-at-hand or ready-at-hand. Art objects are the material condition of a nicer life. And, too, art challenges the scientific worldview. Through art we are exposed to different worlds and contexts and are reminded as well of the face of the other.

Eternity of the Instant

Western artists have all along been trying to catch expressivity: from the archaic smiles of korai to the suffering of Laocoon, the ecstasy of St. Therese, Mona Lisa's smile, from the self-reflecting look of Sapho to Munch's *Scream*. Calm and collected: Michelangelo's *David*. Intense and bursting: Bernini's *David*. To catch, to represent, to show expressions became one of the most important goals of art. It remains unchanged—the viewers might age, but Botticelli's *Venus* will always be just born. In this sense we can hear an echo of what Nietzsche calls "eternal return:" ". . . all things recur eternally, and we ourselves too . . . 'I come again [. . .] not to a new life or a better life or a similar life: I come back eternally to this same, selfsame life, in what is greatest and smallest, to teach again the eternal recurrence of all things' identical and selfsame life, in its greatest and its smallest."[49] Unlike the Platonic shadow of reality, art remains unchanged, frozen within the stability of its form. But that is also exactly what bothers Levinas: in the best examples, art carves out the crystal of existence, a moment of life, but in itself is a closed realm of meaning. It doesn't change, and we do not want it to, but as such it is not life but "still life." We know that the Greek-bronze Poseidon (or Zeus) will never throw his trident, that Bernini's Persephone will never scream. Michelangelo's *Moses* always will always be just about to stand up.[50] They are frozen in time and the future will never come for them. That is why Levinas says that "every artwork is in the statue—a stoppage of time."[51] In this sense a "statue's existing is a semblance of the existing of being."[52] As such, even if it tries to overcome stability, wants to be lifelike, it fails and represents ontological being: *being without event*, without adventure. Levinas calls it "the eternal duration of the interval," "the meanwhile." Orpheus every time is going to turn back, Hamlet every time will raise the same question, Caravaggio's Judith forever is going to hold the sword to Holofernes's neck . . . So although we can recognize the inner duration of the artwork, that duration is not real, it is damned to keep returning, like Groundhog Day. The future and novelty for the artwork will never come—and if it did it would be rather terrifying. (To be sure, to talk about the inner duration, or the narrative might be not true for conceptual or abstract art forms; but this discussion I am going to leave behind as it is not essential for Levinas.) At the same time, Levinas notices that art, like knowledge and ontology, is striving for the eternal but "differs radically from the eternity of a concept" precisely because of this eternal duration. A concept does not have duration while instances of art in some manner—even if frozen—do, as they are "never finished, still enduring."[53] It strives to eternity and tries to keep the flow. What is lively, what is human expression, is locked, captured in the plasticity of form. No doubt this is the most uncanny and monstrous side of representational art: "Whereas a phenomenon is already, in whatever respect, an image, a captive manifestation of its plastic and mute form, the epiphany of a face is alive."[54] That, I suggest, is revealed in the short story "Oval Portrait" by Edgar Allan Poe, which in some sense captures the hidden side of my (and a Sicilian) vase, with "my" face staring blindly at me. In Poe's story, the narrator, while staying in a chateau, sees a painting of a young woman. He is so struck by it that, at first, he closes his eyes. "I had found the spell of the picture in an absolute life-likeliness of expression."[55] The narrator discovers that the painter was painting his wife, and all the love and admiration of the painter for his wife passed into her portrait. With his last brushstroke, he finally achieved what he had been aiming for: "This is indeed Life itself!"[56] But when the liveness passed to the painting, his wife died. For Levinas, Poe stories notably unveil the "forever an interval" "empty interval": "no move can be made to retreat from its approach, but this approach can never end."[57]

Of course, the imitation theory of art does not exhaust the functions of art, which strives to more and more expressivity or closer proximity to a concept (conceptual art)—but what bothers Levinas is that art is always trapped in the "meanwhile." A moment of time taken out of time. Meanwhile, there is the stillness and lifelessness of art. For this reason Levinas finds in art "something inhuman and monstrous."[58] The vase I was given as a gift was made by the artist by assembling some photographs of me. It catches a light, restrained smile. One of my friends, the minute he saw it, spontaneously declared: "That is horrible!" Horrible not because it is done badly, or because my face is distorted. Technically the vase portrait is remarkable. It is horrible because something very lively is captured and frozen there eternally—like a wax figure or corpse in an open casket.

Cohen has already underscored the dimension of time as one of the main characteristics of the face in his early book *Elevations*:

> The face is alive with expressions and impressions. Thus again physiological and ethical-spiritual significations shade off into one another: as the place of so many openings and sensitivities, it is *the place*; as the center of such a multitude of exchanges and passages it is *the center*. No other comparably compact area of the body or world is open to a greater range of give and take. The face is by nature intense, a zone of intensities and exchanges. The true *omphalos* is the face.[59]

The face is expressive and changes in time: "It is active, fluid, moving and moved, physically and emotionally, that it is expressive. But also and more importantly it means that the face is irreversible, that it is indelibly oriented and marked by a past, present, and future."[60] And on the same page:

> face of the Other, is precisely the excessive dimensionality of time, "diachrony," irreversibility, the transcendence of an immemorial irrecoverable past and an always surprising future. At the same time, without contradiction, the face crystallizes a whole life; it gives evidence of accumulated and accumulating vulnerabilities and powers, of experiences etched as character

in lines and wrinkles on its skin. Thus it is at once whole and part, presence and passage, living now and through all its times—a fitting image of the divine-human juncture, where time and eternity meet. (Cohen 1994, 243–44)[61]

I have quoted at some length because in discussing art and face in art the dimension of time is of the utmost importance. We have already noted the nonplasticity of the face, which commentators usually bring into their argument regarding idolatry and image. The claim that Levinas sees art as idolatry and that he is merely prolonging a Jewish ban is quite common, and perhaps the most frequent criticism in the secondary literature. Nonetheless, it is an all-too-easy reading and, in fact, might be quite misleading as it does not address either the specific nature or the value of art. It is an inadequate approach for grasping the specific difference of art, or differences between various arts. It rather obscures such differences, especially inasmuch as art also might try to overcome plasticity, and only some (but not all) art seeks expressivity.

"Art," writes Cohen elsewhere, "is ambivalent, or rather that it is undetermined, neutral or free in relation to the opposition of monotheism to idolatry and mythology. At the same time it seems necessary to both. Art—or artistry, creative design, *poesis*—is on both sides of this great spiritual struggle."[62] In order to grasp the essence of art, as Cohen makes clear in *Elevations* and in "Getting *"Reality and Its Shadow"* Right," we have to look at the notion of time: art is a meanwhile, it is locked in eternal return, as I have suggested, while the face is not. As Cohen points out, "Levinas invokes the famous Jewish proscription of images, then, not as a proof text, or a thundering command from the sky, but rather to highlight two kinds of temporalization, one the temporality of fate, closure, stasis, which Levinas will . . . relate to art qua aestheticism, and the other more challenging temporality of life, which comprises moral freedom, initiative, and genuine novelty."[63] So, art is not simply rejected because it substitutes idol for face but must be approached critically because it remains "partial"; its world is self-enclosed, and its temporality is a closure. In *Otherwise Than Being or Beyond Essence*, for example, Levinas shows how through art essence and temporality resound, that "search for new forms, from which all art lives, keeps awake everywhere the verbs that are on the verge of lapsing into substantives," how in diversity of art works "the essence they modulate is temporalized."[64] But for all this the work of art does not have the temporality of life; it can and does function in isolation. That is why, as has been noted above, its alterity is only exotic. At the same time, art is capable of creating the illusion that its temporality is real, as real as radical alterity. In his essay on the uncanny, Freud reminds us that usually "it is in the highest degree uncanny when inanimate objects—a picture or a doll—come to life."[65] Artwork is in-between: it is scary; it is uncanny because it tries to represent life, sometimes even being more lifelike than life itself. But it is not a life. It is, in Levinas's words, "a caricature of life," "lifeless life" as "the life of an artwork does not go beyond the limit of an instant" and has no power or control over its own "life." And, Levinas says, "Here too we should compare art with dreams: the instant of a statue is a nightmare."[66]

It is against this illusionary character of art that Tertullian and St. Augustine among others were already fighting. It has been said that Aphrodite of Knidos (350–300 BC) by Praxiteles was so lifelike it was coming to life and speaking to people. Ovid's Pygmalion falling in love with his sculpture. Or think of the reverse temporalization in Oscar Wilde's *The Picture of Dorian Gray* where the time of life and change has passed to the painting, which "ages," leaving the living face forever young. Are not the stories of vampires, zombies, and the like stories about the lost temporality of life and the gained temporality of stasis? It may seem as if sculptures or paintings or vases look at you, but they do not. It is not even an empty look—it is no-look, not a look: "like the gods immobilized in the between-time of art, left for all eternity on the edge of the interval, at the threshold of a future that is never produced, statues looking at one another with empty eyes, idols which . . . are exposed and do not see."[67]

Any literary or artistic attempt to overcome this difference between image and the face, between two types of temporalization, leads to tales of the uncanny. Levinas makes us see the difference and sobers us up from that illusion. "Within the life, or rather the death, of a statue, an instant endures infinitely: eternally Laocoon will be caught up in the grip of serpents; the Mona Lisa will smile eternally. Eternally the future announced in the strained muscles of Laocoon will be unable to become present. Eternally, the smile of the Mona Lisa about to broaden will not broaden."[68] It does not mean that we have to ignore art or become iconoclasts, "idol smashers," but rather that we must recognize the limitations of being enchanted by its Sirens' voices. According to Cohen, in the self-understanding of the aesthetic movement of "art for art's sake," argues that what is denied and lost sight of is the moral dimension of art.[69] Art divorced from all else becomes or is susceptible to becoming a tool of ideology or propaganda—or it becomes a comic book. Closing in upon itself and distancing itself from the sociopolitical-economic world can be enchanting, certainly, but it can also be irresponsible and dangerous.

Cohen, in his study on Levinas's theory of art, underlines that the "meanwhile" is only one side of art, its disengagement. Disengagement means that art is not part of life. It "refers to the way an artwork, regardless of medium or artist's intention, sets up a configuration of meaning as a wider or narrower matrix of differential significations, becoming its own world, closing in upon itself, centripetally, independent of everything else, internally coherent or incoherent but always folded upon itself, closed up, wrapped up with itself, in a word, disengaged from everything not subject to its gravitational field" (Cohen 2016a, 169–70).[70] But despite its tendency toward self-enclosure, Cohen reminds us that Levinas insists upon the reality that art occurs within a wider world, a world that does include responsibilities, and is indeed based upon them. Engagement—what Levinas calls "criticism"—is no less a part of art than disengagement, and it is precisely this that aestheticism prefers to forget.

In Lieu of Ending

For Freud the uncanny indicates that something familiar has been repressed, such that the uncanny leads us back to what is known and familiar. For Heidegger, the uncanny is the ontological structure of Dasein. We have seen that different aspects of uncanniness are unveiled in the relationship of art and ethics. There is something dark and monstrous in their knot. No wonder almost all political and religious systems have wanted to control art, to censor it or to force it to endorse a worldview. Conciliate.

Recently the theatrical performance *The Pillowman*, based on the eponymous play by the Irish playwright Martin McDonagh (2003), raises a similar problem.[71] The story at first develops as an investigation of a serial killer. Later it becomes clear that the murders were committed following written stories. As the investigation goes on, we find out that the writer has created several horror stories. For example, one of them is called "The Face Basement," in which the faces of the victims are chopped off, put in a jar, and kept in the killer's basement. The serial killer turns out to be the writer's brother; imaginary stories turned into reality. We might guess that for the writer his stories were a way to deal with his monstrous childhood memories while for his younger brother, who "was slow to get things," they must be real, so he made them real. The play asks the question: What is the moral responsibility of art? What does it mean if art puts monsters in our heads? Is the artist responsible for the effects his work of art has? These questions cannot be answered easily and are not going to be addressed in this essay.

There is always ambiguity, a certain monstrous power, a blindness of art, especially when it seems to take the place of reality and seems to be more real than the real. For Levinas, as Cohen shows, it is important to keep art in the site of ethics, to keep it engaged in the world. That would not (and should not) eliminate the monstrous, uncanny aspect of art, but by keeping it engaged, art itself might preserve the very possibility of the ethical and function as a constant reminder of the alterity of the other. To keep as alert. It does not mean limiting art solely to a didactic function but keeping it as part of our world, our realm of meaning. In this sense it does not diminish art. Quite the opposite. As Levinas puts the matter: "*Face* must not be understood in a narrow way. This possibility for the human of signifying in its uniqueness, in the humility of its nakedness and mortality, the Lordship of its recall—word of God—of my responsibility for it, and of my choosiness *qua* unique to this responsibility, can come from a bare arm sculpted by Rodin" (Levinas 1998, 231–32).[72]

Notes

1. More about it: Umberto Eco, *On Ugliness*. New York: Rizzoli, 2007; J. Baltrušaitis, *Le Moyen Age fantastique; antiquités et exotismes dans l'art gothique* (Paris, A. Colin, 1955); S. T. Asma, *On Monsters: An Unnatural History of Our Worst Fears* (Oxford: Oxford University Press, 2009). Richard Kearney, *Strangers, Gods, and Monsters: Interpreting Otherness* (London and New York: Routledge, 2003); T. K. Beal, *Religion and its Monsters* (New York: Routledge, 2002).

2. In a broader sense it could be connected with the fear of strangeness and otherness as such which even up to now reveals itself in hate, in antisemitism, racism and the like.

3. *Unheimlich* in Heidegger was discussed elsewhere: Jolanta Saldukaitytė, "Dasein svetimybė ir slėpiningumas = On Dasein Being Strange and Uncanny" Žmogus ir žodis: mokslo darbai. *Filosofija* 18 (2016): 29–44.

4. Michel Foucault, *Abnormal: Lectures at the Collège de France, 1974–1975* (New York: Picador, 2003).

5. Latin: *Monstrare*, "to show."

6. D. R. Ellison, *Ethics and Aesthetics in European Modernist Literature: From the Sublime to the Uncanny* (Cambridge: Cambridge University Press, 2001).

7. Sigmund Freud, *The Uncanny. The Standard Edition of the Complete Psychological Works of Sigmund Freud* (London: Hogarth Press, 1955), 220.

8. *The Uncanny*, 225.

9. J. Robbins, *Altered Reading: Levinas and Literature* (Chicago: University of Chicago Press, 1999). R. Eaglestone, *Ethical Criticism: Reading after Levinas* (Edinburgh: Edinburgh University Press, 1997).

10. Richard A. Cohen, *Levinasian Meditations: Ethics, Philosophy, and Religion* (Pittsburgh: Duquesne University Press, 2010), 174, 200–201.

11. Richard A. Cohen, "Levinas on Art and Aestheticism. Getting 'Reality and Its Shadow' Right," *Levinas Studies* 11 (2016), 149–94, 150.

12. Richard A. Cohen, "Emmanuel Levinas" In *The Routledge Companion to Phenomenology*, ed. Sebastian Luft (London and New York: Routledge, 2012), 71.

13. "Levinas on Art and Aestheticism," 166.

14. "Levinas on Art and Aestheticism," 155.

15. "Levinas on Art and Aestheticism," 182.

16. ". . . to not seek, behind the satisfaction of need, an order relative to which alone satisfaction would acquire a value; to take satisfaction, which is the very meaning of pleasure, as a term. The need for food does not have existence as its goal, but food."

17. Emmanuel Levinas, *Totality and Infinity: an Essay on Exteriority*, trans. A. Lingis (Pittsburgh: Duquesne University Press, 2007), 134, 140.

18. "Levinas on Art and Aestheticism," 184.

19. Emmanuel Levinas, "Reality and its Shadow" in *The Levinas Reader*, ed. S. Hand (Oxford: Blackwell, 1989), 142.

20. "Reality and Its Shadow," 132.

21. Emmanuel Levinas *Existence and Existents*, trans. A. Lingis (Pittsburgh: Duquesne University Press, 2001), 47.

22. Emmanuel Levinas, *Nine Talmudic Readings*, trans. A. Aronowicz (Bloomington: Indiana University Press, 1994), 32.

23. *Existence and Existents*, 68.

24. Sandor Goodhart, *Möbian Nights: Reading Literature and Darkness* (New York: Bloomsbury Academic, 2017).

25. Richard A. Cohen, *Elevations: The Height of the Good in Rosenzweig and Levinas* (Chicago: University of Chicago Press, 1994), 135–36. Derrida in "Violence and Metaphysics" notices that in Levinas, thematic development "proceeds with the infinite insistence of waves on a beach: return and repetition, always, of the same wave against the same shore, in which, however, as each return recapitulates itself, it also infinitely renews and enriches itself." Jacques Derrida, "Violence and Metaphysics: An Essay on the Thought of Emmanuel Levinas." *Writing and Difference* (London and New York: Routledge Classics, 2005), 398.

26. *Existence and Existents*, 46.

27. *Existence and Existents*, 46.

28. Richard Kearny, "The Crisis of the Image: Levinas' Ethical Response" in Madison, G. B. & Fairbairn, M. (eds.), *The Ethics of Postmodernity: Current Trends in Continental Thought* (Evanston, IL: Northwestern University Press, 1999), 12.

29. *Existence and Existents*, 46.

30. Emmanuel Levinas, *Otherwise Than Being or Beyond Essence*, trans. A. Lingis (Pittsburgh, Duquesne University Press, 2008), 41.

31. Maurice Merleau-Ponty, *Eye and Mind*, in *The Merleau-Ponty Aesthetics Reader: Philosophy and Painting*, edited by G. A. Johnson and M. B. Smith (Evanston, IL: Northwestern University Press, 1993), 127.

32. Edith Wyschogrod, *Crossover Queries Dwelling with Negatives, Embodying Philosophy's Others* (New York: Fordham University Press, 2006), 390.

33. Emmanuel Levinas, "Is Ontology Fundamental?" in *Basic Philosophical Writings* (Bloomington: Indiana University Press, 1996), 10; Emmanuel Levinas, *Difficult Freedom: Essays on Judaism*, trans. S. Hand (Baltimore: Johns Hopkins University Press, 1990), 8.

34. *Difficult Freedom* 8.

35. Emmanuel Levinas, *Humanism of the Other*, trans. N. Poller (Urbana-Champaign: University of Illinois Press, 2003), 32.

36. Richard A. Cohen, *Out of Control: Confrontations between Spinoza and Levinas* (Albany: State University of New York Press, 2016), 53.

37. *Totality and Infinity*, 198.

38. Emmanuel Levinas, *Collected Philosophical Papers*, trans. A. Lingis (Dordrecht, The Netherlands: M. Nijhoff, 1987), 55.

39. *Existence and Existents*, 31.

40. Emmanuel Levinas, *Entre Nous: On Thinking-of-the-Other*, trans. M. B. Smith (New York: Columbia University Press, 1998), 186.

41. *Difficult Freedom*, 8.

42. *Out of Control*, 237.

43. *Out of Control*, 243.

44. *Difficult Freedom*, 8.

45. *Totality and Infinity*, 140.

46. "Is Ontology Fundamental?," 10. *Difficult Freedom*, 8.

47. *Entre Nous*, 181.

48. *Entre Nous*, 183.

49. Friedrich Nietzsche, *The Portable Nietzsche*, trans. Walter Kaufmann (New York: Penguin Books, 1982), 332–33.

50. Freud in his essay on Michelangelo's *Moses* proposes that the sculpture should be seen as a part of a group "and we cannot imagine that the figure was meant to arouse an expectation in the spectator that it was on the point of leaping up from its seat and rushing away to create a disturbance on its own account" (Freud, *The Uncanny*, 131). Freud argues that more important is that in this sculpture was represented something which does not change and "this Moses

would remain sitting like this in his wrath forever" (Freud, *The Uncanny*, 132). Interesting that Freud did not remark that even if sculpture looks like it is about to move and refers to change rather than stability (like Egyptian sculptures) it nonetheless still remains frozen forever.

51. "Reality and Its Shadow," 137.
52. "Reality and Its Shadow," 138.
53. "Reality and Its Shadow," 141.
54. *Difficult Freedom*, 96.
55. Edgar Allan Poe, "Oval Portrait," *The Works of Edgar Allan Poe* (Project Gutenberg, 2016).
56. Poe, "Oval Portrait."
57. "Reality and Its Shadow," 140.
58. "Reality and Its Shadow," 141.
59. *Elevations*, 234.
60. *Elevations*, 234.
61. *Elevations*, 243, 244.
62. Richard A. Cohen, "Art, Sacred Space and Utopia." *Religija ir kultūra*, 5, 7–23 (2008): 8.
63. Richard A. Cohen, R. A. "Levinas on Art and Aestheticism. Getting 'Reality and Its Shadow' Right." *Levinas Studies* 11 (2016): 149–94, 153.
64. Emmanuel Levinas, *Otherwise Than Being or Beyond Essence*, trans. A. Lingis (Pittsburgh: Duquesne University Press, 2008), 40.
65. But he doubts, for example, that Pygmalion's sculpture coming to life, or Snow White's opening of her eyes are uncanny (Freud 1955, 246). For Freud, of course, the experience of uncanny also relates to psychoanalysis: "An uncanny experience occurs either when repressed infantile complexes have been revived by some impression, or when the primitive beliefs we have surmounted seem once more to be confirmed" (Freud, *The Uncanny* 246, 249).
66. "Reality and Its Shadow," 138–39.
67. *Totality and Infinity*, 221–22.
68. *Collected Philosophical Papers*, 138.
69. *Levinasian Meditations*, 244.
70. Cohen,"Levinas on Art and Aestheticism," 169–70.
71. *The Pillowman*, dir. Varnas, G., Kaunas City Chamber Theatre, Theatre Utopia, 2017.
72. *Entre Nous*, 231–32.

Bibliography

Asma, S. T. *On Monsters: An Unnatural History of Our Worst Fears*. Oxford: Oxford University Press, 2009.

Baltrušaitis, J. *Le Moyen Age fantastique; antiquités et exotismes dans l'art gothique.* Paris, A. Colin, 1955.
Beal, T. K. *Religion and its Monsters.* New York: Routledge. 2002.
Cohen, R. A. *Elevations: The Height of the Good in Rosenzweig and Levinas.* Chicago: University of Chicago Press, 1994.
Cohen, R. A. "Art, Sacred Space and Utopia." *Religija ir kultūra* 5 (2008): 7–23.
Cohen, R. A. *Levinasian Meditations: Ethics, Philosophy, and Religion.* Pittsburgh: Duquesne University Press, 2010.
Cohen, R. A. "Emmanuel Levinas." In *The Routledge Companion to Phenomenology*, edited by Sebastian Luft, 71–81. New York: Routledge, 2012.
Cohen, R. A. "Levinas on Art and Aestheticism. Getting 'Reality and Its Shadow' Right." *Levinas Studies* 11 (2016): 149–94.
Cohen, R. A. *Out of Control: Confrontations between Spinoza and Levinas.* Albany: State University of New York Press, 2016.
Derrida, J. "Violence and Metaphysics: An Essay on the Thought of Emmanuel Levinas." *Writing and Difference.* London and New York: Routledge Classics, 2005.
Eaglestone, R. *Ethical Criticism: Reading after Levinas.* Edinburgh: Edinburgh University Press, 1997.
Eco, U. 2007. *On Ugliness.* New York: Rizzoli, 2007.
Ellison, D. R. *Ethics and Aesthetics in European Modernist Literature: From the Sublime to the Uncanny.* Cambridge: Cambridge University Press, 2001.
Foucault, M. *Abnormal: Lectures at the Collège de France, 1974–1975.* New York: Picador, 2003.
Freud, S. *The Uncanny. The Standard Edition of the Complete Psychological Works of Sigmund Freud.* London: The Hogarth Press, 1955.
Goodhart, S. *Möbian Nights: Reading Literature and Darkness.* New York: Bloomsbury Academic, 2017.
Kearney, R. *Strangers, Gods, and Monsters: Interpreting Otherness.* London; New York, Routledge, 2003.
Kearny, R. "The Crisis of the Image: Levinas' Ethical Response." In *The Ethics of Postmodernity: Current Trends in Continental Thought*, edited by G.B. Madison and M. M. Fairbairn, 12–23. Evanston: Northwestern University Press, 1999.
Levinas, E. *Collected Philosophical Papers*, trans. A. Lingis. Dordrecht, Netherlands: M. Nijhoff, 1987.
Levinas, E. "Reality and Its Shadow." In *The Levinas Reader*, edited by S. Hand. Oxford: Blackwell, 1989.
Levinas, E. *Difficult Freedom: Essays on Judaism*, trans. S. Hand. Baltimore: Johns Hopkins University Press, 1990.
Levinas, E. *Nine Talmudic Readings*, trans. A. Aronowicz. Bloomington: Indiana University Press, 1994.

Levinas, E. "Is Ontology Fundamental?" In *Basic Philosophical Writings*, edited by A. Peperzak, S. Critchley, and R. Bernasconi. Bloomington: Indiana University Press, 1996.

Levinas, E. *Entre Nous: On Thinking-of-the-Other*, trans. M. B. Smith. New York: Columbia University Press, 1998.

Levinas, E. 2001. *Existence and Existents*, trans. A. Lingis. Pittsburgh: Duquesne University Press, 2001.

Levinas, E. *Humanism of the Other*, trans. N. Poller. Urbana: University of Illinois Press, 2003.

Levinas, E. *Totality and Infinity: an Essay on Exteriority*, trans. A. Lingis. Pittsburgh: Duquesne University Press, 2007.

Levinas, E. *Otherwise than Being or Beyond Essence*, trans. A. Lingis. Pittsburgh: Duquesne University Press, 2008.

Merleau-Ponty, M. *Eye and Mind* in Johnson, G. A. & Smith, M. B. (eds.) *The Merleau-Ponty Aesthetics Reader: Philosophy and Painting*. Evanston: Northwestern University Press, 1993.

Nietzsche, F. W. 1982. *The Portable Nietzsche*, trans. W.A. Kaufmann. New York: Penguin Books.

Poe, E. A."Oval Portrait." The Works of Edgar Allan Poe. Project Gutenberg, 2016.

Robbins, J. *Altered Reading: Levinas and Literature*. Chicago: University of Chicago Press, 1999.

Saldukaitytė, J."Dasein svetimybė ir slėpiningumas = On Dasein Being Strange and Uncanny." Žmogus ir žodis: mokslo darbai. *Filosofija* 18 (2016): 29–44.

The Pillowman, Directed by Varnas, G. Kaunas City Chamber Theatre, Theatre Utopia, 2017.

Wyschogrod, E. *Crossover Queries Dwelling with Negatives, Embodying Philosophy's Others*. 1st ed. New York: Fordham University Press, 2006.

Path III

Ontological Contests

12

Review

Levinas's Reading of Spinoza

JACQUES J. ROZENBERG

Richard A. Cohen, *Out of Control: Confrontations between Spinoza and Levinas.* Albany, SUNY, 2016.

The new book by Richard A. Cohen, director of the Institute for Jewish Thought and Heritage at the University of Buffalo, New York, seeks to place in confrontation two philosophers, Spinoza and Levinas, who are largely in conflict on many fundamental themes. It should be remembered that the author is particularly well equipped to conduct such a confrontation. He personally knew Emmanuel Levinas, notably during the academic year 1974–1975 at the University of Paris-Sorbonne, and he translated several of his works into English.[1] He also began his university career in the 1980s, teaching Spinoza's philosophy.

The author justifies the title of his book, *Out of Control*, as characterizing Emmanuel Levinas' anti-Spinozism. He points out that Spinozism represents the control par excellence, in the sense of totalization, of global rationality, of the exclusive unlimited being of duty-to-be, of perseverance for perseverance, similarly enclosing infinity and freedom in the order of necessity alone. In this sense, the *Out of Control* aims to show the height, orientation, and nobility of a freedom that takes charge of moral responsibility toward others, despite all the difficulty of accomplishment and self-sacrifice that it requires.[2] The book covers many themes, expressed in its eight chapters: (1) Levinas, Spinozism, Nietzsche, and the body; (2) the prophetic word in Levinas and Spinoza (and Maimonides); (3) Levinas and Spinoza: loving God without hope of return; (4) Levinas and Spinoza: justice and the state; (5) The Prince of Spinoza: for whom was the *Theological-Political Treatise* written?; (6) Levinas on Spinoza's erroneous understanding of Judaism; (7) thinking of nothing less than death: mortality and morality in Spinoza, Heidegger, and Levinas; (8) Spinoza's spleen: babies, food, and lunatics. Unable to review all these themes, we will limit ourselves to specifying some essential points of this confrontation between Levinas and Spinoza, which we will also interpret in relation to our personal reading of these two authors.

Levinas's Critique of Spinoza

In his 1937 review of Harry A. Wolfson's *The Philosophy of Spinoza* Emmanuel Levinas argued that Spinoza's approach to Judaism is inaccurate for at least three reasons.[3] First, the research of Vaz Dias and Van der Tak shows that Spinoza was not registered on the register of institutions of Jewish studies in Amsterdam. Contrary to what his biographers generally claim, Levinas thought Spinoza did not know the Talmud.[4] He therefore had access only to a "bloodless" biblical text and thus unable to grasp its true meaning.[5] Next, he emphasized that Spinoza reduced the Bible to an entirely human and natural text. Finally, he noted that Spinozist pantheism, by identifying the divine with nature, determined it uniquely within the straitjacket of *The Ethics*, posed as the exclusive standard of truth.[6]

According to Emmanuel Levinas, Spinoza's tour de force was to propose a form of rationalism, that allowed Christianity to be surreptitiously imposed on many Jewish intellectuals, without having himself accepted Baptism. In the words of Richard A. Cohen, Spinoza constituted the Christian "Trojan horse" in the Temple of Judaism.[7] Indeed, Spinoza has, on the one hand, accepted the Pauline supersessionism, according to which Christianity would come to incorporate Judaism, and, on the other hand, Spinoza has greatly promoted secular supersessionism as a cancellation of any form of religion.[8] Like Sabbatai Tsevi, Spinoza contributed to the emergence of secular Judaism, advocating not only the religious freedom of the Jews but also their emancipation from Judaism itself. Also, like Sabbatai Tsevi, Spinoza accelerated the assimilation of Jews to European culture.[9] Spinoza endorsed the double process, the substitution of Judaism by Christianity, and the spiritualization of the biblical letter, without the commandments it is responsible for conveying. He thus asserted that Christians merely interpret in a spiritual sense what the Jews understood in a material way (*quae Judaei carnaliter*), but he jointly naturalized the divine incarnated in the body of Christ, while reading the Jewish Bible in a Christian spirit.[10]

For Levinas, in general Spinozist immanence is self-referenced and thus excludes any possibility of otherness that always implies the notion of transcendence. Indeed, otherness is expressed first in the feminine, which is "other for a masculine being not only because of a different nature but also inasmuch as alterity is in some way its nature."[11] This is why the misogynistic remarks Spinoza wrote in the *Political Treatise* do not seem out of step with the immanentist project of *The Ethics*, where Spinoza took over the misogynistic prejudices of his time.[12] He equated the "pity of women" (*muliebri misericordia*) with superstition (*superstitione*), and also noted "the inconsistency of women" (*mulierum inconstantia*), their "false heart" (*fallaci animo*) and other "vices" (*vitiis*).[13] He put on the same level the "delusional, the talkative, and the child" (*delirans, garrula, puer*), all believing in the illusion of free will, when they cannot contain their impulse to speak (*loquendi impetum*).[14] He also referred to "the inconsistency of women, (to) their deceptive soul and other rebattus vices (from *muffium inconstantia* and *fallaci animo* and *reliquis earundem decantatis vitiis*)."[15] What Richard A. Cohen calls "spleen" toward women, fools, and children, is in fact the Spinozist refusal of free will and human freedom, a freedom that Levinas keeps asserting, but which he supports in relation to responsibility for others.[16]

The Ethics of Spinoza and Levinasian Ethics

Richard A. Cohen emphasizes that Spinoza named his masterwork *The Ethics*, because true knowledge is not just a component of human existence but envelops it entirely within the natural totality. The *Deus sive Natura* thus encompasses all reality, and thus allows us to assimilate every religion, every value and every morality with the only natural necessity.[17]

However, *The Ethics*, according to Levinas, does not lead to a true morality. Indeed, according to Levinas, the absence of transcendence gives free rein to the "natural *conatus essendi* of a sovereign Self," which blurs the "face of others."[18] For Spinoza, it is desire and aversion that completely determine the value of a thing, not the object or the desired person themselves. Pleasure or sorrow, although related to the possession or lack of possession of this thing, result only from our desire or aversion for it.[19] This is why we judge something as good (*bonum esse judicare*) because we "strive, want it, aspire to it and desire it (*volumus, appetimus, atque cupimus*)."[20] Conversely, a thing will be considered bad because we are moving away from it. The value remains purely immanent to desire and concerns the object and others only in a utilitarian way. Even "where men will be most useful to each other is when everyone seeks at the highest point his own useful (*suum utile sibi qu'rit*)."[21] Levinassian ethics oppose Spinozist utilitarianism; the Other must be the highest value, and responsibility for the Other takes the subject hostage to the very fact of the infinite demand of ethics, so that no one "can say: I have done all my duty. Except the hypocrite."[22] Against the immanence of the useful self-referencing, in the service of the only conatus, the presence of the Other, for Levinas, is fundamentally different, that is to say transcendent of the subject herself.[23] The otherness of the Other is incompatible with the monism of the Spinozist substance, which necessarily reduces the Other to the same, and as a result, the absence of transcendence always ends up leading to the destruction of the moral relationship as concern for the Other.[24]

Richard A. Cohen recalls that, for Spinoza, love is mediated by the idea, it is only posed as "the joy that accompanies the idea of an external cause (*quam letitia concomitant idea causæ extern*)."[25] While this love is first immanent to the individual, and remains mediated by the idea, Levinassian love opens to the infinity of the Other, which presents itself both in its corporality and in its alterity.[26] It is the opening of the face of the Other that reveals its infinity, which cannot be reduced to the enjoyment of the loving subject. For Levinas, love shows that "thought and freedom come to us from the separation and from the consideration of the Other—this thesis is at the antipodes of Spinozism."[27] The latter, denying contingency and freedom, is strictly amoral, for it opposes an ethic of responsibility. By this, others seem to me "as if he were unique in the world—beloved."[28] This allows Levinas to define an ethical intelligibility, which preserves both free will and moral action.[29]

The Love of God

Richard A. Cohen underlines the convergence between Levinas and Spinoza concerning the notion of the love of God, for which nothing can be demanded in return, but he also insists on the refusal of the former to the identification of the intellect and the will, which the latter operates precisely: "The will and the intellect are one and the same thing (*voluntas and intellectus unum, et idem sunt*)."³⁰ Levinas contrasts it with ". . . the entire pathetic experience of humanity. . . . This opposition is inspired by the certainty of the surplus. . . an incessant surplus that accomplishes the infinitude of infinity."³¹ This surplus refers to the overflow of the "truth about being," which Levinas illustrates with the metaphor of the "'curvature of intersubjective space,'. . . (that is) perhaps, the very presence of God."³²

Let us remember that, for Spinoza, the intellectual love of God (*amor Dei intellectualis*) derived from the Third Kind of Knowledge, and therefore this love is eternal.³³ This is why, outside of temporal affairs, "God strictly speaking, loves no one and hates no one (*Deus proprie loquendo neminem amat neque odio habet*)."³⁴ It is only indirectly that "God as he loves himself, loves men (*quod Deus quatenus seipsum amat, homines amat*)" Spinoza told Blyenbergh that "all our bliss consists of the love of God, and that this love necessarily follows the knowledge of God (*summa nostra beatitudo in amore erga Deum consists, attendit, quodque ille amor necessario ex Dei cognitione*)."³⁵ However, in the *Ethics*, love for God (*erga Deum amor*) differs from God's intellectual love, for it is attached to all the affections of the body.³⁶ However, even under this type of affection, as Leibniz pointed out in the *Animadversiones*, love for God, for Spinoza, "is merely a parade costume for the people (*non-nisi ad populatulum phaleras esse*)," insofar as "there can be nothing aimiable (*nihil is amabile*) in a God, which produces without choice from all eternity both good and evil. God's true love is not based on necessity, but on bounty (*verus Dei amor fundatur non in necessitate sed bonitate*)."³⁷ With regard to the *amor intellectualis Dei* itself, Spinoza claims, as Arne Naess noted, only a love extending, without ontological distinction, to the whole universe. This love includes both animal species and the inanimate world.³⁸

Against the impersonal eternity of the Spinozist God, Levinas privileges the word of God expressed through the prophets of Israel, expressed in the "infinity of time . . . better than eternity, which is an exasperation of the 'present,' an idealization of the present."³⁹ It is first in the ethical relationship that "my relation to God—comes to me in the concreteness of my relation to the other man."⁴⁰ The latter, on the one hand, opposes any theology, which deals with "God as if he belonged to the being or to perception," and on the other hand inserts responsibility into a "meta-ontological structure" beyond the being itself.⁴¹

It should also be noted that, as Richard A. Cohen points out, though neither Spinozism nor Levinas's philosophy can be considered mystical, it still seems possible to clarify Levinas's opposition to Spinoza through notions close to Kabbalah, such as those of infinity, the face, and the trace.[42] Although Levinas did not see Jewish mysticism in a favorable light, he had nevertheless written the preface for the French translation of Rav Hayym de Volozhin's *Nefesh Ha-Hayym*, in which he referred to the *Zohar*, and the esoteric teaching of the Vilna Gaon. As Charles Mopsik has noted, even though the Levinassian infinity relates more to the Cartesian infinity than to the Kabbalistic *Eyn Sof*, Levinas has nevertheless developed theses that are consistent with several fundamental notions of the Lurianic Kabbalah, notably the *Tzimtzum* (withdrawal or retraction) of infinite divine light.

We have shown, moreover, that Spinoza cannot accept this notion.[43] Applied to intersubjectivity, the theory of *Tzimtzum* allows us to think of the Other as a decentralization of the Ego, and thus as a break of totality. Such a shift does not constitute a loss of perfection, but the condition of existence as a creature.[44]

Justice and the State

Cohen notes that while Levinas and Spinoza seem to agree on the need to establish justice and political authority, they differ profoundly on the how to conceive the nature of this dual necessity. On the one hand, the relationship to morality and religion, and on the other, ontology and metaphysics.[45] In fact, the essential point of divergence between Levinas and Spinoza is the transfer of fidelity from the Creator to absolute loyalty to the state, which Spinoza endows with total authority. According to Spinoza, it is for the state to control religion, whereas for Levinas, religion must guide political and social life.[46] In the *Tractatus Theologico-Politicus*, Spinoza sought to articulate man's love for God and man's love for his neighbor, thus summing up the content of Scripture: "loving God more than anything, and his neighbor as oneself (*Deum supraa omnia amare et proximum tanquam se ipsum*).[47] If God, as a substance made up of an infinite number of attributes that cannot be imitated, how can his justice and charity remain accessible to man? In the words of Jacqueline Lagrée: "The indefinity of ethical requirement is the correspondent of the infinity of divine qualities."[48]

Although, unlike justice, he does not explicitly define charity (*Tractatus Theologico-Politicus*, XVI, 10), Spinoza suggests that these two notions allow man to name God, and refer not to sentiments but only works to be accomplished. However, for Spinoza, justice and charity can only become effective by state law (*ex jure imperii*), which is why their exercise requires obedience to the laws of the state.[49] The *Tractatus Theologico-Politicus* thus sketches a form of morality, founded on obligation and obedience, independent of the real knowledge that man may have of divine necessity, advocated by *The Ethics*. However, because justice and charity only fall under the sovereign, and have no existence in themselves, they cannot have the universal content of adequate ideas.[50] Thus, morality, like religion, cannot compel subjects, except by civil coercion, for Scripture "does not condemn ignorance (*ignorantiam*), but only insubordination (*contumaciam*)."[51] The purpose of the Spinozist state is not so much to defend the freedom of citizens, but first of all its own security and stability. The preservation of the state takes precedence over that of the individual, for "piety towards the homeland is the highest degree of piety" (*quod pietas erga patriam summa sit*). This absolute valuation prevails over all moral considerations, to the point of legitimizing a true reversal of values. Thus, in line with Machiavelli, Spinoza affirmed that it is necessary to consider as "pious an unholy act (*impium committi*) towards the neighbor, if it is done for the conservation of the Republic (*si propter reipublicae conservationem fiat*)."[52] For Levinas, true morality and religion lie beyond state violence.[53] It should be noted that, while idolizing the state, Spinoza actually took up the traditional Jewish idea of the duty to pray for the stability of the state, without which "everyone would swallow alive his neighbor," as well as the obligation to respect the laws of the country where everyone resides (*dyn'a demalkout'a dyn'a*).[54] However, according to the *Talmud*, the obligation to respect the state cannot violate Jewish law, where state laws are in particular opposed to ethical imperatives.[55] As Cohen points out, the conception of the Spinozist state radically contradicts the long prophetic tradition of universal social compassion, as well as the ethical-redemptive policy it implies.[56] Where for Spinoza, pity (*commiseratio*), which does not differ essentially from mercy (*misericordiam*), is a sadness (*tristitia*), for Levinas the ethical responsibility toward others is expressed first in compassion toward him.[57]

Richard A. Cohen emphasizes Levinas's admiration for Spinoza, for his uncompromising rejection of superstition, his critique of anthropomorphic projections, and his critique of childish dependence on the religious. Both called for an "adult religion," even though their conceptions of such a religion were entirely opposed to each other.[58] Because Levinas conceived the human self as this permanent possibility of suspending his "*conatus essendi*" in order to be able to respond to the Other who "is nothing to him," he always opposed the Spinozist totality.[59] Levinas, who denounced in Heidegger the anonymous process of being, "without a carrier, without a subject," could only oppose what could be described as the "strange philosophy" of Spinozism, uniting the finite with an anonymous infinity.[60] Levinas, however, sometimes revealed what Jean-François Rey describes as "admiration and acknowledgement of Spinozism, that is, in the end, for philosophy itself."[61] In this sense, there is an ambiguity in Levinas vis-à-vis Spinoza. According to Dan Arbib, Levinas in fact had a dual relationship with Spinozism: an ontological opposition to *The Ethics*, for all the reasons we recalled in this article; but he also performed a religious rehabilitation of the *Tractatus Theologico-Politicus*.[62] In fact, Levinas even evokes an appreciation of the "internality of rational relations" specific to *The Ethics*, from which Judaism cannot be parted, as it cannot do without mathematics.[63] Moreover, Spinoza is said to have operated an ethical internalization of religion, allowing the desacralization of its pagan ties.[64] However, while Spinoza defined freedom as an existence driven by the "only necessity of its nature" (*sola suae naturae necessitate*), Levinas challenged the primacy of freedom as a measure of being.[65] It is the presence of the Other that calls into question the "naïve legitimacy of freedom" in the name of justice, for the ethical relationship exceeds freedom by the humanity of the Other.[66] At what Antonio Negri calls the "roundness" of the Spinozist being, which presents itself as an exclusive and flawless whole, Levinas contrasts the irreducible experience of the relationship with the other which, in the "face to face," exceeds any set of possible syntheses.[67]

Notes

1. *New Talmudic Readings* (Pittsburgh: Duquesne University Press, 1999); *Discovering Existence with Husserl*, co-translated with Michael B. Smith (Evanston: Northwestern University Press, 1998); *Time and the Other and Additional Essays by Emmanuel Levinas* (Pittsburgh: Duquesne University Press, 1987); *Ethics and Infinity* (Pittsburgh: Duquesne University Press, 1985).

2. Richard A. Cohen, *Out of Control: Confrontations Between Levinas and Spinoza* (Albany: State University of New York Press, 2016), 27–28.

3. Emmanuel Levinas, "Spinoza, philosophe medieval," *Revue des Etudes Juives*, I, 6 (1937): 114–19.

4. A. M. Vas Dias and W. G. van der Tak, "Spinoza Merchant & Autodidact: Charter Other Authentic Documents Relating to the Philosopher's Youth and His Relations" (Published originally in Dutch in 1932). English translation *Studia Rosenthaliana* 16 (1982): 154.

5. Emmanuel Levinas, "Have You Reread Baruch?" in *Difficult Freedom: Essays on Judaism,* trans. Sean Hand (Baltimore: John Hopkins University Press, 1990), 298n5. Concerning Spinoza's lack of interest in the Talmud, cf. M. Chamla, *Spinoza e il concetto della 'tradizione ebraica'* (Milan: F. Angeli), 127.

6. Emmanuel Levinas, "Spinoza's Background" in *Beyond the Verse: Talmudic Readings and Lectures,* trans. Gary D. Mole (London: Continuum, 1994), 164. Cohen, *Out of Control,* 198.

7. Cohen, *Out of Control,* 206.

8. Cf. M. A. Rosenthal, "Spinoza on Circumcision and Ceremonies, *Modern Judaism* 36, no. 1 (2016): 50.

9. Cf. J. J. Rozenberg, "Spinoza, le Spinozisme et les Sources de la Sécularisation" (book to be published).

10. Cohen, *Out of Control,* 191n1.

11. Emmanuel Levians, *Ethics and Infinity: Conversations with Philippe Nemo,* trans. Richard Cohen (Pittsburgh: Duquesne University Press, 1985), 65.

12. Spinoza, *TP* VI, 37 (Paris: Ramond PUF), 205, 158–59.

13. Spinoza, *Ethique* II, 49, scolie de la seconde démonstration (Pautrat, Paris, Ed. du Rééd Seuil, 2010), 206–7; *Ethique* V, 10, scolie, 192–93.

14. Spinoza, *Ethique* III, 2, scolie, Pautrat, 220–21.

15. Spinoza, *Ethique* V, 10, scolie, Pautrat, 520–21.

16. Cohen, *Out of Control,* 296; Emmanuel Levinas, *Otherwise Than Being or Beyond Essence,* tr. Alphonso Lingis (Pittsburgh: Duquesne University Press, 1998), 19–20.

17. Spinoza, *Ethique* IV, Préface, Pautrat, 352–53; *Ethique* IV, 4, démonstration, Pautrat, 366–67; Cohen, *Out of Control,* 108–9.

18. Emmanuel Levinas, *Alterity and Transcendence,* tr. Michael B. Smith (London: The Athlone Press, 1999), 33.

19. Spinoza, *Ethique* III, 9, scolie; *Ethique* III, 39, scolie.

20. Spinoza, *Ethique* III, 9, scolie, Pautrat, 230–31.

21. Spinoza, *Ethique* IV, 35, cor. 2, Pautrat, 408–9.

22. Levinas, *Ethics and Infinity,* 105–6.

23. Emmanuel Levinas, *Existence and Existents,* trans. Alphonso Lingis (Pittsburgh: Duquesne University Press, 2001), 105.

24. Emmanuel Levinas, *Totality and Infinity: An Essay on Exteriority,* trans. Alphonso Lingis (Pittsburgh: Duquesne University Press, 1969), 44.

25. Cohen, *Out of Control*, 86; Spinoza, *Ethique* III, 13, scolie, Pautrat, 236–37.

26. F. S. Scribner, "Extending Spinoza . . . For the Love of God! Spinoza, Levinas, and the Inadequacy of the Body" *International Philosophical Quarterly* 42, no. 2 (2002): 151–60.

27. Levinas, *Totality and Infinity*, 105.

28. Emmanuel Levinas, "The Other, Utopia, and Justice" in *Entre Nous: On Thinking of the Other*, tr. Michael B. Smith and Barbara Harshaw (New York: Columbia University Press, 1998), 227.

29. Cohen, *Out of Control*, 83–92.

30. Spinoza, *Ethique II*, Corollaire de la prop. 49, Pautrat, 194–95.

31. Levinas, *Totality and Infinity*, 217–18.

32. Levinas, *Totality and Infinity*, 291.

33. Spinoza, *Ethique* V, 33, Pautrat, 544–45. For a presentation of the idea of the Intellectual Love of God in Spinoza, cf. S. Nadler, "The Intellectual Love of God » in *The Oxford Handbook of Spinoza*, ed. M. Della Rocca (Oxford: Oxford University Press, 2017), 295–313. Yitzhak Y. Melamed has examined the enigmatic status of this notion in the system of *The Ethics*; "The Enigma of Spinoza's Amor Dei Intellectualis," in *Freedom, Action and Motivation in Spinoza's Ethics*, ed. N. Naaman-Zaudrer and N. Naaman (London, Routledge, 2019), 222–38.

34. Spinoza, *Ethique* V, 17, cor. Pautrat, 524–25; H. A.Wolfson, *Spinoza* II, 283.

35. Spinoza, *Ethique* V, 36, cor. Pautrat, 548–49. Spinoza, *Lettre 21* à Blyenbergh, G. IV, 127, trad. franç. 1147; cf. *TTP*, IV, 4, 186–87.

36. Spinoza, *Ethique* V, 18 cor. Pautrat, 526–27; cf. P. Macherey, *Introduction à l'Ethique de Spinoza - Cinquième partie: les voies de la libération* (Paris: Presses Universitaires de France, 1997), 50.

37. Leibniz, *Réfutation inédite de Spinoza*, ed. L. A. Foucher de Careil (Paris: Ladrange, 1854), 66–67.

38. A. Naess, *Spinoza and the Deep Ecology Movement* (Eburon: Delft, 1992), 5. This theme was studied in greater detail by Eccy De Jonge, *Spinoza and Deep Ecology: Challenging Traditional Approaches to Environmentalism* (New York: Ashgate, 2004), 85–108.

39. Levinas, "Philosophy, Justice and Love," in *Entre Nous*, 114.

40. Emmanuel Levinas, *Of God Who Comes to Mind*, trans. Bettina Bergo (Stanford, CA: Stanford University Press, 1998), xiv.

41. Emmanuel Levinas, *Humanism of the Other*, trans. Nidra Poller (Urbana: University of Illinois Press, 2003), 56. Emmanuel Levinas, *Otherwise Than Being or Beyond Essence*, 126. Cf. M. Nagasaka, "Altérité anarchique—Réconciliation de Descartes et Kant dans la dernière pensée d'Emmanuel Levinas," *ACTA UNIVERSITATIS CAROLINAE. Interpretationes Studia Philosophica Europeanea* 1, no. 2 (2016): 102–17.

42. Cohen, *Out of Control*, 6, 90.

43. J. J. Rozenberg, *Spinoza, le spinozisme et les sources de la sécularisation* (book to be published).

44. C. Mopsik, "La pensée d'Emmanuel Levinas et la Cabale," *Cahiers de l'Herne* (1991): 433, 435, 440.

45. Cohen, *Out of Control*, 103–18.

46. Cohen, *Out of Control*, 104.

47. Spinoza, *Tractatus Theologico-Politicus*, XII, 10, edition bilingue (Paris: Presses Universitaires de France, 1999), 444–45. The translators refer to *Deuteronomy* 6:5, *Leviticus* 19:18, *Matthew* 22:34 and, *Mark* 12:28–31, note 30, 759.

48. J. Lagrée, "Spinoza et l'amour intellectuel du prochain," in *Spinoza, philosophe de l'amour*, ed. C. Jaquet, P. Séverac, and A. Suhamy (Saint-Etienne: l'Université de Saint-Etienne, 2005), 99.

49. Spinoza, *TTP*, XIX 3, 606–7. J. Lagrée, "Spinoza et l'amour intellectuel du prochain" in *Spinoza, philosophe de l'amour*, 100.

50. Cf. E. Garver, "Spinoza and the Discovery of Morality," *History of Philosophy Quarterly* 45, no. 3 (2005): 358–59.

51. Spinoza, *Tractatus Theologico-Politicus*, XIV, 8, 472. S. Frankel, "Spinoza's Response to Maimonides: A Practical Strategy for Resolving the Tension Between Reason and Revelation," *International Philosophical Quarterly* 45, no. 3 (2005): 322–24.

52. Spinoza, TTP, XI, 10, 614–15, cf. note 20 des traducteurs, p. 780, qui réfère à Machiavel, Discorsi, III, 41. Cohen also underlines the Machiavellian character of the Spinozist state. *Out of Control*, 214. On Spinoza's borrowing of the notion of virtue from Machiavelli see cf. L. Althusser, "Spinoza I," *Lignes* 18, no. 1 (1993): 93.

53. Levinas, *Beyond the Verse*, 171.

54. *Pirquev 'Avot* III, 2.

55. Babylonian Talmud, *Bab 'a Qam'a* 133a.

56. Cohen, *Out of Control*, 217.

57. Spinoza, *Ethique* III, Definition of Affects XVIII and Explication, Pautrat, 328–29. Emmanuel Levinas, *God, Death, and Time*, trans. Bettina Bergo (Stanford, CA: Stanford University Press, 2000), 180.

58. R. A. Cohen, *Out of Control*, 24.

59. Emmanuel Levinas, *In the Time of the Nations*, trans. Michael B. Smith (London: Althone Press, 1994), 178.

60. F. Poirié, *Emmanuel Levinas : essai et entretiens* (Arles: Actes Sud, 1996), 101. A. Tosel, *Spinoza ou l'autre (in)finitude* (Paris: L'Harmattan, 2008), 178–79.

61. J. F. Rey, "Levinas et Spinoza," in *Spinoza au XXe siècle*, ed. O. Bloch (Paris: Presses Universitaires de France, 1993), 226.

62. Dan Arbib, "Les deux voies de Spinoza: l'interprétation lévinassienne de l'Ethique et du Traité Theologico-politique in *Revue de l'histoire des religions* 229, no. 2 (2012): 275–300.

63. Levinas, *Difficult Freedom*, 115–16.
64. J. F. Rey, "Levinas et Spinoza" in *Spinoza au XXe siècle*, ed. O. Bloch (Paris: Presses Universitaires de France, 1993), 230. Cf. Hent de Vries, B. Weltman-Aron, "Levinas, Spinoza, et le sens théologico-politique de L'Écriture, *Pardès* 42, no. 1 (2007): 79–94.
65. Spinoza, *Ethique* I, Définition VII, 20–21.
66. Levinas, *Totality and Infinity*, 303.
67. A. Negri, *L'anomalie sauvage. Puissance et pouvoir chez Spinoza* (Paris: Presses Universitaires de France, 1982), 100–105. Levinas, *Ethics and Infinity*, 77.

13

Imagine Freedom

BRUNELLA ANTOMARINI

This essay is a virtual conversation between Spinoza and Levinas. I will try to show how, despite their diverging philosophies, their presuppositions do not always clash—and when they do, it is due to different levels of description of the same phenomenon. My argument will be developed in a kind of narrative in which each divergence will be successively eliminated until one position appears to include and subsume the other. I will take this exemplary phenomenon to be the issue of human vulnerability, in its connection with will and reason. As a matter of fact, Spinoza's radical immanentism, by contrasting the Cartesian dualism and the egotism of the scientific subject of knowledge, though seemingly lending itself to the later scientific reduction of knowledge to rational competence devoid of comprehension, actually does not ignore the issues of human vulnerability that define Levinas's humanism; Spinoza does not deny the sense and value of weakness but rather shifts the issue to a ground wider than the human. In fact, the notion of the human, being deeply jeopardized by the not decreasing (if not increasing) inhumanity of human beings, does not manifest itself through tangible effects and does not rest upon some material pragmatic grounds in such a way that we can find the continuity between the actual immanent world of matter and the urge to ulteriority; it remains therefore mere wishful thinking.

Confronted with a Levinasian philosophy of the Other, Spinoza shows "on his own skin" how the categorical imperative of the Other remains purely normative and regulative if it is not substantiated with actual, material, immanent factors: in his view of a perfectly structured nature, there can be no space for what is not included in that structure, namely the Other. Spinoza's concern with the actual body starts as a Cartesianism and then proceeds as an anti-Cartesian attempt to liberate its automatism from Descartes's mortifying definition of it, emancipating his very philosophy from determinism and offering a pragmatist perspective on right behavior. His emphasis on the actual—and the potential as strife to reach the actual—seems to exclude any indeterminacy of the Levinasian human.

Nonetheless, it is the aim of my essay to show how this opposition paradoxically leads to one and the same conclusion in both philosophers.

Man is a Vulnerable Animal

One of the key notions of Richard Cohen's *Out of Control: Confrontations Between Spinoza and Levinas* is the issue of vulnerability. Rationalism, conceived by its main philosophers as a way to support emerging and increasingly successful science with a metaphysical foundation, eschewed the idea that the strong agent of exact science and philosophy of certainty can ever be vulnerable. In antirationalistic times, Levinas reopened the question: a state of suffering, which thwarts the natural goal of enjoyment, requests patience, postponement, distance:[1] qualities of nonaction, opposed, through the lens of vulnerability, to the early modern masculine philosophies of reason. How to give an account of vulnerability from a Spinozian perspective? Cohen's beautiful quote from Grossman about the "senseless kindness" people sometimes exchange gives the best example of vulnerability as a value.[2] Being kind implies an attitude of support and aid, independently of whether it is needed. Its purpose is to communicate to the other that we know what being vulnerable means. If a principle of sufficient reason is applicable here, it is the simple need for a ritual, or of a pure possibility, or a simple habit. But it exists and is praised. Why then? Does Spinoza's *Ethics*, so focused on actual behavior, offer a perspective on kindness and vulnerability?

That all affect is connected to powerlessness or despondency (*impotentia*) fosters a resistance against its humiliation: humility is ignorance of one's power, incapacity to step out of suffering.[3] All sense of powerlessness here appears through the effect of suffering, and its failed stratagems to counter that effect and to get out of it. This pragmatist view of suffering is not rationalistic in itself, as is the natural course of things in both the human psyche and each and every thing in nature: that "everything, in so far as it is in itself, endeavors to persist in its own being"[4] intimates simultaneously power and limitation.

Power is foundational of all nature and at the same time a reminder of imperfection: (human) nature is exactly the constant search to reach the perfect state of power by *conatus*, by defending the natural pleasure and joy that life consists of, and by avoiding unnatural sorrow. We constantly revolve around the unreachable center of perfection. We correct excess or defect in our behavior according to a circumstantial logic, similar to Aristotle's logic of behavior as described in *Nicomachean Ethics*, according to which striving for the Good is a contingent decision about the proportion of opposites that makes the golden mean of right behavior; we modify the "weight" of a virtue confronted with its opposite and reached as midway (Aristotle, 6, 26–27),[5] a dynamic ideal center of perfection. The infinity of modifications, though seemingly resulting from free choice, actually revolves around an ungraspable radiating center of possibilities, determined by nature.

Although Spinoza replaces the Aristotelian final causes of behavior with material causes, his ethics is deeply indebted to Aristotle's analysis of value and behavior, conceived as objects of rational analysis, aimed at understanding what produces imperfection and, as a consequence, suffering; the issue is re-proposed in Part V of *Ethics*: "For we see that the pain arising from the loss of any good is mitigated, as soon as the man who has lost it perceives that it could not by any means have been preserved."[6]

An empathetic attitude is not a value in itself; it may even become ridiculous, in fact, if we misdirect our pity to the ones who do not need it, as in the case of children's weakness, which is *rationally* (or even better: *instinctively*) considered as natural, transitory and necessary.[7] Although it is true that in Spinoza a vulnerable state is usually associated with a weak mind, it is also true that as a matter of fact a feeling of weakness is accompanied by a feeling of resistance to it, followed by either acceptance (when we recognize its necessity), or an effort to overcome it, in order to reinforce the pleasure of life and our share in the divine nature.

Caught between knowledge of causes and intervention on effects, empathy is governed by imagination and not by anything actual, as is shown in Spinoza's distinction between a disposition to pity things—which as such is *just* a disposition and does not require any action that is not a "ritual" of sympathy—and the particular affect occurring in a particular case,[8] suggesting that the latter is accounted for by the former, called compassion, or, pity: a formal, imagined suffering that, if it is undeniable as a feeling, it is by virtue of its lack of correspondence to actuality, as happens when we imagine a winged horse.[9]

In a continuous line linking the Greeks to Spinoza and Nietzsche, the feeling of empathy toward vulnerability is reduced to self-pity and commiseration. It is only in Romanticism that commiseration, empathy, and indulgence of tears enter the scene of philosophical thinking (and literature) and come to be recognized as a value. In Aristotelian terms, pride (as resistance to weakness, or dishonor) is a subjective golden mean between empty vanity (boasting of strength) and undue humility (*commiseratio*)[10] and, as such, it is a self-regulation of affects in social or circumstantial contexts. Does this systemic relationship deprive empathy of its value?

The twentieth century's concern with the human animal's vulnerability, following psychology and psychoanalysis (through Hegel, Hyppolite, and Nietzsche, and, I would add Peirce, ignored for a long time), may have been prefigured by Spinoza, who first rationally described in depth each and every affect. But what does it mean to include affects in the rational plan? Or, what might be the consequences of including affects in the structure of the mind? Does their description determine a destitution of rationalism, or does it change the definition of reason? Is the aim of reason to guide a human practical-psychological condition out of a state of suffering, or is it to "comprehend" it? In Spinoza's practical view (knowledge as ethics) the role of reason in analyzing affects appears to be comprehension as a means to action: the greater the clarity about affects, the more rational the response. We can imagine a succession of states: weakness, comprehension, reaction (or better, retroduction, as Peirce would call it), which change the body's condition, or its material being. If a body is a complex of functions, and not a substantial fixed entity, "will" is a name for the modifiable body/mind system: even when I think, I simultaneously exert an emotional power, which I call an act of the will. In the same vein, in order to responsibly intervene on the other's pain, I need to gather all of my power. In Spinoza's antisubjective stance, empathizing can only mean comprehending and acting. Saying, "I understand your feelings" can only mean either imparting some ritual comfort or preparing an action of support. In the first case, we do not have any evidence of actual sharing. In the second case we have a pragmatic result, which is the only evidence of the virtue of piety. Actually, the etymological origin of responsibility can be traced back in *respondeo*, answering, reacting: it suggests a self-modification (if only social), or "negative freedom." When I free myself (or the other) from a hindrance, there is in my behavior a game of repulsion/attraction, or rest/motion: I respond, I am free from, I resist a course of events, I correct an amount of energy that would destroy me. I move in order to find some rest. This is common to both the sufferer and the helper, as it belongs indifferently to the "nature of things." Certainly Spinoza's concern is more with a phenomenological description of effects, rather than cause of individual choices, which would remain, in any case, obscure (no example of its authentic intention is possible, as will be later shown by Kantian ethics, or even by Nietzsche, as we will show).

But let's look at Richard Cohen's objection to Spinoza's phenomenological "cynicism": "Here it is a matter of transcendence of the other. . .it is not that the other person must articulate a request, such as 'feed me' . . . ."[11]

Picturing a Gratuitous Gesture

Responding to a request, whether from the other or from oneself, cannot be an act of pure will, as it involves an impulse, or an instinct, which has little to do with choice. In both Spinoza and Levinas an internalist view of empathy is under attack: for the former, each individual is a mode of the whole and individual will is dried up from inside; sharing feelings requires a linguistic expression that cannot be distinguished from falsehood, arbitrariness, or wishful thinking. Spinoza deconstructs freedom and the will in the very moment he destroys the claim that an utterance of empathy may ever correspond to anything substantial. Spinoza's description of the *conatus*, the attempt to keep one's or the other's balance, recalls an original resistance to annihilation that is at the same time automatic (negentropy and homeostasis), willful (emotional), and spiritual (highly evaluated ethically).

For Levinas, on the other hand, if there can be truthful behavior it must start from the arbitrary point determined by a face-to-face connection, external to any individual self.[12] It is true in fact that knowing reasons or causes to act is not at the origin of the action. We may ignore our true reasons—or, even worse, we may ignore the reasons of the other about whom we are bent to care—but we simply act, anyway, on behalf of the other. We stretch out our hand without our own reasons, without the other's reasons. But we do. It is an effort that precedes knowledge and even adequate ideas; on all levels the gratuitous action is contained in the nature of things. It is not beyond nature; what we call the transcendence of the gratuitous gesture is included in the stratagems of nature. So, the question is: Do we *choose* to be aware of the other (to make an "effort")? Or, is it simply a necessity of nature? Or, when we think we choose, do we not actually resist an obstacle, as we do in the face of destruction (entropy)? The fact that the other is not asking seems to suggest a context that is not really intersubjective so much as natural, pragmatic.

Levinas describes a separation in one's inner life that speaks to the phenomenon of self-sensing, a complex sensation between proprioception and consciousness. When we act without self-interest and without guarantee of effectiveness, we reveal to ourselves the deep relationship with another way of our existence with respect to nature. By separating our own self from the goal of the action performed on behalf of someone else, we replace self-interest with disinterestedness. Cohen's analysis of the notion of separation is especially effective when he describes the self-sensing being always divided in itself:[13] it is by virtue of this vulnerability (being torn apart, being easily wounded) that we paradoxically intervene in the vulnerable other's life. Or we might say that an intimation of insufficiency endows us with the necessary strength to help: being divided in ourselves constitutes the possibility of rising beyond ourselves. It is as if nature hinted at the bulk of its totality from the perspective of a lack. (Here we can't help referring to Kant's "superadded thought of totality," as elicited by a *feeling*, in *Critique of Judgment*, Analytic of the Sublime, § 23.)

When I have a chance to *feel* a part of a wider picture in which the other is not alien to myself, do I distinguish between sensing and thinking? When I risk my life to save another's, am I able to distinguish between responding (reaction), thinking (choice), and retroacting (inventing a solution)?

According to Cohen, *responding* to the other's suffering is not evidence that the will and not thinking is at stake;[14] an action that does not bring us any advantage is not immediate, it must be thought-of. We quickly separate ourselves from our immediacy, and my performance is a hybrid between feeling, thinking, and action. In contrast to Spinoza,

Levinas does not describe a disposition so much as he acknowledges a response to provocation[15] that, whatever the result, can be nothing more than amoral "commiseration," or a matter of personal pride or fear of judgment, which we feel *compelled* to accomplish. We are pushed to find the intelligence of the gesture: my action of rescue transcends myself and denies my (and the other's) individual self-sufficiency: so the separation from myself that I undergo requires a transcendence through a virtual connection. To be human means to transcend nature. Yet Spinoza takes the upper hand: being human means to rationally unify, to get *closer* to the totality of nature. It is not that we are "good" but that what is individual is naturally bound to deny its individuality. If a gesture of rescue is gratuitous, it denies a property, an authorship, any self- or mutual recognition, a meaning, an intention; far from being an individual quality and a choice, it is part of the super-organism that we are within the totality of nature.

Although a totality is far away with its closure, human fragility is capable of a gesture of self-despondency that implicitly hints at it and makes it present. It is true, conatus is a constant attempt to stay, whereas transcending in the other is a constant attempt to move on and out. (Spinoza calls it retrieving a lost equilibrium; Levinas calls it seconding a disequilibrium.) Yet can the two gestures fade into one? If we strive to stay in balance (Spinoza), it means that we are moving most of the time; if we surrender to an imbalance (Levinas), it means that we want to persist in our being.

Stability and Instability

Now, following Cohen's challenge: if Spinoza is able to reduce the feeling of pity/empathy to a natural countermotion that has no moral value other than its pragmatic (unguaranteed) results (and not in the actants of a case), how does he define vulnerability in a different way than just "weakness of mind"? Spinoza's readiness to pass to action against weakness is at the same time hypermasculine (a foreshadowing of the over-man?) and fully plausible. When we feel vulnerable, as well as when we witness the other's vulnerability, what we do at our best is to try to get out of that condition or help the other to do the same. If his philosophy does not envisage a moment of expression of pity (which Plato would relate to the feminine or the actor in a tragedy), it is by virtue of resistance against surrender and self-destruction.

It is the entirety of these facets that makes human sensibility transparent to itself. I imagine the war, the political institution, and social conflict as examples of the Spinozian pragmatic attitude of resistance and denial of weakness. And I imagine the poet, the novelist, the composer, the painter, the actor as examples of Levinas's emphasis on expression and comprehension. In both cases, though, there must be (if at stake there is responsibility and not a Romantic swooning) an action.

According to Levinas/Cohen that action is original. It is not a mere reaction if it is intrinsically "good." In reverse, according to Spinoza—and Nietzsche as foreshadowed by him—there is no guarantee of goodness in it.

> This pain, accompanied by the idea of our own weakness, is called humility; the pleasure, which springs from the contemplation of ourselves, is called self-love or self-complacency. And inasmuch as this feeling is renewed as often as a man contemplates his own virtues, or his own power of activity, it follows that everyone is fond of narrating his own exploits, and, displaying the force both of his body and mind, and also that, for this reason, men are troublesome to one another.[16]

The gratuitous gesture is an illusion (empty vanity, in Aristotelian terms); it can be made "theatrically," or by cultural rituality, or for an impulse to be praised, or to show off power. The same gesture can be a good as a negative passion. Later, Nietzsche will say: "Pity is pathological."[17] And Nietzsche offers another example of that "annoying" attitude:

> An accident which happens to another offends us: it would make us aware of our impotence, and perhaps of our cowardice, if we did not go to assist him. Or it brings with it in itself a diminution of our honor in the eyes of others or in our own eyes. Or an accident and suffering incurred by another constitutes a signpost to some danger to us; and it can have a painful effect upon us simply as a token of human vulnerability and fragility in general. We repel this kind of pain and offence and requite it through an act of pity; it may contain a subtle self-defense or even a piece of revenge.[18]

What Nietzsche calls *Mit-Leid* (pity) is not symmetrically shared by the two actors at stake; the feeling of the one differs from and remains obscure to the feeling of the other one. Empathy exits the scene—as it does in Levinas's description of separation—and what is left are two solitudes acting on or undergoing totally different experiences.[19] What seems to be the free purpose of a good action is but a countermotion, which avoids the diminution of the will to power: in Spinozian terms, despondency, diminution, are conditions in which we do not want to stay. Any instinctive subconscious help of the other has a degree of moral value that is not so much higher than it is ignoring the other completely.

As a matter of fact, self-separation is not so different from the distance between the ideal and the error Spinoza describes, that retroactive motion striving for a perfection however unattainable, therefore showing power and powerlessness simultaneously. Self-separation is just a matter of imagination. "But to conceive a thing as free can be nothing else than to conceive it simply, while we are in ignorance of the causes whereby it has been determined to action (II, XXX, note); therefore, an emotion towards a thing which we conceive simply is, other conditions being equal, greater than one, which we feel towards what is necessary, possible, or contingent and, consequently, it is the greatest of all."[20] We picture ourselves free because this affect of freedom seems stronger than necessity and even stronger than contingency. Imagination starts where adequate ideas end.

The fact that understanding the necessary causes a decrease in the power of affects (of imagination, of illusion) and therefore saves us from our own vulnerability, may be read as control of the mind over the body (Spinoza, the scholar of Descartes), or as an intimation of what the body is capable of (the mind lets the body speak: Spinoza the naturalist, or the phenomenologist).

The same can be said of the other basic affects such as fear and hope, love and hate, pain and pleasure, which cannot be appreciated in themselves since they can lead to the wrong path as well as to the right one. Fear of death can be either cowardice, a healthy stance to persist (conatus), or an antiphilosophical attitude (as in Plato's *Phaedo*). Hope can be either the engine of life or mere illusion. Love can be unselfishness as well as blind surrender. It is within the limits of nature (nature making itself: *natura naturans*) that love can exert its right power: "Therefore, although men are generally governed in everything by their own lusts, yet their association in common brings many more advantages than drawbacks. Wherefore it is better to bear patiently the wrongs they may do us, and to strive to promote whatsoever serves to bring about harmony and friendship."[21]

We are back to Aristotle's comparative logic of behavior. The senses are unreal as much as they are incontrovertible[22] and are therefore indefinite modifications of the totality, bounded by an overall stability, which is itself undeniable: any change can occur only within the laws of nature. Matter can do nothing more than what it can, though humans do not know all of its causes and possibilities. Given this premise, what we call transcendence is but a circular mode of endlessly modifying what exists in order to keep everything alive and in motion. Any attempt to invent another nature—a second nature—is an illusory escape from finitude (or from the fetters of nature). Materialism (admission of limit) takes over, by virtue of the very self-separation implied in the constant modification of nature.

Nonetheless, common to these opposed perspectives is the address to behavior as a means to surpass ourselves into what we do not know: whether we call it transcendence (an individual unguaranteed gesture) or conatus, the overall (universal and immanent) impulse to keep everything together. Disequilibrium (overcoming) and equilibrium (search for stability) are mutually implied: we won't ever find one without the other, each being a differential relational notion.

So far, we have seen how Levinas's liberation of transcendence from dogma parallels Spinoza's attempt to save materialism from mechanism. If the ultimate aim of knowledge is right behavior, it is because what happens to the mind happens to the body—and to whatever lives. Body, nature, matter, God, all of these are effects responding to laws (causes) and, if the connection between ideas were not the same as in the order of things, it would arise from an obscure source, unjustified and arbitrary: "We there showed that the idea of body and body, that is, body and mind (II.XIII) are one and the same individual conceived now under the attribute of thought, now under the attribute of extension."[23]

Spinoza's holism does not diverge from Levinas's individualism so much as the first introduces into the Western philosophical perspective an analysis of passions as intelligible phenomena of modifications, as opposed to the Cartesian analysis of mechanical reactions. A geometry of behavior does not necessarily mean to fix choices into rigid rational rules, but to analyze them in the light of their dynamics, in geometrical but vectoral structures; a stance that is not so far from Levinas's intention to liberate an intelligent (not just intelligible) body from its inert materiality. It seems to be both philosophers' general plan to turn knowledge into intelligible behavior. In both cases matter is released from its long-term relegation to passivity.

Although each philosopher uses his own language to allude to the right rules of behavior, in both cases ethics emerges from the limits of knowledge that compel self-sensing humans to understand themselves:[24] it is in this perspective that pity—distinguished from empathy, as we have seen—beside being an affect to be counteracted by a stronger one, in order to avoid self-commiseration and impotency,[25] is also a *recognition* of vulnerability, resulting in the consequent affects of patience, distance, and postponement, inherent in the conquest of the right behavior, and in the effort to coincide with a perfect state—call it a divine state, or ideal condition of stability, or rational lack of suffering. If we are vulnerable, we are also able to respond to it, that is, we must find a way to strengthen ourselves. Contrastingly, if we have the arrogance to feel stronger than we are, we will miss the chance to consider that "human" means just a small part of nature, and nothing special. If humility is wrong as self-diminution, the opposite affect of self-glorification is also wrong ("Extreme pride or dejection indicates extreme ignorance of self"[26]). What Spinoza (and maybe Nietzsche in his wake, as Cohen notices) appears to assume is that the alleged claim to be a kingdom within a kingdom of the human, superior to nature (and its necessary conflicts)—or a "second nature" as retrieved by Hegel from Aristotle—would have produced lasting effects and a deviation from the naturalness of cruelty, and the consequent feelings of fear (and hope) would have disappeared.[27] But this does not seem to be the case. No effects are detectable. Nature is always the same, or, in modern evolutionary terms, nature is *never* the same, and in neither case does it show a tendency, or a progress, or a telos that would be accomplished. A progressive definition of nature is an illusory picture to be replaced—after Darwinism—by its constant readjustment of its occasional unbalance and chaos. The human contribution to the dynamics of re-balancing the unbalance does not need transcendence, nor special faculties nor a special place in the universe. A gesture of unselfishness is part of that effort inherent in the conatus. In this perspective, conatus receives a quality of force vive if it includes the gesture of reaching out into the unknown at one's own risk.[28] In other words, persisting into one's being is more than inertially "obeying" the laws of nature. In fact, as Nietzsche said: there is no evidence of that obedience.[29]

A Living Inertia

Can there be a solution to this (seeming) opposition between a dynamics of nature and a provocation to transcend it? Is inertia dead force, or can we single out a quality of resistance that turns it into creative live force?

Examples are the constant homeostasis we keep in our bodies, in our minds, in the environment itself, by constantly correcting excessive or defective feedback (a field of research called cybernetics and developed by general systems theories). The dynamics of the homeostatic condition, present in any of our human complex reactions and choices that we call emotions and feelings, are the kind of unity of nature that Spinoza seems to refer to when he defines the conatus as the internal modifications that each substance undergoes to keep its stability. But that the conatus is inertial, or live, is modal and not substantial. Substance is nothing other than its modifications, nor are necessity and contingency two different aspects of the same phenomenon. A well-known Spinozian example of that is water: its indivisible unchangeable whole is what gives it the name of water (*sub specie aeternitatis*), but inside of it nothing remains the same; in fact it keeps appearing and disappearing (*sub specie temporis*).[30] So division (contingency, motion) is a *mode* of what is indivisible, a way to make sense of the indivisible. Making sense of the totality in infinite ways is a quality of imagination, if it endows nature with a meaning and aim (*this* water. Or water in a poem). At the same time imagination must rest upon some steady ground, *natura naturans*, or a unifying principle of the infinite modes in which matter manifests itself (the *concept* of water). Antonio Damasio, who considers Spinoza a pathfinder for ongoing neurological research about the role of feelings for rationality, calls this unitary principle the "nesting principle," in which both elementary life forms and complex human choices and decisions connect as one inside the other, the second growing from the first (though Damasio needs to add the *time* of evolution to Spinoza's atemporal descriptions), and each level of action is adjusted to the other by heterogeneous processes that keep somehow *one and the same* outcome:

> Each of the different regulatory reactions we have been considering is not a radically different process, built from scratch for a specific purpose. Rather, each reaction consists of tinkered rearrangements of bits and parts of the simpler processes below. They are all aimed at the same overall goal—survival with well-being—but each of the tinkered rearrangements is secondarily aimed at a new problem whose solution is necessary for survival with well-being.[31]

Damasio visualizes this dynamic as a "messy tree" in which the laws of nature must be constantly modified in order to fit the increasingly complex nest.[32] So, using Nietzsche as mediation, if nature does not "obey" laws so much as it re-arranges the ones it has, we can try to visualize a continuity between conatus (automatic behavior of the elementary vital processes) and free will (intentional, free and therefore ethical behavior of complex processes): at every different level the nest of Being is craved by conatus and transcended by the will.

Persistence (in the totality of what exists) is an ideal that nature in its whole accomplishes in its constant self-reproduction and self-regulation. But (or should I say, therefore?) persistence is also what is bound to transcend itself into the potentiality (*dynamis*) of ulteriority, if it is, as a matter of fact, *kept together* in a unity, as water is. Water does not *want* to persist, but it does have a cohesive force of its moving parts. Although the will may or may not be a human representation (a mental construct), it is undeniable that an *autotelia* must take place in the constant transformation needed to keep together each substance, to protect its homeostatic unity. Otherwise no science could exist, nor ethics.

It is a strange dynamic that makes its appearance here: the function of stability that passes through instability—the one being necessary for the other one; a dynamic detectable as an object of science and as a living being. An autotelic, cosmological auto-poiesis in which persistence and transcendence are parts of one system, which does not deaden life but, on the contrary, revives matter.

Why Do We Believe in Freedom?

After Nietzsche's deconstruction of "freedom" and the Good, we must now see why we cannot get rid of them. Once we see that freedom, altruism, and self-transcendence cannot show their evidence, we might be left with Spinoza's phenomenological description of their being "rational," but that would be begging the question.

To reiterate, we have a duty toward our power. If I am humble, if I fail to recognize my power, I won't be able to help: recognizing the existential vulnerability of the human (but also, why not of animals?) implies a strength. Only if I am strong—and am proud of it, without showing off and annoying others—can I help. Only if I invest all of my strength can I make sense of the other's need for me. Whether I do that out of a solipsistic self-affirmation, or out of my individual responsibility, does not make a big difference to the outcome. Especially for the vulnerable other.

In both cases, I try to *escape* a condition of uneasiness, I respond, I retroact: my freedom is negative freedom. I am free *from*. Is that impulse *force morte* (reaction) or *force vive* (freedom)? (Again, we can imagine Leibniz and Spinoza in dispute about it.)

Is there an original (free) action that is not just a response? I would like to use Hannah Arendt's phenomenological description of the act of forgiving as the evidence of freedom—an act specular to the gesture of help; by forgiving we interrupt time and we cut the continuity with the past. We replace reaction with free action.[33] By doing this for myself, I open the possibility of myself being part of the whole, as a virtual unity with the other. This description, quite similar to Levinas's definition of forgiveness as "acting upon the past,"[34] reinforces the idea that vulnerability (making oneself nonreactive, inertial) and strength (it takes enormous strength to forgive, and it takes a decision) are necessary to one another; they are passions as modes of one Being/matter.[35]

Similarly, Spinoza's notion of "weak mind" can be both the incapacity to react and the incapacity to not-react (as most people are not rational[36]). Through revenge and forgiveness humans appear to share both a state of nature and a divine nature.

Surely, forgiving (as helping) is *appreciated* as a civilized attitude, a noble gesture and a rational choice. But as we have shown, a pragmatist attitude might argue that appreciation cannot ignore cases in which forgiving (or helping) can be worse than revenge. We are back to Aristotle's *Nicomachean Ethics* and its table of virtues, at the same time universal (a work of reason) and circumstantial (a work of feelings). A noble gesture is a golden mean, a function, an environmental systemic relationship. It does not possess a "logic" that is not a minus/plus logic, infinitely modifiable, endowed with some kind of active energy, represented as freedom. A "moral" action is reducible to a natural material mode, whose actants are motion, rest, and the active feedback on each (excessive motion as for rest and vice versa).

Deus sive natura: in which *sive* is inclusive on condition of a mutual transformation, in terms of a motion/rest relationship (I move in order to rest)[37] and in terms of a full potentiality (I rest in order to move), that is, the effort to adapt contingencies to one's needs (causing a shift in a system and increasing its bearability). *Sive* is a bridge between the mechanical and the living, inertia and energy, the creature turned into its own creator. Motion is the very function preordained to God/nature, which allows for the transition. A continuous effort to turn contingency into necessity, chaos into lawfulness, motion is the necessary describable minimum, which must not hypostasize, fetishize, or give the divine and nature a tonality: "Whatsoever brings about the preservation of the proportion of motion and rest, which the parts of the human body mutually possess, is good; contrariwise, whatsoever causes a change in such proportion is bad."[38] The search for equilibrium is a condition of the existence of nature; each body needs many other bodies to survive and either inside of one body or outside we find an infinite number of interrelationships, a network of forces that must work together in order to keep an overall balance. Persistence in one's being means being intertwined, intersubjectively or interobjectively, in continuity with everything else moving and threatening that balance and self-creation.

Vulnerable here means modifiable through resistance and overcoming. No description of freedom escapes the challenge of negative freedom. An implicit resistance (and the necessity of it) is contained in the very definition of affect as potential, *dynamis*, conatus to keep the pleasure, proper to imperfect beings.[39]

A motion toward implies a motion from: *inertia* is not just an effect but also the effector of some (retro)action; it has a life of itself. If giving nature (or God) an end is anthropomorphic, considering dead force the only force in place fails to explain the existence of conatus triggered by an imagined ideal state. We *imagine* everything being explained through everything else, everything being produced by everything else, in infinite modes which do not imitate substance but accrete, co-grow within the living totality.

In consideration of Spinoza's revival (by virtue of Nietzsche's revival?) in the dramatic twentieth century, as an antidote to the illusions of the goodwill—in favor of the rational analysis of desire as a fact—and to the inadequacy of humanism as an annoying attitude of superiority, a redefinition of the feeling of piety appears to be necessary: however deconstructed, it remains the image of a paradoxical ethical *declaration* of nobility. Even if deconstructed as nothing "higher" or "nobler" than resistance to annihilation, it shapes images of nobility. Although when we feel free we acknowledge a psycho-physical state that is an effect whose causes or even its actual presence are not known; the effect is there anyway as a real affection, though sustained only by imagination: "However, no one has hitherto laid down the limits to the powers of the body, that is, no one has yet been taught by experience what the body can accomplish solely by the laws of nature."[40]

From the claim that no one knows "what the body can accomplish," it does not follow that the body can be ignored or even considered a contingent nuisance;[41] on the contrary, it is a deep appreciation of its potential—the extent of which we do not know enough about. A body moves according to physical laws that announce its potential intelligence. Not by chance the passage continues: "Nor need I call attention to the fact that many actions are observed in the lower animals, which far transcend human sagacity."[42]

The intelligence of the body appears through its *impotentia*, starts by the elementary opposition of pleasant/unpleasant, and proceeds with the mental oppositions of good/evil (according to the nest principle). This continuous passage from body to mind depletes the autonomy of conceptual language, which makes sense only if the material effects make a difference (it was Peirce who recognized Spinoza as a proto-pragmatist).[43] The continuity endows the body with a capacity to understand, to imagine and to act accordingly.

When Spinoza insists there is no contingency,[44] he does not mean to block the intelligence of the body in its machinery (otherwise he would not have abandoned the Cartesian legacy) but that there is no individual thing (or body) that can work alone, or by virtue of an individual will not submitted to necessity. Within the nest of Being (or God, or nature) the body finds and uses infinite possibilities. By making a decision, we contribute to the whole an infinitesimal part that leaves all the other parts unknown. But this effort is what we call "freedom." The effects a body detects on itself are all that we can talk about: they constitute the necessity of contingent acting and being acted upon that bodies are.[45] While tracing back the conceptual to the physical, Spinoza elevates the physical to an intelligence that imagines virtual causes of actual effects.

Conclusion

> Spinozian humans are not special beings but they think like angels.
> —Vladimir D'Amora

To recapitulate, there is no evidence of freedom that is not associable to conatus—no evidence of transcendence that is not already envisaged in nature. The power of the body remains partly unknown and the source of its being unselfish is there—and nowhere else—in terms of imagined possibilities. Having adequate ideas saves us from the illusion of being meaningful entities in the universe, endowed with a power that surpasses the power of a limited body/mind. Being unable to connect each singularity to every other singularity, our reason keeps to a few laws of nature that it takes as eternal and universal, and the claim of its own superiority is just a claim to imagine the privilege of freedom.

And, of course, here Kant has the conclusive word: if reason reaches out where it does not have experience (as said in the preface of the First Critique), recognizing at the same time its power and its limitations, its ultimate outcome is ethical, not cognitive. Spinoza appears able to incorporate Levinas; yet, when behaving with a gratuitous gesture of nonrequested generosity, out of which faculty do we act? There seems to be an *imagination* of reason, similar to the free interplay of the two faculties in Kant's aesthetic judgment: acting rationally means to anticipate, or imagine, possible "noble" consequences of our gesture—independently of its actual results. Beyond Being (the Platonic *epekeina tès ousìas*), beyond matter and also beyond knowledge, we have an *imagined* good, an *imagined* justice, which "cannot be abstracted away by thought."[46]

This recalls Kant's essay on progress and his description of the *beholder*, who, passing through the tragic successive betrayals of revolutions and rebellions against injustice, bears witness of and passes over, from generation to generation, the "testimony" of the freedom that was not achieved.[47] It takes imagination to do it. It takes monuments and traces of what did not succeed.

We are unable to think of contingency, unless we endow it with some imaginative cause. In the same mood we do imagine freedom (another way to say the contingency of necessity? Or death?), within whose scope lies a generous gesture uncalled for, of which we cannot exhibit any example but that we can represent to our reason through imagination. In other words, though imagination is the source of illusion, through it we can "represent" freedom to ourselves, that is, we express one of the possible modes of Being.

How to think of totality without an image of it? How to think of freedom without an image of it? Are the laws of nature thought of as logically deduced, or are they imagined as the *right* behavior of nature, as the conatus to keep together what would not, or does not, manage to be kept together forever? The threat of an imagined chaos is implied in the very notion of conatus. If the fetters of scientific laws are not always the same (whether they "evolve," as nature does, or they show to be less exact at the proof of experiment), an imaginative escape from finitude and necessity does exist, in the mind-matter of nature. Is not Spinoza's grand scenario of divine nature winning over a state of nature a visionary thought? Nowhere does he provide an answer about the way phenomena may "be manifest in various regions of meaning."[48]

A body that can do more than we know extracts itself from its own nature and ontologically produces "its ineffaceable testimony."[49]

Levinas wins on the penalty kick.

Notes

1. Emmanuel Levinas, *Totality and Infinity: An Essay on Exteriority*, trans. Alphonso Lingis (Pittsburgh: Duquesne University Press, 1969), 165.

2. The quotation from Grossman: The private kindness of one individual toward another; a petty, thoughtless kindness; an unwitnessed kindness. Something we could call senseless kindness. A kindness outside of any system of social or religious good. . . . This kindness, this stupid kindness, is what is most truly human in a human being. It is what sets man apart, the highest achievement of his soul. No, it says, life is not evil! Vasily Gossman, *Life and Fate*, Trans. Robert Chandler (New York: Harper and Row, 1985), 407–8, 409. Quoted in Cohen, Richard A. *Out of Control: Confrontations between Spinoza and Levinas* (Albany: SUNY Press, 2016), 26.

3. Baruch Spinoza, *Ethics More Geometrico Demonstrata*, trans. R. H. M. Elwes (Waiheke Island: The Floating Press, 2009), IV, 53. References to Spinoza's *Ethics* are given not in page numbers, but in the form of, for instance, Part, Proposition.

4. Spinoza, III, 6.

5. Aristotle, *Nicomachean Ethics*, trans. W. Ross, Kitchener (Ontario: Batoche Books, 1999), 6, 26–27.

6. Spinoza, *Ethics*, V, Note on 6.

7. Spinoza, *Ethics*, V, Note on 6.

8. Spinoza, *Ethics*, III, Definitions of emotions, 18.

9. Spinoza, *Ethics*, II, Concluding Note.

10. Aristotle, *Nicomachean* Ethics, 7, 29.

11. Cohen. *Out of Control*, 33.

12. Levinas, *Totality and Infinity*, 290.

13. Cohen, *Out of Control*, 38, 95.

14. Cohen, 40.

15. Cohen, 40.
16. Spinoza, *Ethics,* III, note on 55.
17. Friedrich Nietzsche, *Will to Power,* ed. Walter Kaufmann (New York: Random House, 1968), 199.
18. Friedrich Nietzsche, *Daybreak: Thoughts on the Prejudices of Morality,* ed. Maudemarie Clark and Brian Leiter (Cambridge: Cambridge University Press, 1997), 84.
19. Levinas, *Totality and Infinity,* 48.
20. Spinoza, *Ethics,* V, 5.
21. Spinoza, *Ethics,* IV, Appendix 14.
22. Cohen, *Out of Control,* 93.
23. Spinoza, *Ethics,* II, note on 21.
24. Cohen, *Out of Control,* 52.
25. Cohen, 84.
26. Spinoza, *Ethics,* IV, 55.
27. Spinoza, III, Preface.
28. Cohen, *Out of Control,* 47.
29. Nietzsche, *Will to Power,* 335.
30. Spinoza, *Ethics,* note 5 on 15.
31. Antonio Damasio, *Looking for Spinoza: Joy, Sorrow and the Feeling Brain* (London: Heinemann, 2003), 38.
32. Damasio, 38.
33. Hannah Arendt, *The Human Condition* (Chicago: University of Chicago Press, 1958), 236–37.
34. Levinas, *Totality and Infinity,* 283.
35. Spinoza, *Ethics,* IV, Appendix 13.
36. Spinoza, IV, Appendix 14.
37. Spinoza, IV, sch. 39.
38. Spinoza, IV, 39.
39. Spinoza, III, 2, 3.
40. Spinoza, III, 2, Note to 2.
41. Cohen, *Out of Control,* 302.
42. Spinoza, III, 2, note to 2.
43. Charles Sanders Peirce, *Collected Papers,* ed. Hartshome and Weiss (Cambridge, MA: Harvard University Press, 1974), 5.412.
44. Spinoza, *Ethics,* I, 29.
45. Spinoza, III, D3.
46. Cohen, *Out of Control,* 241.
47. Immanuel Kant, "A Renewed Attempt to Answer the Question: Is the Human Race Continually Improving?" in *Political Writings,* ed. H. Reiss (Cambridge: Cambridge University Press, 1970), 182.

48. Cohen, *Out of Control*, 291.
49. Levinas, *Totality and* Infinity, 117.

Bibliography

Arendt, Hannah. *The Human Condition*. Chicago and London: University of Chicago Press, 1958.
Aristotle. *Nicomachean Ethics*, trans. W. Ross, Kitchener. Ontario: Batoche Books, 1999.
Cohen, Richard A. *Out of Control: Confrontations Between Spinoza and Levinas*. Albany: State University of New York Press 2016.
Damasio, Antonio. *Looking for Spinoza: Joy, Sorrow and the Feeling Brain*. London: Heinemann, 2003.
Dea, Shannon. "Peirce and Spinoza's Pragmaticist Metaphysics." *Cognitio* 15, no. 1 (2014).
Grossman, Vasily. *Life and Fate*. Translated by Robert Chandler. New York: Harper and Row, 1985.
Kant, Immanuel. *Critique of Judgement*, edited by Pluhar. Indianapolis: Hackett, 1987.
Kant, Immanuel. "A Renewed Attempt to Answer the Question: Is the Human Race Continually Improving?" In *Political Writings*, edited by H. Reiss, 177–83. Cambridge: Cambridge University Press, 1970.
Levinas, Emmanuel. *Totality and Infinity: An Essay on* Exteriority. Translated by Alphonso Lingis. Pittsburgh: Duquesne University Press, 1969.
Nietzsche, Friedrich. *Will to Power*, edited by W. Kaufmann. New York: Random House, 1968.
Nietzsche, Friedrich. *Daybreak: Thoughts on the Prejudices of Morality*. Edited by Maudemarie Clark and Brian Leiter. Cambridge: Cambridge University Press, 1997.
Peirce, Charles Sanders. *Collected Papers*, edited by Hartshome and Weiss. Cambridge, MA: Harvard University Press, 1974.
Sorbi, Luca. *Aristotele: La logica comparativa*. Florence: Olschki, 1999.
Spinoza, Baruch. *Ethics More Geometrico Demonstrata*, trans. R. H. M. Elwes. Waiheke Island: The Floating Press, 2009.

14

Sovereignty in Levinas and Hobbes

Christopher Buckman

Midway through the first Trump administration, Attorney General Jeff Sessions appealed to scripture in defending the enforcement of President Trump's immigration policy. Attempting to tamp down moral outrage stoked by the separation of children from their parents at the Southern Border, Sessions declared: "I would cite to you the Apostle Paul and his clear and wise command in Romans 13, to obey the laws of the government because God has ordained the government for His purposes. Orderly and lawful processes are good in themselves." It is wrong to question government policy splintering asylum-seeking migrant families. Public reaction to Sessions's statement was swift and negative.

Sessions' employment of Romans 13 in this context is indeed shocking, though perhaps not for the reasons pundits assumed. The *Washington Post*, for instance, ran a column connecting the passage to nineteenth-century proslavery arguments, insinuating a sinister connection to Sessions's Alabamian worldview.[1] But this suggestion is unfair: from Augustine through the medieval European kings to the early modern philosophers, Romans 13 has been a locus classicus for debate in Christian political theory, a key text in the attempt to delineate the extent of political obligation of a religious subject to a worldly state. The antebellum South has no special claim on it.

What is truly disturbing is Sessions's evident interpretation of the passage. Romans 13 reads in part: "Let everyone be subject to the governing authorities, for there is no authority except that which God has established. The authorities that exist have been established by God. Consequently, whoever rebels against the authority is rebelling against what God has instituted, and those who do so will bring judgment on themselves." In isolation, and under influence of authoritarian interests, Romans 13 easily reduces to a frightening syllogism: all human authority is established by God's will, and it is wicked to rebel against God's will, therefore it is wicked to rebel against human authority. In no case are the laws or their executors to be questioned.

It should go without saying that this take on the epistle contradicts the central tenets of American political philosophy, traced back to Jefferson and inspired by Locke. It also defies the natural law theory of Augustine and Thomas Aquinas, employed by Martin Luther King Jr. in his indictment of Jim Crow. These sources stand in agreement in declaring that an unjust law is morally invalid and that a person of conscience must on occasion disobey established authority no matter the consequence. The contrary reading of the Bible is fundamentally un-Christian and anti-American.

To formulate a truer monotheistic doctrine of political obligation, other sources must be consulted. The Book of Samuel, containing the account of the reigns of Saul and David, offers a nuanced and perceptive analysis of political power. It is no surprise that, along with Romans 13, key passages from Samuel recur in the works of the political philosophers. The present chapter, following the example set by Richard A. Cohen in his elucidation of Emmanuel Levinas's political philosophy, investigates readings of 1 Samuel, chapter 8, given by Levinas and Thomas Hobbes. While Hobbes agrees with Sessions in asserting the inherent moral authority of the earthly sovereign, Levinas accepts the provisional necessity of human government while staying true to a morally sound suspicion of state power. The source of Hobbes's view is *Leviathan* chapter XX, "Of Dominion Paternal and Despotical," while we look for Levinas's understanding to his 1971 essay "The State of Caesar and the State of David." Both treat the biblical institution of monarchy as metonymic for state power generally; as Levinas writes, "It is the idea of kingship which expresses the principle of state control in biblical texts."[2]

The pairing of Levinas and Hobbes is not arbitrary. In the preface to *Totality and Infinity*, Levinas asks whether philosophical lucidity requires "catching sight of the permanent possibility of war," addressing the claim that the threat of violence grounds the political order.[3] Surely one of his unnamed interlocutors here is Hobbes, who reduces morality to a function of positive law and argues that subjects must transfer all rights to an absolute sovereign to escape the war of all against all. Morality only obliges in the event of a contract ensuring the integrity of further contracts: when no human force guarantees fair play, everything is permitted. For Levinas, the transcendent source of moral obligation, itself a condition of the constitution of subjectivity, demands moral comportment no matter the political situation. The moral law binds, as for Locke, independently of civil society.

Levinas's stance toward Hobbes is not, however, one of straightforward rejection. The continual threat of violence is no illusion. Levinas writes approvingly of the Talmudic commentators' anticipation of modern political theory, meaning, specifically, Hobbes: "Whatever its order, the City already ensures the rights of human beings against their fellow men, taken to be still in a state of nature, men as wolves for other men, as Hobbes would have it. Although Israel would see itself as descended from an irreducible fraternity, it is aware of the temptation, within itself and around it, of the war that pits everyone against everyone else."[4]

The essay from which this quotation is taken is, on one level, a polemic about Zionism. But that is not all: Levinas stakes out a more general political theory applicable to any state assessed from the point of view of morality and religion; he refers here to "the City in its simplest sense."[5] My task is to elucidate Levinas's conception of sovereignty and political obligation in contrast to Hobbes's absolutism. The City in its simplest sense—an earthly power—gains both its legitimacy and its limitations from its relation to the City in its allegorical sense: the divine order, the City of God.

This language—the City of Man, the City of God—which Levinas introduces in the first paragraph of his essay, is, of course, Augustinian. The view of politics taking shape in "The State of Caesar and the State of David" emerges in triangulation between Levinas's ethical philosophy, Augustine, and Hobbes. While the classical Christian conception of politics recognizes the role of "the barbed hooks of the executioner," restraining the wicked from preying on the good, it adds another dimension to the problem by insisting on the higher claim of religious morality, always regarding imperatives of state with mistrust, if not contempt. But Levinas suggests that the Christian theorists failed to properly formulate the relation of City of Man to City of God; "Christian monotheism," he writes, "has been unable to destroy" the idolatry of the state, not only in practice but also in theory.[6] The two towering figures of Christian political philosophy—Augustine and Thomas Aquinas—are ultimately unable to convincingly elaborate a monotheistic politics: Augustine because he tends to limit the activity of the state to the negative role of security (in addition to temporal punishment), deemphasizing a positive function in nurturing community, and Aquinas because, compromising the transcendent ground of morality in grafting his theology to Aristotelian naturalism, he joins the positive calling of earthly power to worldly teleology. He is not suspicious enough of the state. Levinas, by contrast, keeps state power at arm's length while still honoring its potential to alleviate suffering. While the state is a necessary evil, it may also be an imperfect, provisional instrument for securing positive rights.

Hobbes's interpretation of 1 Samuel 8 should be given special weight in this context because of its placement in his writings, within the elaboration of his doctrine in the first half of *Leviathan*, marking it as especially noteworthy or important.

The elders of Israel come to the last judge, Samuel, and inform him that the people, worried about defense against neighboring warlike nations, desire to be ruled by a king. Samuel balks. Until that point, the tribes have survived as a loose confederation, guided by priests and prophets, but recognizing no central authority but that of God. Avoidance of the idolatry of kingship, obedience to God alone has set them apart as a people. But times have changed. The ongoing war against the Philistines presents a continual threat. The Ammonites press from the east. The Amalekites bear a long-standing grudge. Given the no-quarter warfare illustrated in the two books of Samuel, the Israelites have legitimate reasons for prioritizing defense. Centralization of authority seems a necessity. God reluctantly agrees to permit the establishment of a hereditary monarchy but instructs Samuel to inform the people of the cost:

> These will be the ways of the king who will reign over you: he will take your sons and appoint them to his chariots and to be his horsemen, and to run before his chariots; and he will appoint for himself commanders of thousands and commanders of fifties, and some to plow his ground and to reap his harvest, and to make his implements of war and the equipment of his chariots. He will take your daughters to be perfumers

and cooks and bakers. He will take the best of your fields and vineyards and olive orchards and give them to his courtiers. He will take one-tenth of your grain and of your vineyards and give it to his officers and his courtiers. He will take your male and female slaves, and the best of your cattle and donkeys, and put them to his work. He will take one-tenth of your flocks, and you shall be his slaves. (1 Samuel 8, 11–17)

Hobbes favors this passage because it dramatizes his account of the constitution of the commonwealth: through a conscious choice, aware of the consequences, driven by fear of violent death, individuals consent to strict limitation of freedoms and enjoyments in exchange for security. They acknowledge the rights and powers of the sovereign in advance. In Hobbes's terminology, the Book of Samuel illustrates an instance of the establishment of sovereignty by institution, a voluntary contract erecting a human sovereign power where none previously existed.

The biblical prerogatives of the king correspond to Hobbes's rights of the sovereign in *Leviathan* XVIII, Of the Rights of Sovereigns by Institution, which include taxation, the formation and control of the military, the right of punishment, and so forth. The oppression of the people by the monarch is not arbitrary or contingent but of the essence of the sovereign power; it follows from the requirements of national defense. As Moshe Halbertal and Stephen Holmes write in their study of Samuel, "The very act of organizing the people for self-defense inescapably involves a painful degree of tyrannical subordination, resource-extraction, and unfreedom."[7] Hobbes makes the point directly: "Here [in 1 Sam 8] is confirmed the right that sovereigns have, both to the *militia* and to all *judicature*, in which is contained as absolute power as one man can possibly transfer to another."[8]

Hobbes ignores God's concern in granting the right of sovereignty to a human monarch. The emphasis falls squarely on the absolute power wielded by the king, not as an abuse but as divinely sanctioned justice. Hobbes understands Samuel's message as terms of a contract: In order to save yourselves from your enemies, this is what you must agree to pay. God then vests the sovereign with those rightful powers. It comes as no surprise, then, to see among the most commonly cited biblical passages in *Leviathan* Romans 13, in its most authoritarian interpretation.

Levinas divides his political essay, "The State of Caesar and the State of David," into three sections: "Yes to the State," "Beyond the State," and

"Toward a Monotheistic Politics." By this division alone we already see that his intent is to formulate a conception of sovereignty acknowledging the necessity of state power while keeping sight of the "beyond," the exigent moral demand independent of human law. Only the juxtaposition of two realms of order can claim the name of monotheistic politics.

In contrast to Hobbes, Levinas's reading of 1 Samuel emphasizes God's hesitance in granting Israel a monarch. Realpolitik demands moral compromise. As Halbertal and Holmes explain, the reigns of Saul and David offer endless examples of the "double reversal" of ends and means: for the political leader, the sacred becomes a tool for maintaining power, while the instrumental good of power, intended initially for national defense, is elevated to a final goal. To have a king is to entrust the affairs of the people to a man irresistibly tempted by this reversal. Should the people acquiesce to this compromise? Is the individual morally bound to obey an unprincipled sovereign?

Levinas cites the Tractate Temurah of the Babylonian Talmud: "It is better that one letter of the Torah should be uprooted than that the whole Torah should be forgotten," identifying the uprooting of the letter with the establishment of human sovereignty.[9] Staving off total obliteration sometimes requires compromise. But there is never any question of the transfer of divine right to the earthly power, as in Hobbes. This, for Levinas, equals idolatry because it raises the merely human to the level of perfection. The extent of political obligation remains open to continual reassessment and renegotiation.

A second illuminating foil to Levinas's view is the political theory of St. Augustine, which, as Herbert A. Deane observes, resembles that of Hobbes but with the addition of a theological plane, a "beyond" required by monotheism.[10] Levinas implicitly charges Augustine with failing to frame the correct relation between the state and its beyond. This is because, for Augustine, a Platonist, God's law enters history as a completed plan, an eternal template of which this earthly existence represents a fallen shadow. Every moment presents the Christian with a stark choice: accept either the law of God or the law of man; one can follow one but not both, and no servant can serve two masters. It is true that Augustine ultimately acquiesces to the necessity of accommodation with earthly power for the purpose of preserving security, a relationship contained in the injunction to render unto Caesar what is Caesar's. But the legitimate moral power of the state lies within a definite boundary: its only justification is that police authority permits Christians to lead pious lives unharmed by evil men.

This configuration proves unstable. Augustine's initial characterization of government identifies the ruling authority as differing not at all from a large gang of thieves; only the fragile "peace of Babylon" accompanying their monopoly on power offers a public advantage over open warfare between rival gangs. But if the state is an unfortunate necessity, naturally tending toward evil, Augustine reasons, Christians should minimize that evil by participating as government officials when called upon. And if Christians are already involved in the state in this capacity, he comes to believe, it is incumbent upon them to use state power to protect the interests of the Church: Why allow men to pursue evil when the tools exist to stop them? Consequently, Christians should employ state power to discipline heretics. Augustinian politics shuttles back and forth between libertarian wariness of government, on one hand, and authoritarian excess, on the other.

The essential difference in Levinas's position, upending the Augustinian-Hobbesian conception, is in the gradualness of the entrance of God's order in history, the temporality of divine justice, in contrast to its eternal permanence. He writes:

> The ultimate elevation of the Revelation would be due to its need for a response, its quest for interiority. It is precisely in this sense that it is a teaching or Torah. But it thus needs time. The weakness of something that needs time in order to develop must not be regarded abstractly: it points positively here to an order that is greater than the eternity of Platonic Ideas or Aristotelian forms—an order in which a spirit is in relation with the Other, which brings to the spirit more than it is capable of alone. An order in which limits are surpassed, but an order which, by this very fact, exposes itself to risks.[11]

Levinas here rejects the Platonic monotheism of Augustine and the Aristotelian monotheism of Thomas Aquinas for inadequately expressing the moral status of state sovereignty. First, the Platonic view conceives the moral law as already complete, all-or-nothing, granted by an imperious divine act. Guaranteed by a single transformative moment of salvation, Platonic monotheism courts apocalypse: the stark disjunction between the light of heaven and the dark of worldly sin neglects the delicate work of tending the relation to the other, which breathes life into the human spirit. It fails to grasp the intertwining of the good with the world. Second, Thomist Aristotelianism imbeds in nature the eternal hierarchy of moral value, forgetting the elusive relation to that which wholly transcends. Because the moral order, in Levinas's understanding, takes root precariously and grows slowly, exposed to real danger from the harsh elements, aid from worldly forces should not be casually dismissed; neither should we ignore the potential of those forces to advance the demands of justice, despite the essential ambiguity of the sovereign's motivations. Irreducible to the police, government is intimately involved, for better or worse, with the development of the human spirit.

Levinas confirms the Messianic possibility of the state, biblically signified by the promise to the Davidic line to reign over the fulfillment of history. We look to the earthly sovereign for the pacification of this world. Since the rightful function of the state is the formation of earthly good, we must allow it needed tools. Do we then end up in the same place as Hobbes? Must we say with Sessions that lawful processes are good in themselves? Levinas rejects this line of thought by distinguishing between two separate historical goals: "The Messianic State which seems to be entirely incorporated into Israel's destiny . . . mark[s] only a stage, a transition. Indeed, numerous Talmudic passages describe a finite duration to the Messianic era. The true end of eschatology is the future world. It involves possibilities that cannot be structured according to a political schema." He continues: "These texts can . . . be read as announcing new possibilities of the human Spirit, a new distribution of its centers, a new meaning of life, and new relations with the other."[12] By holding apart the provisional role of state power from the final good of human life, Levinas forestalls the absorption of ethics into state authority.

Levinas's central argument indicates that the state of David does not in fact differ from the state of Caesar in the type of justice it metes out, or even in its aim, which in both cases is equitable outcomes for all people. The sole difference between the state of Caesar and the state of David lies in the expected motivations of governmental actors. Governors steeped in the ethical life will be more likely to aim for the good, but the nature of the good remains identical for all states.

The role of the state, defensive in character—though what it defends is defined not only in terms of life and property but also as well-being and spirit—plays a specific historical role with corresponding limitations. The future world, the world beyond politics, measures justice. The state's injunctions bear the weight of compromise and hard necessity. The clash between two distinct points of view adopted within the Hebrew Bible, sometimes referred to as "prophetic" and "kingly," reveals the tension between the imperatives of the two orders. Why does God forswear monarchy at some points and sanctify it at others? While often assumed by historical-critical interpreters to result from the redactive aggregation of promonarchical and antimonarchical sources, it is instructive to read the text as deliberately presenting conflicting aspects of the whole.[13] One of these strands expresses the hostility toward human hierarchy, sometimes fanatical, which Michael Walzer refers to as "antipolitics."[14] We call God "King" not because the term stands in a metaphorical relation to the human institution but in a literal sense: God alone can rule justly over His people. Human kingship usurps divine right. Here is the voice of Samuel warning the Israelites to reject the pagan practice of monarchy, the voice of Nathan brazenly calling David to task for the murder of Uriah.

Opposing antipolitics, the monarchical voice advocates "normal politics"—the accommodation with social reality ensuring peace, prosperity, and human convenience. The problem with the charismatic leaders promoted ad hoc by God to save the people is their unreliability. The normal course of events demands normalized political institutions, and this is why we have kings.[15] Levinas gives normal politics its due when he says "yes" to the state, knowing that the requirements of everyday morality are best met with human initiative and self-organization; he does not, however, turn away from the distant gleam of justice, antipolitics of the future world.

How does the future world make its demands? What is the temporal character of futurity itself, opening the forward-looking horizon of political thought? These questions go directly to the heart of Levinas's philosophical project, which recognizes ethics as first philosophy, insisting that the alterity and transcendence revealed in the face of the other not only ground moral obligations, but precede and make possible the temporal structure of intersubjective experience.

Richard A. Cohen identifies Henri Bergson's break with the traditional philosophical conception of time as decisive for contemporary philosophy.[16] For Bergson, time is not an abstract formal sequence but a vital process of evolutionary development. Husserl recapitulates Bergson's description of lived time as the cumulative growth of being in a more rigorously phenomenological account of retention and protention, which Heidegger then translates into the existential structure of Dasein's being-toward-death. While acknowledging and benefitting from the advantage these theories have over the traditional view, namely that they do justice to the irreducibility of past, present, and future, Levinas supersedes these earlier thinkers in identifying alterity as the only possible break in the totality of being, the only legitimate transcendence able to rupture the enclosed inwardness of the self. Levinas judges the role one's own death plays in the Heideggerian philosophy to be inadequate for gathering subjectivity into "resoluteness," as Heidegger would have it. In its place, Levinas teaches that the call to help the other—to alleviate suffering—realizes the temporal structure resisting being's totalizing reduction. It is because, as Cohen explains, I am always too late to prevent the suffering of the one who stands before me because the past in which the suffering began will never be present for me to fulfill my obligation, that I can have my fixed past at all. This out-of-reach "time immemorial" of the other's need stakes down my temporal structure, which Heidegger conceived of as stretched out, but without anchor. Cohen writes: "Here, then, in moral obligation, the subject morally *subject* to the other, *serving* the other, Levinas finds the source of the ultimate or paradigmatic sense of pastness: a past that never was or can be present."[17] But if the past belongs to the other before me, whose face shatters my inwardness, my obligation to all others releases the future. The future world is the horizon of justice, the field in which conditions will be set for suffering to be healed. In the present we take up the "normal politics" of doing the best we can. But purposefully facing the future means holding back the dispersal of moral obligation in the immediate demands of state policy.

Compare Hobbes. It is true that for us, members of civil society, the open warfare of the state of nature lurks in the past, overcome by the commonwealth established through the social contract. That bellicose world of human suffering, however, is not the irrecoverable "time immemorial" of Levinas. On the contrary: the war of all against all threatens always to burst into the present, dragging us back into primitive conflict. We are never done with it. Traces of the state of nature resurface in the guarded behavior of everyday citizens when they arm themselves for travel and secure their lockboxes in fear of being stripped of valuables by members of their own households.[18] On occasion, upon the disintegration of sovereign power in civil war, the state of nature returns in its full actuality. Hobbes interprets his own experience of the English Civil War in this way. In the rejection of prophetic antipolitics, in the embrace of the normal politics of kingship founded on force and the fear of force, the Hobbesian viewpoint normalizes the random recurrence of violence endemic to security-obsessed civil society.

The future, for Hobbes, promises more of the same. The logic of being, reduced to the lawful development of homogeneous matter and simple motion, dictates a single, inescapable outcome. If an individual fails to signal express consent to the social contract, we assume hypothetical consent: It is what any rational person would do. The choice is no choice at all. God Himself is thought to be a corporeal body, a material substance. Nothing escapes totality.

Levinas, significantly, includes a note in "The State of Caesar and the State of David" calling attention to the Marxist conception of the state. The unknowability of the future world, at least in detail, "oddly calls to mind the strange passages where Marx expects socialist society to bring changes in the human condition, frustrating any prediction by virtue of their actual revolutionary essence."[19] The good of this world grows slowly, forms gradually, and takes on its final meaning and form only in the light of events as of yet unintelligible.

This qualification of the historical mission of the sovereign power defeats its claim to embody the moral law in any absolute sense. While David receives the ongoing favor and promise of God, we must not therefore approve of his sins, or participate in them. Levinas writes in this connection that the ultimate end of a person is "the possibility of listening only to my own conscience, and of rejecting the reasons of state."[20] In his understanding of 1 Samuel 8, God's disinclination to permit the designation of the sovereign invites a constant vigilance, an ongoing concern that state power might be wielded for the wrong ends. For Hobbes such a deviation between the will of the sovereign and the moral good is simply not possible.

Along with Sessions, Hobbes would insist on the total right of the executive to regulate national borders by any means. The sovereign's subjects would be duty-bound to participate: "The measure of good and evil is the law." But conscience, Levinas teaches, resists reasons of state when I am called to attend to human suffering. That the state is needed to keep order does not imply that citizens should never question orders of the state.

Notes

1. See https://www.washingtonpost.com/news/acts-of-faith/wp/2018/06/14/jeff-sessions-points-to-the-bible-in-defense-of-separating-immigrant-families/?noredirect=on&utm_term=.a49e7a5fba56 (accessed January 24, 2025).

2. Emmanuel Levinas, "The State of Caesar and the Sate of David," *Beyond the Verse: Talmudic Readings and Lectures* (Bloomington: Indiana University Press, 1994), 177.

3. Emmanuel Levinas, *Totality and Infinity*, trans. Alphonso Lingis (Pittsburgh: Duquesne University Press, 1969), 21.

4. Ibid., 183.

5. Ibid.

6. Ibid., 186.

7. Moshe Halbertal and Stephen Holmes, *The Beginning of Politics: Power in the Biblical Book of Samuel* (Princeton, NJ: Princeton University Press, 2017), 11.

8. Thomas Hobbes, *Leviathan* (Indianapolis: Hackett, 1994), XX.16.

9. Levinas, "State of Caesar," 179.

10. Herbert A. Deane, *The Political and Social Ideas of St. Augustine* (New York: Columbia University Press, 1963), 234–36. "It might be said that the Hobbesian theory or vision of man and society is the Augustinian vision after God and the City of God have been eliminated. . . . In addition, Hobbes theory demonstrates the effects of the Reformation and Calvinism by grounding the political order on the freely given consent of each member of society, whereas Augustine simply accepts political authority as inevitable after the Fall and does not inquire into its origins" (Deane, 236).

11. Levinas, "State of Caesar," 179.

12. Ibid., 185.

13. Lyle M. Eslinger, *Kingship of God in Crisis* (Sheffield: JSOT Press, 1985), 37.

14. Michael Walzer, *In God's Shadow: Politics in the Hebrew Bible* (New Haven, CT: Yale University Press, 2012), xiii.

15. Ibid., 69.

16. Many of the ideas in this paragraph come from Cohen's "Being, Time, and the Ethical Body," *Levinasian Meditations* (Duquesne University Press, 2010), 37–56.

17. Ibid., 52–53.

18. Hobbes, *Leviathan* XIII.9.

19. Levinas, "State of Caesar," 217, n18.

20. Ibid., 186.

Bibliography

Cohen, Richard A. "Being, Time, and the Ethical Body." In *Levinasian Meditations*, 37–56. Pittsburgh: Duquesne University Press, 2010.

Deane, Herbert A. *The Political and Social Ideas of St. Augustine*. New York: Columbia University Press, 1963.

Eslinger, Lyle M. *Kingship of God in Crisis*. Sheffield: JSOT Press, 1985.

Halbertal, Moshe, and Stephen Holmes. *The Beginning of Politics: Power in the Biblical Book of Samuel*. Princeton, NJ: Princeton University Press, 2017.
Hobbes, Thomas. *Leviathan*. Indianapolis: Hackett, 1994.
Levinas, Emmanuel. "The State of Caesar and the Sate of David." In *Beyond the Verse: Talmudic Readings and Lectures*. Bloomington: Indiana University Press, 1994.
Walzer, Michael. *In God's Shadow: Politics in the Hebrew Bible*. New Haven, CT: Yale University Press, 2012.

15

On Ethics

Levinas and Badiou in the Post-Postmodern Condition

Chung-Hsiung Lai

Introduction: The Ethical Return in the Post-Postmodern Condition

Postmodern philosophy as a philosophy of *difference* takes delight in *decentering* all the unwarranted and unsubstantiated assumptions of modernist thought while emancipating the individual and generating little narratives. However, by showing that the grand narrative picture is never entirely within any human grasp, postmodern philosophy introduces a fatal relativism—there is no objective, universal, and transcendental truth. Truth is only relative to some particular frame of reference, such as power, language, religion, or culture. Moreover, it promotes a radical "de-centered" subject and thus paradoxically constructs a "de-subjected" subject—there is no certainty or fixed humanism for any human subject. By doing so, postmodern philosophy also deprives the subject of its inherent and potential morality regarding the fundamental need for "Being-with" in the world. Admittedly, postmodern philosophy falls short in tackling the new ethical problems arising in the world.

Since the 1990s, it has become possible for us to detect "a return of ethical thought" in what can be called "the post-postmodern condition."[1] The question of the ethical return in this new ontological and epistemological context raises the question of the recent trends in contemporary philosophy, especially Continental philosophy. It has marked the beginning of a new era of contemporary philosophy in an increasingly globalized world, where the greater actual and virtual interconnectedness among people, and thus the greater interconnectedness of thorny problems, requires that "ethics" be applied both ontologically and epistemologically. Since this new human condition is driven mainly by the political, social, cultural, and economic trends of globalization and digitalization, we must acknowledge that the debatable concepts of "truth," "community," "the subject," "difference," and "the Other" definitely come into play when re-conceptualizing "ethics" in the post-postmodern context. Alain Badiou's *Ethics: An Essay on the Understanding of Evil* has been one of the most discussed and debated works on ethics in this ethical return of Continental philosophy.

This book mainly attacks three problems: ethical ideology, Levinas's ethics, and Badiou's "Evil." Specifically, Badiou demonstrates the problems of a humanistic understanding of "the rights of man," the notion of the Other, and a consensus about the existence of the evil (still popular in the twenty-first century), while trying to defend "the anti-humanism of the 1960s" as perceived in the thoughts of Foucault, Althusser, and Lacan. Badiou states: "I was driven by a genuine fury. The world was deeply plunged in 'ethical' delirium. Everyone was busily confusing politics with the hypocrisy of a mindless catechism. The intellectual counter-revolution, in the form of moral terrorism, was imposing the infamies of Western capitalism as the new universal model."[2] Against this commonsensical concept of contemporary ethics, Badiou proposes an ethics that emphasizes the importance of "truth processes" in which human subjects engage to ward off "Evil."

So far, the ethical turn in the post-postmodern condition has left the door open to a great variety of ethical positions. To engage in this ongoing "ethical turn" dialogue, this essay aims to compare the ethical philosophies of Levinas and Badiou, mainly through a careful examination of Badiou's criticism of contemporary ethics. For Levinas, ethics is the ethics of goodness, which can only be realized through a transcendental relation with the Other. Badiou contends that there can be no ethics in general or in a transcendental relation. If ethics is possible, then it is the ethics of truth, which can only be unfolded in "the event" or its four conditions (science, politics, art, and love). Accordingly, this paper aims to explore the following questions: What are Badiou's critiques of ethical ideology, Levinas's ethics, and Evil? What are the problems of Badiou's ethics? What are the differences and similarities between the two thinkers?

Badiou's Critique of Ethical Ideology, Levinas's Ethics, and Three Evils

> No doubt, after the "death of man" pronounced first by Heidegger, but then also by Althusser, Foucault, Lacan, and Deleuze, the works of Levinas have indeed forced the philosophical world to reconsider and once again take seriously the position of ethics.[3]
>
> —Cohen, *Levinasian Meditations*

> Rather than link the word [ethics] to abstract categories (Man or Human, Right or Law, the Other. . .), it should be referred back to particular *situations*. Rather than reduce it to an aspect of pity for victims, it should become the enduring maxim of *singular processes*. Rather than make it merely the province of conservatism with a good conscience, it should concern the destiny of truths, in the plural.[4]
>
> —Badiou, *Ethics*

Since the contemporary politics of difference is not self-sufficient, it requires support from contemporary ethics. In fact, in the twenty-first century, all kinds of difference-oriented politics and aesthetics in postmodern philosophy have reached their limits and have begun to give way to the concepts of "community," "being-with," "singular-plural," "hospitality," and so on—a return of ethics. In brief, if we want to escape the trap of postmodern politics, the political implications of Levinas's ethics provide some positive forms of politics that are forever ethical. That is, Levinas's ethics can preserve the virtuous characteristics of humanity (morality, compassion, love, hospitality, care, and so on) and bring them into the sphere of politics in the post-postmodern condition. Even though Levinas's ethics (and its political implications), as Richard Cohen points out, have forced the contemporary philosophical world to reconsider and once again take the position of ethics seriously, it has also attracted criticism from different quarters. Badiou's *Ethics* may prove to be the most provocative contemporary challenge to Levinas's ethics in the current trend of the ethical turn.

In *Ethics*, Badiou mainly criticizes a contemporary ethical ideology, Levinas's Other, and the idea of Evil to introduce his ethics of truth. As one of the most significant philosophers in France today, Badiou is in a fury about how today's "moral terrorism" imposes the infamies of Western capitalism as the new universal ethical paradigm, especially in the name of "human rights." This is why he wrote *Ethics* after *Being and Event* and *Second Manifesto for Philosophy*. For Levinas, the Other is not only wholly otherwise than being but also the Other only if s/he immediately evokes the absolutely and divinely Other. Badiou argues that it is Levinas's idea of "the Other," which has led to the current ethical ideology (such as human rights), hypocritical moralism (such as generalized victimization), and mindless cultural catechism (such as multiculturalism). Therefore, he believes that if we want to change the current moral terrorism, we must first abandon Levinas's moral radicalism.

Since ethics mainly aims to regulate moral conduct and deals with "how we relate to 'what is going on,'"[5] it can be conceived as a system of social norms that governs judgments and opinions regarding good and evil. Therefore, Badiou asserts that ethics is closer to a Kantian ethics of judgment than to a Hegelian ethics of decisions today. Since a human subject possessing all kinds of "rights" is now held to be self-evident or natural, the term "ethics" usually relates to a system regulating judgments and opinions about "the rights of man" in general (such as natural and legal rights) and "human rights" in particular. These ethical rights are the result of a broad consensus in the world of globalization.

Such contemporary ethics as an ethical ideology, for Badiou, is based on an ethic of difference, of others, or the Other. Its basic feature is to see humans as fragile, needy, and mortal beings whose good consists in the avoidance of pain and death. Ethical ideology "thus defines man *as a victim*."[6] Badiou argues that "because the status of victim, of suffering beast, of emaciated, dying body, equates man with his animal substructure, it reduces him to the level of a living organism pure and simple."[7] Badiou's ethic of truths defines humanity as a human animal whose resistance lies not in his fragile body or the absolute Other but in his stubborn determination to remain "something" other than a being-as-a-victim and a being-for-death. This "something" is what Badiou calls "an immortal" as a truth's eternal status, which makes a human animal genuinely human rather than other mortal animals.

Because man is "*the being who is capable of recognizing himself as a victim*,"[8] it is possible for a man to literally live from hand and mouth, "a biped without feathers." However, man is also the being who is capable of being immortal[9]—one can choose to live as "an immortal" insofar as he is involved in truths. Therefore "if 'rights of man' exist, they are surely not rights of life against death or rights of survival against misery. They are the rights of the Immortal, affirmed in their own right, or the rights of the Infinite, exercised over the contingency of suffering and death."[10] Human subjectivation, Badiou states, is immortal and makes Man. One has to choose between Man as the basis for the uncertainty of truths and Man as being-for-death, being-as-a-victim, or being-for-happiness. It is this same choice that distinguishes philosophy as truth from ethical ideology as nihilism regarding ethics.

One, therefore, must challenge the immortal disjunction that affects any given situation of truth. Badiou argues that since the framework of ethical ideology equates man with a simple mortal animal, constructs the victimized definition of man, and prevents man from grasping the singularity of situations, we must reject this ideology as such. In short, the issues of ethics of truth, for Badiou, happens only in a specific situation and under particular circumstances created by a truth procedure that is essentially indifferent to the differences of universalized others in the world. The ethical ideology of "the rights of man," on the contrary, aims to transcend all situated barriers and to prevail in an ideological consensus beyond divisions of race, gender, class, religion, and country, all the while remaining orientated around the pressing and imperative demands of difference and otherness.

I will summarize Badiou's "three theses" as reasons against ethical ideology. *Thesis one*: man needs to identify himself by his affirmative thought, singular truths, and "the Immortal" (the creation of his infinity in truth procedures), which differentiates him from animals. *Thesis two*: Man should not identify himself with Evil (Badiou's idea of Evil will be elaborated in the next section) because he has positive possibilities and the capability of refusing conservatism and pursuing goodness. *Thesis three*: there is no ethics in general but only in particular, by which Man treats the possibilities of a given situation. That is, all humanity has its root in the identification of the thought of singular situations.[11]

Yet, all these three statements against ethical ideology inevitably attack its theoretical cornerstone (namely, Levinas's ethics) because "the conception of ethics as the 'ethics of the other' or the 'ethics of difference' has its origin in the theses of Emmanuel Levinas rather than in those of Kant."[12] Badiou believes that Levinas's ethics (the ethics of the

Other) subordinates the subject's identity to difference and thus paves the way for the current fashion of ethical difference as "a kind of ethical radicalism." He strategically inserts the voices of those who will object to his argument before critically examining the Levinasian concept of the Other: "At this point, the refined man of ethics will object, murmuring: 'Wrong! Wrong from the beginning. Ethics is in no sense founded on the identity of the Subject, not even on his identity as recognized victim. From the beginning, ethics is the ethics of the other; it is the principal opening to the other, it subordinates identity to difference.' Let us examine this line of argument."[13] Badiou then raises his main objection to Levinas's ethics: "What is it that testifies to the originality of my devotion to the Other?" His criticism of Levinas's ethics is mainly twofold: Firstly, he believes that Levinas's phenomenological discourse fails to "guarantee" the primacy of the ethics of the Other over the truth of the Same.[14] Following Derrida's argument,[15] Badiou draws his criticism first on the ontological ground of Levinas's phenomenological analyses, such as the ideas of the face, the caress, and love. He points out that Levinas proposes a whole series of phenomenological themes to legitimate the originality of the absolute Other in *Totality and Infinity*. All these ethical concepts, for Badiou, cannot by themselves ground "the anti-ontological thesis" or "fleshly epiphany." Without the solid ground of an ontological thesis, Levinas's phenomenological ethics breaks its "logical chains" in favor of the mysterious ground of the Other's alterity. That is, if one wants to consider the ethical primacy of the Other over the Same, one needs to require that "experience of alterity be ontologically 'guaranteed' as the experience of a distance, or an essential non-identity, traversal of which is the ethical experience itself. But nothing in the simple phenomenon of the other contains such a guarantee."[16] Does "the Other" exist ontologically? The answer is "no" for Badiou.

Secondly, he contends that Levinas's ethics is the product of theology rather than philosophy. As we know, Levinas claims that ethics is the "first philosophy" not based on metaphysical or ontological experiences but is a phenomenological description of the rise and repetition of face-to-face encounters with the Other. The face of the Other always already commands me to respond to its calls in an asymmetrical way. When the face of the Other appears to me (the finite being), it must be intelligible. However, how can we know the face we encounter as a phenomenon is not just a "mimetic recognition" (the other reflected as myself)? This question means "ethics requires that the Other be in some sense carried by a principle of alterity that transcends mere finite experience. Levinas calls this principle the "Altogether-Other," and it is quite obviously the ethical name for God. There can be no Other if he is not the immediate phenomenon of the Altogether-Other."[17] It is the encounter with the immediate phenomenon of the Altogether-Other, and its ethical demand under the absolute Other's ineffable authority, which enables Badiou to accuse Levinas of conflating the thoughts of philosophy with those of theology.

Levinas, for Badiou, can be seen as "an inventive thinker" who has no Greek logic, no academic reasoning, and thus no real philosophy. He further explains that Levinas's attributing ethical dominance to the absolute Other over the ontology of the same is not guided by a philosophical axiom but "a religious axiom." Because what Levinas truly has in his ethics are "subjective rigor" and "religious piousness." His philosophy is not even qualified as "the servant to theology;" it is completely annulled by theology.[18] Badiou states: "Levinas's enterprise serves to remind us, with extraordinary insistence, that every effort to turn ethics into the principle thought and action is essentially religious."[19] Accordingly, if we take away all Levinasian ethics' religious aspects, there is nothing left but a "dog's dinner"—"We are left with a pious discourse without piety, a spiritual supplement for incompetent governments, and a cultural sociology preached, in line with the new-style sermons, in lieu of the late class struggle."[20] This twofold criticism leads Badiou to conclude that Levinas's ethics is neither a philosophy nor a theology but rather an antiphilosophical ethics presented as a pious discourse.

After exploring Badiou's criticism of ethical ideology and Levinas's Other, we need to examine his critique of "the problems of evil" to introduce his ethics of truth. Badiou's discussion of evil (as a problem of ethical ideology) constitutes the bulk of the book. It maintains a relationship to key terms (such as event, subject, the void, the multiple, truth, and fidelity) from his *Manifesto for Philosophy* and *Being and Event*. In both post-Kantian theory and liberal communitarianism, ethics, based on Kantian theories of radical evil, is a tool that promotes one's ability to discern evil and make decisions accordingly. Contemporary ethics, following this logic, deems evil a violation of "the rights of man" and "the ethics of difference." However, Badiou argues that this ethical representation of evil itself is an evil of truth.[21] Goodness should not be understood as a divine power against evil. Instead, evil only emerges from what he calls the "truth process" in a particular event.[22] That is, evil for him is not some kind of demon opposed to goodness or God. Instead, it derives from the very possibility of goodness and situational truths.[23] Whereas contemporary ethics excludes the possibility and significance of a truth procedure in its post-Kantian and Levinasian ethics, Badiou believes that only when subjects are faithful to the essence of truth can they ward off evil through a truth process.

According to Badiou, three figures (or forms) of evil can arise in relation to a truth procedure: *simulacrum*, *betrayal*, and *disaster*. The first figure of evil is a *simulacrum* (associated with the *event*). It occurs when a subject, group, or institution is not faithful to the fidelity of the event. In a simulacrum, evil is not understood in terms of goodness but by its imitation. Therefore, to believe that an event convokes the plenitude of the void of the earlier situation is evil to Badiou. Equality, universality, eternity, and the simulacrum of a truth process (as enemies of truth) can establish a legitimate truth process and commit itself to particular features of its situation. Inevitably, a simulacrum brings about the violence of terror directed at everyone.

Badiou uses Nazism as an example worth discussing here. Nazism as a simulacrum represents a single particularity (the flourishing of a particular race over and against other races), not the universal void of the situation (the event). In this case, to think of the singularity of genocide is to think of the singularity of Nazism as a political sequence. This is the problem of a simulacrum. Badiou explains that Hitler attempted genocide as a massive militarized operation because he had taken power, and he took power in the name of a politics whose categories included the term "Jew."[24] In reality, there were many other victims, such as Gypsies, Blacks, homosexuals, Jehovah's Witnesses, communists, and so on. Nonetheless, the name "Jew" was the name of names, "serving to designate those people whose disappearance created, around that presumed German 'National Socialist revolution' simulacrum, a void that would suffice to identify the substance."[25] The "Jew" was thus a particular invention of the political sequence of Nazism. For Hitler, the multiple (or the void) of this particular situation must be eliminated for the fullness of the anti-Semitic political situation to be established. Badiou concludes that "I have pursued the example of Nazism because it enters to a significant extent into that 'ethical' configuration (of 'radical Evil') opposed by the ethics of truths. What is at issue here is the simulacrum of an event that gives rise to a political fidelity." [26]

The second figure of evil is *betrayal* (associated with *fidelity*). It occurs when a subject, group, or institution succumbs to the pressure of its animality and thus fails to live up to the fidelity to truth. After simulacrum, betrayal is the second name of the Evil made possible by a truth. It is Evil in the sense of betrayal, betrayal of a human subject's "the Immortal." One facing the simulacrum of an event is always tempted to betray a truth from the demands of self-interest because the formal characteristics of this evil are precisely those of truth. Moreover, when there is confusion between one's common interests and disinterested interest, between human animal and subject, between mortal and immortal, one is bound to be confronted with a genuine choice between the "Keep going!" (even when one no longer feels caught up in the truth process) proposed by the ethics of this truth. Following the collapse of the sole maxim of consistency (and thus of ethics), a crisis of fidelity is always what is put to the test.[27] As a result, one can easily betray the becoming-subject in himself and thus become the enemy of that truth whose subject is the "some-one" that one is composed of. Therefore, "it is that the defeat of the ethics of a truth, at the undecidable point of a crisis, presents itself as a betrayal. And this is an Evil from which there is no return."[28]

The final figure of evil is *disaster* (associated with the naming of *truth*). It occurs when a subject, group, or institution mistakes an open moment of truth process for the fixed reality and thus attempts to name the *unnamable* of the event (such as Nazism, the 9/11 event, and the war in the former Yugoslavia). Since the powers of the language of the situation are themselves unrestricted, every element of an event can be named and judged from the perspective of a given interest in the communication between human subjects. Consequently, the evil naming activity of the "subject-language" (the language of the militant, the researcher, the artist, the lover, and so on) will produce "the particular *coherence* of a subjective truth," and "claim the power, based on its own axioms, to name the whole of the real, and thus to change the world."[29] Such an evil becomes possible when a truth procedure starts to reorganize "the multiple" in a situation.

Accordingly, the "subject-language" as disastrous evil always desires to subjugate the unnamable related to the undecidability of the truth process at its very beginning. However, it is possible, Badiou believes, for a human subject to eliminate this naming evil. If the subject-language covers the same ground as the language of the situation, then the power of truth may manifest itself not by the mere distortion of pragmatic or totalized meanings, but by the absolute authority of truthful nomination. In this case, a truth would "force the pure and simple replacement of the language of the situation by a subject-language. That is to say: the Immortal would come into being as the wholesale negation of the human animal that bears him."[30] In short, these are the three figures of Evil that, according to Badiou, dwell in the three dimensions of the process of truth respectively: the simulacrum is linked to the event of the void, betrayal is related to the uncertainty of fidelity, and the disaster concerns the naming of a truth. Badiou's ethics aims to ward off these three evils through a truth process for the truths to come.

The Problems of Badiou's Ethics and a Comparison between Levinas and Badiou

> Badiou's book [*Ethics*] does nothing less than evacuate the foundation upon which every deconstructive, "multicultural," or "postcolonial" ethics is built: the (ethical) category of alterity. The whole tangled body of doctrine variously associated with the Other—and developed by Levinas, Derrida, Irigaray, and Spivak, among so many "others"—is here simply swept away.
>
> —Peter Hallward, "Translator's Introduction," *Ethics: An Essay on the Understanding of Evil*

> Once again, it is propelled by a claimed quest for truth. Everything must be shattered; all pasts must be unmasked in their naivete, all present "truths" must be surpassed for the truth that will come. Perhaps his [Badiou's] enthusiasm for the future comes less from a genuine desire for truth than from the frustration of a romantic nihilism that devalues everything it touches beforehand. . . . Ethics is far more serious, and far more serious than Badiou would prefer.
>
> —Cohen, *Levinasian Meditations*

After exploring the critique of Badiou's ethics, I want to point out two reservations I have regarding Badiou's criticism of Levinas. Firstly, it is not convincing to exclude religious ethics from the philosophy of ethics. This point has been the most discussed counter-criticism against Badiou's criticism of Levinas so far. Scholars like Richard Cohen, Simon Critchley, and Bettina Bergo argue that religion should not be excluded from the domain of ethics but be treated as "the paradigm of ethical action" or "the condition of philosophy." Admittedly, Badiou is right to point out that there are problems with the recent secularization of the Other in ethical ideology. This is particularly problematic in this case because Levinas's ethics is fundamentally religious and, in a sense, tied to religious piety. For Levinas, to know God is to know what must be done ethically.[31] Therefore, if we read Levinas's philosophy and his Talmudic readings together, we can hardly find any clear boundaries between "ethics in service to religion" and "religion in service to ethics."

Nevertheless, Levinas's insights into the ethics of Judaism are clearly philosophical rather than dogmatic. Cohen rightly states that "the real point is that for Levinas there is no rupture between philosophy and religion. Instead, 'there is communication between faith and philosophy and not the notorious conflict. Communication [is] in both directions.'"[32] Take "thou shalt not murder" as a moral imperative, for example. "One can call this 'religious,' but I think Levinas prefers to call it ethical."[33] This communication between religion and philosophy is both affirmative and necessary insofar as we can recognize religion not as the defender of the irrational but as sustaining and sustained by the irreducible surplus of the ethical.

Moreover, Philippe Nemo, in the "foreword" of *Levinas, His Life, and Legacy*, rightly points out that "Levinas devoted all of his spiritual energy, all of his philosophical genius, to providing an entirely universal form to biblical ethics. He restricted himself neither to theology nor to exegesis, but completely embraced philosophy, the language of reason."[34] Although the status of philosophy, religion, and even ethics remains to a certain degree indeterminate throughout Levinas's major works, we may say that his most significant contribution to philosophy is that he reconceptualizes the humanistic ethics in the Bible with the philosophical language of Greece. Since Levinas's messianic thinking motivates our concern with the creation of what is "good" for others, Bettina Bergo also points out that "it is even possible to say that Levinas is a messianic thinker *before* he is an 'ethical' thinker, although these really exist in a relation of reciprocity in his thought."[35] Though Levinas's philosophy constantly hovers between Athens and Jerusalem, he always keeps his sights on one cast-iron determined direction beyond these two cities, namely, *peace*. That is, we can say that Levinas is devoted to exploring the diasporic Jewish soul with the rational pen of ancient Greece and develops his lifelong philosophy to realize his deepest desire for human beings—*peace*. Badiou's militantly maintained boundary between the ethics of religion and truth and the exclusion of the former from the latter may lead us, I believe, to a more suffocating truth of ethics.

My second reservation is that it is also unreasonable to accept the primacy of the ethics of antiphilosophical[36] and antihumanistic *greatness* over the ethics of humanistic *goodness*. Following Nietzsche's belief that creating new humanity always demands that the old one first be destroyed, Badiou's ethics is necessarily a philosophy of antihumanism. For Badiou, unless we keep questioning and destroying the old humanism, we will be left with nothing but an animality-oriented humanism. Thus, Badiou's ethics upholds the antihumanist stances of Foucault, Althusser, and Lacan, resisting the traditional humanist Man, anthropological goodness, commonsensical ethics, and Levinasian Other. Furthermore, in *The Adventure of French Philosophy*, Badiou claims that *greatness* is a road toward something that one does not know in advance, and contemporary French philosophy is fundamentally an adventure in such greatness—choosing a philosophical action or intervention over wisdom and meditation. That is, "the French philosophical moment was more interested in greatness than in happiness. We wanted something quite unusual, and admittedly problematic: our desire was to be adventurers of the concept."[37] As a result, Badiou argues that what took place in late twentieth-century France was ultimately a moment of philosophical adventure, including his own philosophy.

Unlike Badiou's ethics as a challenge against all humanistic philosophy to follow the French antihumanist tradition of greatness, Levinas's ethics aims to develop a humanistic philosophy of radical goodness from Judaism. If exploring Levinas's philosophy and his lifelong commitment to ethics, one can observe, on a deeper level, that Levinas's philosophy not only critically *reflects* the thousand-year-old problems of Western philosophy but also actively *responds* to the Jewish people's collective anxiety and their dedication to their post-Nazism mission: How can we humans prevent such a brutally violent historical calamity from happening again? As a philosopher, he realizes that only by arousing people's genuine humanistic compassion for others (with what he calls "the wisdom of love") can we conquer the egoistic consciousness and inhumanity of the "I," and develop a "hospitality" to the third party in politics. Responding to the most shocking violence and tragedy in human history philosophically and seeking for the possibility of world peace characterize the epochal significance of Levinas's ethics of the Other. Levinas's ethics of goodness is, by all means, a sincere and creative philosophy to achieve the height of the "humanity of the human." Perhaps there is no necessary conflict between aesthetic and moral excellence in philosophy; however, I contend that goodness must precede greatness in ethics, especially when the heroic greatness has been overemphasized in the postmodern condition. In short, Levinas's ethics of goodness for the care of others should have primacy over Badiou's ethics of truth for the sake of greatness in the philosophy of ethics today.

In summary, we can say that there are three main points where Levinas and Badiou sharply part ways regarding their ethics. Firstly, the goal of Levinas's ethics is *goodness*, whereas the goal of Badiou's is *greatness*. Secondly, Levinas's ethics is a product of *humanism*, whereas Badiou's ethics is an outcome of *antihumanism*. Finally, as we know, Levinas's ethics is a philosophy of *transcendence*, whereas Badiou's ethics is a philosophy of *immanence* (I will elaborate on it later). Despite these three significant differences between them, and despite Badiou's posing his ethics in opposition to Levinas's ethics, their philosophies share at least three common elements.

Firstly, both Levinas and Badiou pursue a higher mode of a human being or a noble humanity. For Levinas, ethics occurs as the moral height of the other person. That is, to be an ethical subject, one must lift one's selfhood to its proper moral height through one's relation with the ethics of the Other. Helping others before oneself, creating a just society for the third party, and pursuing the world's peace are the three main aspirations of human ethical life. These goals are what Levinas calls the very "humanity of the human." Badiou also pursues this philosophical aim of being a noble human in the name of "the Immortality." For Badiou, although humans are mortal beings, their relation to truth provides them with opportunities to become immortal—something other than mortal creatures. It is a truth procedure that opens all humans up to the possibility of being immortal. Thus, Badiou's ethics affirms that we humans should be confident that we have a place in the truth-procedure, and we should develop the courage to pursue a higher form of the subject concerning the ethics of truth.

Secondly, both Levinas and Badiou emphasize the unknowable and inaccessible aspect of the real. Although Levinas does not use terms like "event," "situation," or "void," he develops an originally material concept of the real: the "*il y a*" (*there is . . .*). Levinas argues that existence (the real) always already precedes existents (human beings, for instance). The *il y a* thus precedes our consciousness of the real. In the *il y a*, "the things of the day world then do not in the night become the source of the 'horror of darkness' because our look cannot catch them in their 'unforeseeable plots'; on the contrary, they get their fantastic character from this horror."[38] The darkness of the *il y a* reduces the nonvisual real to unknowable, anonymous, and inaccessible being. Accordingly, the idea of the *il y a* signifies a consciousness without my consciousness or without me when I face the unknowable being of the real (the Other). In the *il y a*, I am neither an "I" nor an "other." We may say that Levinas's *il y a* not only illustrates the real as a mysterious being but also prioritizes the significance of the *il y a* over my consciousness of the Other. As an anonymous being, the *il y a* thus can be seen as the first and constitutive escape from the Heideggerian neutral Being and Nothingness. It shows the unimaginable being of the real where dwells the absolute Other.

In Badiou's account, there is no "absolute Other" but the "void" that conditions the (sensed and represented) real. What situates an event is its location at "the edge of the void" of the situation in which it takes place. Without the void, the real cannot attach the situations of an event to their beings. Badiou writes that "the void, the multiple-of-nothing, neither excludes nor constrains anyone. It is the absolute neutrality of being—such that the fidelity that originates in an event, although it is an immanent break within a singular situation, is none the less universally addressed."[39] Being the vital condition of Badiou's ontology, the void does not *become* (which is privileged by Deleuze and other postmodern philosophers). Instead, it remains forever *void* and *ideal* as it is. Due to the preexistence of the void, Badiou's ontology is *mathematics* in general and *set theory* in particular. That is, the void illustrating a material infinitism can be seen as a radical mathematical set of all sets in the real.

Moreover, there is no clear or fixed frame of this mathematical set to contain all other sets. Mathematics knows only the pure, subtractive, and inconsistent multiple and thus cannot be reduced to the One or any totality. As a result, philosophy can be seen as a truth process of rigorous deduction inflected by mathematics. Philosophy is not the universal truth but the very site where thinking *seizes* the truths of an event happening in the void. In other words, a truth is produced when the subjective process (of a philosopher, for example) is put into the faithful thinking in a given situation, making this process of philosophical subjectivization possible. When it comes to emphasizing the unknowable and inaccessible aspect of the real in philosophy, Levinas and Badiou may be closer to one another than generally thought.[40]

Finally, both Levinas and Badiou challenge the violence of totality. In *Totality and Infinity,* Levinas introduces the "first philosophy" by opposing it to "a philosophical thought which reduces the Other [*l'Autre*] to the scale of the Same and the multiple to the totality, making of autonomy its supreme principle."[41] Levinas's ethics is fundamentally based on his powerful critique of ontological violence and the totality of the Same. Similarly, in Badiou's philosophy, there is no "the one," no possible overarching totality of beings, and no all-embracing infinity, as a totalized set of all things. There are only "a multiple of multiples" in an event. Under the imperative to "Keep going!" Badiou's ethics combines resources of discernment (do not fall for simulacra), of courage (do not give up), and of moderation (do not get carried away by the extremes of totality).[42] Blind fidelity and totalitarianism are thus targeted. The militant pursuit of truth, for Badiou, aims to eliminate the totality of the one from philosophy. Accordingly, "it is essential that politics renounce the category of totality."[43]

In brief, there are differences as well as similarities between Levinas's ethics and Badiou's in the post-postmodern condition. Where there Levinas explores the transcendental relation with the Other in terms of the ethics of goodness to pursue the height of humanity, Badiou believes that only through the courageous fidelity of mathematical ontology can we develop a rigorous ethics of truth to pursue the greatness of the Immortal. Badiou's ethics has its problems, as discussed above. However, we also need to admit that Levinas's ethics has been questioned by many due to its Jewish mysticism, ontological grounding, and political implications. Badiou, being the most provocative critic of Levinas's philosophy, is not the only one.[44] For instance, Critchley asserts that politics is the Achilles' heel of Levinasian philosophy. In "Five Problems in Levinas's View of Politics and the Sketch of a Solution to Them," Critchley summarizes five problems in Levinas's discourse of politics: fraternity, monotheism, Eurocentrism, family, and Israel-related issues. Considering these and other criticisms (such as hyperbolic language and radical idealism) also need more examination, it is fair to say that Levinas's philosophy is radical and original but not perfect. It has its own limits.

Nonetheless, I agree with scholars like Richard Cohen, Richard Sugarman, and Robert Bernasconi, who would not accept the accusation that the ethics of the Other lacks a sense of reality in ontology and politics and has no actual discourse intervening between the political issues. Strictly speaking, Levinas's ethics of the Other is an original and rigorous discourse that attempts to pursue both goodness and truth. To a certain degree, it has a sense of reality that is strong enough for Levinasian scholars to look into the political problems in our contemporary thought. However, the political implication of Levinas's ethics does require further explanation and new exploration in this new trend of ethical thought.

Conclusion: Toward a New Ethico-Political Philosophy

Postmodern philosophy draws decentralizing, antilogocentric, and antiutopian conclusions from the postwar era (the failed hope of modernism). Yet, it does not construct its own telos or grounds for little narratives. As a result, postmodernists more often than not find themselves trapped in a dilemma: how to justify or rationalize the foundation of critiques that are antifoundational. Hence, a new trend of thought in the "post" postmodern condition reflects and yearns for a return of ethics—an ethical ethos that demands that we respond to urgent ethical issues at both the global and local scales. Within this new trend, there are significant philosophers and promising scholars who not only critically examine the postmodern philosophy of difference but also conceptualize what kinds of ethics we need for the twenty-first century. Suppose postmodern philosophy is right to decenter all grand narratives. In that case, it is equally right that the rise of little narratives cannot go without a sense of ethical bounding or totalities among them. For instance, Nancy's "singular plural," Derrida's "deconstructive hospitality," and Agamben's "the coming community" all try to bring the radical politics and aesthetics of postmodern decentering back to an ethical sense of "togetherness."

Given the pressing and imperative demand for global ethics and politics to cope with so many urgent ethico-political issues today, what will guide a future ethico-political philosophy, I believe, is an increasingly pressing longing of *ethical humanity* and a new conception of the function of a *messianic now* that can be produced by our globalized society and acquired from it. Thus, my contention is that if postmodern philosophy is to legitimize its radical politics of decentering for a new ethico-political philosophy in the twenty-first century, it may need to prioritize immediate responsiveness and demonstrate constant responsibility to others. If contemporary politics is to avoid postmodern relativism or nihilism, it may need to be based on the "(*im*)patience of the messianic response" that I have proposed elsewhere: the persevering patience of waiting (political ethics) coupled with the impatience required to prepare today for what is to arrive tomorrow (ethical politics).[45]

Regarding the rigorous reconceptualization of ethics in this ethical turn, the significance of Levinas's works and Badiou's are undeniable and thus deserve more careful examination and detailed evaluation. For Levinas, the ethics of transcendence precedes both ontology and immanence. For Badiou, ethics is the ontology of truth that sees transcendence as an evil of simulacrum against truths. Both Badiou's criticisms of Levinas's ethics (no ontological guarantee and no philosophical reasoning) actually originate from the indirect attack on Levinas's idea of transcendence. That is, if there is no transcendence but immanence (or ontology) in philosophical truth, then Badiou is right to state that all Levinasian ideas of ethics (such as the Other, alterity, Desire, responsibility and the face) are "inventive" and "pious" concepts without philosophical rationality. The problem is: how can Badiou or other contemporary immanent philosophers *know* for sure that there is no transcendence beyond immanence? Specifically, since the universal *void* of all events is unknowable and inaccessible, how can Badiou guarantee that the *void* is not embraced or conditioned by transcendence? How can he distinguish his idea of the void phenomenologically from Levinas's idea of *il y a*? Can immanence *exist* without its nonimmanence (which can be transcendence)? As Agamben points out, transcendence and immanence as two lines of contemporary thought set up the basic arguments of metaphysics that have haunted Western philosophy since its inception. However, it is at the ethical level that the difference between these two lines of thought is brought into sharp relief. The conflict between Levinas's ethics and Badiou's highlights this difference in contemporary Western philosophy.

After comparing Levinas to Badiou regarding ethics, it is reasonable to conclude that both Levinas and Badiou pursue radical idealism in their own ways. However, Levinas's ethics of otherness-oriented goodness is more humanist, subtle, and constructive, while Badiou's ethics of greatness-oriented truth is more courageous, material, and situational. The former signifies the ethics of transcendence, while the latter represents the ethics of immanence. Although the two modes of ethics are not in a binary opposition relation, it is almost impossible to reconcile them. Moreover, the ethical turn in the post-postmodern condition has provided us with a broad diversity of new situations, discourses, and thinkers and promises a more insightful discussion and further constructive ventures into ethics to erect a new contemporary ethics of goodness as well as greatness. Doubtlessly, both Levinas and Badiou have made significant contributions to this re-conceptualization of ethics in philosophy. However, what is needed in the highly calculating and techno-capitalist reality of today, I believe, is a more contextualized and goodness-oriented philosophy that may help us to better cope with today's urgent ethico-political problems.

Notes

1. Since the 1990s, a group of well-known thinkers and rising-star scholars have come together to re-conceptualize the idea of ethics to cope with the problems of postmodern thought. In fact, there are more and more works that exemplify "the return of ethics" in the new condition that goes beyond the postmodern condition of little narratives: Jean-Luc Nancy's *The Inoperable Community* (1991) and *Being Singular Plural* (2000), *God, Justice, Love, Beauty* (2011), Jacques Derrida's *Of Hospitality* (2000), *On Cosmopolitanism and Forgiveness* (2001), and *The Animal That Therefore I Am* (2008). Giorgio Agamben's *The Coming Community* (1993), Alain Badiou's *Ethics: An Essay on the Understanding of Evil* (2001) and *Saint Paul: The Foundation of the Universal* (2003), Michael Hardt and Antonio Negri's *Multitude* (2004) and *Commonwealth* (2009), Heather Widdows's *The Connected Self: The Ethics and Governance of the Genetic Individual* (2013), Peter Singer's *Ethics in the Real World* (2016), and various other theoretical publications related to contemporary ethics.

2. Alain Badiou, *Ethics: An Essay on the Understanding of Evil* (New York: Verso, 2001), liii.

3. Richard Cohen, *Levinasian Meditations: Ethics, Philosophy, and Religion* (Pittsburgh: Duquesne University Press, 2010), 193.

4. Badiou, *Ethics*, 3.
5. Badiou, 2.
6. Badiou, 10.
7. Badiou, 11.
8. Badiou, 10.
9. Badiou, 12.
10. Badiou, 12.
11. Badiou, 16.
12. Badiou, 18.
13. Badiou, 16–17.
14. Badiou, 19–22.

15. Derrida, in "Violence and Metaphysics," argues that Levinas's notion of ethics as a critique of ontological violence is also presented in his ethical discourse, which presupposes the very ontological language that it claims it overcome. That is, doesn't Levinas's critique of philosophy itself arguably use the assimilating language of philosophy as discourse of the Self (Derrida, *Grammatology* 131)?

16. Badiou, *Ethics*, 21–22.

17. Badiou, 22.

18. Badiou, 22–23.

19. Badiou, 23.

20. Badiou, 23.

21. Unlike Foucault, truth, for Badiou, is not something produced by power; rather it always arises in a plural form (truths) that is materially and militantly produced in a specific situation. Each situation starts from an event that eludes the prevailing logic or knowledge that governs the situation. Therefore, unlike Levinas, true ethical questions, for Badiou, cannot arise from the preontological face-to-face situation; rather it can emerge only in a specific situation of an event.

22. Badiou, *Ethics*, 87.

23. Badiou, 91.

24. Badiou, 64.

25. Badiou, 75.

26. Badiou, 77.

27. Badiou, 78–79.

28. Badiou, 80.

29. Badiou, 83.

30. Badiou, 83–84.

31. Levinas, *Difficult Freedom*, 17.

32. Cohen, *Levinasian Meditations*, 201.

33. Cohen, 194.

34. Philippe Nemo, Foreword to *Emmanuel Levinas: His Life and Legacy*, by Salomon Malka, trans. Michael Kigel and Sonja M. Embree (Pittsburgh: Duquesne University Press, 2006), xi.

35. Bettina Bergo, "Levinas's Weak Messianism in Time and Flesh, or The Insistence of Messiah Ben," *Journal for Cultural Research* 13, nos. 3–4 (2009): 247.

36. Following Pascal, Badiou believes that to "dismiss philosophy is to be a true philosopher," so philosophy should engage with the great anti-philosophers to refute them. Anti-philosophy thus aims to seek to a "clear mind" for a fundamental resistance to conceptual explanation in ineffable or transcendent meaning. For example, Saint Paul's "discourse of Life" is opposed to the pretensions of Greek philosophy and Wittgenstein's "in-articulable" is opposed to the abuse of the language of speculative idealism (Badiou, *Saint Paul*, 62).

37. Alain Badiou, *The Adventure of French Philosophy*, ed. and trans. Bruno Bosteels (London: Verso, 2012), 259.

38. Emmanuel Levinas, *Existence and Existents*, trans. Alphonso Lingis (The Hague: Nijhoff, 1978), 54.

39. Badiou, *Ethics*, 73.

40. For me, Levinas's *il y a* seems closer to *the real* than Badiou's void in terms of ethics—the former signifies an inaccessible *ethical condition of the Other* while the latter illustrates an inaccessible *material condition of nothingness*.

41. Levinas, *Totality*, 294.

42. Badiou, *Ethics*, 91.

43. Badiou, 115.

44. For a discussion of other criticisms of Levinas's ethics (such as Derrida, Lyotard, Ricoeur, Irigaray and Zizek), see Richard Cohen's "Defending Levinas: Interview with Chung Hsiung (Raymond) Lai" in *Levinasian Meditations: Ethics, Philosophy, and Religion* (Pittsburgh: Duquesne University Press, 2010), 169–98.

45. Chung-Hsiung Lai, "On (Im)Patient Messianism: Marx, Levinas, and Derrida" in *Levinas Studies*, vol. 11, ed. Richard A. Cohen (Pittsburgh: Duquesne University Press), 87–89.

Bibliography

Badiou, Alain. *The Adventure of French Philosophy*. Edited and translated by Bruno Bosteels. London: Verso, 2012.

Badiou, Alain. *Ethics: An Essay on the Understanding of Evil*. New York: Verso, 2001.

Badiou, Alain. *Saint Paul: The Foundation of Universalism*. Cultural Memory in the Present. Stanford, CA: Stanford University Press, 2003.

Bergo, Bettina. "Levinas's Weak Messianism in Time and Flesh, or The Insistence of Messiah Ben." *Journal for Cultural Research* 13, no. 3–4 (2009).

Cohen, Richard. "Defending Levinas: Interview with Chung Hsiung (Raymond) Lai." In *Levinasian Meditations: Ethics, Philosophy, and Religion*. Pittsburgh: Duquesne University Press, 2010.

Cohen, Richard. *Levinasian Meditations: Ethics, Philosophy, and Religion*. Pittsburgh: Duquesne University Press, 2010.

Derrida, Jacques. "Violence and Metaphysics." In *Writing and Difference*. Translated by Alan Bass. Chicago: University of Chicago Press, 1978.

Hallward, Peter. "Translator's Introduction." In *Ethics: An Essay on the Understanding of Evil*, by Alain Badiou. New York: Verso, 2001.

Lai, Chung-Hsiung. "On (Im)Patient Messianism: Marx, Levinas, and Derrida." In *Levinas Studies*, vol. 11, edited by Richard A. Cohen and Jolanta Saldukaitytė. Pittsburg: Duquesne University Press, 2016.

Levinas, Emmanuel. *Difficult Freedom: Essays on Judaism*. Translated by Sean Hand. Baltimore: Johns Hopkins University Press, 1990.

Levinas, Emmanuel. *Existence and Existents*. Translated by Alphonso Lingis. The Hague: Nijhoff, 1978.
Levinas, Emmanuel. *Totality and Infinity: An Essay on* Exteriority. Translated by Alphonso Lingis. Pittsburgh: Duquesne University Press, 1969.
Nemo, Philippe. "Foreword." In *Emmanuel Levinas: His Life and Legacy*, by Salomon Malka. Translated Michael Kigel and Sonja M. Embree. Pittsburgh: Duquesne University Press, 2006.

16

On the Importance of Importance
Emmanuel Levinas on the First Challenge to Jewish Thought Today

RICHARD SUGARMAN

Richard A. Cohen has played a pivotal role in making the philosophy of Emmanuel Levinas central to contemporary Jewish thought. At the same time, he helped incorporate the place of Levinas as the next step in Continental philosophy and phenomenology after Merleau-Ponty. Reflecting on his early interest in Levinas, Cohen wrote something for which he is justifiably well known, regarding Levinas's philosophy: "I thought to myself, this is true." In 1981, I received an inquiry from Professor Cohen, asking whether I would like to contribute an essay to a book he was editing that would later be published as *Face to Face with Levinas*. I was happy and surprised to know that Cohen was aware of my interest in Levinas, which had originated with my own teacher, John D. Wild, who published the significant introduction to the English edition of *Totality and Infinity*. What struck me then and now was Cohen's fearlessness as a philosopher. He always went right to the heart of the matter.

What I learned over the years was that Cohen understood, appreciated, and wrote about the rupture between Heidegger and Levinas. Heidegger had influenced Levinas deeply, but his Nazism remains a scandal in Continental philosophy. What took me longer to understand was his critique of Jacques Derrida whom Cohen repeatedly, and in my view correctly, criticized as a Heideggerian while retaining his admiration for Levinas. Cohen was properly skeptical of Derrida's claim that Levinas had not escaped the phenomenon of Heidegger's ontology as he had thought. As the 1980s unfolded, the texts and thought of Levinas became better known in America and in the English-speaking world. And this was partly owing to Derrida, who had become even better known in circles of literary criticism and philosophy than perhaps Levinas himself.

In 1984 Cohen authored the introduction to a book that has remained one of the most readable and popular introductions to Levinas, *Ethics and Infinity: Conversations with Philippe Nemo*.[1] It is from this book that Levinas's distinctively Jewish and religious writings were first juxtaposed with his philosophical endeavors. As Cohen would later write, he did not see the kind of separation that most other scholars saw between the Jewish and philosophic writings of Levinas. Along the way, Cohen published more books considered important. He edited and co-translated a book that would appear in English under the title, *Discovering Existence with Husserl*.[2] In this book, Levinas recounts his discovery of phenomenology, the experience of studying with Husserl's foremost student and later critic, Martin Heidegger. Anyone wishing to understand phenomenology in its formative stages is encouraged to read this book. Several years before that, Cohen produced a systematic work comparing Rosenzweig and Levinas that did not shy away from one of the most important questions between the ancients and the moderns.[3] This question concerned the way that the Good, for Levinas, is, as it was for Plato, "beyond or otherwise than being."

In his brilliant work *Out of Control: Confrontations between Spinoza and Levinas*, Cohen shows the importance and dynamism of Spinoza's rejection of this notion of the Good in Plato, along with his rejection of the teachings of the Torah and how this leads to a demystified world of religious life. Along with the demystification, however, as Cohen correctly argues, an effacing of Judaism itself occurs. It is not until the philosophy of Levinas that Judaism fully returns to philosophy without diminishing the necessity to dispel the illusions of mystification and to reattach philosophy once again to the Good.

By the year 2000, Levinas had become much better known in American philosophical circles. In addition to the fact that translations from French into English were virtually a yearly event, so too was the exponential growth of secondary literature on Levinas. These included important contributions from Richard Cohen.

In March of 2000, the University of Vermont hosted a conference on Levinas and the Humanities that I chaired. I invited Richard Cohen to be the keynote speaker. He did not disappoint. Almost always clear, reasoned, and explicit in his views, positions, and statements, Cohen made a remark that I shall not soon forget. He said that what distinguished Levinas from other thinkers was his insistence on *the importance of importance*. A student listening to Cohen, not known as an academic to be sure, was asked by a faculty member what *he* was doing there, listening to a talk on Levinas. The student responded in a way that gave Cohen great satisfaction on his central subject: "I believe that studying Levinas makes me a better person." Cohen opposed minute philosophy and the evasion of the major ethical challenges facing humanity at the turn of the millennium. The conference lasted three days, and Cohen showed up at every session seeking to find that which was meaningful in each presentation. However, it could not be said that he suffered fools gladly. Nor was he afraid of speaking to me as a friend. He visited with me at my office on several occasions where students drifted in and out at will. He added, "Now I see why you don't write anything. Don't you believe in office hours, or do you just have hours to write that are left over?" He also upbraided me for not going to conferences and sharing my own insights on Levinas and phenomenology. This, however, turned out to have benefited me, and by 2002 I was already speaking at the first International Conference on Levinas in Jerusalem. Cohen and I discovered over the years that more often than not our views on philosophy, religion, and politics had more in common than either of us was aware. During this time, Cohen had moved from the University of North Carolina at Charlotte to SUNY Buffalo where he was the chair of the Department of Jewish Studies. While he was a progressive on most things in politics, he was a staunch defender of Israel's right to exist and to defend itself as a state. He was unafraid to speak in hostile environments and to state his views clearly, rationally, and insist on an ethical and reasoned response in return. There is only one relatively technical issue on which I disagree with Cohen concerning Levinas. Unlike Cohen, I believe that Levinas continued to use the phenomenological approach throughout his later years as well. But this is a small matter. Perhaps we could agree that Levinas enlarged the scope of phenomenology, and by insisting on "Ethics as First

Philosophy," he muted much of the criticism properly directed at so-called Continental philosophy. These focused on charges of moral relativism, and even nihilism, especially in the case of Heidegger.

It should be stressed that Cohen pursued his research in relation to the thinking of Levinas, yielding other books devoted in whole or in part to his thinking. Cohen charts a new path in hermeneutics in this book *Ethics, Exegesis, and Philosophy: Interpretation after Levinas*. What he expresses is that Levinas has a theory of interpretation where this is always an interpretation *to* someone else, and often *for* another person or persons. In this way, Cohen shows that Levinas manages to restore the notion of *transcendence* to philosophy proper after its deconstruction since the time of Spinoza.

Upon receiving the Nietzsche Prize in Italy in the mid-1980s, Levinas remarked: "Remember that I am receiving the Nietzsche Prize, not the Nobel Prize." He added: "This is very strange, for I have written virtually nothing about Nietzsche."[4] While Levinas's comments on Nietzsche are indeed quite spare and appear to be derisive, the question at the beginning of *Totality and Infinity* is in fact raised by Nietzsche and responded to by Levinas. It is, therefore, left to Levinas to demonstrate that morality—or as he more often calls it, ethics—is first philosophy. What does this mean? It means, in the words of William James, that "morality says some things are better and therefore, more important, than other things."[5] This in turn brings us to the question of theodicy and its presumed end. Theodicy, distilled, means justifying the ways of God to human beings. Levinas notes that the term "theodicy" was coined by Leibnitz in 1710. Before it was named, it "corresponded to one Biblical strain in reading Scripture,"[6] where we would arrogate to ourselves the capacity to understand and to justify everything from God's point of view, even the suffering of others. For Levinas, in the aftermath of the Holocaust, theodicy has worn out its philosophical significance as a meaningful category for understanding human suffering. We cannot, as Job's friends did, with all the best intentions, become God's "little helpers" going to and fro in the earth, like the prosecuting attorney pointing out the moral and religious failures of others that led to such unprecedented suffering. The reader will note, however, that there is a serious alteration of perspective by Job in chapter 24. Job moves from speaking about his own pain and suffering to that of every man. In this way, perhaps, his having been challenged by his consolers has had an effect upon him.

Above all, what Levinas is trying to banish is not the notion of transcendence, but the rationalizing of what he calls the "useless sufferings" of others. Levinas affirms that if we take the moral drama of our relation with others seriously, then we must appeal to reasoning rather than rationalizing. Reason, for Levinas, is linked to the act of justification in relation to transcendence. In other words, in opposition to Nietzsche, Levinas argues that *ressentiment* depends upon the very excellence of Justice, which it seeks to devalue. The case against morality presupposes morality, as such. Reasoning comes before the fact, when something still may be done for the other. This expresses what Levinas calls the "new rationality of transcendence."[7]

What Levinas advocates in relation to human suffering is a diachronic logic. For myself and my own sense of shame, guilt, and righteous indignation, there is nothing to prevent me from rationalizing my own sorrows. The sufferings of the other, on the other hand, belong to "useless suffering"—that is, a suffering that cannot be explained by me to the other on behalf of some higher authority, not even God Himself.[8] Should I tell the other in all seriousness that his children were taken from him and defiled and destroyed because he did not keep strictly kosher, or for some other violation of Jewish law? This position is not unknown in Jewish theology, and has various expressions ranging from the assault on Zionism to the attack on assimilation to that on irreligiosity, expressed by the well-known position of Rabbi Joel Teitelbaum, the *rebbe* of Satmar.

To borrow the language of art and music, we might call Levinas a philosophical minimalist. As I see it, he remains completely committed to the phenomenological approach to philosophy from the beginning of his philosophical career to the end. From *The Theory of Intuition in Husserl's Phenomenology* in 1931, to his last publications in the late 1980s, Husserl remains a touchstone for Levinas's phenomenological approach. Levinas never ceased his efforts to answer the last sentence of *Theory of Intuition*: "But isn't the possibility of overcoming this difficulty or fluctuation in Husserl's thought provided with the affirmation of the intentional character of practical and axiological life?"[9]

Levinas's position that ethics is "first philosophy" derives from a careful analysis of the face-to-face relation. In this relation, which is always present even when the other turns away from me, explanation is made intelligible by becoming an explanation to and for a *someone else*. As such, it permits the other to perpetually interrogate me and presents me with the responsibility of justifying what I am saying to the other. The personal Other transcends me; this is even more the case with the divine Other. This links reason to transcendence. In other words, this is the beginning of a "new rationality of transcendence."[10]

Levinas wants to know what is irreducible in our quest to explain what we mean when we give explanations to one another. What is it that we cannot do without if we are to advance the claim, as Levinas does, that to be human is a *normative* as well as a descriptive term? Put most simply, Levinas wants to describe what it means to be, in the colloquial Yiddish sense of the term, a *"mensch."*

Rabbi Menachem Mendel of Kotzk was asked by his followers why he never wrote a book. He responded: "I have been working on a book for many years. It's a short book. It has two words and my signature: 'A Mensch, by Menachem Mendel of Kotzk.' I start every morning and by evening I see I have fallen short. I have to tear it up because I have to start over again and every year I take the scraps and burn them with the *chameẓ* before Passover."[11]

A Jewish Philosophical Response to the Holocaust

Surely, Levinas is bothered every bit as much as every other Jewish thinker by the question: Where was God during this hour of extremity and greatest need, abandoning the just to a world without justice? How, though, might this question possibly be framed in the expectation of an answer? Still, it is not Levinas's central question. His question might be put simply: Where were other human beings? Where were other people? Above all, we are left to take responsibility for the question, Where was the *humanity* of the human being?

Is it possible, then, to speak of Jewish theology in the absence of theodicy? In his preface to *Of God Who Comes to Mind*, Levinas notes that

> we have been reproached for ignoring theology; and we do not here contest the necessity of a recovery, or, at least, the necessity of choosing the opportunity for a recovery of these themes. We think, however, the theological recuperation comes after the glimpse of holiness which is primary. This is all the more true that we belong to a generation—and to a century—for which was reserved the pitiless trials without consolation or

promises; and because it is impossible—for us, the survivors, to witness against holiness, in seeking after its conditions.[12]

If there is a theological dimension to Levinas's philosophy, it becomes more minimal in his later works. Rather than contesting the idea of theology, he sees it as subordinate to philosophy. It is holiness that he wishes to affirm and explain. He will later do this in five new Talmudic readings in *From the Sacred to the Holy*. Unlike students of comparative religion, Levinas makes a sharp distinction between the sacred and the holy.[13] The sacred need not have anything in common with the realm of the ethical. Levinas regards the sacred as too closely bound up with the merely mythic as opposed to the factual. Sacred belongs to the realm of ontology. Therefore, since "to be" is to persevere in being for each being's survival, in what he calls (borrowing from Spinoza) the "*conatus essendi*," is a function of power where each person is set off against the others in a war of all against all. The sacred, then, orders itself according to principles of exclusion, where outsiders remain unwelcome. It is dominated by the category of sameness.

Levinas views the holy, on the other hand, as the surplus of morality, where morality is presupposed and yet heightened by a responsibility that borders on the Infinite. In this sense, holiness is something that can be embodied and practiced. It is emblematic of a different kind of human relation from that of "each against each." To love your neighbor as yourself means this for Levinas: "In order to become yourself, truly, you must love the other person."[14] He means this in terms of elevating that which is good for the other to a place of primacy. Moreover, holiness works on the principle of inclusion rather than exclusion, as is frequently the case in the establishing of systems of sacred order. Hence the repeated emphasis both in the Bible and in Levinas on those who are most vulnerable and therefore most likely to be excluded: the widow, the orphan, the stranger, the poor. In this way, the vision that emerges is one of each *for* each or all *for* all.

This means that it is necessary to study the morality inscribed in the Torah that is enacted through laws. These laws are expressed concretely in actions that are accompanied by an exacting range of details. Human freedom is a burdensome freedom, a *difficile liberté*, that expresses itself through the assumption of responsibility. In Jewish law such responsibility is measured by the Torah, always understood through the Talmud, analyzed and debated ad infinitum by the sages of the Talmud, continuing through into the present. Such responsibility inscribed in laws is not a mechanistic exercise, or one that easily divides itself into parts. "Faith," here, is understood not as something "I have," but rather as fidelity to a way of life. It is only through this original sense of fidelity that it makes sense to speak of "having faith." "Jewish theology," then, is *less* than the sum of the laws that embody its morality: it remains tied to an ethical rationality of transcendence that is the product of the incessant give-and-take of Talmudic inquiry.

Levinas is very much aware that the sages of the Talmud were not overly keen on matters of theodicy, especially when it interrupted their own discourse. In a heated discussion recorded in the Talmud,[15] Rabbi Eli'ezer is outvoted by his colleagues on a matter of law. After exhausting every imaginable argument, Rabbi Eli'ezer performs several miracles in support of his position but is rebuked by Rabbi Yehoshu'a: "When scholars are engaged in halakhic discussions, what right have you to interfere?" His esteemed colleagues point out to him that such matters are to be decided according to the principles of Rabbinic hermeneutics, and even a heavenly voice confirming one opinion or another is bracketed. Even a heavenly voice is considered impermissible evidence in such a sober conversation. Were the sages of the Talmud also, then (as Levinas himself has been), reproached for being unconcerned with matters of theology, let alone theodicy? Still, the Talmud retains a trace of transcendence, both for the rabbinical commentary tradition and for the human sciences. What makes Levinas's phenomenological interpretation distinctive is the fact that he explores the great existential questions of our own time by focusing on the specifically moral and philosophical dimension of the Talmudic tradition, or the aggadic, as opposed to the legal, or halakhic, dimension of the texts.

Rather than theodicy, Levinas appeals in *Totality and Infinity* to the phenomenon of a moral eschatology to advance his position. He rejects the absolutist position now unexpectedly ascendant in the Abrahamic religions, advanced in an oracular fashion, that would behave "as though eschatology added information about the future by revealing the finality of being."[16] Rather, as he states in the preface, moral eschatology "does not introduce a teleological system into the totality; it does not consist in teaching the orientation of history. Eschatology institutes a relation with being beyond the totality or beyond history and not with being beyond the past or the present."[17] In such a case morality would be founded on politics and would be accepting of "the ontology of totality issued from war."[18] Already we can see Levinas moving to his most mature metaphysical position, which is beyond essence, or the "otherwise than being."

Levinas is advocating a nonapocalyptic eschatology. He argues that it is reflected *within* the totality and history *within* experience—what he calls the "beyond" of history—leaving us fully responsible for judging our own conduct. He puts it this way: "Submitting history as a whole to judgment, exterior to the very wars that mark its end, it restores to each instant its full signification in that instant, all the causes are ready to be heard. It is not the last judgment that is decisive, but the judgment of all the instants in time when the living are judged."[19]

The Meaning of Order and the Order of Meaning

The meaning of order may be discerned in the syntax of grammar, where one term succeeds another. Is grammar, then, the ordering of sense? Is it not already a covert appeal to "theodicy"? As Nietzsche said, "'Reason' in language . . . we are not rid of God because we still have faith in grammar."[20] Levinas recognizes this question as already belonging to the Talmudic tradition; it arises for him with a contemporary existential urgency as "the arbitrariness of extermination."[21] Citing the commentator Maharsha (1555–1632), he notes: "One term always precedes another. Can one deduce from the impossibility of terms being simultaneous a teaching on the chronological order of the events they designate?"[22]

First, it is necessary to introduce a distinction with a difference. *This distinction concerns the difference between the meaning of order and the order of meaning.* The meaning of order is familiar to us in a variety of ways. The key term is "order." Order may be founded on necessity—it need not have an internal purpose or aim. As Kafka has Joseph K. say at the conclusion of the parable "Before the Law": "It is not necessary to accept everything as true, one must only accept it as necessary."[23] Administration, bureaucracy, politics, and war all belong to the realm of the meaning of order. This is what Levinas calls "totality." Every subject must find his or her place in the realm of such order; otherwise, its existence lacks function. Totality is, for the most part, an inescapable *formalism*. This does not mean that we can do without it. However, one can lose sight of its human significance when our sense of what is beyond totality, infinity, makes it possible for human beings to relate to each other in the most primary face-to-face manner.

When we speak, however, of the "order of meaning," we cannot escape from issues of purpose, justification, and for that matter, even explanation. In a brilliant Talmudic reading, "Damages Due to Fire,"[24] Levinas explores this difference between the meaning of order and the order of meaning. Following Maharsha, Levinas notes that Abraham asks first about the just when he appeals to God on behalf of Sodom: "Will you sweep away the righteous with the wicked . . . so the righteous be as the wicked?"[25] The same chronological priority is given by Moses when he intercedes on behalf of Israel after the debacle of the golden calf. What Moses most wants to know during the moment when God shows him his eclipse side is "why the righteous *sometimes* suffer and the wicked sometimes prosper."[26] Here we are dealing with the meaning of order, that is, with grammar. Levinas probes further.

According to Levinas, Moses does not fear even such a diabolical universe; rather, what he cannot abide is a world that is completely arbitrary, that is, one where even the priority of the just, in suffering extermination, could still retain a semblance of reason. For example, there is an argument over whether or not Moses received any kind of response to his question. In the Talmudic passage, Rabbi Me'ir holds that he received no answer, while Rabbi Yehoshu'a holds that he did.[27] Levinas cannot accept any kind of rationalization when it comes to the theme of extermination. Neither the preservation of the righteous, nor even their being taken before the unjust are taken so they would not have to suffer from what they see in an unjust world, is acceptable to him. Levinas goes on to ask: "Or does the madness of extermination retain a grain of reason? That is the great ambiguity of Auschwitz."[28] He notes that the text under consideration from the Talmud "does not resolve it. It underlines it. The text does not resolve it because the answer here would be indecent as all theodicy probably is."[29] If this is the case, then what is left to say?

Still, the object of Levinas's inquiry is the order of meaning that cannot be resolved by appealing to the logic of grammar. It is the order of meaning, and therefore it is the very possibility with which Levinas wrestles. This returns him to the Talmudic argument over what Moses yearned to see and to understand when the glory of God is as it passes by.

Levinas notes that the Talmud indicates that Moses asked, "Why are the righteous *sometimes* prosperous, *sometimes* not, and the unrighteous *sometimes* prosperous, *sometimes* not?"[30] Moses reserves for the moment of supreme intimacy with God the question that must have mattered to him most. Levinas astutely notes, "Moses does not ask: Why do the righteous suffer and the wicked prosper?"[31]

From his commentary on Yosel Rakover, "To Love the Torah More Than God," it appears that Levinas later radicalized his thinking. In his reflection on Rakover, Levinas carefully notes that Rakover is comparable to Job in doubting not the existence of God but His justice. When Levinas speaks of loving the Torah more than God, he is referring to the unconditional obligation to follow the prescribed course of conduct set out in Jewish law regardless of what God may and may not be doing. What is important to keep in mind is what Levinas, in his spare autobiographical statement, appended to *Difficult Freedom*, notes about his life and thought: "It is dominated by the presentiment and the memory of the Nazi horror."[32]

The Face, Absence, and Transcendence

What we do see is a certain movement, perhaps even a radicalization, in Levinas's thinking about theodicy from 1955 to 1975, and thereafter. In "To Love the Torah More Than God," Levinas concludes: "Religious life cannot be achieved in this heroic situation. It is necessary that God unveil his face; it is necessary that justice and power be rejoined. There must be just institutions on this earth. But only the man who has recognized the veiled face of God can demand that it be unveiled. In such vigorous dialectic the equality is established between God and man even in the midst of their disproportion."[33] What we see in Levinas's position here is consonant with the tradition of *hastarat panim*, or "the hiding of the Face." What the absence of the Face signifies, according to Jewish tradition, is reversion to the laws of nature—including human nature. This indicates a time when divinity, as it were, brackets the appearance of its own benevolence, leading to a war of each against each and all against all. However, this is not considered the norm. The norm, to use the language of the medievals, is not *Deus absconditus*—God Who conceals Himself—but rather a God Who reveals Himself, *Deus revelatus*. What will progressively interest Levinas is the way in which Transcendence can express itself altogether.

According to Levinas, it is through the trace that Transcendence can appear in a positive way, not simply as a "privation." The trace is "the insertion of space in time, the point at which the world inclines toward a past and a time."[34] What it does is to form an absolute past that unites, "anachronically," all of the phases of time. In this way, the trace is what makes memory possible and philosophically intelligible for Levinas.

Here we must introduce a distinction between memory and that which is remembered. It is not sufficient simply to say that we remember something while at the same time refusing to describe that which is remembered as having happened outside of memory. The trace is analogous to "fingerprints" that make it possible to identify the event right after it has passed. While it may be taken for a sign, it is not a sign like any other. The trace is like the DNA of that which is beyond Being or, to use Levinas's formulation, the "otherwise than Being."

Closely related to the notion of the trace is that of Illeity, which correlates to the earlier category of the *Il y a*. The *Il y a*, as described much earlier by Levinas, expresses raw existence, or impersonal being. The *Il y a* unfolds as isolated instants temporally without orientation, direction, or purpose. As such, it corresponds to the biblical notion of *tohu va-vohu*, the chaos and void prior to Creation. While the *Il y a* expresses an inescapable immanence, Illeity refers to a radical alterity of the absolutely Other, which is, to use the words of Levinas, "transcendent to the point of absence."[35] These two categories help situate the phenomena of being and "the otherwise," or "better than being." In this manner, Levinas avoids the kind of dualism that would separate the realms of "totality" and "infinity." Let us remember that the work is entitled *Totality* and *Infinity*—not *Totality* or *Infinity*.

What binds totality to infinity, sameness to otherness, truth to justice? Let me suggest that it is the diachronic sense of time, governed by urgency before meaning and number, where I am pledged to responsibility for the other that illuminates the "and" between totality *and* infinity. Such time has a promissory dimension: it is the promise of time that secures a future as well as a past and present to human experience. It is for this reason that Levinas can say, as he does in *Time and the Other*: "I breathe, I hope" ("*spiro spero*").[36] Hope, however, must be based upon a sense of promise if it is not to be blind hope. A sense of promise originates with the Other, where I enter into a covenant prior to all contract. This by itself does not yet give a telos to time. At least, time does not have a sense of telos in the Aristotelian sense, because there is a dimension of time that remains open and radically contingent, more visibly open in the future, but still open in the present and even in the past. Still, it leaves room for a time of promise, where the future can be better than the present. This Talmudic notion depends upon the responsible conduct of free human beings toward one another. It is not, as is the case with the Enlightenment notion of progress, thought to be a necessity. The time of promise is messianic, or, as Levinas puts it, "where I must regard myself in the accusative mode of taking on responsibility for the sufferings and well being of all the others."[37]

In the notion of Illeity, it is my sense that there is a doubling of the trace. In other words, the other in her absence is someone to whom I am faithful and answerable. In fact, this is the case with the multiplicity of others. While it is true that some are more proximate, it is the very fact that I am responsible for all the absent others that makes it possible for us to speak of ethical life—even when justice appears as postponed, compromised, or inverted. Otherwise, I should be drawn simply after that which appears on the screen of my senses. This means that I can change the channel with my remote at virtually every moment. But there is a way in which the other remains constantly "on" for me. This is how Levinas grounds his distinction between need and desire. Need is something that may be filled, whereas desire, he says, is like the "hunger that begets hunger," or what Levinas calls metaphysics, as opposed to ontology, which is based strictly on need. This yearning, as we may call it, permits us to speak of love in relation to the Other, who transcends me. It is in this manner that love is, for Levinas, originary and therefore irreducible.

Let me make a suggestion for the metaphysical minimalism of Levinas. On the ethical level, the irreducible stance is the domain of the *for-the-other*. Practically, as has been noted by some critics of the utopian nature of the politics of Levinas, this is not achievable. That is to say, it is not possible to be always for the other, and even more so for a multiplicity of others. Still, Levinas does not regard utopianism as a reproach. What I think we can say, without compromising the spirit of the philosophy of Levinas, is that there must also be a way in which the Infinite appears as the "Other-for." In other words, the Other-for makes it possible for me to be turned around, to face the concrete Other, who comes to me from without. It is the Other-for who makes it possible for us to render prayer philosophically intelligible.

The reason we can speak of the absence of the Other-for at Auschwitz is that "before the other" was transmuted into the absolute war of each against each and all against all. Whether this philosophical expansion is legitimate from the standpoint of Levinas is not clear. Nor does it address the problem of providence in traditional Jewish theology. Nonetheless, this does not imply that Levinas is outside the bounds of normative Jewish thinking. Let us keep in mind that Levinas is first and foremost a philosopher who treads gingerly when it comes to theological issues. Levinas's work emphasizes the inseparability of humanity and morality. For Levinas, *what was unique to the Holocaust was the crisis of morality itself*. Part of his philosophic project, as we have noted, consists of searching for those minimal conditions and categories that make ethical and religious discourse possible.

Levinas speaks of the sense of abandonment between 1940 and 1945, the peculiar kind of loneliness, and what appears to be the disappearance of just institutions: "Who will say the loneliness of those who thought themselves dying at the same time as Justice, at a time when judgments between good and evil found no criterion but in the recesses of subjective conscience, no sign from without?"[38] How does one live in the absence of justice? Our ability to recognize the absence of justice, where justice is postponed or deformed, without therefore succumbing to a belief in its nonexistence is a necessary precondition grounding the possibility for all ethical life. More precisely, the demand for justice depends upon our capacity for reckoning with the claims of all the absent others, where it is not necessarily a case of spatial separation or temporal proximity. There is a decisive metaphysical difference that phenomenology has helped make clear between absence and nonexistence, a distinction long obscured in the history of philosophy.

What is absent can reappear. My attachment to someone who no longer lives is very different from my attachment to one who never lived at all. My relation to the absent other tests my fidelity, my assumption of responsibility, and calls forth restraint and patience on my part. Absence is not convertible to presence by a change of position, perspective, or interpretation. That which is absent is not necessarily an entity in another place, hidden from view, or unintelligible. It is important to stress this difference between absence and non-existence. Rather, the phenomenon of absence appears positively and forms our understanding of everyday events with concrete significance. The disbelieving look of the innocent one in her agony horrifies us just because it expresses the absence of justice. Our ability to recognize the suffering of the innocent is conjoined with this absence of justice that has the power to inform us that what passes for truth, under the sway of institutional power, is not exhaustive of reality. Awareness of this distinction offers scant consolation but nonetheless permits a degree of intelligibility to emerge.

For Levinas, echoing the Talmud, since the destruction of the Second Temple, what we have before us is only the "four cubits of Halacha,"[39] or Jewish law. This is why, for Levinas, a difficult freedom means a teaching that is inscribed as responsibility. This teaching is the continuing version of the rationality of transcendence. It is in this manner that we can glimpse a Jewish theology with an integrity of its own but nonetheless dependent upon the rehabilitation of Continental philosophy by Levinas, after Heidegger. This means that ethics rather than fundamental ontology must take its place as first philosophy. To paraphrase Se'adyah Ga'on, in an infinite amount of time, everyone would agree to recognize those laws of the Torah for which reasons are given and which are ethically intelligible—in Hebrew, "*mishpatim*." In other words, these laws extend to everyone. We do not, however, as yet, have the luxury of an infinite amount of time. For this reason, the Torah as a teaching, according to Se'adyah, is given. It is governed by a sense of urgency. This is what is meant by the phrase "we will do and we will understand."[40] There is a paradox mentioned by Kierkegaard in his journal: "We live forward and think backward." After Sinai it is affirmed that we can live forward and think forward, thus averting an otherwise inescapably tragic sense of life.

Levinas in no way seeks to devalue the ritual laws (*edot*) or the supra-rational laws (*ḥukkim*); rather, he tries to the extent possible to extract the ethical dimension of all these laws and practices. Moreover, they may have significance for everyone. This subject is much too complex for us to begin to investigate, especially since its wisdom is said to have exceeded even that of King Solomon. Levinas merely points out that the paradox of rendering oneself impure by burying someone else may be linked to overcoming an "always already sordid egoism."[41] This implies that for Levinas, the concern for the death and life of the other takes priority over my own, but not without a temporary cost.

Regarding the phrase "the four cubits of Halacha," the commentators on the Talmud indicate that this refers to the space where a sage who learns and understands the Torah may be found. In *Difficile Liberté*, Levinas, commenting on the first blessing uttered in the morning in the Jewish prayer book, asks why we thank God for the rooster, which can distinguish between night and day. Levinas, as only he can, asks: *Why the rooster and not some other animal?* Surely other animals distinguish between night and day! Yet only the rooster vocally communicates the dawning of the day to others who perhaps enjoy a bit more sleep in the morning. When does night end and the dawn of day begin? This is the very first question taken up in the Mishnah,[42] the core of the Talmud.

Why should we care that the first rays of dawn are evident? Before we ask, Levinas gives us an intimation of the answer. In the Jerusalem Talmud there is an opinion voiced that these four cubits are the distance at which we can make out the face of another person. In other words, as soon as the face of the other can appear, the human breaks in upon humanity. This is *our* world. The night has now passed.

Richard A. Cohen has labored long and successfully to place Levinas in the forefront of philosophy and Jewish thought. By continuing his efforts on the importance of importance, Cohen has helped us to better understand how Levinas remains the first challenge of the twenty-first century to philosophy and Jewish studies.[43]

Notes

1. Levinas, *Ethics and Infinity: Conversations with Philippe Nemo*, trans. Richard A. Cohen (Pittsburgh: University Press, 1985).

2. Levinas, *Discovering Existence with Husserl*, trans. Richard A. Cohen and Michael B. Smith (Evanston, Illinois: Northwestern University Press, 1998).

3. Cohen, Richard. *Elevations: The Height of the Good in Rosenzweig and Levinas* (Chicago: University of Chicago Press, 1994).

4. Levinas, *Is it Righteous to Be?* (Stanford, CA: Stanford University Press, 2001), 149.

5. William James, *The Will to Believe* (New York: Dover, 1956), 25.

6. E. Levinas, *Entre Nous: On Thinking-of-the-Other* (New York: Columbia University Press, 1998), 96.

7. This phrase first appears in an article on Gabriel Marcel. It is the title of one of the very best books written on Levinas: *The Rationality of Transcendence* by Theodorus de Boer (Amsterdam: J. C. Gieben, 1997).

8. Levinas, "Useless Suffering," in *Entre Nous*, 91–101.

9. Levinas, *The Theory of Intuition in Husserl's Phenomenology* (Evanston: Northwestern University Press, 1973), 158.

10. This phrase first appears in an article on Gabriel Marcel. It is the title of one of the very best books written on Levinas: *The Rationality of Transcendence* by Theodorus de Boer (Amsterdam: J. C. Gieben, 1997).

11. This story was told to me by Chaim Feinberg in 1991 in Monsey, New York. Feinberg authored *Leaping Souls: Rabbi Menachem Mendel and the Spirit of Kotzk* (Hoboken: Ktav, 1993).

12. Levinas, *Of God Who Comes to Mind*, Preface to the Second Edition (Stanford: Stanford University Press, 1998), ix–x.

13. Sugarman, "Through the Lens of Levinas: Preliminary Reflections on Holiness," *Levinas Studies*, vol. 8 (Pittsburgh: Duquesne University Press, 2013).

14. Emmanuel Levinas, *Of God Who Comes to Mind* (Stanford: Stanford University Press, 1998), 90.

15. BT Bava Mezi'a 59b.

16. Levinas, *Totality and Infinity: An Essay on Exteriority* (Pittsburgh: Duquesne University Press, 1969), 22.

17. Levinas, 22.

18. Levinas, 22.

19. Levinas, 23.

20. Friedrich Nietzsche, *Twilight of the Idols* (New York: Viking Press, 1954), 167.

21. Levinas, *Nine Talmudic Readings* (Bloomington: Indiana University Press, 1990), 187.

22. Levinas, *Nine Talmudic Readings* (Bloomington: Indiana University Press, 1990), 187.

23. Franz Kafka, "Three Parables," in *Existentialism from Dostoevsky to Sartre*, ed. Walter Kaufmann (New York: Penguin, 1975), 151.

24. Levinas, "Damages Due to Fire," in *Nine Talmudic Readings* (see note 19 above), on BT Bava Kamma 60a–b.

25. Genesis 18:23, 25.

26. Levinas, *Nine Talmudic Readings*, 187.

27. Yehuda Nachshoni, *Studies in the Weekly Parashah: Sh'mos*, trans. Shmuel Himelstein (New York: Mesorah, 2002), 583.

28. Levinas, *Nine Talmudic Readings*, 187.

29. Levinas, 187.

30. Levinas, 186.

31. Levinas, 186.

32. Emmanuel Levinas, *Difficult Freedom: Essays on* Judaism, trans. Sean Hand (Baltimore: Johns Hopkins University Press, 1990), 291.

33. Emmanuel Levinas, "To Love the Torah More Than God," trans. H. A. Stephenson with commentary by Sugarman, in *Judaism* (Spring 1979), 220.

34. Levinas, "Meaning and Sense," in *Emmanuel Levinas: Basic Philosophical Writings*, ed. Adriaan Peperzak (Bloomington: Indiana University Press, 1996), 62.

35. Levinas, *God, Death, and Time* (Stanford, CA: Stanford University Press, 2000), 224.

36. Levinas, *Time and the Other*, trans. Richard Cohen (Pittsburgh: Duquesne University Press, 1987), 73.

37. Sugarman, "Messianic Temporality: Preliminary Reflections on Ethical Messianism and the Deformalization of Time in Emmanuel Levinas," in *Recherches lévinassiennes*, ed. Roger Burggraeve et al. (Leuven: Peeters, 2012), 428ff.

38. Levinas, *Proper Names* (Stanford, CA: Stanford University Press, 1996), 96, 119.

39. Levinas, 423, quoting Berakhot, 8a.

40. Exodus 24:7.

41. Levinas, *New Talmudic Readings* (Pittsburgh: Duquesne University Press, 1999), 116.

42. Mishnah Berakhot 1:1.

43. Part of this essay was first published in the book *As a Perennial Spring*, edited and published by Bentsi Cohen, 2013, who was a student of both Rabbi JB Soloveitchik and Rabbi Dr. Norman Lamm. I would like to thank Bentsi Cohen for permission to republish parts of this essay here.

Bibliography

Levinas, Emmanuel. *Ethics and Infinity: Conversations with Philippe Nemo*. Translated by Richard A. Cohen. Pittsburgh: Duquesne University Press, 1985.

Levinas, Emmanuel. *Discovering Existence with Husserl*. Translated by Richard A. Cohen and Michael B. Smith. Evanston, IL: Northwestern University Press, 1998.

Cohen, Richard. *Elevations: The Height of the Good in Rosenzweig and Levinas*. Chicago: University of Chicago Press, 1994.

Levinas, Emmanuel. *Is it Righteous to Be?* Stanford, CA: Stanford University Press, 2001.

James, William. *The Will to Believe*. New York: Dover. 1956.

Levinas, Emmanuel. *Entre Nous: On Thinking-of-the-Other*. New York: Columbia University Press, 1998.

Boer, Theo de. *The Rationality of Transcendence: Studies in the Philosophy of Emmanuel Levinas*. Amsterdam Studies in Jewish Thought, V. 4. Amsterdam: J. C. Gieben, 1997.

Levinas, Emanuel. *The Theory of Intuition in Husserl's Phenomenology*. Evanston: Northwestern University Press, 1973.

Feinberg, Chaim. *Leaping Souls: Rabbi Menachem Mendel and the Spirit of Kotzk*. Hoboken, NJ: Ktav, 1993.

Levinas, Emmanuel. *Of God Who Comes to Mind*. 2nd ed. Meridian, Crossing Aesthetics. Stanford, CA: Stanford University Press, 1998.

Sugarman, Richard. "Messianic Temporality: Preliminary Reflections on Ethical Messianism and the Deformalization of Time in Emmanuel Levinas" In *Recherches lévinassiennes*, ed. Roger Burggraeve et al. 428 ff. Leuven: Peeters, 2012.

Sugarman, Richard. "Through the Lens of Levinas: Preliminary Reflections on Holiness." In *Levinas Studies*, vol. 8. Pittsburgh: Duquesne University Press, 2013.

Levinas, Emmanuel. *Totality and Infinity: An Essay on* Exteriority. Translated by Alphonso Lingis. Pittsburgh: Duquesne University Press, 1969.

Nietzsche, Friedrich. *Twilight of the Idols*. New York: Viking Press, 1954.

Levinas, *Nine Talmudic Readings*. Translated by Annette Aronowicz. Bloomington: Indiana University Press, 1990.

Kafka, Franz. "Three Parables." In *Existentialism from Dostoevsky to Sartre*. Edited by Walter Kaufmann. New York: Penguin, 1975.

Nachshoni, Yehuda. *Studies in the Weekly Parashah: Sh'mos*. Translated by Shmuel Himelstein. New York: Mesorah, 2002.

Levinas, Emmanuel. *Difficult Freedom: Essays on Judaism*. Translated by Sean Hand. Baltimore: Johns Hopkins University Press, 1990.

Levinas, Emmanuel. "To Love the Torah More Than God" Translated by H. A. Stephenson with commentary by Richard Sugarman. *Judaism* Spring 1979, 79–86.

Levinas, Emmanuel. "Meaning and Sense." In *Emmanuel Levinas: Basic Philosophical Writings*. Edited by Adriaan Peperzak. Bloomington: Indiana University Press, 1996.

Levinas, Emmanuel and Jacques Rolland. *God, Death, and Time*. Translated by Bettina Bergo. Meridian. Stanford, CA: Stanford University Press, 2000.

Levinas, Emmanuel. *Time and the Other*. Translated by Richard Cohen. Pittsburgh: Duquesne University Press, 1987.

Levinas, Emmanuel. *Proper Names*. Translated by Michael B. Smith and David E. Wellbery. Stanford, CA: Stanford University Press, 1996.

Levinas, Emmanuel. *New Talmudic Readings*. Translated by Richard A. Cohen. Pittsburgh: Duquesne University Press, 1999.

17

Levinas and the Ethics of Sacrifice
Reading "Dying For . . ." Adverbially

SANDOR GOODHART

The emergence, in the life lived by the human being . . . of the devoting-of-oneself-to-the-other. In the general economy of being in its inflection back upon itself, a preoccupation with the other even to the point of sacrifice, even to the possibility of dying for him or her; a responsibility for the other. Otherwise than being! It is this shattering of indifference—even if indifference is statistically dominant—this possibility of one-for-the-other, that constitutes the ethical event. . . . It is as if the emergence of the human in the economy of being upset the meaning and plot and philosophical rank of ontology: the in-itself of being-persisting-in-being goes beyond itself in the gratuitousness of the outside-of-itself-for-the-other, in sacrifice, or the possibility of sacrifice, in the perspective of holiness.

—Emmanuel Levinas, *Entre Nous*

In this chapter I will do three things.[1] First, I will summarize Emmanuel Levinas's text, "Dying for . . . ," which is one of the later texts of *Entre Nous*.[2] Next, I will explicate certain themes of "Dying for . . ." that seem to me to confirm—at least for those of us familiar with *Totality and Infinity* and *Otherwise Than Being*—expectations that we may have on the basis of that writing (I am thinking especially of the adverbial versus the adjectival). Thirdly, I will consider Levinas's take on Heidegger's treatment of "my death."[3] And in conclusion, I will pose some questions raised by the text itself concerning substitution, temporality, and their somewhat ambivalent status here and elsewhere in Levinas's writing.

Part One: Reading "Dying For . . ."

The great revolution of Heidegger's philosophy, Levinas tells us, is to understand being as a verb, as an event. The "event of being," the adventure of being, in its *Eigentlichkeit*, its authenticity, reveals itself as "existential," as "being-there" or *Da-sein*, as fundamentally adverbial. The fact of its existence—of its ec-stasis, the fact of its being human—is revealed not as preceding and gathering objects, nor as a transcendental subject. Rather this study of being reveals itself in Levinas's view as independent of subject and object, and, as a consequence, independent of consciousness. Heidegger calls this new approach "ontology," and for Levinas it signals—whatever the disastrous politics in which the author of this approach would become embroiled—a new approach to the meaningful.

But Levinas will show that this fact of its being human in fact escapes ontology, that in declaring existence or *Da-sein* to be the secret of being, as Heidegger does, we have not gone far enough in our effort to understand "first philosophy," the axiological starting place from which all speculation on being and beings proceeds (and which is Heidegger's philosophic project). Such first philosophy will only be found in the ethical understood as infinite responsibility for the other individual.

Here is how Levinas does this. There are two alternative ways of understanding the human: the human as identity, and the human as devotion to the other, a responsibility that is also an election. Being near things means being near things that are ready-to-hand, *Zu-handenheit*. But these things are ready-to-hand because they are part of being-in-the-world, and being-in-the-world means being-with-others. Section 26 of *Sein und Zeit*, Levinas points out, studies being with others as *Sorge*, care, or *Fürsorge*, care for, the care of one for the other, and this care of one for the other is constitutive of being-there; Heidegger calls this being with others *Miteinandersein*.

But such *Miteinandersein* of the everyday then gets mixed up in Heidegger's analysis (as Levinas reads it) with the "they," with the being of **all** the others that takes over in a kind of subtle "dictatorship." The "they" disburdens the everyday of its particular being; it "accommodates" the everyday, but it does so to its own advantage since it thereby enhances its own "domination" over that everyday.

Thus, in Heidegger, the return to the authentic is no longer sought in identity, in subject and object; but neither is it sought through some sort of reaching out toward the other that escapes the "with" and the "for" of *Miteinandersein* and *Fürsorge*; rather this return to the authentic is sought in ontology; and at the heart of this ontology is an "upheaval" brought about by a being-for-death that is anticipated with the courage of an anxiety, the "courage of an anxiety" that Levinas calls, somewhat sarcastically, a "perfect authenticity" since it replaces a concern with fears and evasions of the everyday. "With death," Heidegger writes, "*Da-sein* stands before its ownmost potentiality-for-being."[4] And this encounter with death undoes all relations with the other. Thus, "the *Eigentlichkeit* par excellence of being-there," Levinas writes, "is not a beyond being."[5]

"Dying for" opens the way for Levinas to that which is beyond being. In Heidegger's philosophic project, our potential encounter with others is thwarted in one of two ways: either we proceed through the "they" that lacks authenticity, or we proceed through authenticity and its anticipation of death, which undoes all relations. Thus we have an ontology, a being-there concerned with being, and a being-in-the-world privileging *Eigentlichkeit* in relation to care for the other person but conditioned by occupations and works, not faces, and without the death of the other signifying for the survivor any more than "funerary behaviors and emotions, and memories."[6]

Without attempting to "improve upon" Heidegger, Levinas concludes by telling us briefly what matters for him. Levinas notes that he titled his remarks "Dying for . . ." or "Dying for another" (the phrase "Dying for . . ."—*Mourir pour* . . . in French—is taken from section 47 of *Sein und Zeit*).[7] He tells us that he considered calling it "dying together," despite the common sense we have that death means separation. He recalls a biblical text from II Samuel 1:23 in which the prophet, weeping for the death of King Saul with his son Jonathan in battle, says that they were "swifter than eagles," "stronger than lions," and notes that in death they were "not divided."[8] Levinas suggests that this passage is not referring to some life after life, nor is it just a metaphorical way of talking; but it may suggest that the human as living may surpass or exceed "the animal effort of life," the effort he describes as "purely life." The newness of this idea of the human thus conceived "would not be reduced to a more intense effort" at "persevering in being" (which is the Heideggerian assumption, and, we might add, the Freudian assumption as well) but rather would refer to a human that "would awaken in the guise of responsibility for the other man,"

> the human in which the "for the other" goes beyond the simple *Fürsorge* exercising itself in a world where others, gathered round about things, *are* what they do; the human, in which worry over the death of the other comes before care for self. The humanness of dying for the other would be the very meaning of love in its responsibility for one's fellowman and, perhaps, the primordial inflection of the affective as such. The call to holiness preceding the concern for existing, for being-there and being-in-the-world—utopian, a dis-interestedness more profound than the *with-the-others* or *for-the-others* of the *Fürsorge* involved in the being-in-the-world, in which the being of the other equals his occupation and is understood only in terms of "one's things" and vested interest. Care as holiness, which is what Pascal called love without concupiscence. A no-place prior to the *there* of *being-there*, prior to the *Da-* of the *Dasein*, prior to that place in the sun that Pascal feared was "the prototype and beginning of the usurpation of the whole world."[9]

"Dying for . . ." is for Levinas then the adverbial modality of the human as such, the human conceived as a beyond being, as an opening to a limitless responsibility, a responsibility I can no more shirk than I can have another die in my place. It occurs to Heidegger, as *Sterben für* (in section 47 of *Sein und Zeit*), as a "simple sacrifice," without death for this other person being capable of releasing the other person from death, or challenging the truth of "everyone dies for himself." The "ethics of sacrifice" in Heidegger, Levinas tells us, "does not succeed in shaking the rigor of being and the ontology of the authentic."[10]

Does not the "relationship to the other in sacrifice," Levinas asks, "in which the death of the other preoccupies the human *being-there* before his own death," indicate precisely a beyond (or before) ontology disclosing at the same time a responsibility for the other and through that responsibility a human "I" that is neither subject nor object, an I that is chosen to answer for his fellowman and in this way and only this way identical to itself and constitutive of the self?[11] A uniqueness that derives from chosenness rather than an "ownmost potentiality" before death? Beyond humanism as we still currently conceive of it, which is a humanness of life and knowledge (the *conatus essendi*) and thus not human enough? Priority of the other over the I, of the Thou over the I in Buber's (or Marcel's) famous formulation of the "I-Thou," is in the view of Levinas the human response to the nakedness or vulnerability of the face and its mortality. It is there in the other's face "that the concern for the other's death is realized, and that 'dying for him', 'dying his death', takes priority over authentic death."[12] This gesture does not issue from some hope for a resurrection, for some *post-mortem* life, but rather from the very excessiveness of sacrifice, a gesture that constitutes holiness in charity and mercy. This maintenance of death as a perpetual future from a present of love (rather than imagining death as a present before a future love)—and thus a schema of temporality cognate with Franz Rosenzweig's triad of creation, revelation and redemption rather than Aristotle's past, present, and future, or Christianity's messianic age and second coming—Levinas tells us, is probably one of the "original secrets of temporality itself and beyond all metaphor."[13]

Part Two: "Dying For . . ." As Adverb

To Die For, as some readers may know, was the title of at least two Hollywood movies released in the United States. The first, released in 1989, directed by Deran Sarafian and starring Brendan Hughes, concerned a group of vampires who fought their battles in the streets of Los Angeles. The second, directed by Gus Van Sant in 1995 and starring Nicole Kidman and Matt Dillon, chronicled the story of a beautiful though cold young woman who seduced a young man into killing her husband for her so that she could escape small town-life and advance herself in her chosen career: the popular news media. (Perhaps the earlier movie could be viewed as one of the consequences of the latter one.) The title thus referred in this second context to both the beauty of the woman (billed, so to speak, as "drop dead gorgeous"), to the fate of the two men affected by her charms (both the young man who kills "for" her and his—and her—victim), and perhaps as well to the nature of the valuation of the human that has allowed for this kind of behavior. In fact, in common parlance in America the phrase "to die for" has become something of a postmodernist synonym for extreme desirability overlaid upon objects of little or no consequence. We speak of certain kinds of foods (attractive desserts, for example), as being "to die for;" or we speak of other aspects of popular culture as being "to die for."

I think that it is appropriate that the translators of the present text, Michael Smith and Barbara Harshav, decided against such an adjectival rendering of Levinas's original "*mourir pour . . .*" and chose instead to follow the English rendering that Joan Stambaugh introduces into her translation of *Sein und Zeit*,[14] namely, "dying for . . .," a phrase that highlights the adverbial function of these words, which is to say, modifying not a noun or another adjective, as in the above example, where the beauty of the character played by Nicole Kidman is characterized as "to die for," but modifying rather a verb, answering not "which, what kind of, how many," but "how, when, or where."

This distinction between adjective and adverb is an important one since Levinas makes a great deal out of Heidegger's description of being as an "event" or "adventure" that assumes various modalities or manners of being—being-in-the-world, being-there, being-in-itself, being-for-itself, being-with, being-a-self, being-toward-death, being-a-whole, potentiality-of-being, and so forth—all of which, Levinas points out, Heidegger calls, somewhat curiously, "existentials."

The first point that I want to suggest is that Levinas does the same with "dying for . . . in that he uses the concept he finds in Heidegger to name a manner or modality of an action (in this case the action of responsibility rather than of being) rather than using it to describe a substantive or a description of a substantive (as he might well have done); but (and here is my second point) that he takes a phrase to which Heidegger assigns a somewhat minor importance (a minor modality of being-toward-death) and reassigns it a major role.

The phrase, in Levinas's hands, is already a kind of philosophic pun (the phrase in German is *Sterben für*). It reminds us on the one hand of phrases like "being for itself" and "being in itself," which of course is a fundamental distinction in phenomenology (one thinks of the être *pour soi* and être *en soi* in Sartre's vocabulary), or the *Fürsorge* ("solicitude") in Heidegger's vocabulary of which Levinas makes so much, phrases in which "for" appears to designate orientation or direction and points us toward words like "towards" or "unto."

Levinas and the Ethics of Sacrifice | 263

But the phrase also derives its tension in Levinas's usage from the fact that "dying for" appears to mark an event, an action on behalf of another; yet "dying" is the one action you might think you should not be able to do "for" or on behalf of another. It denotes an extreme or ultimate of action since it designates a point in one's relationship with another necessarily conceived without one present. "I can no more give up my responsibility for the other individual than I can have another die in my place," Levinas is fond of saying.

Part Three: Levinas's Notion of Death and Heidegger's

Part of the reason for Levinas's insistence upon death as unique in this way has to do with his critique of Heidegger's notion of death. For Heidegger, death is what guarantees being, as its "nonrelational ownmost possibility." "Death," Heidegger writes in Levinas's citation, "is a possibility of being that *Da-sein* always has to take upon itself. With death, *Da-sein* stands before itself in its ownmost potentiality-of-being. . . . This nonrelational ownmost possibility is at the same time the most extreme one. As a potentiality of being, *Da-sein* is unable to bypass the possibility of death. Death is the possibility of the absolute impossibility of *Da-sein*."[15] Now Levinas will qualify this Heideggerian understanding of death in two ways. Death for Levinas is not the "possibility of impossibility" (as Heidegger formulates it) but the "impossibility of possibility." "The impossibility of escaping God lies in the depths of myself as a self, as an absolute passivity. This passivity is not only the possibility of death in being, the possibility of impossibility. It is an impossibility prior to that possibility . . . . It is the birth of meaning in the obtuseness of being, of a 'being able to die' subject to sacrifice."[16] He makes this qualification for two reasons. If death is the "possibility of impossibility," as it is in Heidegger, then it remains a structure of possibility (rather than one of impossibility)—whatever follows from that possibility, which is to say, it remains a structure of ego, of defense. One of those possibilities of this line of thinking is that this particular event, death, may not be the end of possibility. Therefore, to say it is the *possibility* of impossibility is to say that it is also possible that it is *not* impossible, that it is not the end of possibility, that death is the possibility of a possibility, of an openness to capability or capacity. Heidegger's definition, in other words, keeps open the door to the resurrectional or some other type of life after death. This option for Levinas will become problematic when he talks about time and, in particular, Rosenzweig's notion of temporality.

There is a second reason Levinas qualifies it. The possibility of my death for Heidegger, which is to say, of impossibility, guarantees in a curious way my possibility. "With death," Heidegger writes, "*Da-sein* stands before itself in its *ownmost potentiality-of-being*" [my italics].[17] For Heidegger, all concepts derive their most authentic being from the possibility of their own impossibility (and Jacques Derrida's working out of the path of this impossibility in just about every text he undertakes to examine is well known).[18]

But in doing so, in defining death and being this way, from Levinas's perspective, Heidegger has defined life by death, precisely by including death within it. Levinas, on the other hand, would like to formulate a notion of life that excludes death, that defines itself as other than death, that sees death as the end of possibility and thus the end of the human, a limiting strategy that ironically may prove more hopeful than its Heideggerian counterpart. Levinas gives the biblical example of Saul and his son Jonathan whose "dying together" does not promise an afterlife, a life after death for Levinas, but ironically a defeat by the human of death.

In defining death the way he does, in other words, Heidegger (in Levinas's view) excludes the notion of the human that Levinas finds critical. Why "critical"? Part of the crisis is the confrontation of National Socialism with the enthusiasm of the young German philosopher admired by so many—Levinas among them. But the "crisis" to which Levinas refers is older. It concerns a Platonic gesture by which the diachrony of time is expelled and replaced with the synchrony of representation. "Dying for . . ." in this context names an adverbial mode of behavior, a prophetic diachronic mode, that precedes being, that is beyond or before being. How so? It escapes being because it concerns the other individual, not as I represent him, but as he encounters me, not as an it but as a Thou, not as a figure who reflects the round trip journey of my Ego from the same to the other and back again but as one who jumps over my starting place to a heteronymous relation with the other individual prior to my self-constructing autonomy—in short, not as an object to a subject but as a face to face.

As such, "dying for . . ." is a modality of responsibility, one of the ways I can enact my infinite responsibility for the other individual (*autrui*). In these terms, Levinas calls it the "ethics of sacrifice" and he links it to the notion of time, to what he calls absolute futurity.

Conclusion

My thesis, then, is that Levinas takes a minor reference in *Sein und Zeit* and reads it adverbially, the way Heidegger has taught us to read being in general. But perhaps here the student has surpassed the master. For in Levinas's hands, this idea opens us to a beyond being and allows us to wonder whether in relating being in its ownmost and most authentic capacity in death, its capacity to undo all other relations at the moment of death (as Heidegger says), Heidegger has betrayed his own purpose. What if the "ethics of sacrifice" opens us to a living in the wake of death, to a world envisioned, for example, by the biblical universe, in which "dying with another" defeats the egoistic conception that would regard death as simply one more modality of possibility, even if that possibility is of impossibility itself?

Such a re-conceptualization would require new conceptualizations. It would require in the first place a new notion of substitution, one no longer conceived according to the model of exchange, of the one for the other, but rather according to the model of gestation or maternity, of the other in the same, of a participation or sharing in the fortunes of the other that precedes my free and conscious choice and for which my very subjectivity is a modality not of being but prior to being of responsibility, a responsibility to which I was elected before choosing and that I can own or disavow but not escape. But secondly, perhaps, it requires a new notion of time or temporality, one that no longer presupposes the pastness of the past or the futurity of the future as in clock time, but envisions an infinite within the finite: one capable of being disclosed as the ongoingness of the past and the future anteriority of the future in whose wake my ownership of my infinite responsibility for the other human being allows me to live.

But those conceptions are another story for another day.

Notes

1. The following essay was delivered as a talk at a conference in London, England, in 2004 (read by my colleague at Purdue University, Thomas Ryba) and again at a joint meeting of the North American Levinas Society and the Société Internationale de Recherche Emmanuel Levinas in Toulouse, France (read by the author), in 2016. The current version is offered in honor of the work of Richard A. Cohen.

2. Levinas, *Entre Nous*, 207–17.

3. See Levinas, *Totality and Infinity*.
4. Quoted in Levinas, *Entre Nous*, 214.
5. Levinas, *Entre Nous*, 214.
6. Levinas, *Entre Nous*, 215.
7. Compare Heidegger, *Being and Time*, 221–24.
8. Levinas, *Entre Nous*, 215.
9. Levinas, *Entre Nous*, 216. Here is the French original: de l'humain où le « pour l'autre » déborde la simple *Für-sorge* s'exerçant dans un monde où les autres, autour des chose sont ce qu'ils font ; de l'humain où l'inquiétude pour la mort d'autrui passe avant le souci pour soi. Humain du mourir pour l'autre qui serait le sens même de l'amour dans sa responsabilité pour le prochain et, peut être, l'inflexion primordiale de l'affectif comme tel. Appel de la sainteté précédant le souci d'exister, le souci d'être-là et d 'être-au-monde, utopie, désinteressement, plus profondes que l'avec les autres ou le pour les autres de la *Fürsorge* impliquée dans l'être-au-monde où l'être de l'autre équivaut à son métier et ne s'entend qu'à partir des « affaires » et de l'intéressement. Souci comme sainteté, ce que Pascal appelait amour sans concupiscence. Non-lieu préalable au là de l'être-là, préalable au Da du Dasein, à cette place au soleil où Pascal redoutait « l'image et le commencement de l'usurpation de toute la terre». Emmanuel Levinas, *Entre nous. Essais sur le penser-à -l'autre* (Paris: Grasset, 1991), 213.
10. Levinas, *Entre Nous*, 217.
11. Levinas, *Entre Nous*, 217.
12. Levinas, *Entre Nous*, 217.
13. Levinas, *Entre Nous*, 217.
14. Heidegger, *Being and Time*, 223.
15. Heidegger, *Being and Time*, 232.
16. Levinas, *Otherwise Than Being*, 128.
17. Heidegger, *Being and Time*, 232.
18. "The least bad definition," Derrida is reported to have said concerning deconstruction, was that deconstruction was "a certain experience of the impossible." See Peter Conradi, *The Sunday Times*, October 10, 2004. Conradi's remark in the above obituary for Jacques Derrida is all the more remarkable for being one of the few accurate statements about Derrida's work within a largely misinformed and unappreciative article.

Bibliography

Conradi, Peter, "France's Radical Chic Philosopher Dies at 74," *The Sunday Times* (London), October 10, 2004.

Girard, René. *Violence and the Sacred*. Baltimore: The Johns Hopkins University Press, 1977.

Heidegger, Martin. *Being and Time. A Translation of Sein und Zeit*. Translated by Joan Stambaugh. Albany: State University of New York Press, 1996.
Levinas, Emmanuel. *Entre Nous: Thinking-of-the-Other*. Translated by Michael B. Smith and Barbara Harshav. New York: Columbia University Press, 1998.
Levinas, Emmanuel. "Aimer la Thora Plus Que Dieu," *Difficile liberté. Essais sûr le judaisme*. Paris: Albin Michel, 1976. Translated by Seán Hand as Emmanuel Levinas, *Difficult Freedom. Essays on Judaism*. Baltimore: Johns Hopkins University Press, 1990.
Levinas, Emmanuel. "Man-God," *Entre Nous. Thinking-of-the-Other*. Translated by Michael B. Smith and Barbara Harshav. New York: Columbia University Press, 1998, 53–54.
Levinas, Emmanuel. *Otherwise Than Being or Beyond Essence*. Translated by Alphonso Lingis. Pittsburgh: Duquesne University Press, 2000.
Levinas, Emmanuel. *Totality and Infinity: An Essay on Exteriority*. Translated by Alphonso Lingis. Pittsburgh: Duquesne University Press, 2001.

Path IV
Ethical Religion

18

The Small Goodness Never Wins, But Is Never Defeated

On How Emmanuel Levinas Finds Inspiration in Vasily Grossman for His Vision of a Humane Society

ROGER BURGGRAEVE

The reference to the "small goodness" (*la petite bonté*) appeared in the work of Emmanuel Levinas from 1985, together with the reference to the novel *Life and Fate* by the Russian-Jewish writer, Vasily Grossman (1905–1964). Concretely, it concerns a full paragraph of a Talmudic reading "Beyond Memory," which Levinas delivered in December 1985 on Memory and History, the 25th "Colloque des intellectuels juifs de langue française" in Paris. From that period on, mainly in interviews, Levinas refers to Grossman's novel as a real source of inspiration.[1] Levinas's interest in this novel is not that of a literary academic or historian concerned about an objective-scientific report on the origin, background, and content of the book. His reading and interpretation take place from the perspective of his own thought, in particular the relationship between society and ethics inspired by the face-to-face responsibility. In line with his thought, we would like to develop the significance of the "small goodness" for the humanization of society. Starting from Grossman's critique of the Stalinist regime, we reflect along with Levinas on the risk of totalitarianism that slumbers within every sociopolitical order. This sets us on the track of the "small goodness," not only as a surpassing of but likewise as leverage within social, economic, juridical, and political organizations. Last, but not least, we will make clear how the small goodness correctly understood can imply a reversal of the traditional view on the future of human society, including a redefinition of messianism.

When the Sociopolitical Order Raises Itself into a Definitive Regime

In his reading of *Life and Fate*, Levinas recognizes his own suspicions in Grossman's critique of Stalinism. Interpreting in his own way the style of socialist realism propagated and imposed for the glorification of the Communist Revolution, the book reported "coldly and boldly" on the organized terror and depersonalizing horror of the Stalinist regime.[2]

The Totalitarian Perversion of the Collective Good (Grossman)

Although he initially, and for quite some time, saw in the communist regime the arrival of eschatological, messianic events, Grossman also saw the enormous machinery—with its "mythological grandeur" and infallibility—deployed by the Stalinist regime to pressurize, spread propaganda, and to keep its own people, and especially its scientists, intellectuals, and artists, in a stranglehold.[3] He saw the achievements of the new workers state but also had to acknowledge and reflect its reverse side, namely the so-called evident and necessary violence of the government. During the "general collectivization" he saw the sufferings of the peasantry with his own eyes. He saw the arrests, killings, and deportations of thousands and thousands of kulaks (expropriated wealthy farm owners), considered class enemies of the farm laborers and poor peasants.[4] Hence the initial fascination was converted, not without hesitations and strategic considerations, into its own opposite.[5] Grossman even goes so far to situate Stalinism on the same level as the terrors of the Nazi regime.[6] Both embody the idea of total war, resonating with the "final and total war" of Gog and Magog in Ezekiel 38.[7] (This was one of the reasons why Grossman's book was confiscated but the author was not arrested nor exiled).[8]

Still more important is that Grossman shows how the terror of the Stalinist regime legitimizes itself in the name of the collective Good and thus presents itself as "utopia," the only alternative for the derailment of the bourgeois-capitalism of the Czars (and of Western Europe). What is shocking is that the general collectivization, with the enforced regulation they demanded, "was carried out in the name of Good."[9] Grossman puts the following words in the mouth of Ikonnikov: "I saw people annihilated in the name of an idea of good as fine and humane as the ideal of Christianity. The idea [of social good] was something fine and noble—yet it killed some without mercy, rippled the lives of others, and separated wives and husbands and children from fathers."[10] It is a painful insight that evil is usually not committed as evil but is legitimized as a form of the Good, particularly of the sociopolitical order proclaimed as the common or universal Good.[11] Hence the challenging conclusion of Grossman (Ikonnikov), which is likewise cited by Levinas: "I do not believe in the Good," "this terrible Good with a capital 'G.'"[12]

In the short article "Le surlendemain des dialectiques" (1970), long before Grossman, Levinas unmasked the Stalinist regime as turning the sociopolitical Good into evil: "the very alienation of the work of de-alienation: Stalinism": "the very alienation of de-alienation"). In the name of the future sociopolitical Good, one is allowed "here and now" to murder, to persecute, to lock up without due process. Moreover, that politics was based on the presupposition that the "bearers" of the regime availed of the truth of the future and the present.[13]

For Levinas, the shock is even greater because "the Russian Revolution refuting itself in Stalinism" finds its inspiration and justification in Marxism.[14] In Marxism, Levinas finds a certain affinity with his own thought on the priority of the other and our radical responsibility for the other.[15] It is for this reason that it is even more shocking that Marxism has turned into its own opposite precisely thanks to Stalinism: "Its noble hope consists in healing everything, in installing, beyond the chance of individual charity, a regime without evil. And the regime of charity becomes Stalinism."[16] This change from the inside-out of Marxism into Stalinism is "the greatest offence of the human, because Marxism bore the hopes of humanity."[17] Stalinism has made its original prophetic generosity of "the one for the vulnerable and alienated other" into its own opposite: "the philosophical masquerade of disguising evil as good," "the supreme paradox of the defense of man and his rights being perverted into Stalinism," which Levinas calls "the greatest spiritual crisis in modern Europe.[18]"

THE PERVERSION OF THE GOOD INTO ITS OPPOSITE IS A PERMANENT TEMPTATION.

The reversal of the Good into its opposite as an access to the final Good is for Levinas not only a past historical fact but shows a permanent possibility: "General and generous principles can be inverted in their application. Every generous thought is threatened by its Stalinism. (. . .) Ideology is the generosity and clarity of the principle which have not considered the inversion which keeps a watch on this general principle when it is applied." The perversion of the idea of the Good as a consequence of its organization adheres to every economic, social, juridical, political organization, even when it flows forth from the best ethical intention of responsibility for the other. An autocratic, totalitarian ideology is the inexorability of the general principle that "runs the danger of becoming its own contrary and forgets—or refuses—to consider the general in the light of the particular."[19]

However indispensable a sociopolitical order may be for the realization of the humane to give shape to the responsibility of all for all, every such order tends to absolutize and sacralize itself, which in the Bible is called the temptation of idolatry: "A justice that has no patience to strive only for a better justice but raises itself above time into an absolute and immutable regime leads us to a totalitarian politics."[20] In this regard, Levinas refers to "the state of Caesar": "Despite its participation in the pure essence of the state, the state of Caesar is also the place of corruption par excellence and, perhaps, the ultimate refuge of idolatry. Incapable of being without self-adoration, it is idolatry itself."[21] Political power is tempted to make itself permanent and autocratic, and to install itself—or perhaps "wrap" itself—in its own power, making use of available structural and legal means: direct (tyrannical) and indirect (populist), for instance in all sorts of "bread and games," financial or other concessions, "carriages and horses" (to use a biblical image).[22] "The state of Caesar, the pagan state, is jealous of its sovereignty, in search of hegemony: the conquering, imperialist, totalitarian, oppressive state, attached to realist egoism."[23] Every political order comes to stand under the pressure of this 'imperial' temptation: "The conquering march is probably in the invincible logic of political power, whatever be the limits of that power. Political power wants to expand, it wants to be an empire."[24] It makes use of the repressive potentiality of the rigor and the harshness of structural justice itself, with its controlling and sanctioning regulations (dura lex).[25] In case a "secular sacralization" is at hand, and thus not a theocracy (as was the case with Stalinism), a remarkable paradox takes place in the sense that it then is about a "divinization without God" that at the same time implies a replacing of God: "enlightened tyranny" and "the diabolical tricks by which the civilizations which rest on truths that rush forward, do not keep their own promises."[26]

Not only a political system but also every social system—for instance, in somatic and psychological health care, in the environmental sector, in education, in development cooperation (with its nongovernmental organizations)—is by nature conservative, in the sense that it can turn into its own contrary by raising itself up as a definitive regime or "system of salvation" that gives a final answer to the needs of its "subjects" or "clients." Levinas pointed out how not only Stalinist politics suffocated itself in all sorts of centralist administration and bureaucracy, but how this fate threatens just as much our so-called democratically designed and controlled forms of politics, a paradoxical form of violence, namely a form of "non-violent violence."[27] "The history of modern Europe is the permanent temptation of an ideological rationalism, and of experiments carried out through the rigor of deduction, administration and violence": administration, with its "gluttony for dossiers," is a self-multiplying system whereby organizations and institutions consolidate and develop their power, at the cost of the unique subject.[28] These systems not only become more and more complex but, like octopuses, have a long reach with their tentacles. And it is not because these systems arise out of an ethical responsibility of the one for the other that they are ensured against the "systemic aberration" and "perversion from the inside-out" into institutionalism. Notwithstanding their original goodwill, they can be developed in such a manner that they undermine their noble goals and thus bring about evil as the reverse-side of the good.

Small Goodness as Leverage to Humanize Society

Hence according to Levinas, "the political," with all its social and economic levels and all its juridical and institutional forms, should never get the final word about the realization of justice and a humane society.

Ethically speaking, there is a need for a transcendence of the political, which implies refusal of resignation as refusal of the sociopolitical "status quo."[29]

Ethical Appeal to Surpass the Sociopolitical Order

This appeal to transcend the sociopolitical order and its economic, social, and legal mediations and institutions shows an important difference between Grossman and Levinas. Confronted as Grossman (and Ikonnikov) were with Stalinist terror, they lose all trust in the state as an organized form of collective well-being. Even Levinas acknowledges how the book *Life and Fate* is marked by a "constant pessimism," as the already cited quote shows: "I do not believe in the Good."[30] Levinas shares wholeheartedly the distrust toward totalitarian states and regimes. But with him, this does not imply that he loses sight of the importance of the "the political" or the "polis" (Aristotle). Time and again, he emphasizes the ethical necessity of organized society and politics, which for him, moreover, also implies that he deems possible that which is an ethical must. The possibility and reality of the multifaceted sociopolitical order is indeed linked to the condition of the "liberal" principle, namely that a considerable and constant vigilance is needed to prevent the structural, institutional, and legal forms from deteriorating into (brutal or subtle) forms of autocracy and institutionalism, police state and totalitarianism. Precisely because Levinas retains his belief in the possibility and the task of the sociopolitical order—in contrast to Grossman (and Ikonnikov) who have lost their trust in the Soviet state entirely—he also keeps on hammering away time and again on the "liberal state" that draws its liberal character from the space it creates for criticism on the justice achieved and thus for "an always better justice" (*une justice toujours meilleure*).[31] A just social, economic, and political system always falls short with regard to its source and intention, namely the face-to-face and the responsibility of everyone for everyone. The options, priorities and achieved balances that are established in the sociopolitical order create ever-new injustices. For this reason, Levinas explicitly puts forward the ethical necessity of "a justice behind justice" (*une justice derrière la justice*), to prevent or to remedy—as a critical corrective—every degeneration of the structural socioeconomic and political justice.[32]

In order to concretize this "justice which is more just," Levinas ascribes a central role to human rights: to be understood as the rights of

The Small Goodness Never Wins, But Is Never Defeated | 277

the vulnerable other. It is indeed characteristic how "in a totalitarian state, a mockery is made of the rights of man, and the promise of an ultimate return to the rights of man is postponed indefinitely."[33] For that reason, it is important to affirm the prophetic extra-territoriality of human rights: "The concern of the rights of man is not a function of the state, it is an institution in the state which is not of the state."[34] Human rights surpass all political power and all reason of state, and they can be invoked by every human person as a person—and thus not only by every legally recognized citizen of a state. "This also means (and it is important that this be emphasized) that the defense of the rights of man corresponds to a vocation outside the state, disposing, in a political society, of a kind of extra-territoriality, like that of prophecy in the face of the political powers of the Old Testament, a vigilance totally different from socio-political intelligence, a lucidity not limited to yielding before the formalism of universality, but upholding justice itself in its limitations. The capacity to guarantee that extra-territoriality and that independence defines the liberal state and describes the modality according to which the conjunction of the 'socio-political' and ethics is intrinsically possible."[35]

Goodness and Smallness: Ethical Individualism

The final word "beyond the socio-political," according to Levinas, is given to the "small goodness" of which he finds direct inspiration in Grossman's novel, namely Ikonnikov-Morzh, or Ikonnikov for short. We come to know that Ikonnikov had studied at the Technological Institute of Saint Petersburg, and that at the end of his studies "he had been converted to the teachings of Tolstoy" and given up his studies to become a teacher in some small village.[36] After moving to Odessa, where he worked as a mechanic in the engine room of a cargo ship, and after wandering in Japan and India, he resided for a time in Sydney, Australia. After the Bolshevik Revolution, he returned to Russia and joined a farmers' commune, where, after some time, he began to preach the gospel. The horrors of the thirties affected him mentally, whereby he was coercively confined in the psychiatric hospital of the prison. When he was released, he went to live with his older brother in Belarus. When Belarus was occupied by the Germans during the war, he relapsed into his former hysteria, especially when he witnessed the suffering of the Jews. When he tried to save Jewish children and women, he was soon denounced and locked up in a camp. There he quickly became known as "a strange man who would have been any age at all" and "unhinged."[37] He was also taken by his fellow-prisoners as "a holy fool," or as "that holy fool, that seeker after God," "one who in Russia is called *yourodivyi*, the son of a priest (pope), but without theologically orthodox faith."[38] With Grossman, Levinas discovers in him "a feeble-minded" person.[39] And he immediately adds: "A feeble-minded person can be inspired. This is the type that exists in Russia. It is The Idiot of Dostoevsky."[40] Only the voice of such a "madman and simpleton" can speak so clear and ringing.[41] He was executed because "he refused to work on the construction of a new extermination camp [*Vernichtungslager*].[42]

In his scribblings, the "feeble minded" Ikonnikov defends that "good is to be found neither in the sermons of religious teachers and prophets, nor in the teachings of sociologists and popular leaders, nor in the ethical systems of philosophers . . . ," but in the love and pity that ordinary people bear in their hearts for all life.[43] These ordinary people, who are considered by the "powers that be" as "simpletons" or "feeble minds," bring back among the people and in the systems the "lost kernel"—the "sacred kernel"—that has fallen away from the hypocritical, literally sanctimonious, husks of the final and violently organized good (cf. supra).[44] We read literally the following from Ikonnikov, which has also been cited by Levinas:

> There exists, side by side with this so terrible greater good, human kindness in everyday life. It is the goodness of an old woman carrying a piece of bread to a prisoner, the goodness of a soldier allowing a wounded enemy to drink from his water-flask, the kindness of youth towards age, the goodness of a peasant hiding an old Jew in his loft. It is the goodness of those prison guards who risk their own freedom, smuggle the letters of prisoners out to wives and mothers.[45]

It is clear that we can only understand small goodness correctly if we have an eye for the contrast or the contradiction in which it arises. It is no sentimental outburst in a context of satisfaction and a care-free society. It shows its meaning and strength in a context of power and threat, institutional violence, autocracy, totalitarianism, and terror (cf. supra). But with this contrast, not everything has already been said about its true nature. This requires a reflection on the two aspects that are invoked by the category "small goodness," namely "smallness" and "goodness."

First and foremost, it is goodness. And that idea has been present since the beginning of Levinas's work. It even receives a prominent place in his thought from the beginning: "You find elsewhere this word goodness in my work, in *Totality and Infinity*, which preceded significantly my reading of Grossman."[46] For Levinas, goodness is a "work" through "effective" incarnation, going beyond every kind of "affective" emotionality. But there is more, because of its internal quality. Goodness has both an asymmetrical as well as an exuberant dynamism, insofar as it is rooted in desire—which is distinguished from need. What immediately stands out, even in the spontaneous understanding of goodness, is that it intends to surpass every form of reciprocity—*do ut des*. It is not connected to the condition of utility. It does not calculate and goes beyond all self-interest ("being").[47] It happens for the sake of the other, without the one exercising it having to 'contribute' something. And hence, according to Levinas, it is an expression of desire (*désir*) and not of need (*besoin*). Need after all starts with my hunger, my necessity, and the satisfying answer that the sought-after object can give me. Desire does not start from an emptiness but from a fullness that wants to "pour out" itself.[48] Desire does not lock itself up within itself but moves outward, not because it needs something else, but to give itself to the other. Hence, Levinas characterizes desire as "insatiable desire—not because it corresponds to an infinite hunger, but because it is not an appeal to food. This desire is insatiable, but not because of our finitude."[49] Precisely because desire does not ensue from need, it does not approach the other functionally ("for me"—"for my sake") but for the sake of the other: "A desire without satisfaction hence takes cognizance of the alterity of the other."[50] In other words, desire is an expression of our infinity, a fullness that is awakened and struck within us by the other and simmers up in us into an "abundant profusion," an infinity that "infantizes" itself and thus never ceases. What is out of the question here is a "commandment" or a "law," and thus of a must, unless we understand desire's internal impetus toward self-surpassing as an "internal must"—which is the very essence of desire. "Desire is revealed to be goodness" (*Le désir se révèle bonté*).[51]

But despite its exuberance and infinity, Levinas takes over Ikonnikov-Grossman's characterization of it as "small." This is because it is an "ethics without ethical system," which is to say that it rises above or beyond any system of norms and rules. Stronger still, its vocation is to surpass the political as a system, with its alienations, including its totalitarian aberrations.⁵² That is why it neither can nor may be of the same caliber as the social, economic, juridical, and political regime. Hence, Ikonnikov-Grossman and Levinas call it "small," or "unsightly," weak, and powerless, fragmentary, and partial, unostentatious, and casual. It is anything but lofty and awesome, like the idea of the collective Good announcing itself as something "great and threatening." It is so commonplace that it usually happens unnoticed. It takes place without much reflection or "deductive argumentation"—"thoughtlessly," as Ikonnikov calls it. It happens unplanned and coincidentally. It is so meager that you barely hear any testimonials about it. It usually remains invisible, certainly to the media that makes things public. It is like tiny particles spread here and there through life, so that we also easily overlook them. "One might just as well be afraid of a freshwater fish carried out by chance into the salty ocean," says Ikonnikov ironically.⁵³ Its powerlessness is so huge that we also begin to doubt it. In its smallness it is also foolish, silly, even insane and to a certain extent meaningless, says Ikonnikov. But it is and remains "as simple as life itself."⁵⁴ In its weakness, it possesses a hidden force, a mild force that does not impose anything or impose itself on anyone, for it never enforces itself.

Hence, according to Levinas, it can never be raised into an ideology, theory, or thought construct.⁵⁵ And it should never be the object of preachment or edifying and persuading discourse, or worse still of dogmatic argumentation or propaganda that in a sly manner presents or imposes it as the truth.⁵⁶ Actually, it must remain under the radar of every argumentation . . . whatever the philosophical discourse may be that tries to make it seem suspicious. Despite the awareness that it cannot be hushed up, the uneasy awareness must remain that this speech can degrade into an oppressive persuasion speech. It is only thanks to this self-restraint that the modest and at the same time effective force of the small goodness can remain intact.

Levinas thus attempts to summarize what Ikonnikov has scribbled on the gentle, hidden force of small goodness:

> In the decay of human relations, in that sociological misery, goodness persists. In the relation of one person to another, goodness is possible. The impossibility of goodness as a government, as a social institution. Every attempt to organize the human fails. The only thing that remains vigorous is the goodness of everyday life. Ikonnikov calls it the "small goodness."

It's a goodness without witnesses. That goodness escapes all ideology: he says that "it could be described as goodness without thought." Why without thought? Because it is a goodness outside all systems, all religions, all social organizations. Gratuitous goodness! The feeble-minded are those who defend it and work at its perpetuation from one being to another. It is so fragile before the might of evil. It is a "mad goodness," the most truly human in a human being. It defines man, despite its powerlessness, and Ikonnikov has another beautiful image to qualify it: "It is beautiful and powerless, like the dew." What freshness in this despair.[57]

However banal the small goodness may seem, "in it the human turns the inhuman of being, always preoccupied with itself, upside down."[58] In contrast to "being" as "interest" it reveals noiselessly but stubbornly the "otherwise than being" of disinterestedness as a "seed of folly" (grain de folie), "the breathlessness of the spirit, or the spirit holding back its breath."[59]

Precisely because this small goodness is an "ethics without ethical system" it can only be authenticated by "individual consciences," which leads Levinas to the idea of slightly anarchical "ethical individualism."[60] "There are, if you like, the tears that a civil servant [of state or sociopolitical order] cannot see: the tears of the [unique] other. In order for things to develop an equilibrium, it is absolutely necessary to affirm the infinite responsibility of each, for each, before each. In such a situation [of social and political systems], individual consciences are necessary, for they alone are capable of seeing the violence that proceeds from the proper functioning of [socio-political] Reason itself. To remedy a certain disorder which proceeds from the Order of universal Reason, it is necessary to defend subjectivity. As I see it, subjective protest is not received favorably on the pretext that its egoism is sacred but because I alone can perceive the 'secret tears' of the other, which are caused by the functioning—albeit reasonable—of the hierarchy [and the administrative and legal system of the socio-political order]."[61] The individual conscience can or rather should never be eliminated. However good the intention may be, laws can be or become unjust, namely because they no longer satisfy as new problematic situations arise. There is the dictatorship of bad laws but also of good laws. The worst dictatorship is perhaps the one with the "best" laws, which then elevate themselves as such to "final" laws. Precisely for that reason the unique, responsible subjectivity is indispensable for assuring the nonviolence that the sociopolitical order searches for in equal measure, but that is again painted into a tight corner by that order as system and regime. In and through the small goodness, the one and only "I" accords acknowledgment and confirmation of the unique other. In its modest and almost casual, unnoticeable movement, it actualizes a form of respect by means of making no claims on the other, nor humiliating the other, but by approaching the other and assisting the other in word and deed.[62] In spite of itself, the small goodness reveals that "the substance of the I is made of saintliness. It is perhaps in this sense that Montesquieu rested democracy upon virtue."[63]

Reversal of the View on the Future of a Humane Society

With this, not everything has already been said about the "small goodness." As "unselfishness," not only does it surpass the sociopolitical order, but it also likewise introduces a reversal of the view on the future of a humane and humanizing society.

At first glance, the idea of small goodness evokes the indulgent-cynical reproach of "cheap and silly altruism" or "love as amusement" (*amour rigolo, amour rigolade*).[64] That is also what happens when in *Life and Fate* Mostovskoy has read through the scribblings of Ikonnikov. Grossman notes how he first remains seated for a few minutes with his eyes half closed and then reacts contemptuously: "Yes, the man who had written this was (. . .) the ruin of a feeble spirit! The preacher declares that the heavens are empty . . . He sees life as a war of everything against everything [cf. Hobbes]. And then at the end he starts tinkling the same old bells, praising the goodness of old women and hoping to extinguish a world-wide conflagration with an enema springe. What trash!"[65] The reproach, which also ridicules small goodness, shall recur time and again and at times such a ridiculing reproach will be convincing and effective. Namely when the small goodness is reduced to an isolated burp of feelings of empathy or sympathy, without effectively doing something; whereas the small goodness precisely develops its own decisiveness in contrast with the powers of a system that threatens to flood everything over and is impossible to fight against.

Now the question is how small goodness installs a new view on history. For that purpose, we start with the last paragraph of the scribblings of Ikonnikov, to which Levinas also refers in the conclusion of his Talmudic lesson "Beyond Memory":

> My faith was steeled, reinforced in Hell. It has emerged from the flames of the crematoria, from the concrete of the gas chambers.[66] I have seen that it is not human beings who are impotent in the struggle against evil, but the power of evil that is impotent in the struggle against human beings. The powerlessness of small goodness, is the secret of its immortality. It can never be conquered. Evil is impotent before it. Prophets, religious teachers, reformers, social and political leaders are impotent before it. This dumb, blind love is human's meaning. Human history is not the battle of good struggling to overcome evil. It is the struggle of a great evil trying to crush the tiny seed of humanity. But if even now [by Stalinism, Hitlerism, genocides, terrorism . . .] the human has not been destroyed in human beings, evil will never prevail.[67]

This quote presupposes a classic view on history, namely that it can be read globally as a struggle between good and evil, or rather as a struggle of good against evil. Moreover, this dynamism of history is interpreted from a certain Messianic or eschatological perspective, in the sense that one "hopes" and "believes" that history will end well. Concretely, good shall defeat evil. There will be a new world without blood and tears, without hate and persecution and extermination . . . Time and again, in the heat of the struggle and alienation, we envision a liberation as a conquering of that alienation . . . thanks to the struggle that was waged! But has that not precisely been the concept of history that Stalinism employed? Through its struggle, it promised the ultimate victory of the good, of which it saw itself as its incarnation and guarantee. But then one should not forget how that victory of the good over evil was only possible through all those forms of censure and repression, persecution and violence, deportations and camps . . . and so much more that actually should not have seen the light of day, but indeed were 'revealed' by Grossman in plain terms, without exaggeration, in his novel. For Marx, and especially for Lenin and Stalin, history apparently had a goal, namely the communist society. But Grossman saw how that was striven for at the price of innumerable inhumanities, meaning to say how the ideology of an ideal—entirely humane, 'messianic'—society legitimized all coercive measures and state violence, including ideological purifications, as necessary. This shakes not only Ikonnikov, but also Levinas, to his senses, who indeed interprets Grossman's book as a true "revelation." This book reinforces his view on history, which actually becomes a view without a view on a "telos" or "end goal" of history. Hence Levinas, with a feeling for some paradoxical exaggeration, states that he has no philosophy of history in the sense that he rejects every idea of a dialectically teleological process that is directed toward the final victory of good over evil. He lets go of this view once and for all.[68] There is no such thing as a fulfilment of history, to which we—in history—would be on our way and, furthermore, where such fulfillment would be ensured by God's promise or by divinized human powers. Since Auschwitz, he no longer subscribed to such a promise since the Lord of Hosts did not intervene to protect his people from the absolute evil of extermination.[69] Apparently, God had abandoned his people of Israel, who stood for humankind. That is why God can no longer be thought of as someone who intervenes in history and directs it toward messianic fulfillment.[70] Auschwitz is the end of every theodicy, and thus also the death of God ("Has he not died in the extermination camps? Isn't his death thus almost an empirical fact?").[71] Auschwitz has introduced the inexorable end of the traditional view on "salvation history." Hence Levinas's radical thesis that we must dare think not only of history and ethics but also of religion as a "religion without promise": "Is one loyal to the Torah because one counts on the promise? Must I not remain faithful to its teachings, even if there is no promise? One must want to be a Jew without the promise made to Israel being the reason for this faithfulness. Judaism is valid not because of the 'happy end' of its history, but because of the faithfulness of this history to the teachings of the Torah."[72]

Is history then entirely without prospect? Is there no promise at all anymore? In his Talmud lesson "Beyond Memory," despite impressions to the contrary, Levinas hangs on to the idea of a view of the future, just as it is also expressed in the Bible, namely in Isaiah: "Do not remember the former things, or consider the things of old. I am about to do a new thing; now it springs forth, do you not perceive it?" (Isa 43:18–19).[73] And this radically new thing, that no ear has heard and no eye has seen, is declared precisely in the preceding verses, namely the annulment and surpassing of the battle as the only way toward the good: "Thus says the LORD, who makes a way in the sea, a path in the mighty waters, who brings out chariot and horse, army and warrior; they lie down, they cannot rise;

they are extinguished, quenched like a wick" (Isa 43:16–17). The new and unheard of that is mentioned should certainly no longer be understood as the awesome and fanatic battle of the good and its victory over evil, but the goodness that takes place in and through the face-à-face of the responsibility-of-the-one-for-the-other. Levinas discovers therein the true meaning of messianism, namely that every person, being responsible for the other, is Messiah: a personal, unique vocation. We do not have to wait for a mythic Messiah, appearing at the end of history, installing a "perfect society" as achievement of every social and political promise by suppressing all suffering and violence.[74] Levinas makes the Talmudic comment of Rabbi Nahman his own: "The Messiah is the King who no longer commands from outside. The Messiah is Myself; to be Myself is to be the Messiah. The one who suffers, who has taken on the suffering of others is the Messiah. (. . .) All persons are the Messiah. (. . .) In concrete terms this means that each person acts as though he were the Messiah. Messianism is therefore not the certainty of the coming of a man who stops History. It is my power to bear the suffering of all. It is the moment when I recognize this power and my universal responsibility."[75]

Inspired by the Talmud and confirmed by Grossman-Ikonnikov, Levinas arrives at a reversal—not at an abolishment—of eschatology: "The small goodness does not win, but will never be defeated" (*la petite bonté n'a pas vaincu, mais n'a pas été vaincue non plus*).[76] As "incarnation" of the "one responsible for the other" the small goodness is invincible, although it never wins! In contrast to the traditional—spectacular and violent—eschatology (comparable to the apocalyptic battle of the good against the evil ones in *The Lord of the Rings* by J.R.R. Tolkien), the small goodness does not engage in an ultimate battle against all evil in the world, for it realizes it will not cope against it. But in its paltriness and weakness, it still maintains its strength, in the sense that it does not let itself be destroyed in the battle of evil against good. It stubbornly clambers to stand up, like a downtrodden blade of grass pokes fun at us behind our backs by again, slowly but resiliently, raising itself up. It is eternal, indestructible, even though it is powerless in assuring a world without violence. And note well that what is essential for its significance is that it comes without guarantees that all will be well. It is not meaningful because it is indestructible, for then its invincibility would be a condition for its meaning and fulfillment. It takes place without worrying whether it will survive or endure. In this regard, it is unreflecting, also without any thought on quid pro quo. It is also valuable when it is aimless. If it does something here and now for the other, then that is enough, and "tomorrow and the day after tomorrow" of a lasting significance is not needed in order to have value. In its expression, it has no need for compensation, not even for the condition of compensation of its indestructible eternity. Of course, this unconditional character does not preclude that it is unassailable: "invincible but unarmed."[77]

This reversal of eschatology does not mean that the battle against evil becomes redundant. Racism and anti-Semitism, genocide and terrorism cannot be left undisturbed. We cannot remain indifferent to evil. It is only that the battle can never acquire an ultimate significance. It remains a battle with a bad conscience, or rather it must remain a struggle with a bad conscience. The bad conscience of that battle should never be suppressed or undone. Even the battle against evil remains standing before the ethical appeal of the non-violent face-to-face: "Thou shalt not kill." In other words, the bad conscience is the space for the small goodness that simmers up in the heart—or the soul—of people in the most impossible and abominable circumstances. Beyond and within every battle, however historically inevitable or necessary it may be, the small goodness breaks into the open from within the "soul"—the desire (cf. supra)—without promise as a condition for its fulfilment, that is, without the certainty and "assurance" ever of coming to fulfilment in a world "without death and tears." It is precisely its smallness and vulnerability that makes it dynamic, that namely entices it to "infantizing," an infinity that is never infinite enough. A dynamic, ever breaking-out promise in a history without view to an end—because that history of people in this world will also never be without evil and terror.

Conclusion: "The Good Must Be Loved without Promises."[78]

This view resonates entirely in the question of Levinas: "Are we entering a moment in history in which the good must be loved without promises?"[79] And we know his answer: "I was once asked if the Messianic idea still had meaning for me, and if it were necessary to retain the idea of an ultimate stage of history where humanity would no longer be violent, where humanity would have broken definitely through the crust of being, and where everything would be clear. I answered that to be worthy of the Messianic era one must admit that ethics has a meaning, even without the promises of the Messiah."[80] We saw how both Grossman-Ikonnikov as well as Levinas distrust the moment in which the "for the other"—in the form of the small goodness—becomes the object of "ideological preaching" because—precisely on the basis of that defense and argumentation—it runs the risk of being betrayed.[81] From the ethics of the responsibility of the one for the other, that does not count on a "completed time" when everything "will be in order" ("the dream of a happy eternity"), but that lives in the perspective of an "infinite time" in which the practice of goodness—however small it may be—can always be done again and again, flows forth a radically new, ethical and religious spirituality.[82] "[The small goodness] bears witness to a new awareness of a strange (or very old) mode of spirituality or a piety without promises, which would not render human responsibility—always my responsibility—a senseless notion. A spirituality whose future is unknown."[83] The one-for-the-other has meaning, even though there are no prophecies or "eschatological consolations" that announce a prosperous future like a 'reward in heaven' for the trials and humiliations suffered.[84] This is a hope without boastfulness, without a promise that everything will be all right. It is the hope that fulfills itself in the daily practice of the "small goodness" that—notwithstanding all dread and terror—rises yet again in the soul, the heart, and the body of ordinary, simple people. The small goodness crawls unbroken like a downtrodden blade of grass that again stands upright and mockingly laughs behind the back of those who trample it underfoot, ridicule it and abuse it. Is that not "the enigma of a God speaking in man and of man not counting on any god?"[85] Levinas recognizes in it the '*rahamim*' of the Bible, the name for mercy and the Merciful One.[86] In other words, he not only discovers in the small goodness—as face-to-face responsibility—the basis and inspiration for a humane and humanizing society but also "the enigma of a God speaking in man and of man not counting on any god."[87] That is precisely what deeply touched Levinas in the novel of Grossman: "the sovereignty of that primordial goodness or mercy that evil cannot overcome (a goodness uncovered in the turmoil, the sign of a God still unheard-of but who, without promising anything, would seem to assume meaning beyond the theologies of a past shaken to the point of atheism) is perhaps the conclusion reached by Life and Fate."[88]

Pro manuscripto: Roger Burggraeve (KU Leuven)—
Leuven, July 25, 2018

Notes

1. Emmanuel Levinas, *Éthique comme philosophie première*, préfacé et annoté par Jacques Rolland (Paris: Éditions Payot & Rivages, 1998), 133.
2. Emmanuel Levinas, *A l'heure des nations* (Paris: Éditions de Minuit, 1988), 103.
3. *A l'heure des nations*, 101. Emmanuel Levinas, *Difficile liberté. Essais sur le judaïsme*. 2nd ed. (Paris: A. Michel, 1976), 266.
4. Vasily Grossman, *Life and Fate,* translated and with an introduction by Robert Chandler (London: Vintage, 2006), 12–13.
5. *A l'heure des nations*, 102.
6. Emmanuel Levinas, *Altérité et transcendance* (Montpellier: Fata Morgana 1995), 116.
7. *A l'heure des nations*, 102.
8. *A l'heure des nations*, 101–2.
9. *A l'heure des nations*, 104.
10. Grossman, 390–91. *A l'heure des nations*, 104.
11. Grossman, 388–90.
12. Grossman, 13, 391. *A l'heure des nations*, 104.
13. *Difficile Liberté*, 360.
14. *Difficile Liberté*, 360.
15. Emmauneul Levinas, *Entre nous. Essais sur le penser-à-l'autre* (Paris: Grasset, 1991), 138.
16. Emmanuel Levinas, 'Entretiens,' in *Emmanuel Lévinas. Qui êtes-vous?*, ed. F. Poiré (Lyon: La Manufacture, 1987), 134.
17. Emmanuel Levinas, *Altérité et transcendance* (Montpellier: Fata Morgana, 1995), 116.
18. *Difficile Liberté*, 265. *Alterité et Transcendence*, 139. "Entretiens," 134).
19. Emmanuel Levinas, *L'au-delà du verset. Lectures et discours talmudiques* (Paris: Minuit, 1982), 99.
20. Emmanuel Levinas, *Éthique et Infini. Dialogues avec Philippe Nemo* (Paris: Fayard & France Culture, 1982), 85–86. Emmanuel Levinas, *Dieu, la mort et le temps*, ed. J. Rolland (Paris, Grasset, 1993), 211–12. Emmanuel Levinas, *Autrement que savoir* (Interventions dans les Discussions & Débat général) (Paris: Osiris, 1988), 62.
21. *L'au-delà du verset*, 216.
22. *Difficile Liberté*, 109.
23. *L'au-delà du verset*, 216.
24. Emmanuel Levinas, *Nouvelles lectures talmudiques* (Paris: Minuit, 1996), 71.
25. *Entre Nous*, 260.

26. *Nouvelles lectures talmudiques*, 69–70.
27. "Entrétiens," 135.
28. *A l'heure des nations*, 157. Emmanuel Levinas, 'Trancendance et hauteur.' in *Liberté et commandement* (Montpellier: Fata Morgana, 1994), 62.
29. Emmanuel Levinas, *Dieu, la mort et le temps* (Paris: Grasset, 1993), 212.
30. *A l'heure des nations*, 103.
31. *Entre Nous*, 125. Emmanuel Levinas, *Autrement que savoir* (Paris: Osiris, 1988), 62.
32. Emmanuel Levinas, '*Entretien préparatoire avec Emmanuel Levinas sur l'argent, l'épargne et le prêt* (le 10 avril 1986 à Paris chez Levinas' in: Roger Burggraeve, *Emmanuel Levinas et la socialité de l'argent. Un philosophe en quête de la réalité journalière. La génèse de 'Socialité et argent' ou l'ambiguité de l'argent* (Leuven: Peeters, 1997), 61.
33. "Entretiens," 97/51. *Hors sujet*, 184/123.
34. "Entretiens, 119.
35. *Hor sujet*, 185.
36. Grossman, 10.
37. Grossman, 10, 394.
38. Grossman, 10, 304, 394. *A l'heure des nations*, 103.
39. Grossman, 394. *A l'heure des nations*, 103.
40. Emmanuel Levinas, 'Portrait—Emmanuel Levinas se souvient . . .' (en dialogue avec Myriam Anissimov), in *Les Nouveaux Cahiers*, 21 (1985), nr. 82, 30–35. *Is It Righteous to Be?* 34/90.
41. Grossman, 11.
42. Grossman, 515.
43. Grossman, 391.
44. Grossman, 389.
45. *A l'heure des nations*, 104–105. Grossman 391–92.
46. "Entretiens," 135.
47. Emmanuel Levinas, *Autrement qu'être ou au-delà de l'essence* (La Haye: Nijhoff, 1974. *Otherwise Than Being or Beyond Essence*, trans. A. Lingis (The Hague: Nijhoff, 1981), 4–5.
48. Emmanuel Levinas, *Humanisme de l'autre homme* (Montpellier: Fata Morgana, 1972). *Humanism of the Other*, trans. N. Poller (Urbana and Chicago: University of Illinois Press, 2003), 45.
49. Emmanuel Levinas, *Totalité et Infini: Essai sur l'extériorité* (La Haye: Nijhoff, 1961). *Totality and Infinity. An Essay on Exteriority*, trans. A. Lingis (The Hague: Nijhoff, 1979), 34.
50. Emmanuel Levinas, "La philosophie et l'idée de l'Infini' in *En décourvrant l'existence avec Husserl et Heidegger* (Paris: Vrin, 1967). *Collected Philosophical Papers*, trans. A. Lingis (Dordrecht: Nijhoff, 1987), 175.

51. *Humanisme* 46.
52. "Entretiens," 135.
53. Grossman, 393.
54. Grossman, 393.
55. Répondre d'autrui, 15.
56. *Entre Nous*, 116, 139.
57. *Altérité et transcendance*, 117–18.
58. Emmanuel Levinas, "La vocation de l'autre" in Emmanuel Hirsch, *Racismes. L'autre et son visage* (Paris: Cerf: 1988), 89–102. "The Vocation of the Other," *Is it Righteous to Be?*, 92.
59. *Autrement qu'être*, 180, 5.
60. "Trancendance et hauteur," 82.
61. "Trancendance et hauteur," 81.
62. *Entre nous*, 48–49.
63. "Trancendance et hauteur," 81.
64. "Entretiens," 115.
65. Grossman, 394.
66. Grossman, 394. *A l'heure des nations*, 105.
67. Grossman, 394.
68. "Entrétien," 15. "Portrait—Emmanuel Levinas se souvient . . . " in *Les Nouveaux Cahiers* 21 (1985), nr. 82/*Is it Righteous to Be*, 30–35.
69. *Entre Nous*, 114.
70. *Entre Nous*, 196.
71. *Entre Nous*, 115.
72. "Entretiens," 130. *Entre Nous*, 242–43.
73. *A l'heure des nations*, 96.
74. *Difficile liberté*, 85.
75. *Difficile liberté*, 120.
76. 'Emmauel Levinas, "Entretien préparatoire avec Emmanuel Levinas sur l'argent, l'épargne et le prêt (le 10 avril 1986 à Paris chez Levinas)," in "Emmanuel Levinas et la socialite de l'argent: Un philosophe en quête de la réalité journalière," *La génèse de 'Socialité et argent' ou l'ambiguité de l'argent* (Leuven: Peeters, 1997).
77. *A l'heure des nations*, 103.
78. *Altérité et transcendence*, 119.
79. *Altérité et transcendance*, 119.
80. *Éthique et Infini*, 122.
81. Entrétien," 15.
82. *Totalité et Infini*, 261.
83. *A l'heure des nations*, 157.
84. *Altérité et transcendence*, 122; *A l'heure des nations*, 104.
85. *Altérité et transcendence*, 196.
86. *A l'heure des nations*, 135.

87. *Altérité et transcendence,* 196.
88. *A l'heure des nations,* 103.

Bibliography

Burggraeve, Roger. *Emmanuel Levinas et la socialité de l'argent. Un philosophe en quête de la réalité journalière. La génèse de 'Socialité et argent' ou l'ambiguité de l'argent.* Leuven: Peeters, 1997.

Grossman, Vasily. *Life and Fate,* translated and with an introduction by Robert Chandler London, Vintage, 2006.

Levinas, Emmanuel. *Altérité et transcendance.* Montpellier: Fata Morgana, 1995. *Alterity and Transcendence,* translated by M. B. Smith. New York: Columbia University Press, 1999.

Levinas, Emmanuel. *L'au-delà du verset. Lectures et discours talmudiques.* Paris: Minuit, 1982. *Beyond the Verse. Talmudic Readings and Lectures,* translated by G. D. Mole. Bloomington: Indiana University Press, 1994.

Levinas, Emmanuel. *Autrement qu'être ou au-delà de l'essence.* La Haye: Nijhoff, 1974. *Otherwise Than Being or Beyond Essence,* translated by A. Lingis. The Hague: Nijhoff Kluwer, 1981.

Levinas, Emmanuel. *Autrement que savoir* (Interventions dans les Discussions & Débat général) (Paris: Osiris, 1988), 62.

Levinas, Emmanuel. *Dieu, la mort et le temps.* Établissement du texte, notes et postface de J. Rolland. Paris: Grasset, 1993. *God, Death, and Time,* translated by B. Bergo. Stanford, CA: Stanford University Press.

Levinas, Emmanuel. *Difficult Freedom: Essays on Judaism.* Translated by Seàn Hand Baltimore: Johns Hopkins University Press, 1990.

Levinas, Emmanuel. *Entre nous. Essais sur le penser-à-l'autre.* Paris: Grasset, 1991. *Entre nous. Thinking-of-the-Other.* Translated by M. Smith and B. Harshov. New York: Columbia University Press, 1998.

Levinas, Emmanuel. *Éthique comme philosophie première,* préfacé et annoté par Jacques Rolland. Paris: Éditions Payot & Rivages, 1998.

Levinas, Emmanuel. *Éthique et Infini. Dialogues avec Philippe Nemo* (Paris: Fayard & France Culture, 1982. *Ethics and Infinity. Conversations with Philippe Nemo,* translated by R.A. Cohen. Pittsburgh: Duquesne University Press, 1985.

Levinas, Emmanuel. *A l'heure des nations.* Paris: Éditions de Minuit, 1988. *In the Time of the Nations.* Translated by Michael B. Smith. Bloomington: Indiana University Press, 1994.

Levinas, Emmanuel. *Humanisme de l'autre homme.* Montpellier: Fata Morgana, 1972. *Humanism of the Other.* Translated by N. Poller. Urbana and Chicago: University of Illinois Press, 2003.

Levinas, Emmanuel. *Nouvelles lectures talmudiques* Paris: Minuit, 1996. *New Talmudic Readings*, translated by R. A. Cohen. Pittsburgh: Duquesne University Press, 1999.

Levinas, Emmanuel. "Portrait—Emmanuel Levinas se souvient . . . " (en dialogue avec Myriam Anissimov), in Les Nouveaux Cahiers, 21 (1985), nr. 82, 30–35. *Is It Righteous to Be?*

Levinas, Emmanuel. *Totalité et Infini: Essai sur l'extériorité.* La Haye, Nijhoff, 1961. *Totality and Infinity. An Essay on Exteriority.* Translated by A. Lingis. The Hague: Nijhoff, 1979.

Levinas, Emmanuel. 'Trancendance et hauteur.' in *Liberté et commandement.* Montpellier: Fata Morgana, 1994. 'Transcendence and Height' in *Emmanuel Levinas. Basic Philosophical Writings* edited by A.T. Peperzak, S. Critchley, R. Bernasconi. Bloomington: Indiana University Press, 1996.

Levinas, Emmanuel. *En décourvrant l'existence avec Husserl et Heidegger.* Paris: Vrin, 1967. Hirsch, E. *Racismes. L'autre et son visage.* Paris, Cerf: 1988.

Poiré, F. *Emmanuel Lévinas. Qui êtes-vous?* (Lyon: La Manufacture, 1987) 'Interview with François Poirié,' in *Is It Righteous to Be. Interviews with Emmanuel Levinas*, edited by J. Robbins J. and translated by J. Robbins, M. Coelen, with T. Loebel. Stanford, CA: Stanford University Press, 2001.

19

Sympathy for the Devil

On Richard Cohen's Levinasian Meditations on Sartre and Theology

JAMES M. MCLACHLAN

> Satan, who was vanquished, fallen, guilty, denounced by the whole of Nature, banned from the universe, crushed beneath the memory of an unforgivable sin, devoured by insatiable ambition, transfixed by the eye of God, which froze him in his diabolical essence, and compelled to accept to the bottom of his heart the supremacy of Good—Satan, nevertheless, prevailed against God, his master and conqueror, by his suffering, but that flame of non-satisfaction which, at the very moment when divine omnipotence crushed him, at the very moment when he acquiesced in being crushed, shone like an unquenchable reproach.
>
> —Jean-Paul Sartre, *Baudelaire*

The title "Sympathy for the Devil" has much more to do with Sartre's theological critique of theology than Richard Cohen's devilish nature. But a connection can be made between Cohen's Levinasian critique of theology, his reading of Sartre, and Sartre's own theological interests. I will focus on three chapters from Cohen's *Levinasian Meditations*: the final two chapters on theology and theodicy: "Against Theology: 'The Devotion of

Theology without Theodicy," and "Theodicy After the Shoah: Levinas on Suffering and Evil," and his discussion of Levinas and Sartre that takes place primarily in "The Choosing and the Chosen: Levinas and Sartre." In relation to Cohen's critiques, I want to show the importance of theology to Sartre's early work, to indicate how what Kate Kirkpatrick calls Sartre's participation in a "diffuse Augustinianism" is strongly present in the ontological framework of Sartrean existentialism.[1] Sartre is an atheologian who is caught in the theological character of his own ontology. But, more importantly, Sartre's atheology can be enlisted in Levinas's and Cohen's critiques of theology.

Much of *Being and Nothingness* has a theological character. This might sound ironic since we're talking about one of the twentieth century's most famous atheists, but it is nonetheless true. The theological elements include Sartre's description of a failed eschatology and theodicy in relation to the human desire for totality. In fact, the projected totality of the in-itself-for-itself is reiterated again and again. The for-itself, consciousness, is seen as an emanation from the in-itself that aims at a return to positivity and totality. In this Sartre resembles some forms of traditional Western theology that he reappropriates in support of his atheism. The for-itself, like human creatures, is completely dependent on a transcendent being on which, because of its perfection, human being has no effect. The for-itself's efforts to create a basis for its own existence are all doomed to failure. These theological themes are well known and both Paul Tillich and Karl Barth, the most important theological voices of the twentieth century, wrote lengthy discussions of Sartrean ontology.[2] From a Levinasian standpoint this makes perfect sense because much of Western philosophy has been theological in its aim at the ideal of totality. It is to Sartre's credit that he did so much to show the failure of the theological enterprise.[3]

The irony of the discussion of Sartre and Levinas is that the atheist Sartre, through his ontology, remains in the grips of theology. But Sartrean resources also offer a powerful critique of the theological project as it has been practiced in the West.

Cohen's Levinasian Meditation on Theology

In an interview given in 1983, Levinas is asked whether the face of the other person is a mediation of God. Levinas replied with a question. "Hold on a minute, '[n]ow we're getting into theology . . . To me, the other is the other human being. Would you like to do a bit of theology?" For Levinas, reading the other as a conduit to God, to the higher being, thus "doing theology" would reduce the person to a mere conduit of a greater alterity. Levinas insists that it is given without the "odor" of the "numinous" and, by extension, a "holiness" as such.[4] The irony here is that Levinas is often accused of having a theological agenda.[5]

In his *The Origin of the Other: Emmanuel Levinas Between Revelation and Ethics*, Samuel Moyn argues for a theological source to ideas of the Other in Levinas. Tracing ideas of the other to Rudolf Otto's notion of the divine as the wholly Other in *The Idea of the Holy* and later in the theology of Karl Barth,[6] Moyn stresses the import of Kierkegaard to Barth in post– First World War thought in Germany and later in 1930s France with the publication of Jean Wahl's *Études Kierkegaardiennes* and Lev Shestov's *Kierkegaard and the Existential Philosophy* which Levinas reviewed.[7] Moyn sees Kierkegaard, Rosenzweig, and Barth as Levinas's allies in his liberation from Heidegger. Moyn argues that Levinas converts Rosenzweig from an alley of Heidegger to his opponent. Moyn finds evidence for the Kierkegaardianization of Rosenzweig in Levinas in his project of opposing Heidegger and related to the hallmark words "transcendence" and "the Other." Moyn argues Levinas's Rosenzweig goes from being Heidegger's partial alley to his "pitiless enemy."[8] It is the Kierkegaardian and Barthian ambience of interwar philosophy and theology that Levinas recruits in this effort. The Barthian Otherness of God is enlisted as the otherness of the Other. The absolute otherness of God in Kierkegaard and Barth becomes that absolute otherness of the Other in Levinas.

But whatever inspirations Levinas might have taken in his effort to escape ontology, it is certainly clear that he opposed the ontological structure of Western theology in a more radical fashion than Heidegger's attack on ontotheology and has little sympathy with ideas like Otto's notion of the holy, which is so close to Heidegger's descriptions of openness to Being. Levinas's distinction between the **"Holy"** and the **"Sacred"** is well known. He sees the usual ways that these terms are defined as the essence of idolatry.[9] In *The Idea of the Holy* Rudolf Otto describes an experience of "the Holy" in terms quite similar to Levinas's characterization of "the Sacred."

Otto calls "The Holy" the "*Mysterium Tremendom et Fascinans*" that fills us with awe and terror. It resembles Heidegger's Being and is the creative source that gives a ground to beings. The young Heidegger was fascinated with Otto, recommended *The Idea of the Holy* to Husserl, and at one point planned to review it.[10] Otto claims the experience of the Holy is qualitatively different from any other experience. Otto's "holy" is not morality, rather "to be *rapt* in worship is one thing; to be morally uplifted by the contemplation of a good deed is another." [11] Otto calls this feeling of the Holy "creature consciousness"; it is an awareness of being in the presence of something totally different than anything in the mundane world. This totally other he calls the *"mysterium tremendum."* The *mysterium* shatters the categories of our understanding, which Otto thinks is basic to all religions. The Holy is an experience of the "overplus of meaning," which he refers to as the *numinous* from the Latin word *Numen* or spirit. Otto describes the experience as anything from a gentle tide sweeping over the person to an intoxication and wild frenzy: in short, something absorbing the person.[12]

What Levinas calls "the Sacred" is similar to Otto's "Holy" as a notion of a ground of religious experience in which the individual person is swallowed up in anonymous power. Levinas describes the experience of the sacred as provoking the kind of enthusiasm in which the self is lost in the mystic sacred. The sacred is the unknown, mysterious and life-giving force. It is being itself. The *numinous* power of the sacred wraps the individuals and absorbs them into the group and into the mystery. It is mysterious and something that we can only feel or experience. "The sacred, then, in this sense, is the loss of the sincerity of meaning ("saying") and the initiative of selfhood ("responsibility") through the "proliferation" of anonymous significations and personae."[13]

> The numinous or the Sacred envelops and transports man beyond his powers and wishes, but a true liberty takes offence at this uncontrollable surplus. The numinous annuls the links between persons by making beings participate, albeit ecstatically, in a drama not brought about willingly by them, an order in which they founder. This somehow sacramental power of the Divine seems to Judaism to offend human freedom and to be contrary to the education of man, which remains action on a free being. . . . The Sacred that envelops and transports me is a form of violence.[14]

Levinas defines the Holy, rather, as the ethical, the respectful relation to another person who "transcends" all my ideas and perceptions. The Holy is not an idolatrous relation but the sacred is idolatrous. The *numinosity* of the sacred transports us beyond. The person is absorbed in the beyond. Human freedom is lost to the uncontrollable surplus of power. The *numinous* annuls the relations between persons, making them participate in a drama that these beings lose themselves in, as they are transported in the ecstatic experience. As individuals, they are damaged by it. This is a form of violence.

Otto's idea of the Holy, as the *numinous,* the *mysterium*, is the powerful mystery that crushes the person. Levinas points to a different idea of the "Holy" as the ethical. He says it is the still small voice of conscience. The divine truth doesn't differ from the human. Levinas writes: "the truth of angels in not of a different order to truth the truth of men."[15] Human truth includes suffering, uncertainty, and self-criticism, which calls into question the self-certainty of ecstasies that intuit truth directly as the impersonal, numinous, sacred.

Like Otto, Heidegger sees the sacred as Being. It is the *es gibt,* the overflowing gift of Being. In Levinasian terms the "*Il y a*" or "There is," the Totality that is beyond all finite beings. Levinas characterizes the *Il y a* as a totality "from below." Being, or the sacred I, is the basis of existence from which all beings fall into their separate existences. Heidegger famously contended that the metaphysical tradition shows the forgetfulness of being in placing a being, God, as Being. Barthian theology of God as the absolutely transcendent other is both an attempt to escape the Heideggerian critique but perhaps also its chief example. It is a totality "from Above." The God of revelation breaks in on history, and as Barth tells us, is beyond religion. But such a God is understood as the creator, ex nihilo, of all that is, and the revelation ultimate truth, the totality. Barth tells us that in religion/theology/onto-theology man talks to God, but, in revelation, God talks to man. Being/the Sacred speaks to the overwhelmed individual.[16] Here revelation is beyond critique, even an ethical one.

In "Against Theology: The Devotion of a Theology without Theodicy" Cohen writes that the Levinasian critique of theodicy is not to rid us of theology but rather to "puncture the pretentions of theology precisely in order to awaken theology from its slumbers, to awaken theology to religion."[17] The problem with theology is that it has been a branch of ontology. It totalizes the world from above or below. A critical moment in the association of God with being was Augustine's reading of the Latin translation of *"ehyeh 'asher' ehyeh"* as "I am" (Exodus 3:14), which he associated with a Neoplatonic perfect being theology.[18] God is for Augustine and later Barth identified with all powerful Being. The phrase can and has been translated differently, ethically as opposed to ontologically. Buber translated is "I shall be present."[19] Rosenzweig translated it as "I will be there as I will be there."[20]

Cohen discusses the critique of theology first in a critique of the sacred a totality from below. One loses herself before the "there is" of the sacred much as in Otto's description of the experience of the "Holy." But theology can also be totality from above in Barth's sense as God/Eternal Being breaking into history from above. Cohen stresses, this is not a symmetry where the totality that emerges from the sacred is, if anything, nonrepresentational. Cohen claims that theology, as a project, is representational. Thus, even in their apophatic forms, theologies are about Being. In this respect, says Cohen, Levinas opposes both the sacred and the holy of theology. Theology, for all its protestations that it only speaks by analogy, constantly forgets that it doesn't speak directly about God. Western theology, even in its negative incarnations, has actually given us a pretty straightforward description of God, as omnipotent, omniscient, simple, sovereign, and eternal Being. Cohen cites Levinas in *Otherwise Than Being or Beyond Essence*: "Thus theological language destroys the religious situation of transcendence. The infinite 'presents' itself anarchically, but thematization loses the anarch that alone can accredit it. Language about God rings false or becomes mythic, that is, can never be taken literally."[21] This is why, claims Cohen, "Theology, in other words, is not an accidental aberration of religion, but a permanent, if pernicious, temptation of it. The subversion of theology, then, is not merely a negative enterprise but is in fact a necessary and positive component of true religion."[22] We, as theologians, are always tempted to say something ultimate, final, and static about God, the ultimate being and reality. The critique of theology is the critique of a position that sees religion primarily as a matter of belief. In other words, an orthodoxy that sees the essence of religion as "true belief." For Levinas there is nothing mystical or theological behind the analysis of the idea of religion. It is wholly ethical and a matter of praxis more than belief. The word *religion* should announce the ethical relation between human beings that is irreducible to comprehension and thereby distanced from the exercise of power. Ontology becomes fundamental to religion when it becomes necessary to know or to experience directly that "personal perfection and personal salvation are, despite their nobility, still selfishness."[23] The Christian emphasis on the proper object of faith, proper doctrine, or even proper experience is selfish because it focuses on the individual, knower or believer, and the correctness of his knowledge or faith. Cohen writes: "We must realize that it is no accident that theology and Christianity in particular are intimately entwined if not synonymous. Indeed, in the final account, one can say that Christianity does not simply have a theology, but is a theology. Christianity is, in any event, the theological religion par excellence."[24]

Cohen's Levinasian critique is biting, and perhaps too much so, because it becomes difficult to see a way out for Christianity, if indeed Christianity is essentially the theological religion. Is it the case because of its emphasis on belief that Christianity is simply an error, and worse than a simple factual error, an ethical one? Notice also that here the relation of the absorption of the individual in the One of the sacred and the ego expansion of theology come together in the totalizing exclusivism of Christian theology. As one passes from immediacy of the experience of mystical union with the sacred to the said of theology the ego expands into its commanding knowledge of the whole of being. Cohen argues that somehow theology must become secondary for Christianity and must be humbled, taking a secondary role to ethics. This is a position taken by some Christian thinkers. For example, Alfred North Whitehead thought the history of Christianity constitutes a tragic failure. Its failure consisted in the theological/political idea that chose to conceive of God as the divine despot imposing laws on the world. Whitehead claimed the whole of Christian theology, with the possible exception Quakerism, from a tragic failure that valued power and totality over morality. Christian theology, as valuable as it is and has been for the growth of Western civilization, conceived God as a coercive power in the form of a Roman emperor or Byzantine Bazeleaus.[25]

Cohen's critique follows Levinas's Critique of Western ontology and philosophy. Levinas claims the predominant tradition of Western Philosophy has been an egology in which the many finite beings are absorbed in the totality of the one Being/God/Absolute.[26] What is experienced immediately in mystical and religious experience as the loss of self in the sacred, the "there is," is said explicitly in the ontology of God's relation to the world. Although this appears as though the self is lost in the One, we might as easily say that the self has expanded in the thinker/theologian, the mystic, or believer, who knows the One to encompass the totality of Being. There may not be perfect symmetry between the totality from below and totality from above, but there is a striking resemblance. In one the self is lost, absorbed in being, and in the other it is annihilated by the all powerful Deity/Being. Ironically, in both, the self expands to take in everything. The self is identified with the real. But the self is also lost in that it no longer relates to anything beyond itself. In the self's absorption or annihilation into being or deity there is no longer anything but the self. There is no beyond. There is no real Other. The self has expanded back into eternity. This is the sense in which Western philosophy/ontology is an egology and is what unites the two types of egology from below and above. Levinas describes this in an interview.

> As egology yes. If you read the *Enneads,* the One doesn't even have consciousness of the self; if it did have consciousness of self, it would already be multiple, losing perfection. In knowledge, one is two, even when one is alone. Even when one assumes consciousness of self, there is already a split. The various relations that can exist in man and in being are always a split. The various relations that can exist in man and in being are always judged according to their proximity to or distance from unity. What is relation? What is time? A fall from unity, a fall from eternity. There are many theologians from various religions who say that the good life is coincidence with God; coincidence that is, the return to unity. Whereas in the insistence to the relation to the other in responsibility, the excellence of sociality itself is affirmed: in theological terms proximity to God, society with God.[27]

Levinas points out that to know is to admit a split between the knower and the known. This is to admit a relation. Sartre will see this problem in his critique of Christian theism. The irony will be that in many respects, Sartre's ontology strongly resembles Plotinus.[28] The in-itself gratuitously emanates the for-itself. This is also the Augustinian theological structure that runs through existentialist works like *Being and Nothingness, Baudelaire,* and *Saint Genet* and becomes part of Cohen's critique of Sartre. I believe this critique is correct, and yet Sartre also offers resources for the critique of theology put forward by Levinas and Cohen.

Cohen on Sartre and Levinas: "Choosing and the Chosen"

Sartre the existentialist is an ontologist/metaphysican as well as a phenomenologist; a good deal of Sartre's ontological framework is not based on his phenomenological analysis. Sartre's famous distinction between the in-itself and for-itself in *Being and Nothingness* owes more to a type of Augustinian theology as it does to phenomenology.[29] I want to show that though Cohen's Levinasian critique of Sartre is essentially correct, Sartre both fits within and yet offers an important critique of the Western theological tradition in ways that supplement Levinas's and Cohen's critique of theology.

Cohen begins his discussion of Levinas and Sartre noting the affinities between the two thinkers: the independence, freedom, or atheism of the human subject; responsibility as the very selfhood of the subject; and the asymmetry of social relations.[30] He then moves to three Levinasian critiques:

1. Metaphysical Desire versus Being for Being. The human subject does not ultimately aim for being but for the beyond being.

2. Difficult Freedom versus Absolute Freedom. Freedom is not pure, transparent, impregnable, a matter of consciousness alone, but embodied, vulnerable, or as Levinas expresses it, "created" and difficult."

3. And finally, Being for the Other versus the Evil Genius. The other person has priority—being "for—the other" is higher, better, more excellent, and hence more genuinely oneself than being "for-oneself." The Face of the Other activates my freedom. Sartre both sees and, yet also, obscures this idea.[31]

I agree with each of Cohen's critiques. Despite the striking similarities, there are major differences between Sartre and Levinas. I want to add that they center on Sartre's nonphenomenological ontology. I will center Cohen's first critique, which relates to the critique of theology. This relates to the Augustinian theology that colors Sartre's ontology. But first, let me very briefly mention the latter two critiques. Freedom is not pure, transparent, impregnable, a matter of consciousness alone, but embodied, vulnerable, or as Levinas expresses it, "created" and "difficult." For Levinas, the other "activates" my freedom. My encounter with the other, and the question this poses for me, is the basis of this decision. How do I respond? In *Being and Nothingness* the other does not activate my freedom but grants me my being. My freedom is grounded in the negativity of my nothingness. The for-itself negates the being, the objectification, foisted or granted to me by the Other. I negate his/her image of me. Levinas writes

> Imperialism of the same is the whole essence of freedom. The "for-itself" as a mode of existence designates an attachment to oneself as radical as a naïve will to live. But if freedom situates me effrontedly before the non-me in myself and outside of myself, if it consists in negating or possessing the non-me, before the Other it retreats. . . . [T]he Other imposes himself as an exigency that dominates this freedom, and hence as more primordial than everything that takes place in me.[32]

Sartre's for-itself can choose, indeed it must choose, but never chosen, it is never responsible for what is not its own but better, the Other.

Cohen is correct when he says Being-for-itself is an artificial intellectual abstraction. The Augustinian ontology of *Being and Nothingness* weakens Sartre's ontology. The Godlike nature of Being and of the abyss between the in-self and the for-itself both causes and is the source of the frustration of the desire to be God. But I will take the position that in Sartre's critique of Western theism, the theological element of Sartre's ontology works to show the emptiness of traditional Western theology.

Cohen cites Levinas's interview with Richard Kearney where Levinas "criticizes Sartre's adherence to ontology and his consequent inability to put into question the immanence or 'sameness' of being, his inability, that is to say, to appreciate the *alterity* of the other person." Thus for, Levinas, Sartre falls into the same difficulty that has always been found in the Western philosophical/theological tradition. Levinas says of Sartre:

> I was extremely interested in Sartre's phenomenological analysis of the "other," though I always regretted that he interpreted it as a threat and degradation, an interpretation that also found expression in his fear of the God question. . . . In Sartre the phenomenon of the other was still considered, as in all Western ontology, to be a modality of unity and fusion, that is, a reduction of the other to the categories of the same. This is described by Sartre as a teleological project to unite and totalize the for-itself and the in-itself, the self and the other-than-self. It is here that my fundamental disagreement with Sartre lay.[33]

Like Levinas, for Sartre, our immediate awareness of the other is not a matter of knowledge. But, for Sartre, Levinas maintains, the phenomenon of the other is still a modality of being of the totality of being. But this is only partially so, for Sartre, the relation to the other in Sartre sits quite uncomfortably with the ontology of the in-itself and for-itself. It is in this conflict, more clearly than anywhere else, that Sartre's phenomenology conflicts with his ontology.

> There, is indeed a confusion here between two distinct orders of knowledge and *two types of being which cannot be compared.* We have always known that the object in the world can only be probable. This is due to its very character as object. *It is probable that the passerby is a man; if he turns his eyes towards me, the although I immediately experience and with the certainty the fact of being looked at. I cannot make this certainty pass into my experience of the other as object.* In fact, it reveals to me only the other as subject, a transcending presence in the world and the real condition of my being as object. In every causal state therefore it is impossible to transfer my certainty of the other as subject to the other as object which was the occasion of that certainty, and conversely it is impossible to invalidate the evidence of the appearance of the other as subject by point to the constitutional probability of the other as object. . . . What is certain is that I am looked at: what is only probable is that look is bound to this or that mundane presence.[34]

We are immediately aware of the other not as object but as subject. We attempt to bring this into our experience and into our knowledge. But then the other of whom we are aware as subject turns into an object. Notice we don't arrive at the existence of the other through the ontology. We could not. Phenomenology allows us to talk about the encounter with the Other. We are aware of it through certain emotions like shame. We never grasp it. The other is not my inner experience. My inner experience of shame only makes me aware of something beyond. When I step back and place the experience into the frame on ontology/theology, it is changed.

Sartre's analysis of shame is quite different from Levinas's analysis of the same emotion. For Sartre, shame is not ethical, though it may have the potential to become such, but is my sense of becoming an object for the other. It's my transcendence, my freedom, being frozen into facticity, into an object, into being. My escape is disrupted. But I don't experience the subjectivity of the other; I'm only aware of it. The other's subjectivity is still other to me.

The theological character of Sartre's ontology becomes quite clear in his essay "Cartesian Freedom." The important point to grasp in Sartre's discussion of "Cartesian Freedom" is that he believes that, for Descartes, liberty and human autonomy only exist in the realm of the negative. From the point of view of being as evil, negation, deviation.[35] This is one of the ontological sources of our shame. Cohen is correct in seeing that despite Sartre's humanistic attempts, his representation of freedom ends up like Heidegger's depending on the "light of Being" or the way that Being reveals itself to us as freedom (the *es gibt*).[36] In "Philosophy and the Idea of the Infinite" Levinas maintains this is no different than classical idealism where mere free will is the lowest form of freedom. For theology, the highest form of freedom was to identify with true freedom that obeys universal reason. This is just as true of Augustine as it is for the Stoics, and Spinoza. Levinas claims it's also true that the Heideggerian "freedom is obedient," but such obedience has nothing to do with injustice but with the acceptance of Being. This is the "demonic" element of Sartrean freedom that is tied to the negative, to rebellion.

Levinas says such an idea of freedom "hardens the will" rather than making it "ashamed" before infinity. This is certainly true of Sartre who sees encounters with the other as duels. My encounter with the other hardens me against her. In Sartre's analysis of possession, I possess things, not simply to dwell, but to create a wall that protects me from the Other. Sartrean freedom is also about the self who fails to fulfill his project "in which every deficiency is but weakness and every fault committed against oneself."[37] The self is ashamed because he has failed to be "authentic," to have constituted his life in a resolute manner. It is important to remember that, for Sartre, these efforts are also acts of bad faith. It is to Sartre's credit that he sought to avoid this trap and saw human beings as rebels against the trap, even if their negation of being is a doomed one. Unlike Heidegger and the theologians, Sartre is not happy about the human subordination, to the sacred, to being, but in Sartrean ontology the human cannot escape. Still Sartre doesn't stare at the sacred with the sense of cosmic rapture as do Heidegger and the theologians. For him it is dead—an object of disgust, of nausea.

Sartre's Augustinian Ontology

Sartre's Ontology is the negative mirror of an Augustinian two orders of being.

1. Uncreated Being (God)
2. The Nothingness of created being. (Created ex-nihilo)

Sartre claims Godness, Totality, haunts consciousness (being-for-itself); but these intentions are doomed to frustration in that even our finite aspirations are impossible. An eschatological conception that unites the disparate elements of reality into a totality is a part of many religious metaphysical systems from Plotinus to Augustine, to Barth. Sartre's "eschatology that fails" resembles the eschatology of the fall and original sin found in traditional theism. Roughly, in the Neoplatonic Christian eschatology, human being is a fall from finite innocence and perfection and can only return through the grace of God. In the Sartrean eschatology the fall from the in-itself starts a pilgrimage in which the soul seeks to perfect itself in Godness.

The nihilated in-itself is the first phase of the process of the growth of consciousness. The nihilating for-itself is the second phase, but it lives in isolation from the in-itself. The projected third phase is the unification of the for-itself and the in-itself in a new in-itself-for-itself, a plenum that is also conscious of itself. It involves the fullness and substantiality of a body with the emptiness and agility of Spirit. One does not return through the negation of the negation to previous structures of the for-itself. Rather, the for-itself aims at the being that it projects, **being as for-itself**. The for-itself would become the foundation of its own being, it would encompass Being itself. It would be God.

The Impossibility of the Theological God

Early in the introduction to *Being and Nothingness* Sartre shifts from the phenomenological to the ontological level. His ontological proof for grounding his notion of the being of the phenomenon is not a phenomenological description but an ontological one that is similar to Descartes's use of the ontological proof of the existence of God. Sartre wants to show the presence of the in-itself as neither determinate nor indeterminate being. The phenomenon has to be, for its material content, dependent on a transcendent being of the phenomenon (being in-itself). Cohen quotes Sartre in this respect: "Consciousness is congenitally orientated toward a being which it is not."[38] The in-itself is the basis of all phenomena perceived by consciousness, and there is little else that can be said about it.

Through the dichotomy of the in-itself and the for-itself, Sartre attempts to create a philosophy with an objectively ontological perspective (being-in-itself) on the one hand and a subject-oriented perspective (being-for-itself), in terms of phenomenology and transcendental ontology, on the other.

The conflict between the subjective and objective orientation of Sartre's thought is reflected in the two types of being: the in-itself and the for-itself. Being-in-itself is uncreated; it does not depend causally on anything else. There is not supposed to be a metaphysical first cause. Being-in-itself is without essence. It is not dependent on anything; it is "de trop," simply there, overflowing, superfluous, absurd. There is no reason for its existence—it simply is. The in-itself is solid or "massif," "filled with itself," "opaque to itself." It has no "inner" and "outer" and no reference to what it is not. The in-itself is identical because it is only what it is and has no relation to another. It is completely positive. There is nothing negative about it. There are no distinctions within it.[39] It's easy to see a comparison with God of theology except that such a God could not be conscious.

Sartre approaches the demonstration of the for-itself through a regressive analysis that begins with concrete examples and moves back to the origin of negation. Sartre endeavors to offer what amounts to a "me-ontological" proof, one that will show the presence of nothingness in the world of phenomena. The objective negative is the original starting point from which he works back toward the original negation in consciousness. Not nothingness but consciousness is the opposite of being-in-itself because consciousness is a combination of being and nothingness. Nothingness is encountered in the object world, but it cannot be being-in-itself because being-in-itself is pure positivity. Neither can it proceed from nothingness because nothingness is not; therefore, it must proceed from a being concerned with its own nothingness, a being that "must be its own nothingness."[40] It is not simply nothingness but both being and nothingness. Just as we cannot explain why God chose to create ex-nihilo, how nothingness emerges from the Being upon which it depends is not clear, and indeed this cannot be made clear. But the regressive analysis is intended to show that without it there is no other possible explanation for negation and negativities. It is through its own nothingness that the for-itself negates being and thus creates objects. Its negative action has no effect on being-in-itself, which is absolutely transcendent; the being that the for-itself negates is itself. The for-itself is absolutely dependent on being-in-itself for its being; it creates the objective negative. The plural character of phenomena is projected by the for-itself on the in-itself.[41]

With the in-itself and the failed eschatology of the for-itself Sartre falls into the kind of fixation on perfect being that Cohen sees at the foundation of Western philosophy and that Levinas highlights in "God and Philosophy."[42] Like Parmenides, Plotinus, and the Western theological tradition Sartre gives no reason for the relation of the way of truth (being-in-itself) and the way of appearance (being-for-itself) other than to say that they are related. The falleness of the for-itself has a theological character. How the perfection of wholly positive being-in-itself could have generated the negative being-for-itself remains a mystery, somewhat like the mystery in traditional theology's version of the fall of creation from grace or the reason that a perfect God had no need but decided to freely create a world with billions of suffering, imperfect beings. In Augustinian theodicy the fall represents an ex-nihilo creation of evil by perfect creatures created by the Perfect Being. Somehow "unqualifiedly good (though finite) creatures" were capable of evil that God did not create in them, otherwise we could blame God who gave him his imperfect nature. In the same sense there is no reason and no explanation for the ex-nihilo creation or emanation of the for-itself from the in-itself. Sartre would argue, simply, that we are presented with the brute fact of the existence of these two categories of Being—the one dependent on the other.

The form of Sartre's relation of the for-itself to the in-itself has Neoplatonic/Augustinian overtones. It is quite similar to the Plotinian emanations from Being. The emanations refer to the Transcendent Being and to the One, but the One is more than its emanations and is in no way lessened by their emanation. The relation of the in-itself and for-itself and the relation of the for-itself and the in-itself are also similar to traditional theological conceptions of God and creatures, wherein the creature is related to the creator but not the creator to the creature. This similarity is important because of Sartre's claim that he is not involved in a theological/metaphysical exercise but in a phenomenological investigation that requires neither God nor first principle. But the proof of the existence of the in-itself and the use of the regressive analysis to establish the existence of the for-itself are at least similar to metaphysical efforts to explain reality. So, one of the questions that follows from Sartre's description of the for-itself is how does being-for-itself ever come to be? If being-in-itself is pure positivity, then why is there an original upsurge of consciousness at all? In this respect Sartre's being-in-itself is quite like the Parmenidean being that founds Western philosophical and theological tradition. There is something unreal about negation—and hence consciousness—in Parmenides, Plotinus, Augustine, and Sartre. Being/God can only be described in positive terms. In being-in-itself there is no change; reality is stable. Being-in-itself does not come to be. There is no becoming, no time, and no differentiation. Sartre, like the onto-theological tradition itself, never deals with the question of why negation comes to be, or in Sartre's terms, why there are beings rather than just being-in-itself. For although Sartre eschews metaphysics in his rhetoric, he lets metaphysics in the back door with his ontological proof. The way we get to the in-itself is not through phenomenological analysis but by way of logical proof. He wants to return to the phenomenological method to arrive at the description of consciousness, but even here the proof of the existence of the for-itself is provided by a regressive analysis. Sartre, like Parmenides and the theologians, offers no clear account of the relation of the way of truth (being-in-itself/God) and the way of appearance (being-for-itself) other than to say that they are related. The falleness of the for-itself has this kind of theological character. How the perfection of wholly positive being-in-itself could have generated the negative being-for-itself remains a mystery somewhat like the mystery in Christian theology's version of the fall of creation from grace. John Hick argued that for traditional Augustinian theodicy the fall represents an ex-nihilo creation of evil by perfect creatures.[43] In the same sense there is no reason and no explanation for the "ex nihilo" creation or emanation of the for-itself from the in-itself. How does negation arise from all that positivity? Sartre, the existentialist, can argue in a way that Augustine the theist cannot. Very simply, we are presented with the brute fact of the existence of these two categories of Being the one dependent on the other. It is, as he says, absurd.

Sartre's ontology resembles Neoplatonic and theistic eschatology in a pessimistic way. One does return to the pleroma, but it is as only Being-in-itself. There is no sense in which, as was claimed by German idealism, that Being comes to know itself. This resemblance to mystic union with the sacred has been noted by several writers. Simone de Beauvoir says that Sartre studied the mystics during the early thirties.[44] For consciousness it appears as the in-itself seeks to ground itself but this is not the case. The problem of God is not a peripheral problem for humans. It is central "everything within me demands God and that I cannot forget."[45] It would seem theologically there should be a reason for all this and in the conclusion of *Being and Nothingness* Sartre discusses the metaphysical implication of the ontological structures of the in-itself and the for-itself in these very terms.

> On the ontological level nothing permits one to affirm that, from the beginning and in the very womb of the in-itself, the for-itself means the project to be the cause of itself. . . . [And yet] everything ***happens as if*** the in-itself, in a project to ground itself, gave itself the modification of the for-itself. (The for-itself is the in-itself losing itself as in-itself in order to ground itself as consciousness). . . . Thus everything happens as if the in-itself and the for-itself were presented in a state of disintegration in relation to an ideal synthesis.[46]

From the point of view of consciousness, it appears as though being has emanated consciousness to come to know itself. It is important to realize that this is only the projection desire of the incomplete consciousness, the for-itself toward completion. Even though the in-itself has emanated the for-itself, which consists of the negation of being. Consciousness, being-for-itself, is a lack and this is the real meaning behind the traditional notion that God is the good. God is the totality, the lacked, the standard of value, the ideal. So, God haunts the whole of life, for consciousness, because God is the goal we are aiming for. But God could not serve the function of being the ideal goal if God existed. God is so good, so perfect (the combination of the in-itself and for-itself) that God cannot exist even as an ideal because even the ideal is a magical entity. Being itself, being complete, cannot be conscious. Sartre believes, like Levinas, that consciousness requires plurality, and for Sartre this is to lack completion.

Under Sartre's interpretation of the relationship of consciousness and doubt, which is based in part on the idea of the cogito that emerges in Descartes's *Meditations*. God cannot be conscious because consciousness implies doubt and lack. Consciousness, like thought, is based on the ability to doubt, to experience the imperfection and finitude of human being that creates the ideal of perfection and infinitude Descartes sees as being "in the mind." For Descartes, God's consciousness must be radically unlike human consciousness; it is immediately one with its objects. But in Sartre's interpretation of consciousness (which may be implied in Descartes as well) this cannot be consciousness at all but only pure, positive, brute being-in-itself. Consciousness is negation and imperfection. The theological tradition destroys itself.

Sympathy for the Devil: The Critique of Theology

Let's return to Sartre's sympathy for the devil in his reading of Baudelaire. Sartre lays out in theological/mythical language the theme of the gratuitousness of the for-itself that figures so prominently in *Being and Nothingness* and runs through his work from *Nausea* to *Saint Genet*. The freedom and even the identity of the for-itself is in its nothingness before the pure positivity of Being, the in-itself. The individuality, the freedom, and the personhood of the for-itself is found in negativity. In *Baudelaire*, he describes this freedom of negation in terms of Satan's rebellion against the absolute positivity of God/Being.

> Satan, who was vanquished, fallen, guilty, denounced by the whole of Nature, banned from the universe, crushed beneath the memory of an unforgivable sin, devoured by insatiable ambition, transfixed by the eye of God, which froze him in his diabolical essence, and compelled to accept to the bottom of his heart the supremacy of Good—Satan, nevertheless, prevailed against God, his master and conqueror, by his suffering, but that flame of non-satisfaction which, at the very moment when divine omnipotence crushed him, at the very moment when he acquiesced in being crushed, shone like an unquenchable reproach.[47]

Satan is a heroic figure because, in his defeat before that mighty positive creative power of God, he does not simply accept it, nor worship it; rather, he rebels against it. Satan prevails against God in the only way the for-itself can prevail against the pure positive power of Being. He does not go gently into the night of being but rages, hopelessly, against it. Freedom is purely negative. The theme of freedom as negativity is present in *Saint Genet* where, Sartre explains, like all humans, I may escape God's infinite being and objectifying power by the fact that such a being could not conceive nothingness. To be conscious is to be a presence of nothingness to itself. It is in my nothingness that I am free. This is the point of human rebellion but also its despair.

> And furthermore, nonbeing attracts me, or, if one prefers, I attract myself from the depths of nonbeing: as a being, I am encircled and hemmed in by being, God's eye sees me. But since God, the infinite Being, cannot even conceive nothingness, in nothingness I escape him and derive only from myself. Not that I annihilate myself, but in absorbing myself in conceiving nonbeing I am still a consciousness or, if one prefers, a presence of nothingness to itself.[48]

We have here something like another Augustinian, Pascal, had: his famous idea about the superiority of the human to the universe. "Man is a reed, the weakest of nature, but he is a thinking reed. It is not necessary that the entire universe arm itself to crush: a vapor, a drop of water suffices to kill him. But if the universe were to crush him, man would still be nobler than what kills him, because he knows that he dies and the advantage that the universe has over him. The universe knows none of this."[49] But unlike Pascal, Sartre doesn't rush into the arms of the God that both associate with Being. Sartre sees that for traditional theology, one is only free, really free, to do evil from the point of view of Being, that is, to rebel against Being and to negate it. This is part of the point of "Cartesian Freedom." This is Sartre's claim that consciousness is pure negation. But this also is why he cannot shake free of theology as ontology, as part of the great chain of being that the for-itself so wishes to escape.

> Cartesian man and Christian man are free for Evil, but not for Good; for Error, but not for Truth. God takes them by the hand and, through the conjunction of natural and supernatural lights which He dispenses to them, leads them to the Knowledge and Virtue He has chosen for them. They need only let themselves be guided. The entire merit in this ascension reverts to Him. But insofar as they are nothingness, they escape Him. They

are free to let go of His hand on the way and to plunge into the world of sin and non-being.[50]

Sartre accepts the idea that freedom and creation are the same. A free act is an absolutely new production, the germ of which could not be contained in an earlier state of the world and that, consequently, freedom and creation are one and the same. But human creativity is only for the negative. In this respect, Sartrean existentialism acts as an important critique of theology. It reveals theologians' obsession with Being. The only possible escape is beyond Being.

In Sartre, Levinas and Cohen have an ally in the critique of theology. For although Sartre's atheist ontology mirrors the theological tradition, it also shows its emptiness.

Notes

1. Kate Kirkpatrick, *Sartre and Theology* (London: Bloomsbury, 2014). Kate Kirkpatrick, *Sartre and Sin: Between Being and Nothingness* (Oxford: Oxford University Press, 2017). The relationship of Sartre and theology has been discussed before in Thomas M. King, *Sartre and the Sacred* (Chicago: University of Chicago Press, 1974). Jacques Salvan, *The Scandalous Ghost: Sartre's Existentialism as Related to Vitalism, Humanism, Mysticism, and Marxism* (Detroit: Wayne State University Press, 1967).

2. Karl Barth, *Church Dogmatics*, vol. 3. Trans. J. W. Edwards, O. Bussey, Harold Knight (Edinburgh: T&T Clark, 1958); Paul Tillich, "The Nature and Significance of Existentialist Thought," *Journal of Philosophy* 53, no. 23: 739–48.

3. Emmanuel Levinas, "God and Philosophy" in *Of God Who Comes to Mind*, trans. Bettina Bergo (Stanford, CA: Stanford University Press, 1998), 55.

4. Emmanuel Levinas, *Is it Righteous to Be: Interviews with Emmanuel Levinas*, trans. Jill Robins (Stanford, CA: Stanford University Press, 2001), 17.

5. Dominque Janicaud, "The Theological Turn in French Phenomenology," in *Phenomenology and the Theological Turn: The French Debate*, trans. Bernard Prusak (New York: Fordham University Press, 2000).

6. Samuel Moyn, *The Origin of the Other: Emmanuel Levinas Between Revelation and Ethics* (New York: Columbia University Press, 2005), 126–27.

7. Emmanuel Levinas, "Review of Lev Shestov's *Kierkegaard and the Existential Philosophy*," trans. James McLachlan, *Levinas Studies* 11, 237–43.

8. Moyn, *Origin of the Other*, 168.

9. Emmanuel Levinas, "A Religion for Adults," in *Difficult Freedom* trans. Sean Hand (Baltimore: Johns Hopkins University Press, 1997), 14. John Caruana,

"Not Ethics, Not Ethics Alone, but the Holy: Levinas on Ethics and Holiness," *Journal of Religious Ethics* 34, no. 4 (December 2006): 561–83.

10. Todd A. Gooch, *The Numinous and Modernity: An Interpretation of Rudolf Otto's Philosophy of Religion* (Berlin: Walter de Gruyter, 2000). See also Heidegger's outline for lecture on mysticism "The Philosophical Foundations of Medieval Mysticism" in Martin Heidegger, *The Phenomenology of Religious Life*, trans. Matthias Fritch and Jennifer Anna Gosettie-Ferencei (Bloomington: Indiana University Press, 2004). Heidegger recommended Otto's *The Idea of the Holy* to Husserl as particularly significant and intended at one point to review this text. See John Van Buren, "The Earliest Heidegger: A New Field of Research," in *A Companion to Heidegger* (New York: Blackwell, 2005), 21; Katlyn Creasy, "Martin Heidegger's Changing Conceptions of the Holy: From the Phenomenology of Religious Life, "The Origin of the Work of Art," and "Elucidations of Hölderlin's Poetry," Unpublished, http://kaitlyncreasy.weebly.com/uploads/8/5/2/3/85234142/heideggers_changing_conceptions_of_the_holy.pdf

11. Rudolf Otto, *The Idea of the Holy*, trans. John Harvey (Oxford: Oxford University Press, 1958), 35.

12. Otto describes the experience of the "Holy" in the following:

The feeling of it may at times come sweeping like a gentle tide, pervading the mind with a tranquil mood of deepest worship. It may pass over into a more set and lasting attitude of the soul, continuing, as it were, thrillingly vibrant and resonant, until at last it dies away and the soul resumes its 'profane', non-religious mood of everyday experience. It may burst in sudden eruption up from the depths of the soul with spasms and convulsions, or lead to the strangest excitements, to intoxicated frenzy, to transport, and to ecstasy. It has its wild and demonic forms and can sink to an almost grisly horror and shuddering. It has its crude, barbaric antecedents and early manifestations, and again it may be developed into something beautiful and pure and glorious. It may become the hushed, trembling, and speechless humility of the creature in the presence of whom or what? In the presence of that which is a *mystery* inexpressible and above all creatures; Otto, *The Idea of the Holy*, 37.

13. Emmanuel Levinas, *Nine Talmudic Readings*, trans. Aron Aronowiz (Bloomington: Indiana University Press, 1994), 152. Levinas is probably also referring to Durkheim's descriptions of the sacred in *The Elementary Forms of Religious Life*. Durkheim describes "the sacred" as the interests of the group. Durkheim describes the experience as being overpowered by enthusiasm in relation to group ritual. In many ways Durkheim's "sacred" is a naturalist explanation of Otto's description of the experience of the holy. In Levinas's critique of the sacred, the individual is lost in the communal experience of the sacred. See Emile Durkheim, *The Elementary Forms of Religious Life*, trans. Joseph Ward Swain (New York: The Free Press, 1965).

14. Levinas, "Religion for Adults, 14.

15. Levinas, "Religion for Adults," 15.

16. Richard A. Cohen, *Levinasian Meditations: Ethics, Philosophy, and Religion* (Pittsburgh: Duquesne University Press, 2010), 308–9; Karl Barth, *Dogmatics in Outline*, trans. G. T. Tomson (New York: Harper and Row, 1959).

17. Cohen, *Levinasian Meditations*, 298.

18. Richard Kearney, *The God Who May Be: A Hermeneutics of Religion* (Bloomington: Indiana University Press, 2001), 26–28.

19. Martin Buber, *Moses: The Revelation and the Covenant* (New York: Harper and Row, 1958), 52–53.

20. Kearney, 27.

21. Emmanuel Levinas, *Otherwise than Being or Beyond Essence*, trans. Alfonso Lingis (Pittsburgh: Duquesne University Press, 1998), 197. Cohen, *Levinasian Meditations*, 305.

22. Cohen, *Levinasian Meditations*, 298.

23. Emmanuel Levinas, *Nine Talmudic Readings*, trans. Annette Aronowicz (Bloomington: Indiana University Press, 1990), 87.

24. Cohen, *Levinasian Meditations*, 308.

25. Alfred North Whitehead, *Adventures of Ideas* (Detroit: The Free Press, 1961), 164–66.

26. In "God and Philosophy" Levinas claims that rational theology and all forms of discourse accept are in "vassalage" to philosophy, and the dignity of being is the ruling discourse of Western philosophy: "Not to philosophize is still to philosophize." The philosophical discourse of the West claims the amplitude of an all-encompassing structure or of an ultimate comprehension. It compels every other discourse to justify itself before philosophy. Rational theology accepts this vassalage. If, for the benefit of religion, it reserves a domain from the authority of philosophy, one will know that this domain will have been recognized as philosophically unverifiable. See Emmanuel Levinas, *Of God Who Comes to Mind*, trans. Bettina Bergo (Stanford, CA: Stanford University Press, 1998), 55.

27. Levinas, *Is it Righteous to Be?*, 173.

28. Richard E. Aquila, "On Plotinus and the "Togetherness" of Consciousness," *Journal of the History of Philosophy* 30, no. 1 (January 1992), 7–32. Richard E. Aquila, "The Cartesian and a Certain "Poetic" Notion of Consciousness" *Journal of the History of Ideas* 49, no. 4 (October–December 1988), 543–62.

29. Kate Kirkpartrick, *Sartre and Theology* (London: T&T Clark, 2017), 93.

30. Cohen, *Levinasian Meditations*, 131.

31. Cohen, *Levinasian Meditations*, 132.

32. Emmanuel Levinas *Totality and Infinity*, trans. Alfonzo Lingus (Pittsburgh: Duquesne University Press, 1969), 87.

33. "Dialogue with Emmanuel Levinas," trans. Richard Kearney, in *Face to Face with Levinas*, ed. Richard A. Cohen (Albany: State University of New York Press, 1986), 17.

34. Jean-Paul Sartre, *Being and Nothingness: An Essay in Phenomenological Ontology*, trans. Hazel Barnes (New York: Washington Square Press, 1956), 368–69.

35. Jean-Paul Sartre, "Cartesian Freedom," in *Literary and Philosophical Essays*, trans. Annette Michelson (New York: Collier, 1962), 195.

36. Cohen, *Levinasian Meditations*, 134.

37. Emmanuel Levinas, "Philosophy and the Idea of Infinity" in *Collected Philosophical Papers*, trans. Alphonso Lingis (Dordrecht: Martinus Nijhoff, 1987), 52.

38. Jean-Paul Sartre, *Being and Nothingness: An Essay in Phenomenological Ontology*, trans. Hazel Barnes (New York: Washington Square Press, 1993), 108–10.

39. Sartre, *Being and Nothingness*, 27.

40. Sartre, *Being and Nothingness*, 27.

41. Sartre, *Being and Nothingness*, 28–29.

42. Emmanuel Levinas, "God and Philosophy" in *Of God Who Comes to Mind*, tr. Bettina Bergo (Stanford, CA: Stanford University Press, 1998), 55–56.

43. John Hick, *Evil and the God of Love* (San Francisco: Harper and Row, 1977), 174.

44. Cited in King, *Sartre and the Sacred*, 43. Kirkpatrick, *Sartre and Theology*, 44. Salvan, *The Scandalous Ghost*.

45. Jean-Paul Sartre, "Cartesian Freedom," in *Literary and Philosophical Essays*, trans. Annette Michelson (New York: Collier, 1962), 195.

46. Sartre, *Being and Nothingness*, 760, 762.

47. Jean-Paul Sartre, *Baudelaire*, trans. Martin Turnell (New York: New Directions, 1967), 99.

48. Jean-Paul Sartre, *Saint Genet: Actor and Martyr*, trans. Barbara Frechtman (New York: Pantheon, 1963), 159.

49. Blaise Pascal, *Pensées*, trans. A. J. Krailsheimer (New York: Penguin, 1995), 347.

50. Jean-Paul Sartre, "Cartesian Freedom," in *Literary and Philosophical Essays*, trans. Annette Michelson (New York: Collier, 1962), 193.

Bibliography

Aquila, Richard E. "On Plotinus and the "Togetherness" of Consciousness." *Journal of the History of Philosophy* 30, no. 1 (January 1992): 7–32.

Barth, Karl. *Church Dogmatics*, vol. 3. Translated by J. W. Edwards, O. Bussey, Harold Knight. Edinburgh: T&T Clark, 1958.

Buber, Martin. *Moses: The Revelation and the Covenant*. New York: Harper and Row, 1958.

Cohen, Richard, ed. *Face to Face with Levinas*. Albany: State University of New York Press, 1986.

Cohen, Richard. *Levinasian Meditations: Ethics, Philosophy, and Religion*. Pittsburgh: Duquesne University Press, 2010.
Kearney, Richard. *The God Who May Be: A Hermeneutics of Religion*. Bloomington: Indiana University Press, 2001.
Kirkpatrick, Kate. *Sartre and Theology*, London: Bloomsbury, 2014.
Kirkpatrick, Kate. *Sartre and Sin: Between Being and Nothingness*. Oxford: Oxford University Press, 2017.
King, Thomas M. *Sartre and the Sacred*. Chicago: University of Chicago Press, 1974.
Levinas, Emmanuel. "God and Philosophy" in *Of God Who Comes to Mind*. Translated by Bettina Bergo. Stanford: Stanford University Press, 1998.
Levinas, Emmanuel. "A Religion for Adults" in *Difficult Freedom*. Translated by Sean Hand. Baltimore: Johns Hopkins University Press, 1997.
Levinas, Emmanuel. *Is it Righteous to Be: Interviews with Emmanuel Levinas*. Translated Jill Robins. Stanford, CA: Stanford University Press, 2001.
Levinas, Emmanuel. *Nine Talmudic Readings*. Translated by Aron Aronowiz. Bloomington: Indiana University Press, 1994.
Levinas, Emmanuel, "Philosophy and the Idea of Infinity" in *Collected Philosophical Papers*. Translated by Alphonso Lingis. Dordrecht: Martinus Nijhoff, 1987.
Levinas, Emmanuel. *Otherwise than Being or Beyond Essence*. Translated by Alfonzo Lingus. Pittsburgh: Duquesne University Press, 1969.
Levinas, Emmanuel. *Totality and Infinity: An Essay in Exteriority*. Translated by Alfonzo Lingus. Pittsburgh: Duquesne University Press, 1969.
Moyn, Samuel. *The Origin of the Other: Emmanuel Levinas Between Revelation and Ethics*. New York: Columbia University Press, 2005.
Otto, Rudolf. *The Idea of the Holy*. Translated by John Harvey. Oxford: Oxford University Press, 1958.
Salvan, Jaques. *The Scandalous Ghost: Sartre's Existentialism as Related to Vitalism, Humanism, Mysticism, and Marxism*. Detroit: Wayne State University Press, 1967.
Sartre, Jean-Paul. *Baudelaire*. Translated by Martin Turnell. New York: New Directions, 1967.
Sartre, Jean-Paul. *Being and Nothingness: An Essay in Phenomenological Ontology*. Translated by Hazel Barnes. New York: Philosophical Library, 1956.
Sartre, Jean-Paul. "Cartesian Freedom" in *Literary and Philosophical Essays*. Translated by Annette Michelson. New York: Collier, 1962.
Sartre, Jean-Paul. *Saint Genet: Actor and Martyr*. Translated by Barbara Frechtman. New York: Pantheon, 1963.
Tillich, Paul. "The Nature and Significance of Existentialist Thought." *Journal of Philosophy* 53, no. 23: 739–48.
Whitehead, Alfred North. *Adventures of Ideas*. Detroit: The Free Press, 1961.

20

Incarnate Religion

MARK K. SPENCER

Emmanuel Levinas's and Richard Cohen's major claims about genuine religion or "religion for adults" are all founded on their attention to the central role of the body in human life.[1] This attention leads, especially in Cohen's work, to a critique of other forms of religion on the grounds that many of their claims are inconsistent with true claims about human life, and especially about our corporeality. In this chapter I present Levinas's and Cohen's criteria both for a religion being "adult" and for critiquing their own conclusions, both of which are based on their analysis of the body's role in experience. These criteria should impact, I argue, the view of religion and holiness taken even by those who disagree with their conclusions—for example, those committed to sacramental life, exclusive universalism, theodicy, or rational theology, each of which is critiqued by both thinkers.[2] I argue that some of their criteria are established beyond complete challenge—that is, any religion must abide by them to be a viable view for a morally responsible adult. But these same criteria provide a basis for challenging some of their conclusions. It is a testament to the excellence of their thought and their commitment to the phenomenological ideal that they provide a way to challenge their own conclusions.

My argument proceeds in three steps. First, I argue that while Levinas and Cohen show that Husserlian and Heideggerian phenomenology are inadequate to grasp real transcendence, they provide a new phenomenological method for doing so.³ This method can also be used to assess their conclusions, and this becomes apparent when their method is compared to those of the "theological turn" in French phenomenology, exemplified by Jean-Luc Marion, and of the early "realist" phenomenology developed by thinkers like Max Scheler and Dietrich von Hildebrand. Second, I show how they use their phenomenology to elucidate the role of the body in religion, I present the bodily criteria by which any adult religion must abide, and I synthesize an account of religious views that they take to be thereby excluded from adult consideration. Third, I show how, utilizing the method outlined in the first section, and the criteria in the second, a critique may be mounted against those exclusions. My main intention is to show the unshakeable contributions of Levinas and Cohen to any discussion of religion.

∽

Phenomenological Method and Transcendence. From his earliest works, Levinas sought a route of "escape" from modes of thought that reduce all things to the self or to another sphere of sameness—for example, reducing persons to their role in a community, or reducing beings to Being conceived as the impersonal unfolding of history.⁴ He sought an account of "real transcendence," that is, of relating to others without reducing self or other to one another or to some third thing.⁵ Most other philosophical attempts to describe alterity or transcendence end up reducing persons to some conceptualizable or propositional content, or to being just an intentional object, that is, an object whose meaning is constituted, at least partly, by the intentional act by which it is grasped.

Levinas, and, following him, Cohen, see phenomenology, as developed by Edmund Husserl and Martin Heidegger, as the best philosophical method for remaining rooted in what is given in conscious experience.⁶ That such an approach cannot grasp real transcendence does not negate the fact that it clarifies many other aspects of experience. There is neither the space nor the need in this chapter to consider Husserlian or Heideggerian phenomenological methods in detail; a few remarks suffice. Husserlian phenomenology describes any object in its essential characteristics as it gives itself in intentional acts, such as perceiving, knowing, or feeling. An object's meaning is at least partially constituted by the kind of act through which it is received and intended. On Husserl's method we set aside consideration of the real existence of objects, so as to focus on how they give themselves in intentional acts. Phenomenological claims are based on what is given in immediate insight and are revisable in light of more precise insights.[7] Heideggerian phenomenology considers beings in relation to Being, which reveals beings in their historical situation and renders them intelligible. This method considers the ways in which phenomena exist, rather than considering them just as intentional objects.[8]

But some levels of human experience cannot be considered on either approach. These include sensibility, which is not an intentional act of perceiving an object, but bodily immersion in one's environment, for example, enjoying sensing oneself being caressed by the sun or the breeze on one's face. This everyday bodily experience does not involve representing, intending, or considering the being or meaning of the environment but is just bodily, self-sensing immersion.[9] Experiences of self-sensing, sensibility, and enjoyment underlie what, for Levinas, is the most important bodily aspect of human life, the ethical relation, in which the expressivity of the other's face commands me not to murder or harm, but to serve, him or her, placing me under obligation and responsibility. To see the expressivity of another's face or hear the expressivity of another's voice is not to grasp the content of what is said, but to find oneself claimed by what is uncontrollable and unpredictable in the other, to be called to response and responsibility, that is, to find oneself ethically obligated to the other in a way one did not choose.[10] When I hear another's expressivity and feel myself required to respond, or when I see another person hungry when I have more than enough to eat, or when I would pass by a homeless person but see the appeal in their eyes to help, I find myself troubled in my bodily sensibility. I no longer just enjoy my environment, but I find that my bodily goods and my body itself could have been used to serve the other. To be able to sense and enjoy is to also be able to misuse that enjoyment at the expense of others but also to be able to devote my bodily life to others' enjoyment, even to the point of suffering and dying for them.

Husserlian or Heideggerian phenomenology, being focused on knowledge and experience, cannot give an account of being bodily claimed to serve the other. But it is better to serve others than to know things. We cannot understand why it is worthwhile to pursue knowledge unless we are first given an impulsion outward to speak to others, and this requires that we first be called to responsibility. Left to myself, I am oriented to my own enjoyment, but encountering others pulls me out of myself and reorients me toward them. Only on this basis do I seek to know anything outside myself.¹¹ I do not deduce that I am called to respond and be responsible to others from a consideration of my nature, or of being, or of communal relations. Rather, I find myself called to respond prior to any such considerations.¹² I always find that I had already been called and am now "too late" to do all that I could have done for the other; being ethically related to others is a bodily state in which I find myself already with a weight of responsibility that I alone can and must bear.¹³

Since these relations cannot be fully cognitively grasped, two dangers arise: first, someone describing ethical relations could take him or herself to be able to assert anything he or she wanted about them; second, the ethical relation could be taken to be indescribable and thus irrelevant to rational discourse. If claims about ethical relations were arbitrary or impossible, there would be no way to critique Levinas's and Cohen's claims about that relation. But they avoid both extremes by devising a method for describing how I find the other's call in me; they thereby allow for assessment and revision of their claims about the ethical relation. This is an expansion of phenomenology so that it is a method for describing real transcendence.[14]

Transcendence is a relation in which I receive the other as infinite, as beyond my capacity to grasp intentionally, and in which both I and the other remain separated from each other and from the relation, even while we are related.[15] Given the structure of this relation, I cannot examine it or the other as I would an object or a being. Rather, I can only examine its effects: this new phenomenological method directs me to consider it as it shows up in my bodily response to the other—for example, how I find myself called by, substituted for, suffering for, or responsible for the other.[16] When I encounter the other in the cases described above, I sense myself called to certain bodily responses: to speak to the other, to give the other the food I would have eaten, to serve the other's needs with my bodily labor. All subsequent thinking about how to accomplish these tasks is based on this prior sensing of the other's call in me. I find my body is not just an organ of perception but can be used ethically to serve or unethically to harm.

Levinas and Cohen thus make definite claims about the structure of the call that I find in me and, on that basis, about the structure of the relation of real transcendence. If I were to apply their method and find my calling to have a different structure, then I would have good phenomenological reason to revise their claims. But what is *not* open to revision is the claim that we are in relations of transcendence, including ethical and bodily relations. I must be called to responsibility, or, as we have already seen, I would have no reason to seek knowledge or to communicate about anything. And I find that this calling is indeed felt in my bodily sensibility, so that it is distinct from, and so can be prior to, knowledge and intentionality. But this does not preclude my receiving other calls and entering into other relations of real transcendence besides the ethical ones. We find evidence for these calls and relations and so for challenging some of Levinas's and Cohen's claims by comparing their phenomenology with two other phenomenological movements that significantly parallel Levinas's and Cohen's approach.

A first, which was influenced by Levinas, is the "theological turn" in contemporary French phenomenology, best exemplified by the work of Jean-Luc Marion. His project is to describe "saturated phenomena," phenomena whose meaning exceeds any content or act through which I intend them. For example, I might approach a painting considering it according to what I have learned from art history, but find that what I see in it exceeds any conceptual content I have learned.[17] Cohen shows that one such phenomenon does *not* parallel Levinas's claims, despite Marion's intention that it do so. Early in his career, Marion described the phenomenon of "counter-intentionality," in which I look at another person only to find him or her looking back, giving meaning to me, rather than vice versa. With this description, Marion intends to give an alternative phenomenology to Levinas's phenomenology of real transcendence.[18] But Cohen shows that he fails in this intention: real transcendence is not an intentional relationship, whether from the self to the other or vice versa.[19] However, Marion has since developed his phenomenology. The saturated phenomenon does not constitute me as intentional object, but like the other's face in Levinas renders me impelled to respond, with the ability to respond and the response itself given to me. But, in examining saturated phenomena, and how the relation of real transcendence shows up in me, Marion finds a wider range of calls than just the ethical call found by Levinas. Each encounter with another person or with any saturated phenomenon reorients my self-sensing flesh such that it is responsive in some way. Some such encounters call me to ethical response but others to erotic response, self-development, or other responses.[20] Marion's claim is that transcendence has more forms than Levinas describes. Regardless of whether he is correct, this shows that Levinas's method for describing transcendence can be used to challenge or expand on his claims.

A second movement that parallels[21] Levinas's and Cohen's approach is the "realist" phenomenology of the early twentieth century, as practiced, for example, by Max Scheler and Dietrich von Hildebrand, who rejected

Husserl's method of setting aside consideration of real existence, in favor of describing reality as it gives itself in actual experience.[22] Levinas argues that Husserlian and Heideggerian phenomenology must be surpassed by a more fundamental axiology,[23] and consideration of feeling and values are fundamental to Hildebrand's and Scheler's phenomenology. On their view, I discover values—such as justice, kindness, and beauty—in finding myself affected by them and called to give them their due response. The relation to values is one of real transcendence: values are important-in-themselves, not avenues to fulfilling my needs or desires, constituted by my intentional acts, or as reducible to Being.[24] Different values call for different responses. Paradigmatic among values is the unique value of each person, which calls for a response of charity.[25] Being affected by values, like encountering the other's face in Levinas, is prior to and guides all other action and cognition. But—and here the realists offer a phenomenological revision of Levinas's claims—many acts of cognition are themselves relations of real transcendence, where the two enter into relation while remaining distinct from that relation. For example, face-to-face personal knowing of another person is a genuine relation to the other: one in which the other is known in him or herself without being reduced to anything in the self like a concept or proposition.[26] Hildebrand and Scheler, like Marion, describe relations of transcendence other than those described by Levinas, and so corroborate my claim that Levinas's phenomenological method can be challenged from within his own method.

Having seen the ways in which Levinas and Cohen develop phenomenology, and in which their phenomenology can be developed, we are now in a position to see how this method provides criteria for adult religiosity and how they thereby reject a number of religious views.

~

Corporeal Criteria for a Religion for Adults. The ethical relation is a relation with the infinite, that is, with what cannot be reduced to any kind of sameness—anything that would reduce the infinite other to something possessable by me. It is a singular election or call to infinite ethical responsibility, to devote my body, even in its suffering, to the service of others.[27] As a relation to the infinite, this is the truly religious relation, on Levinas's and Cohen's view.[28]

Cohen shows how all of bodily life can be rendered ethical in his remarkable explanation of circumcision, which inscribes ethical commands in the most private and animal aspects of a boy's flesh before he can even be aware that he is called. This captures a key religious claim for Cohen and Levinas: spiritual calls cannot be separated from physical acts or from ethics. Any religion that reduces our spiritual life to lofty sentiments or aspirations, or to cognitive acts or experiences, fails to grasp the corporeality of our call to goodness.[29] I am called to goodness in my flesh in a way prior to any representational, conceptual, or propositional thinking, discovered in my proximity to the other. The call to infinite responsibility is a condition of being "ill at ease in my own skin," in the ways described above, when I encounter the other, and, on that basis, a condition of desiring to transcend myself in good bodily actions toward the other.[30] This is to acknowledge the superiority of the other in ethically commanding me, not merely to pity the other person's suffering, and so infantilize the other person. It is to act as one adult toward another adult.[31]

Levinas and Cohen argue that any responsible religious stance must base itself on this relation of transcendence with the infinite. Most religions relate to the sacred, understood as something of supernatural power, capable of miraculous acts, and which illumines the religious seeker and brings about cognitive or affective religious experience. But all such relations, they claim, reduce to the self, for they seem be about gaining knowledge or experience for myself, or about liberating me for more spontaneous, self-directed free acts. No real transcendence, no relation to the infinite, has occurred. Levinas takes this criterion for adult religiosity to exclude any religion that relates to God through sacraments: physical acts that purport to make God present and available for knowledge or personal gain.[32]

By contrast, in finding myself ethically related to another person, placed under obedience and responsibility, I find myself in real transcendence. The ethical relation is a command to move in "transascendence" toward an infinite moral height, which is not reducible to experience or to my free and spontaneous will and that is never definitely reached—yet calls me ever upward to becoming better.[33] The ethical relation of one human body to another, of finding myself called to provide food and drink to the other, is for these reasons more genuinely "religious" because it is more closely related to what is infinite and truly transcendent to me than any classic "religious experience." By contrast, Levinas says, the attempt to relate to the sacred is far more "materialist," and he calls for a "desacralization" of the sacred, an unmasking and rejecting of such experiences as idolatrous, worshiping what is not genuinely infinite and ignoring the infinitude found in the ethical relation.[34]

A "religion for adults" requires leaving behind a religious stance that is focused on seeking religious experiences, including a static state of enjoyment in heaven, or that relies on God to miraculously provide those things which I in my responsibility can or ought to provide.[35] The relation to the infinite invests me with responsibility and does not allow me to shift this responsibility to anyone else, even God. I must desire this responsibility more than union or friendship with God, for this is desire for what is genuinely infinite and religious.[36] Because of its infinitude, this desire presents itself "as though" it was given by God, though I can never assert that it *is* given by God since that would substitute a cognitive relation for the ethical relation.[37] In Levinas's trenchant phrase, I find myself in a condition in which God commands me to "love the Torah," God's ethical commands, "more than God."[38] I am not thereby a mere project of God's; rather, I find myself separated from all others, "created" as a unique, separate being, capable of freely but responsibly acting on my own. My freedom is not an autonomous power for self-determination but is always invested with responsibility by others and so is troubled and bodily. God's appeal to do ethical work in the world is an appeal to human maturity, not a call to escape the world for union with God. The "being created" relation is not, on this view, a miraculous act in the past that must be accepted on faith—for that would be to reduce the transcendent to thinkable content, which would not be transcendent—but an aspect of the ethical relation.[39]

These criteria allow Cohen and Levinas to reject as nonadult and irresponsible, and hence dangerous and even evil, any religion that would move in these other directions. But they do not thereby reject traditional religion in favor of secular, Enlightenment-style ethics.[40] This move is one of their great religious insights. Being rooted in a religious tradition, including its liturgy and devotions, is a key part of the training in perception that is required for entering into the ethical relation and for seeing the universal call to morality in my particular circumstances. The universal call to responsibility requires attention to particularity.[41] This is not to instrumentalize liturgical practice by making it mere training for ethical actions. Rather, liturgy is an essential part of the ethical life, which initiates me into receptivity to God's command to act ethically and justly and into finding that command already implanted in me; it is part of the "ethical interhuman relation" that, on Cohen's view, is the essence of genuine religion.[42] To be a bodily being is to be rooted in kinship, nation, and history.[43] The religious relation relates us to others as the bodily, historical persons that we actually are, and I discover this in liturgy. In addition to liturgy, a further aspect of religious tradition that must be retained in adult religion is the sober study of tradition, debating with others throughout history how best to live an ethical life.[44] What is rejected are forms of religiosity based purely on enthusiasm, passion or friendship for God, aesthetic enjoyment of God, or being taken out of ourselves irrationally.[45] The ethical call is prior to rational activity, but it invests reason with responsibility, and a religion for adults must use reason responsibly.

The ethical call is given universally to each person in each other person's face. This requires rejecting religions that only recognize particularized experiences and calls, like many forms of paganism, and religions that violently exclude nonbelievers in pursuit of a "universality" centered on the acceptance of cognizable theological claims by all those remaining after the violence is over. Cohen sees triumphalist forms of Christianity, in their exclusion from salvation of members of all other religions, as forms of this "exclusive universality."[46] This is not a critique of all aspects or forms of Christianity; for example, Levinas positively invokes the Christian notion of Christ the Man-God, understood as humiliation taken on by God as expiation or substitution for others, as an excellent phenomenological expression of the ethical relation.[47] Also to be rejected is any religion or morality, such as many forms of Enlightenment morality, that sees ethics as universal in the sense of not being embodied in particular, bodily relations.[48] Each of these approaches fails to recognize real transcendence; in each case, the other and the infinite are reduced to cognizable content. For this reason, Levinas and Cohen reject any view on which religion is focused on personal salvation or on a God who rewards, punishes, or pardons.[49] One must rather desire to be responsible and not seek anything in return, to "love God for nothing;"[50] anything less would reduce this love to self-love and so not be real transcendence.

Religion for adults also requires seeing that suffering is itself rooted in the basic structure of human life. Suffering is a negative form of "sensibility." It is literally meaningless and useless in itself, and any attempt to impose a meaning upon it with a theodicy—for example, as divine punishment or as an opportunity for penance—is problematic not only because it is insensitive and cruel to those who are suffering, but more fundamentally because suffering takes place at a more fundamental layer of human life than meaningful, intentional relations such as reasoning or use. Because rationality is always posterior to sensibility in the structure of the layers of human life, no rational explanation or practical effect can alleviate or make up for suffering.[51] Suffering is, in another of Levinas's fine phrases, "a wound that bleeds forever," as if only another suffering could staunch it.[52] The only thing that can make suffering meaningful is something else that takes place on the self-sensing, bodily layer of human life: I must, as part of my response to the ethical call, suffer for others. To find myself called to serve the other is a wounding but a wound by which I am called to substitute myself for others. On this basis, I can dedicate all my wounds and sufferings to others, not, on Levinas and Cohen's view, in the sense that this will magically take away their suffering: but in the sense that my suffering can be undergone for them, as part of the liturgy of my life whereby I live increasingly for others.[53]

Given all of this, religion must be embodied, not lived entirely in rational or "spiritual" experiences. Indeed, Levinas and Cohen take these criteria to exclude any rational theology from adult religiosity, where such a theology would purport to prove things about God's existence or attributes; the level of human life in which we can have adult religiosity is the bodily level, prior to and excessive over any rational, cognitive act.[54]

But none of this is to say that the other person *is* God, or that God is incarnated in the other person. The other's face reveals God by manifesting the height and infinitude of the moral command to substitute myself for the other, but this requires seeing the other entirely *as other*, as one who requires moral regard, not focusing on the particular sense-perceivable aspects of this other, like the color of his or her eyes.[55] God is not present in the other's face as an object or property able to be grasped; rather, I see God's call in the other's face as a "trace" left by God, revealing that He has already passed by and left His commands to me.[56] This trace also reveals to me that there are many other others besides this one; God manifests Himself as the "third" Who troubles any relation among two persons, even an ethical relation, with others' need for justice.[57] God is always "other than the other," turning me away from Himself to a stance of justice for all; God is "transcendent to the point of absence," making Himself entirely unavailable in the present.[58] It is not enough to respond ethically to one another; I must also take up the work of building a just world. This requires, and lays the foundation, for all reasoning.[59] Adult religion is this work, this endless liturgy, of living ethically and justly, with every layer of my life, with the universality and traditionary particularity that these works require. It is not a matter of being taken out of myself into a drama entirely imposed on me from above, but an investing of my freedom and corporeality with responsibility, such that I am God's partner in bringing about a just world.[60]

~

Critique of Claims Regarding Non-Adult Religion. Levinas and Cohen's account of the transcendence and relation to the infinite that can and does occur in the bodily layer of human life is a phenomenological clarification of our experience that no religious or philosophical engagement with the human person can plausibly deny. The bodily layer of experience, the layer of self-sensing, suffering, and the ethical call, really is foundational to the intentional and existential acts described by Husserl and Heidegger, none of which can be removed from their ethical and sensible context, and none of which involve real transcendence. These acts cannot grasp their foundation in sensibility but rely upon it for their existence and moral justification.[61]

However, given the comparisons between Levinas's expanded phenomenological method, and the methods worked out by Marion, Scheler, and von Hildebrand, a critique can be made of Levinas and Cohen's claims regarding some of the forms of religiosity they take to be non-adult. It is beyond the scope of this chapter to fully defend those forms of religiosity, but I shall outline such an argument, while still holding to their bodily criteria for adult religiosity. In this way, we shall better see the permanent value of those criteria, while also seeing that these criteria can be used and expanded in ways differing from how Levinas and Cohen use them. I do not intend to defend specific religions but rather just consider formal features of the kinds of religions that are critiqued by Levinas and Cohen.

The first form of religiosity that they reject is that which aims at being in the presence of the sacred, for example, through sacramental means. Such a method seems to remain at the level of intentional acts, without the possibility of real, and while setting aside ethical responsibility for others in pursuit of extraordinary experiences and self-fulfillment.[62] It seems to involve refusing to take responsibility, as every adult must do, for one's free actions but instead letting those actions be controlled or overwhelmed by enthusiasm or faith in mysteries, both of which fail to involve real transcendence.[63]

But the wider range of real transcendence described by Marion, Scheler, and von Hildebrand gives reasons to reject this criticism for at least some sacred or sacramental experiences. Levinas and Cohen's criteria for adult religion require that one really transcend oneself toward the infinite—not merely have intentional experiences that seem to be of transcendence—and they require that this transcendence involve the investing of one's freedom and bodily life with responsibility. They claim that this occurs only in the face-to-face relation with another person. But Marion has shown us that the face-to-face relation can already arouse many different calls in me, not just the ethical call. A religion would clearly be nonadult if it claimed to dispense with the ethical call, or if it undermined my responsible freedom. But there is no a priori or experiential warrant to claim that we *only* encounter calls to ethical or just action. Real transcendence can involve being called to a wide range of responses, including erotic and noetic responses, through the particularities of the persons I encounter. Furthermore, I can find myself in a relation of real transcendence, receiving a call to responsibility, with things other than the faces of other persons, such as nonhuman living things. As von Hildebrand and Scheler phenomenologically argued, we find ourselves opened to a relation of transcendence by values of many sorts in many different things. If these claims are correct, there is a space for a really transcendent relation to the sacred, including through sacraments. Physical things, in the right contexts, invest my freedom with responsibility and with calls to certain sorts of action or knowing, and this is experienced in the self-sensing body, rather than purely spiritually, such that those physical things are rightly called "sacraments."[64]

Levinas would object that such experiences purport to make God present and thereby reducible to an intentional object of religious or mystical experience; such experiences cannot be genuinely religious because they fail to relate to the infinite, for we can only relate to the infinite if it is unavailable for intentional consideration. God can only be regarded as if He has passed by and left His trace and call, as always irrecuperably in the past, never as present.

But it is not clear that this temporal claim is required or warranted by Levinas's phenomenological findings. Von Hildebrand, as we have seen, describes a cognitive relation that is simultaneously a real transcendence, in which the other is experienced without his or her meaning being constituted by the intentional act and without being reduced to me. In this relation, my mind is invested with meaning and a call to further self-transcending cognition, but in a way that leaves both subject and object free of reduction to the relation—that is, the person or value that is contemplated is revealed in itself, and not just in its conceptualizable or representable content.[65] This is a nontotalizing mode of presence. We find such an experience in friendships, in which we get to know other persons not in the sense of accumulating facts about them but in coming to know them personally, and in meeting strangers as well, in which we both find ourselves called ethically to respect them but also experience them cognitively as irreducible persons.[66] The possibility of such an experience allows for the possibility of religious experiences of God as personal within Levinas and Cohen's criteria for adult religion. It allows a rejection of Levinas's claim that nothing present can be infinite,[67] since the cognized other appears as infinitely excessive over all representable content, but not merely as mysterious (since mysterious presence shuts down, rather than invests, rationality).[68] All this retains Levinas's central claims regarding real transcendence.

On this foundation, a second form of religiosity can be defended: certain forms of exclusive universalism and natural theology. "Exclusive universalism" refers to any view on which one asserts that a particular religious doctrine is true and therefore should be held by all persons and to the exclusion of all other religious views. It is clear that Levinas and Cohen's criteria exclude any violent exclusion of religious views; whatever else it may be, the call that we encounter in the face of another person is ethical. If the bodily and ethical criteria for adult religion are correct, then violent or triumphalist religious views are indefensible. Likewise, any theology that threatens human freedom must be rejected given these criteria. But this does not discount all exclusive universalisms. The ethical relation is already a relation with cognizable content.[69] In encountering the face of another person, I receive the knowable content "Thou shalt not kill" and the call to justice, and, if Marion is right, other knowable content as well. An opening is provided here for receiving doctrinal content in other encounters: the mind can be invested with content such that it is responsible to think certain things and irresponsible to think others. Any content received in this way always exceeds its unpacking in particular intentional acts; what is necessary is a sober, studious, free tradition of debate and discussion. The original content received, however, constrains what one can responsibly think and so allows for theologically articulable doctrines.

The fact that all relations to the infinite include cognizable content further opens the possibility of defending, within Levinas and Cohen's criteria for adult religion, a third form of religion, theodicies. Levinas and Cohen conclusively show, I think, that suffering cannot have meaning imposed on it through intentional acts. Intentional acts are finite and do not have real transcendence, but suffering, due to its place in self-sensing, is infinite. Accordingly, no finite meaning can account for suffering. However, on their view, suffering can become meaningful by being invested with ethical meaning through my choice to suffer for the other. Yet as we have seen above, this call gives cognizable content. The meaningfulness of suffering for the other, while fully grasped in sensibility and not through intentionality, can still be unpacked cognitively, in the manner of theological doctrine described above. Some theodicies—such as the one Levinas and Cohen give, in terms of suffering for others on the basis of a divine call—can thereby be given. It is possible to find oneself called to suffer for others through hearing the content of such theodicies and so to find one's suffering invested with meaning not entirely through one's own choice, but through the meaning one receives.

There is more that should be said about how Levinas and Cohen's bodily criteria constrain the range of religions that any responsible adult can consider, and about how their criteria allow for a wider range of religions than they themselves allow. These remarks are meant to lay the groundwork for further consideration of particular religious views. But they are also meant in praise of Levinas and Cohen's remarkable phenomenological elucidation of the genuine locus of a really transcendent relation to the infinite in human experience. These claims must be retained in any consideration of religious claims by a responsible adult.

Notes

1. Richard Cohen, *Levinasian Meditations* (Pittsburgh: Duquesne University Press, 2010), 38–9; Levinas, Seán Hand, trans., *Difficult Freedom* (Baltimore: Johns Hopkins University Press, 1990), 11.

2. See Cohen, *Levinasian Meditations*, 264–65, 297–98, 305, 315–16; Cohen, *Out of Control* (Albany: SUNY Press, 2017), 98–101; Levinas, "Transcendence and Evil," in Alphonso Lingis, trans. *Collected Philosophical Papers* (Dordrecht: Martinus Nijhoff, 1987); *Difficult Freedom*, 6–7.

3. Levinas, *Entre Nous*, Michael Smith and Barbara Harshav, trans. (New York: Columbia University Press, 1998), 216.

4. See, for example, Levinas, *Discovering Existence with Husserl*, Richard Cohen and Michael Smith, trans. (Evanston: NWU Press, 1998); Levinas, *On Escape*, Bettina Bergo, trans. (Stanford, CA: Stanford University Press, 2003).

5. Levinas, *Totality and Infinity*, Alphonso Lingis, trans. (Pittsburgh: Duquesne University Press, 1969), 41–42; "God and Philosophy," in *Collected Philosophical Papers*, 166.

6. Levinas, *Discovering Existence*; *Totality and Infinity*, 42–48.

7. Cohen, *Elevations* (Chicago: University of Chicago Press, 1994), 275–78; *Ethics, Exegesis, and Philosophy* (Cambridge: Cambridge University Press, 2001), 41–77. See Husserl, *Ideas*, v. 1, F. Kersten, trans. (The Hague: Martinus Nijhoff, 1983), part 2.

8. See Heidegger, *Being and Time*, Joan Stambaugh, trans. (Albany: State University of New York Press, 1996), intro, part 2.

9. Levinas, *Totality and Infinity*, 110ff.; Levinas, Richard Cohen, trans., *Time and the Other* (Pittsburgh: Duquesne University Press, 1987), 63.

10. These themes are ubiquitous for Levinas and Cohen. See, for example, Levinas, *Totality and Infinity*, 194–201; *Otherwise Than Being*, Alphonso Lingis, trans. (Pittsburgh: Duquesne University Press, 1998), 110–18, 153ff; Cohen, *Levinasian Meditations*, 323–24.

11. Cohen, *Elevations*, 282; *Levinasian Meditations*, 50, 216–19.

12. Levinas, *Entre Nous*, 60; Cohen, *Ethics, Exegesis, and Philosophy*, 291–93, 306.

13. Levinas, *Otherwise Than Being*, 150; Cohen, *Levinasian Meditations*, 236.

14. Levinas, *Entre Nous*, 216; Cohen, *Levinasian Meditations*, 241.

15. Levinas, *Totality and Infinity*, 51–52, 195.

16. Levinas, *Otherwise Than Being*, 114: in encountering the other, I find myself obsessed with the other; the responsible, biblical saying "Here I am" is drawn out of me by the encounter.

17. See especially Marion, *In Excess*, Robyn Horner and Vincent Berraud, trans. (New York: Fordham University Press, 2004). For a comparison of Levinas's approach with Marion's see Cohen, *Levinasian Meditations*, 241.

18. Marion, *Prolegomena to Charity*, Stephen Lewis, trans. (New York: Fordham University Press, 2002), 71–101.

19. Cohen, *Elevations*, 284.

20. Marion, *In Excess*, 118.

21. On this parallel see John F. Crosby, "Introductory Study" to Dietrich von Hildebrand, Crosby, trans. *The Nature of Love* (South Bend: St. Augustine's Press, 2009), xxxi–xxxvi.

22. See, for example, Scheler, "Phenomenology and the Theory of Cognition," "The Theory of the Three Facts," and "Idealism and Realism," in David Latcherman, trans., *Selected Philosophical Essays* (Evanston: NWU Press, 1973); von Hildebrand, *What Is Philosophy?* (New York: Routledge, 1991), 273–76.

23. Levinas, *Entre Nous*, 211.

24. These claims are the major themes in the entirety of Scheler, Manfred Frings and Roger Funk, trans., *Formalism in Ethics and Non-Formal Ethics of*

Values (Evanston: NWU Press, 1973); von Hildebrand, *Christian Ethics* (New York: McKay, 1953).

25. Hildebrand, *Love*, 23–24.
26. Hildebrand, *Love*, 7–8; *What is Philosophy?*, 229–36.
27. Levinas, *Entre Nous*, 211–17; *Totality and Infinity*, 194ff; Cohen, *Levinasian Meditations*, 253–54.
28. Levinas, *Totality and Infinity*, 80; Cohen, *Elevations*, 182–87.
29. Cohen, *Levinasian Meditations*, 288–92.
30. Levinas, *Entre Nous*, 58–59.
31. Levinas, *Difficult Freedom*, 139.
32. Levinas, *Difficult Freedom*, 6–7; Cohen, *Levinasian Meditations*, 221–23, 299.
33. Levinas, *Totality and Infinity*, 78–79; Cohen, *Elevations*, 185; *Out of Control*, 39.
34. Levinas, *Difficult Freedom*, 7.
35. Cohen, *Levinasian Meditations*, 255, 326.
36. Levinas, *Difficult Freedom*, 143–45; *Totality and Infinity*, 33–34.
37. Cohen, *Elevations*, 268–71.
38. Levinas, *Difficult Freedom*, 142; Cohen, *Levinasian Meditations*, 326.
39. Levinas, *Difficult Freedom*, 141; *Totality and Infinity*, 293–94; *Otherwise Than Being*, 111–12; Cohen, *Elevations*, 180–82, 217; *Levinasian Meditations*, 222–23.
40. Cohen, *Levinasian Meditations*, 259–61.
41. Levinas, *Difficult Freedom*, 13, 20.
42. Cohen, *Levinasian Meditations*, 215; Levinas, *Totality and Infinity*, 79. See also Michael Purcell, *Levinas and Theology* (Cambridge: Cambridge University Press, 2006), 138–39.
43. Levinas, *Totality and Infinity*, 278–80; Cohen, *Ethics, Exegesis, and Philosophy*, 299–300.
44. Levinas, *Difficult Freedom*, xiv, 18, 138–39; Cohen, *Levinasian Meditations*, 242, 246–47.
45. Levinas, *Difficult Freedom*, 6–7, 20, 27; Cohen, *Levinasian Meditations*, 212–14.
46. Cohen, *Levinasian Meditations*, 259–65.
47. Levinas, *Entre Nous*, 53–60.
48. Cohen, *Levinasian Meditations*, 266–67.
49. Levinas, *Difficult Freedom*, 143–45; *Time and the Other*, 69; Cohen, *Levinasian Meditations*, 308. Levinas is not rejecting the notion of punishment altogether; indeed, to be guilty and worthy of punishment is one possibility for a responsible adult (*Difficult Freedom*, 139). What he rejects is seeing God as entirely meting out rewards and punishments, instead of investing us with the responsibility to perform these works of justice.
50. Levinas, *Out of Control*, 83.

51. Levinas, "Transcendence and Evil," 180; Cohen, *Levinasian Meditations*, 315-24; *Out of Control*, 97-98.
52. Levinas, *Difficult Freedom*, 148.
53. Levinas, *Otherwise Than Being*, 77-90; Cohen, *Out of Control*, 99.
54. Cohen, *Levinasian Meditations*, 210ff., 296ff.
55. Levinas, *Totality and Infinity*, 79, 194 Cohen, *Levinasian Meditations*, 243.
56. Levinas, "God and Philosophy," 162-70.
57. Levinas, "Meaning and Sense," in *Collected Philosophical Papers*, 104-7; *Otherwise than Being*, 159-60; Cohen, *Levinasian Meditations*, 54, 237.
58. Levinas, "God and Philosophy," 165-66.
59. Cohen, *Levinasian Meditations*, 302-3.
60. Levinas, *Difficult Freedom*, 14.
61. Levinas, *Difficult Freedom*, 16.
62. A separate critique of such forms of religion is that, given that they are carried out at the level of cognitive acts, their claims can be critiqued and rejected on the grounds of other intentional evidence, for example, the evidence of the sciences, internal contradictions among theological claims, or the conflict between theological claims and human freedom. See, for example, Cohen, *Levinasian Meditations*, 199-200, 210-14, 298. I shall not address these critiques here, since the critique in terms of the deeper, bodily layer of life is a stronger, more fundamental critique.
63. Levinas, *Difficult Freedom*, 9; *Entre Nous*, 56.
64. See Thomas Aquinas, *Summa theologiae* III q. 60 a. 4. For the way in which sacraments invest our freedom with responsibility, see e.g., *Summa theologiae* III q. 79 a. 6; q. 85 a. 1. In Aquinas's use of the term, circumcision as described by Cohen is a sacrament; cf. *Summa theologiae* III q. 70 a. 2 and 3. For parallels between the structure of ethical subjectivity in Levinas and in Thomas Aquinas see my "Ethical Subjectivity in Levinas and Thomas Aquinas: Common Ground?" *Heythrop Journal* 53 (2012): 137-47.
65. On another form of transcendence involving love, see Hildebrand, *Nature of Love*, chs. 4 and 9.
66. Richard Kearney, in building on Levinas's phenomenology, argues that our encounter with other persons and the infinite in them is both ethical and cognitive. See "Epiphanies of the Everyday," in *After God*, ed. John Panteleimon Manoussakis (New York: Fordham University Press, 2006).
67. Levinas, *Otherwise Than Being*, 146.
68. Cf. Marion, *In Excess*, ch. 5. It is beyond the scope of this chapter, but this may allow for a defense of Buber's dialogical view of the relation among persons and with God, within, not in distinction to, Levinas's criteria for genuine religion.
69. See my "An Ethical Neo-Platonism: Levinas and Bonaventure in Dialogue." *Quaestiones Disputatae* 1 (2011): 226-40.

Bibliography

Cohen, Richard. *Elevations*. Chicago: University of Chicago Press, 1994.
Cohen, Richard. *Ethics, Exegesis, and Philosophy*. Cambridge: Cambridge University Press, 2001.
Cohen, Richard. *Levinasian Meditations*. Pittsburgh: Duquesne University Press, 2010.
Cohen, Richard. *Out of Control*. Albany: State University of New York Press, 2017.
Heidegger, Martin. *Being and Time*. Joan Stambaugh, trans. Albany: State University of New York Press, 1996.
von Hildebrand, Dietrich. *Christian Ethics*. New York: McKay, 1953.
von Hildebrand, Dietrich. *The Nature of Love*, John Crosby, trans. South Bend: St. Augustine's Press, 2009.
von Hildebrand, Dietrich. *What is Philosophy?* New York: Routledge.
Kearney, Richard. "Epiphanies of the Everyday," in John Panteleimon Manoussakis, ed., *After God*. New York: Fordham University Press, 2006.
Levinas, Emmanuel. *Collected Philosophical Papers*. Alphonso Lingis, trans. Dordrecht: Martinus Nijhoff, 1987.
Levinas, Emmanuel. Seán Hand, trans., *Difficult Freedom*. Baltimore: Johns Hopkins University Press, 1990.
Levinas, Emmanuel. *Discovering Existence with Husserl*. Richard Cohen and Michael Smith, trans. Evanston: Northwestern University Press, 1998.
Levinas, Emmanuel. *Entre Nous*. Michael Smith and Barbara Harshav, trans. New York: Columbia University Press, 1998.
Levinas, Emmanuel. *On Escape*. Bettina Bergo, trans. Stanford: Stanford University Press, 2003.
Levinas, Emmanuel. *Otherwise than Being*, Alphonso Lingis, trans. Pittsburgh: Duquesne University Press, 1998.
Levinas, Emmanuel. *Time and the Other*. Richard Cohen, trans. Pittsburgh: Duquesne University Press, 1987.
Levinas, Emmanuel. *Totality and Infinity*. Alphonso Lingis, trans. Pittsburgh: Duquesne University Press.
Marion, Jean-Luc. *In Excess*, Robyn Horner and Vincent Berraud, trans. New York: Fordham University Press, 2004.
Marion, Jean-Luc. *Prolegomena to Charity*, Stephen Lewis, trans. New York: Fordham University Press.
Scheler, Max. *Formalism in Ethics and Non-Formal Ethics of Values*. Manfred Frings and Roger Funk, trans. Evanston: NWU Press, 1973.
Scheler, Max. *Selected Philosophical Essays*. David Latcherman, trans. Evanston: NWU Press, 1973.
Spencer, Mark K. "Ethical Subjectivity in Levinas and Thomas Aquinas: Common Ground?" *The Heythrop Journal* 53 (2012): 137–47.

Spencer, Mark K. "An Ethical Neo-Platonism: Levinas and Bonaventure in Dialogue." *Quaestiones Disputatae* 1 (2011): 226–40.

21

The Ethical Event

A Phenomenology of חסד *Chesed* for Asylum-seeking Refugees

Devorah Wainer

This article is written to honor Richard Cohen, who had the impossibility of knowing to what extent he brought this author out of isolation and into conversation with a community of Levinas scholars. Levinas teaches that "unlike theoretical reasoning that aims for closure . . . the ethical relationship is . . . open" and as such is the source of knowledge—through relating in conversation. At the Levinas Summer Schools, facilitated by Cohen (and other scholars), the relating, studying, and conversing produced knowledge in me and a sense of belonging that continues to resonate in me. Cohen wisely re-asks, in his own inimitable style, Levinas's question: "How can we retain an ethical sensibility in the face of senseless suffering?"[1]

This question qua question is posed by the *Shoah*.[2] With Levinas in mind, I propose that postmodern Jewish thinkers' response to suffering has been an intensification of ethics and responsibility:[3] "They have shown a passion to think about responsibility more radically and more honestly in the face of suffering . . . to protect others from suffering."[4] Scholars and authors together with Cohen declare that after Auschwitz, "final solutions" are an impossibility.[5]

I suggest that any attempt to answer Cohen's question that aligns with Levinas's thinking must therefore be dynamic and open, like the "human I . . . which is the beginning of the human and of spirituality."[6] Equally, this author, a Jewish thinker, attends to the tragic suffering of people who, by fleeing their home countries, escape rape, torture, and death. In turn, they request asylum in a different country where a moral responsibility, a morality that is "the imperatively demanding and transcendent face of the other person" (Cohen 2010, 113), is absent. The plight of people who seek asylum is universalized. Each individual, a unique human, is lost in what Levinas calls "an abuse of logic" or what Ricoeur identifies as "hyperbole."[7]

With his question, Cohen has once again inspired me to write in my own idiosyncratic voice—albeit not with the signification of the philosophers. How else can I bear witness to the devastating neglect of legal responsibilities—required by international law—that causes meaningless suffering and a suffering of meaninglessness for persons who flee from death, torture, and trauma, leaving all that they have to seek refuge elsewhere? Across oceans and deserts and islands, I have come face to face with the "humanity of those who suffer." Suffering that began in their home countries where the "evil" that "rends" it made life unbearable and their deaths possible. Incarcerated, their suffering is compounded and continuous in prisons constructed by Western democracies. I have encountered "impasse of life and being" and have witnessed persons become watery, bent, prematurely aged versions of themselves who, due to wrongful indeterminate imprisonment, have acquired detention-induced psychoses.[8]

Contra the shrill shriek of politicians and the public to "Go back to where you came from" that totalizes all persons requesting asylum, the pages that follow contain intentionally open-ended narratives that illuminate the lived experiences and felt memories of distinctive individuals who seek asylum. These narratives—some cameos and some excerpts—are somewhat analogous to Levinas's philosophical reflections "which are not rigorously intellectual" (Levinas 1988, 96). All are written to illuminate the human, the soul, the *holiness* if you will of each person locked in a cage, a cell, or a remote, inaccessible island.

Their backgrounds and reasons for fleeing their home countries are little known to most citizens.[9] Typifying what Levinas condemns as "indifference," they are invisiblized—Operation Streamline in action.[10] The Southwestern Federal Courts try seventy-five people per day as criminals for illegal entry or reentry. In Arizona, at the Tucson Federal Court, it is impossible to identify the rattling, clanging, banging sounds that herald the start of the trials and equally unbearable to identify the source of the commotion. As Fernanda Santos reports, men and women of different sizes and heights are chain-ganged with hand, foot, and waist cuffs that cut through their skin to the bone, even as the chains bang against their shins as they shuffle forward: "In Streamline proceedings, judges typically combine the initial appearance, arraignment, plea, and sentencing into a single hearing, sometimes taking as little as 25 seconds per defendant."[11] Alternatively, those who arrive at the Australian border and are not tried are detained in maximum security jails or on inaccessible prison islands—some for seven or more years.

How then does a witness communicate the vicious fallacious policies perpetrated in the name of the citizen? What method does a researcher use to communicate the experiences of people who are tried and convicted in twenty-five seconds or incarcerated for years? Already all of these individuals lack agency and are criminalized and totalized. Eschewing theorizing the phenomenology of refugeeism and captivity, I will lift my pen and write narratives. The register of these narratives that I write is *midrash*.[12]

Midrash מִדְרָשׁ

Midrash is a Hebrew word that derives from the root *-drash*, meaning to carefully seek, inquire, or require. Initially midrash was a teaching tool in the form of a story, the purpose of which was to explicate lines and verses in the Torah.[13] These narratives are employed to search for or to investigate the meaning of the text. The term is no longer univalent and is contemporaneously employed to create critical awareness and challenge dominant ideologies. I write *midrashim*[14] to answer the non-Socratic questions, as above. *Midrashic* questions are dialogic—raised to engage the reader with the narrative (or the text). Buber[15] stresses that we do not tell stories to find our collective "I" but to awaken the telling of others: "Our telling is a cry, a search, not for ourselves but for the Other. . . . The search for the other, the search for the Thou must be carried to the unfamiliar, the foreign and the stranger" (Kepnes 1992, xi).[16] I write creative midrashim that are intentionally without explication, remaining open for the reader to interpret—so that they may find the Other.

The excerpts of midrashim are organized to incrementally unfold dialogically with the reader as an opening toward Cohen's question. Levinas's life project eschews prioritizing rational thought over relating as he urges us to "engage in living dialogue in which it is more important to find out *who* is speaking and *why*, than merely to know what is said."[17]

Who then are the people—let us say it, the souls—crying out to us, "Please protect me"? And *why* have they arrived unwittingly in Australia? The Torah teaches the value of life: "Choose life that you may live." At multiple places in the Torah, it is written that saving a life is the highest action that one might choose. Equally within the Torah, a schema is presented such that attunement to making a good and valuable life, for the self and for the Other, is manifest in active choice and action. Judaism, Cohen explains, lives in the active work of transformation: "In the concrete everyday labors and details that conserve and develop morality and justice on earth."[18]

What, then, is it to choose life? For me, choosing life means mitigating, assuaging, and alleviating the meaningless suffering of marginalized and incarcerated persons, who, in the act of fleeing their home countries chose life and yet are punished by countries like Australia and the USA.

Let us now attend to the phrase "ethical sensibility." In the face of cruel and punishing policies and treatment to which asylum seekers are subjected, a brief delineation of terminology and context is required. First is my corrective linguistic turn. The designation *asylum seeker* has become a misnomer loaded with negative connotation. An asylum seeker is a person looking for protection because they fear persecution, or they have experienced torture, trauma, or human rights violations. Not every asylum seeker meets the legal criteria to qualify as a refugee. However, within the context of international law, every *refugee* is initially classified as an asylum seeker.[19]

The Refugee Convention (1951) and subsequent Protocols (1967) declare that while awaiting the outcome of the application for refugee status, the host country has legal obligations to protect the asylum seeker.[20] In Australia and concomitant islands, about 95 percent of those incarcerated are found to meet the criteria for refugee status. Some even arrive already with the UNHCR determination of refugee status and are thus termed *asylum seeker*. No longer a neutral legal ascription, it is instead currently a fear-inducing term, abused by politicians, the media, and gullible citizens.

According to Levinas, and as Cohen so clearly elucidates, the fundamental ethical problem is "not the sufferer's, the one subject to the pain of meaningless suffering, the victim, but that of the witness in relation to the sufferer" (2010, 320).[21] It is here, with language, that an ethical sensitivity to asylum seekers initiates the hyphenated term *asylum-seeking refugee*. I instantiate the hyphenation of the combined words of the asylum seeker who becomes a refugee. The asylum-seeking refugee transcends the ubiquitous negative spin to become unique and dignified, worthy of an ethically sensitive approach—at least according to this author, perchance to be promulgated by others!

"The least one can say about suffering is that, in its own phenomenality, intrinsically, it is useless: 'for nothing' (Levinas 1988, 93)," the corollary of which is, according to Levinas, sensibility that is a vulnerability: "Such is embodied existence," Cohen writes, "hence there are moral consequences to embodiment."

Poetry in Supermax

Let us turn our attention to two asylum-seeking refugees incarcerated in a "Supermax" maximum security prison. We will read an excerpt from the midrash *Poetry in Supermax* that explicates an "ethical sensibility" to "meaningless suffering." When I first met the two men, they had for the past six months shared their room, a converted container so small that one had to stand on his bed for the other to enter through an open door. I had traveled by air to their location specifically to visit any asylum-seeking refugees who requested visitors.

I had passed through three different security checks performed by nasty prison guards that would have sent a novice visitor running scared through the electric wires and gates. A guard with a highly visible gun in his holster talks as we walk on the boardwalk through gates controlled by the central guard room to the visitors' room—another small container. He says he hopes I have applied mosquito repellent. It has just rained, and it feels as though we are in the tropics. "Oh," I respond naively. "Do you give all the detainees mosquito repellents?"

"Don't be stupid, they can be bit. Their fault for coming here."

By the time I left I needed to bathe my legs in that repellent!

In the visitor's room, a guard sits expressionless, like a wax imitation of a human as he looks at security monitors.

I notice Kavan[22] standing, nervously scrunching his cap. Knowing he is the person I have come to visit doesn't make me a culturally perceptive genius. I know he is from Iran and, besides, he is the only person other than the wax man in the room.

With gentle politeness I offer him tea, coffee, or water from the tiny-easy-to-miss server. Kavan's bewildered face reveals his lack of comprehension. Not only is he already accustomed to being frog-marched and rough handled by the guards, he doesn't speak English.

I say my name. Much nodding, smiling, and head bobbing ensues when suddenly Kavan jumps up and rushes to the door. Banging on it for wax man to open with a click of the security technology. Now I am confused and bewildered. I wait.

Huffing, out of breath, and triumphant, Kavan returns with another detainee.

"English . . . English," he repeats with an impossibly huge grin. It seems he has not smiled in so long that his face doesn't quite accommodate the full expansion of his smile. All the while he is thumping the second man on the back. Number Two bends and nods and grins, also now repeating "English . . . English." Miraculously our halting conversation in the language of words, translations, arm-waving, nods, and frowns become more fluent and we begin understanding each other.

During our uniquely crafted conversation, I learn that Kavano likes to recite poetry. "Yes," he knows to recite Rumi, the thirteenth-century Persian poet, Sufi mystic. With genuine excitement, I ask him to recite any Rumi poem that he knows. This once-nervous, cap-scrunching man sits up taller and straightens his spine. His eyes are slowly coming alive as he starts a few lines. Goosebumps cover my arms. I force the tears of emotions back into their ducts. A few more words. Although I don't actually know the poem he is reciting, I am immersed in an exquisite moment. Time stops.

Then he stops. Again he starts. A different poem. He stops. And then comes the wet behind his eyes. Kavan no longer remembers. "Too long. Too much worry. No sleep," he explains.

More of our unique language flows as we turn to Mr. English. Up to that moment, Mr. English had remained mostly invisible as a unique individual. Now, to take the pressure off Kavan, I ask Mr. English about himself.

The two were strangers when they were brought, separately, to the Detention Center. For the first time they are hearing about each other's families. Tears flow as they speak of their sons.

How have we now moved from sons back to poetry?

It seems as if *chesed* was waiting to descend. Firouz offers: "I like to write poetry. But what's the point here in hell?"

Kavan's eyes reenlighten.

Now, the one roommate writes his poetry for the other to recite.

Chesed חסד

I would like to propose that the retention of an ethical sensibility in the face of senseless suffering is achieved through *chesed*. Chesed, a Hebrew word, is often translated as comparable to the English words "mercy," "compassion," and "kindness." Yet none of these words adequately convey the meaning of *chesed*. At the heart of Levinas's ethic is *chesed*—חסד–as the self's responsiveness to the Other at the concrete level of action. *Chesed* is a kind, expansive act. Although *chesed* is used in the Torah more than two hundred times, there is one specific context that connects us to the ability to retain an ethical sensitivity, and as such is worthy of our attention. I am referring to the use of *chesed* in the book of Micah, in the Jewish Bible. Micah, (760–690 BCE) a prophet, was a contemporary of the perhaps better-known prophet, Isaiah. Micah (6:8) tells the people, us, what is considered to be the "good" that the Divine requires of us. "Only to do justly, and to *love chesed*, and to walk humbly with God."

Here we have the phenomenological response to senseless suffering where *chesed* חסד is one of two words in Micah's phrase: אהבת חסד—*ahavat chesed*. An explication of these two words is instructive. The word preceding *chesed* חסד in is *ahavat* אהבת, which is the (contracted) third-person singular possessive of "love" *ahavah* אהבה. The translation of *ahavat chesed* is thus "the love of" *chesed*—the love of *loving-kindness*.

Chesed is thus an act of kindness, or, as also often translated it means "loving-kindness." Thus we see that Micah's message encouraging us to "*ahavat chesed* "can be translated as "the love of loving-kindness." Additional to the translation, one needs to discern the context in order to convey the feeling and thereby the deeper meaning derived from the language.

The "good" required of us is "to do justly, and to love *chesed*, and to walk humbly with your God." Micah does not elaborate to offer what might prompt the "love of loving-kindness." Simply, it is the good required of us! To walk humbly and do good is foundational to Levinas's ethics qua ethics—the face, the Other, responsibility. To retain an ethical sensitivity is to inculcate *ahavat chesed*.

The power here evoked lies in action as the first move. In defiance of indifference (and perhaps also of solipsism), Levinas raises the necessity of initiating an act of generosity by raising to consciousness and almost entreating to action what the "decent person ought to do."

Upon arrival at Australian borders, *asylum-seeking refugees* are immediately locked away. Despite seeking asylum and refugee status being entirely within their international legal rights, the Australian regime denies them dignity, care, and protection. Instead, they are construed by governments (and citizens) as being stranger than strange for risking their life (i.e., possibly drowning at sea) by choosing life. With a cruel twist that shatters international law, Australia subjects the innocent to senseless intolerable suffering. According to Levinas, this suffering is evil. In defiance of "indifference" and to destroy it, I go to where they are destitute, broken and alone. I meet them behind walls and wires, on islands and in deserts. Their pain, tangible and intolerable, urges me to envelop myself with meaning.

It is not entirely unlikely that I turn to Emmanuel Levinas (ז'ל 1906–1995) in seeking a path beyond such meaninglessness and despair. Indeed, it is precisely because Levinas's personal experiences are not separate from his philosophical adjurations that he provides a response for my aching heart and critical-thinking mind. Detained asylum-seeking refugees are invisibilized, silenced, and othered. Like Levinas, who poignantly tells us he suffered and felt "no longer part of this world" (Levinas 1988a), so too asylum-seeking refugees are the reviled, unwelcome, and unwanted Others.

Rubbish Persons

When Rami arrived at Sydney airport seeking asylum, he was taken directly to Villawood Detention Centre[23] and locked in Stage 1, as were all asylum-seeing refugees. Except Stage 1 is the maximum-security section of the jail for tried and convicted criminals. Rami, a young Iraqi student, was terrified in a dormitory amid criminals. He didn't dare allow himself to sleep in the dark of night. He knew he was not a criminal, so each day he would dress in his suit, believing "they" (prison guards) would realize their mistake and come to release him. He wanted them to see that "Rami is not a rubbish person."

After one month of waiting, he no longer dressed "as a gentleman." After two months of sleeping on the floor, he was told to make room for another "rubbish person." After three months, feeling forgotten and alone, he was so depressed that he no longer cared what happened.

Not only was suffering the strangeness of the stranger and being othered a recurrent theme in the life of the philosopher, but Levinas too was incarcerated.[24]

During World War II, Levinas, an officer in the French army, was held in Fallenbostel prisoner-of-war camp, near the infamous Bergen Belsen extermination camp. There, as a Jew, he was separated from his fellow French officers and, together with other Jewish POWs, he was traumatized by the relentlessly harsh conditions, not the least being hard labor. The linguistic phenomenology of the detained asylum-seeking refugees that I met is chillingly almost identical to that of Levinas.

One sharp contrast is the horror, anguish, and deaths from hard labor as a Jewish POW, whereas in the purpose-built maximum security jails, the asylum-seeking refugees languish, develop psychosis, and some die due to medical neglect and suicide.[25] Both contexts—detained Jewish POWs (1942–1945) and detained asylum-seeking refugees (1998–) produce complex post-traumatic stress disorder (PTSD) and survivor guilt of which Levinas, without explicitly spelling out the mental health terms, as such, has described as "a tumor in the memory." The Shoah, during which his entire family was murdered in Lithuania (his wife and daughter were hidden in France), lingered with him like a malignant tumor. Such was his pain that he wrote: "Over a quarter of a century ago, our lives were interrupted and doubtless history itself. There was no longer any measure to contain monstrosities. When one has that tumour in the memory, twenty years can do nothing to change it. Soon death will no doubt cancel the unjustified privilege of having survived six million deaths."[26]

The pattern of separation and segregation—being made to feel strange and unwanted—occurs with notable regularity in the stories and accounts of the asylum-seeking refugees. Inside the visitors' yard at Villawood Detention Center, Rami, now housed in Stage 2 with other asylum-seeking refugees, approaches me during one of my visits. He has a "big secret" to tell me. "Devorah, I don't know that I am human here inside Villawood Detention Center. You visit me and make me feel human for a few hours." The mechanisms of separation, isolation, loss, and dehumanization are malevolently employed to break the prisoner.

In response to his lived experiences, Levinas tells us that his life project is to "search for what is genuinely human . . . . the relationship to the other man . . . seemed to me to be . . . the grand mystery if you will . . . of humanity . . . genuine dialogue a real conversation . . . the essence of which is in relationship."[27]

Is the philosopher here approaching the concrete essence of *ahavat chesed*? Levinas writes honestly about the memories that haunted him, saying "it is incontestable that in every philosophical reflection, in every philosophical essay, there are memories of a lived experience, which is not rigorously intellectual."[28] The "lived experience" to which he refers causes unalleviated, unmitigated suffering "that is not merely a restriction of one's freedom, constricting possible spontaneous movements, but an overwhelming of one's humanity so concretely violent and cruel that we can only describe such pain as "evil" or "absurd." Suffering is intrinsically "useless," in the sense that it serves no purpose and is "for nothing." Suffering, and by this Levinas means "innocent suffering," is meaningless.

Freedom

Our next cameo *midrash* takes place four years after we first met Rami in Stage 1 of Villawood Detention Center.

I'm remembering that terrible day under the big tree, near the fence, at the bottom of the Villawood Detention Centre visitors' yard of surveillance: it was the day when the negative judgment in Rami's court case was passed down. We still had options within the legal application processes for him to be recognized as a refugee and so be freed from incarceration. Yet I realized how that judgment shattered me. Not only would the incarceration of Rami continue, so too, *mutatis mutanda*, would I have to continue those interminable drives to Villawood Detention Center, queue outside regardless of the weather, endure body checks before entering the compounds, spend less time with my family, and carry the burden of the next legal process on which his life depended. I was tired.

Cohen (on Levinas) writes that one must stand on one's own feet. To that I might add, I had to draw on my inner fortitude to fulfill the responsibilities—the ethical responsibilities—as inspired by the Divine's "demand for compassion and justice."[29] More simply, Cohen writes: "The other person suffers: I must help."[30] My singularity, that calls forth my responsibility already begun, lies in my nonsubstitution. I am ethically and morally responsible to show up for Rami (and the other detainees). Consequentially, I gather up my "being-for-the-other," my "higher self," to guide me as I drive off to Villawood Detention Center to discuss our next plan to obtain that precious visa.

Thinking back, I remember my felt sense of anguish under that big tree near the fence that drove me to desperately shake Rami's shoulders saying: "Give me something. You HAVE to give me a character reference from someone that the Government will accept," for his next visa application that I was preparing. Rami hesitantly says that a priest from his home country, now in the secretariat of the Vatican, knows him very well, "like family." He even has his phone number in the Vatican. Rami's big brown eyes look to me silently inquiring if this person might be suitable.

"Let's try," I calmly suggest despite my pounding heart. I am cautious to avoid getting his hopes up. "Please phone urgently . . . don't wait!" I add. "Inside,"[31] lethargy, boredom, endless sorrow, and anxiety re-creates time akin to Macbeth's "tomorrow and tomorrow and tomorrow."[32] "Yes," says Rami in his quiet demeanor, to which I am now accustomed.

I leave Rami to phone his priest in the Vatican. A few weeks slowly drag by, and the letter does not arrive. This application process is time sensitive. Failure to submit in the specified timeframe leaves the detainee in danger of forced removal and return to the country from which he escaped. Our crucial window of time to submit the visa application to the minister is closing. In response to my questions born of my sense of urgency, Rami assures me that, yes, he had phoned the priest; yes, he spoke to the priest himself; yes, his priest who knows him very well, "like family," understands the situation and its urgency. His priest has agreed to write the letter, Rami patiently explains to me. Adding: "Rami is not so important as the Pope."

And then, one night, well before dawn, my phone rings. I almost don't answer. Then I do. Sleepily, somewhat irritably, I respond to the thickly accented voice: "Who is calling, please?" Why did I not end that 3 a.m. thick-voiced call? It was Rami's priest phoning me from the Vatican!

That night he faxed his letter with the Vatican stamp on it. I cried with relief and the next day, or was it that same day, I completed Rami's submission for a refugee visa and after my "day job," I drove out to Villawood Detention Center for Rami to sign the precious papers.[33]

Yet another nine months passed without any communications from immigration regarding the visa. Rami, untried and innocent, remained incarcerated—suffering the meaninglessness of "tomorrow and tomorrow and tomorrow." His anxiety became so extreme that he stopped eating. To engender hope, I asked him what he would most like to do the day he is released from detention with a visa.

"I want to see nature. I want to go where there are trees and grass. And I want to see the sea—the horizon, as far as the eye can see." As always, Rami was clear, his request simple.

The only time in four years Rami had ever requested anything from me was then, when he was so depressed and anxious that his throat had constricted and he couldn't eat. "What can I bring you?" I was concerned. He was getting very thin. All Rami wanted was a McDonald's burger.

"What sort?" I asked.

"You choose."

I am a vegetarian. What did I know about McDonald's burgers? But I went to McDonald's and bought him burgers that I happily presented to him. Gentle, kind Rami never mentioned that they were always cold by the time I passed the security checks to enter the visitors' yard of surveillance.

Another phone call.

It was a Friday afternoon when the unanticipated insistent ringing of my phone cut through my reverie. "Devorah?" was the simple question addressing my "Hello."

"Yes, I'm Devorah."

"You need to fetch Rami now. What time can you be here?"

Bewilderment clouding my brain induced my response: "I can't come today. It's Friday and my family is having dinner with my parents . . . ." As I said "my parents" the light broke through the clouds and I shrieked "What? . . . What did you say?"

Rami, who referred to my parents as Mummy and Daddy, had received his visa. He was to be released immediately with, in his words, "stamped documents to show the world who is Rami."

The day after, Rami left his "rubbish clothes" inside and walked away from the wire, free, we went to Manly Beach (North of Sydney) as he had asked that day, nine months earlier, under that big tree near the fence, at the bottom of the Villawood Detention Centre visitors' yard of surveillance. Although only a half-hour drive to Manly, after four-plus years of incarceration, Rami was unaccustomed to the motion of the motor car. It caused him severe motion sickness. As we stroll along the Manly Corso, amidst tourists and bikini-clad youth, I suggest he eat something to settle his stomach.

"Perhaps McDonald's?"

I give him cash, show him where to queue, how to order; I gladly albeit nervously wait outside.

Rami emerges with a grin showing me the food bag, to which I say triumphantly:

"Now THAT is freedom. Buying your own McDonald's."

"No, Devorah," Rami declares. "Freedom is having a HOT McDonald's. Now, as freedom, all I want is to see my name and picture on a visa that says I belong. I want to discover who is Rami."

Cohen makes the point, contra many academic commentators, that Levinas's thinking is in fact "political—a radical politics."[34] The accuracy of Cohen's assertion becomes clear: juxtapose the politics that incarcerates the sick (cancer, diabetes), the disabled, gang-chaining people making freedom of movement impossible and inaccessible.

In defiance of the political systems that seek to criminalize and invisibilize them, I have come to visit, bringing a modicum of decency, dignity, and hopefully respite to the hours of sitting and waiting with ever increasing desperation. Here follows a midrash complete and open so that the reader might feel what it's like to search for the other, as Buber has stressed is the purpose of midrash. Equally this midrash breathes life into Levinas's words: "More, for my position as *I* consists in being able to respond to this essential destitution of the Other, finding resources for myself. The Other who dominates me in his transcendence is thus the stranger, the widow, and the orphan, to whom I am obligated."[35]

The Visiting Room

Far north in the tropics, beyond deserts, country towns, and wide expanses of Australian land lies the city of Darwin, where there is a detention center for asylum-seeking refugees—women, children, and men. During the monsoon season, I visit a young woman and her six-year-old son. Two weeks ago, they were taken directly from a boat and incarcerated in a prison with boardwalks, which are intended to make movement possible when monsoon rains are torrential. Here, state-of-the-art, automatic lockdowns happen when unbidden, inconvenient rains pour down. There is no protection from the masses of marauding mosquitoes at this marshy, damp prison.

After passing the intimidating prison security checks, I sit tense and uncomfortable on a hardwood kitchen-like chair at a long refractory-style table in a too-small enclosure.

This is the visitors' room, which is small enough to ensure a lack of privacy. And it's cramped enough to ensure we all reach for accoutrements to mop brows and wipe sweaty necks. The constant, edgy hum of conversation in close proximity further disquiets me. The brusque, monosyllabic security guard manages to make me feel tense and guilty. Yogic breathing settles me when my attention is drawn to the door at the opposite end of the room that now slides open. A woman and little boy are escorted to sit opposite me at the table. No words are spoken. They are clearly bewildered.

She sits upright and silent. The little boy leans in toward her as his big eyes brim with curiosity. With a sweeping open palm, I offer Mum the cool drinks and Middle Eastern sweets I have brought for them, and I also motion to the little boy. Mum's head shakes as she keeps her eyes fixed on me. Following his mum's cue, the little boy withdraws his outstretched, about-to-take-a-lolly arm and shakes his head too. My heart aches. When were such delicacies last available to them? Of course Mum initiates a refusal. She has no concept of "visitor" in this inhospitable jail. I am the Stranger, the Other. The guards brought her to this visitor's room with no explanation. "Just come," she was instructed. As the little boy withdraws his hand, I feel tears welling up, yet I don't dare tear up. I am here for them.

Slowly I begin to see Mum. She is beautiful. Clearly a refined woman. Her fine skin is of a smooth texture. I imagine she had once tended to herself with regular facials, eyebrow threading, hairstyling. Like others I have seen in detention centers, her allocated clothes are lumpy and un-rememberable, her hair not quite unkempt but not freshly washed or styled. Mostly I notice her quiet, contained demeanor. Her guarded eyes recede into dark, swollen puffs in her expressionless face. Ordered and brought to me by the prison guards, she was made "to sit" (opposite me) as the guard indicatively pushed his hand on her head. Never taking her eyes off me, she pulls her little boy to herself even tighter even as sitting upright. I see pain and confusion. I am her first visitor. She's never been into the visitors' room with its hum and buzz of chatter. A dystopia from the boardwalks and rooms in which they are locked and left. Here, a disabled asylum-seeking refugee in her wheelchair; there, a school-age young girl denied education, condemned to boredom in this prison.

In that silent moment, sitting face to face, something gentle passes between us. I look into her eyes. In the absence of a spoken language known to both, I place my hands on the table between us. And in a movement that is exquisitely not of my own volition, my palms slowly open and turn upward as they rest on the table between myself and Fatima—for that is her name. Holding my eyes with hers, never glancing away, she slowly, tentatively, lowers her palms onto mine. Eyes together.

Buber's meristic rule between I and Thou.
Palms only just touching.
Eyes holding each other.
Tears.

∼

> I write midrashim as witness to the otherwise unpresentable—the indescribable.
>
> —Devorah Wainer, *Beyond the Wire*

I write midrashim because I am my children's mother.

I write midrashim for my children who embody *ahavat chesed*, who never complain when I am bone-tired after visits to Villawood Detention Center.

I write midrashim so that they may one day read of their generosity toward the asylum-seeking detainees to whom I devoted my most precious resources: time and money.

I write midrashim for the children to be born to parents who were asylum-seeking refugees and are now Australian citizens. As Yuval Harari, the historian, says in a podcast with Sam Harris, neuroscientist, that the way he lives influences the way he thinks "because just to reach a theoretical conclusion that has no influence on how you actually live, what is the point?"[36]

I write midrashim to be included in archives where otherwise asylum-seeking refugees would remain invisible, their unique selves lost, flattened, in the totalization of rational thought and political spin.

Mostly I write midrashim to heal my own vicarious trauma and suffering born of too many shocks: too many hours with too many incarcerated, broken humans.

I write midrashim so those humans will know they are the lights that shine into the dark, dank cracks of Australia and Australians.

Shabbat

"*Na'ase v'nishma*—We will do, and we will hearken."

Chronologically, we do first. These action-oriented words from the Torah float around my head and settle within. It's *Shabbat*. The peaceful, floating juxtaposition of the incessant, pounding beat of the workweek. Suddenly an unanticipated and therefore shrill ring from my mobile cuts through my silence.

Unusual for Ahmed to call so early in the day, I thought, as I notice his caller number. Jarred . . . Alert . . . Vigilant. What prompted him to call on the phone I smuggled into Villawood Detention Center? Usually, the detainees sleep until visiting hours. Their stress, trauma, thoughts of family back home (alive or dead now?) chases away sleep at night.

"Thank you, Cousin. Thank you for the lovely food I had last night." About three years ago, Ahmed, who is Palestinian, and I bonded as "cousins." (He added that his mum and I should be the prime ministers of Palestine and Israel, respectively.)

Now I am confused.

"What food?" I probe gently.

"The food, cousin; the food you sent in for Shabbat. Hummous, pita, kebab, salad. The food!"

Usually able to think quickly, I draw a blank. I am perplexed.

Ahmed's "other cousin," in his own words, referring to a young Israeli woman, had been incarcerated on a Friday afternoon with no explanation of why she was locked up or for how long.

"But who will tell me?" The guards met her near-hysterical repeated question of how long she would be incarcerated with a disinterested "we've-heard-this-terror-before."

"It's Friday. Everyone has gone home."

"When do they come back?"

Immigration operating procedure is to incarcerate people on Friday afternoon, leaving them in the zone of terror until Monday. Sarah had been inside for just long enough to learn that some had been locked up for three or four years and sometimes more. This, too, is part of the villainous method of breaking people down.

I met her, spoke Hebrew, and as she wrapped her arms around me, she collapsed onto my shoulder, her very long, now matting, blonde hair entwining us. And she sobbed. Not hysterically. Sarah sobbed the sob of shock, of fear turned terror, of the helplessness that precedes anger and with the life-force that precedes the automaton. I have seen people there as they slowly, month-by-month, release their life force and begin to droop. I see the tear-ridden, sleepless, baggy dark eyes; untoned bodies, unstyled hair, and shoddy, unkempt clothes.

For each incarcerated asylum-seeking refugee there arrives a moment when there no longer seems any purpose for holding on. They enter, each according to their past circumstances: in touch with reality, demonstrating appropriate responses, speech patterns, healthy bodies, alert minds, spunky personalities, hopeful. Slowly after months of waiting . . . waiting. No release, no visa, no family, no work. No autonomy. No exercise. No friends. No shade. No sun. No shelter. No clothes. No relating. No believing. No trust. No sleep. No relief. No release. No name. Ongoing, timeless incarceration with no end in sight, literally and liminally. The desert stretches out in front of them. The concrete wall of their compound is all there is.

"They took my shampoo," she self-consciously explains. Silent still, I look deeply into her eyes. "And my money. Can you get my credit card? My cash?"

With that list, she remembers her mobile phone.

"My phone—" Her voice quavers and becomes a wail.

"My dad; I can't call my dad, Devorah." It all pours out in Hebrew. Her Israeli accent gets to me, and I have to look away. My elder daughter is on university exchange in Israel at this time. She shouldn't see my tears. Right?

After two weeks of being dehumanized, institutionalized, invisibilized, Sarah made a claim to kosher food.

"At least I must have kosher food for Shabbat. Devorah, I am Jewish. I must eat kosher on Shabbat." Behind the wire, confused and terrified, this was more of a brave protest for life, to be witnessed and heard, than a religious requirement. Sarah was not religious. Sarah demanded living. She had not yet reached that letting-go-of-life moment. The food was brought in, after visiting hours—after 7 p.m. to reduce the visibility of a situation that could become inflammatory. Sudden, unanticipated escalations of drama were inevitable where people were "buried alive." What could discovery of fresh food for one individual do to stir up and release dangerous angry explosive behavior inside the locked-down detention center?

It was Friday night, Shabbat, in Villawood Detention Centre. Sarah was locked into the single women's accommodation yard, and Ahmed was locked into his section, Stage 2, where single men were housed amid couples, families, and children.

Sarah's at the wire. Surreptitiously rattling the security wire between the two yards to attract someone's attention. She asks them to fetch Ahmed.

Now, while writing, I am less numb. Then being just numb enough was a survival mechanism. Questions flow to consciousness. I wonder who she asks to bring Ahmed. How long it takes for Ahmed to get the message. Was he lying aimlessly on his bed when someone he knew or didn't know knocked on his door? Did he first grab some other clothes? Did he take or hide his illegal mobile phone? Was he having coffee and chatting with another incarcerated person?

Are these the questions of the vicarious witness?

It was there, in the most unlikely of spaces, the space of no place, that Sarah, fiercely proud and independent, waited at the wire. Her eyes had recently acquired dark shadows from sleeplessness, fearing for Ahmed, who came unquestioningly to the wire.

"The food was so yummy! The best in more than five years. Thank you, Devorah," I hear him continue on the telephone.

"You mean the kosher food I sent in for Sarah?"

"YES!" with the "Duh, what else?" tone.

"But . . . but . . . " His "duh" inhibits my freedom to inquire further. Not wanting to hear that the food arrived during visiting hours, I brace myself to ask: "But how did you get the food? I asked them to deliver after visiting and lock-up time. Did they deliver early? Did you get permission to eat together?"

"HUH?" Ahmed speaks five languages, and apparently, *English-nuance* is his sixth language, learned during his five years of incarceration. He's learned "duh" and "huh" with the appropriately withering tones.

The "huh" is his incredulity that I could even think, never mind utter, the question out loud: "Did you get permission to eat together?"

"No, Devorah," showing his sixth language of nuance and then returning to his soothing Arabic accent.

He's enjoying himself. Momentarily, he savors having a private life. Nothing in the detention center is private. All is known. But I don't know how he got the food.

"She fed me."

Silence.

"She fed me, Devorah, through the wire, piece by piece. My hands were too big to take it. I put my mouth to the wire. Nothing even spilled. The best food I had—in more than five years."

Notes

1. Richard A. Cohen, *Levinasian Meditations: Ethics, Philosophy and Religion* (Pittsburgh: Duquesne University Press, 2010), 322.

2. *Shoah* is the Hebrew word for the Holocaust.

3. Steven Kepnes, Peter Ochs, and Robert Gibbs, *Reasoning After Revelation: Dialogues in Postmodern Jewish Philosophy, Radical Traditions* (Boulder, CO: Westview Press, 1998).

4. Kepnes et al., *Reasoning after Revelation*.

5. *Auschwitz* is the name of one of the death camps that has become synonymous with Shoah. See Cohen, *Levinasian Meditations;* Kepnes, Ochs, and Gibbs, *Reasoning after Revelation*, 1994; and Emil L. Fackenheim, *To Mend the World: Foundations of Post-Holocaust Jewish Thought* (Bloomington: Indiana University Press, 1994).

6. Emmanuel Levinas, *Is It Righteous to Be? Interviews with Emmanuel Levinas*, trans. Jill Robbins and Thomas Loebel and ed. Jill Robbins (Stanford, CA: Stanford University Press, 1984), 182.

7. Fackenheim, *Levinasian Meditations*, 113.

8. Emmanuel Levinas, *Entre Nous: On Thinking of the Other*, trans. Smith and Harshav (New York: Columbia University Press, 1988), 93.

9. An exception to unknown refugee producing causes is the recent and ongoing civil war in Syria that has caused millions to flee. At the time of writing, food and water insecurity, for example, in Egypt is already producing civil unrest and refugees the numbers of which are predicted to be greater than those from Syria.

10. Fact Sheet, Operation Streamline, https://immigrationforum.org/article/fact-sheet-operation-streamline/.

11. Fernanda Santos, "Detainees Sentenced in Seconds in 'Streamline' Justice on Border." *New York Times*, 2014. http://www.nytimes.com/2014/02/12/us/split-second-justice-as-us-cracks-down-on-border-crossers.html.

12. One of the better known midrashim directly related to the Torah is the legend of Abraham as a young child smashing his father's idols. He tells his father that the idols destroyed each other, and his father didn't buy it, because idols aren't living beings. To which little Abraham says, "Exactly." This midrash explains why God would choose Abraham in particular to be the father of the Jewish people. He was willing to challenge the conventional wisdom of his time. A recent midrash written with a feminist lens in order to reimagine the Torah, is *The Red Tent* by Anita Diamant (Mankowitz 2020).

13. The Torah is considered sacred within the context of Judaism and comprises the first five books of the Jewish Bible.

14. Midrashim is the plural form of Midrash.

15. Martin Buber (1875–1965) Jewish philosopher and mystic. Author of *I-Thou*. Also known for re-authoring Hasidic tales.

16. Steven Kepnes, *The Text as Thou* (Bloomington: Indiana University Press, 1992), xi.

17. Emmanuel Levinas, *Totality and Infinity*, trans. Alfonso Lingus (Pittsburgh: Duquesne University Press, 1969).

18. *Levinasian Meditations*, 269.

19. The term *asylum seeker* is invoked as a legal sub-clause of refugee for a person who is awaiting a decision on their application for international recognition and protection as a refugee.

20. A total of 148 countries including Australia are party to the Refugee Convention. As such Australia has international obligations to protect the human rights of all asylum seekers and refugees who arrive in Australia, regardless of how or where they arrive and whether they arrive with or without a visa.

While asylum seekers and refugees are in Australian territory (or otherwise engage Australia's jurisdiction), the Australian government has obligations under various international treaties to ensure that their human rights are respected and protected. These treaties include the International Covenant on Civil and Political Rights (ICCPR), the *International Covenant on Economic, Social and Cultural Rights* (ICESCR), the Convention against Torture and Other Cruel, Inhuman or Degrading Treatment or Punishment (CAT) and the Convention on the Rights of the Child (CRC). These rights include the right not to be arbitrarily detained (https://humanrights.gov.au/our-work/asylum-seekers-and-refugees/asylum-seekers-and-refugees-guide#rights).

21. *Levinasian Meditations*, 290.

22. Names have been changed.

23. The complete name of Villawood Detention Center is always used as that is exactly how the detainees spoke.

24. Levinas, *Is It Righteous to Be?*

25. B. Boochani and A. K. Servastani, "Chauka, Please Tell Us the Time [iPhone]," 2017; Behrouz Boochani, *No Friend But The Mountains: Writing from Manus Prison* (Picador/Pan Macmillian, 2018).

26. Emmanuel Levinas, *Proper Names* (Stanford, CA: Stanford University Press, 1996), 120.

27. Emmanuel Levinas, *Dieu, la Mort et le Temps* in *Philosophy*, ed. Michael Field (France, 1993).

28. *Entre Nous*, 96.

29. *Levinasian Meditations*, 204.

30. *Levinasian Meditations*, 205.

31. "Inside" is the language of prisoners indicating inside the prison.

32. Indicating the futile and monotonous passing of time.

33. It is important to note that I am not a migration agent or lawyer and have never acted as such. During my years acting and advocating for detainees if a lawyer was required I assembled pro-bono lawyers and barristers with whom I worked on behalf of the asylum-seeking refugees.

34. *Levinasian Mediations*, 110.

35. *Totality and Infinity*, 215.

36. Yuval Harari, "The Edge of Humanity" in *Making Sense with Sam Harris*, ed. Sam Harris (New York: HarperCollins, 2018).

Bibliography

Boochani, B., and A. K. Servastani. "Chauka, Please Tell Us the Time [iPhone]," 2017.
Boochani, Behrouz. *No Friend But The Mountains: Writing from Manus Prison*. Sydney: Picador in Pan Macmillian, 2018.
Cohen, Richard, A. *Levinasian Meditations: Ethics, Philosophy and Religion*. Pittsburgh: Duquesne University Press, 2010.
Fackenheim, Emil L. *To Mend the World: Foundations of Post-Holocaust Jewish Thought*. Bloomington: Indiana University Press, 1994,
Harari, Yuval. "The Edge of Humanity." In *Making Sense with Sam Harris*, edited by Sam Harris. New York: HarperCollins, 2018.
Kepnes, Steven. *The Text as Thou*. Bloomington: Indiana University Press, 1992.
Kepnes, Steven, Peter Ochs, and Robert Gibbs. 1998. *Reasoning after Revelation: Dialogues in Postmodern Jewish Philosophy, Radical Traditions*. Boulder, CO: Westview Press.
Levinas, Emmanuel. *Totality and Infinity*, translated Alfonso Lingus. Pittsburgh: Duquesne University Press, 1969.
Levinas, Emmanuel. *Is It Righteous to Be? Interviews with Emmanuel Levinas*. Translated by Jill Robbins and Thomas Loebel. Edited by Jill Robbins. Stanford: Stanford University Press, 1984.
Levinas, Emmanuel. *Entre Nous: On Thinking of the Other*. Translated by Smith and Harshav. New York: Columbia University Press, 1988.
Levinas, Emmanuel. *Dieu, la Mort et le Temps*. Paris: Grasset, 1993.
Levinas, Emmanuel. *Proper Names*. Stanford, CA: Stanford University Press, 1996.
Mankowitz, Rachel. "Why Can't I Write a Midrash?" *The Cricket Pages*. https://rachelmankowitz.com/2020/12/26/why-cant-i-write-a-midrash/. 2020.
Santos, Fernanda 2014. "Detainees Sentenced in Seconds in 'Streamline' Justice on Border." *New York Times*. http://www.nytimes.com/2014/02/12/us/split-second-justice-as-us-cracks-down-on-border-crossers.html.
Wainer, Devorah. *Beyond the Wire*. Perth: Boffin Books, 2014.

Conclusion
Cohen Responds

Response to Contributors

Richard A. Cohen

I am honored by the present volume, grateful for the toils of its editors, encouraged by the intellectual attentions of its contributors, and awakened by the acumen and originality of their many insights. If my own work has facilitated theirs, what could be more gratifying? The real honor remains Levinas's. He is our teacher. His thought awakens philosophers to the *intelligibility*, the *significance* of a vigilance beyond and above being, signification and ideation, to the disrupting exigencies of ethical responsibility, of service to and for the neighbor, and service to all persons, near and far. Against all the intellectual's well-wrought complacencies, whether positivist or postmodern, whether antihumanist or posthumanist, his writings bear witness to the *importance of importance*, to the piercing transcendence of ethical elevation, starting with the face of the other, arousing us to "proximity and not truth about proximity." Levinas at once respects and surcharges our much prized knowing, our self-consciousness, and our cleverness as well, with the surplus of ethical exigency, the priority of responsibility to and for the other person. "This antecedence of responsibility to freedom would signify the Goodness of the Good." Not the Idea of the Good, not even the idea of proximity, but proximity, a pre-original indebtedness, to alleviate the other's suffering, to facilitate the flourishing of all. Such are not empty phrases, cynical or prudential, but rather the most concrete difficult exigencies, the imperatives of morality and justice: to help you, to help everyone.

The authors of present volume are all touched by Levinas, by the radical and irreducible sting of the ethical as the priority of the other person, perhaps to extend or limit its range, perhaps to question this or that formulation, but ever awakened by its imposition. No doubt there have always been philosophers and theologians as well (and politicians) who dismiss ethics for a mirage, who reduce "ought" to this or that "is," whether true or beautiful or both or neither. But analogous to the contradiction that implodes sophistry, the truth that all is false, theirs is also a deceptive posturing, punctured by its very advocacy, its "better that there is no better." As for the philosophers who, along with common sense, maintain the legitimacy of ethics, they have always bound it to the priority they give to knowledge, to science. Even Socrates and Kant, who more than any others have acknowledged not only the legitimacy but the primacy of ethics, they too, still awed by knowledge, bind it to that Procrustean bed, betrayed. Not Levinas. Ethics is no handmaid, not to knowledge, not to God, not to anything else. The originality and greatness of his thought is *to think ethics ethically*, ethics as first philosophy. Not only the thought of responsibility but a responsible thought. Only by such a route, oriented by ethical responsibility, can the meaning, truth, and status of all the registers of signification, from ontology, to science, technology, art, rhetoric, sociality, politics, and so on, find their deepest sense. So, for instance, politics serves justice, and not justice politics. So, too, knowledge, scientific and philosophical, beyond all its circular posturing, finally finds it justification, its *raison d'être*—the holy grail which has hitherto eluded it—in justice. Or as Levinas puts it in *Otherwise Than Being or Beyond Essence*: "Justice, society, the State and its institutions, exchanges and work are comprehensible out of proximity. This means that nothing is outside of the control of the responsibility of the one for the other."[1]

But it is time I responded, albeit too briefly owing to limitations of space, to the chapters of the present volume.

Don Ihde was my dissertation director. His contribution ("*Cohenfest*: Did Rich Cohen Eat Al Lingis's Octopus?") brings a smile to my face. It was not an octopus but a skunk, not a matter of eating but of vacating. That episode of the *fest* was early summer 1980. Having finished my dissertation and doctorate (on time in Levinas), I quit my "day job" of nearly two years in northern Indiana at the Burns Harbor plant of the Bethlehem Steel Corporation. I'd already been there too long, but I needed the company health plan to cover the medical costs of my son's birth. And I'd been fortunate enough to have been offered an assistant professorship in philosophy at the Scranton campus of Penn State, starting in fall 1980. But the job had only a one-year contract. So when Al Lingis, who had been my teacher and mentor when I was an undergraduate philosophy major at Penn State, and who was for the upcoming year leaving State College on sabbatical, he offered me his lovely cottage for a year gratis, I happily accepted. With one proviso: what with a newborn baby, Lingis's pet skunk would have to move out. Lingis being Lingis, however, when we arrived at the cottage, exhausted from a long drive, baby in car, car packed, Lingis gone—the skunk remained. That I was exasperated is not the issue. The issue is the denouement of the oft-told tale Lingis forever after told, namely, the ungrateful Cohen coldheartedly evicting the beloved de-skunked pet skunk, indifferent to its unlikely survival in the wild. So what actually happened? It is true is that after that fateful first day the skunk was never seen again. But its disappearance, so I conjecture, was its own doing, taking advantage of a front door opening and shutting as we moved in, scooting away at the first opportunity, escaping its cottage cage for the great unconfined wilds, never to be seen again. For me it's break for freedom was a stroke of good luck. For Lingis it became another Aesop's fable, illustrating man's inhumanity toward nature via Cohen's callousness. Many years later, in my last conversation with David Allison (also Lingis's student, and also, with Lingis, on my dissertation committee) before his untimely death in 2016, this story came up. Dave being Dave, however, and not Lingis, he laughed out loud at the recollection, letting me know that his favorite part was exactly the denouement, except that he heartedly approved my alleged wickedness when I had, in Dave's words, "kicked the damn skunk out!"

I smile too for Ihde's recollections of those heady festive days and years at Stony Brook, where I did my graduate studies, part of a cohort of ten graduate students more or less products of the largehearted idealistic experimental '60s, riding the seas of existentialism, phenomenology, structuralism, deconstruction, sometimes literally on the Long Island Sound aboard Ihde's sailboat. Ihde, who was already a leading expositor of phenomenology, was just then setting out into the uncharted field of "philosophy of technology," where his many pioneering studies were at the forefront. So too Ihde was department chair, guiding the newly created graduate program into the forefront of Continental philosophy. And New York City was an hour and a half away by car. My first year at Stony Brook four of us, graduate students, carpooled to commute weekly to the New School to audit Aron Gurwitsch's graduate course on Husserl's *Formal and Transcendental Logic*, and to forage at the many nearby used bookstores (including the Strand). In November 1975, back from a year in Paris, I attended the now-celebrated "Schizo-Culture" conference at Columbia University, attending presentations by Foucault, Deleuze, and R. D. Laing, among others. What an amazing assembly of speakers, what a vibrant critical, demanding audience. Thank you, Don, thank you for welcoming me into such a world, and for creating it as well.

More pertinent to the task at hand, Ihde and I sat together on several conference panels dedicated to issues in technology. These conference presentations resulted for me in three papers (2000, 2006, 2010) on the meaning and status of technology vis-à-vis ethics, to which Ihde, in his contribution to the present volume, raises fundamental objections. On the issue of technology and ethics, Ihde criticizes my position, which he labels an "engineer's instrumental functionalism." The latter takes technology to be ethically neutral in the sense that it can be used for good or for evil, for injustice or for justice. So in one sense it is not neutral because it always has an ethical valence, for good or evil, but in another it is neutral because such valuations come to it from the exterior, as it were, depending on how it is put to use, and not as a result of its own character. Hence Ihde's label. It is a criticism because Ihde argues that technology is not simply used for good or evil but has its own ethical slant, skews the ethical playing field, as it were, and is never neutral. So, for instance, nuclear fission can not only be used for good or ill, for electricity or for bombs, say; its very scale is an ethical game changer, both regarding energy and war.

Now one way I could respond to Ihde is to countercharge that he has not fully grasped the true depth of ethics, which is to say, the Levinasian conception of ethics as first philosophy. Here I would argue that while he is correct that my position treats technology as an "instrumental functionalism," it does not do so from the perspective of an *engineer* but rather the context of ethical responsibility. So in saying that technology is never neutral, I would be saying that nothing is ethically neutral, that intelligibility arises from the exigencies of moral responsibility, all the way to social justice, and that nothing escapes this ethical nexus. Nonetheless, I admit that Ihde's point is well taken: technologies come with ethical consequences, such as the unprecedented magnitude of energy resulting from nuclear fission, or the magnitude of storage, access and availability of data resulting from new information technology, or the accelerated magnitudes of speed resulting from transportation technologies (trains, planes, automobiles), and so on, challenging norms of decision-making fitting for smaller, slower technologies, to say nothing of challenges to human biological reflexes. While Ihde and I agree in rejecting blanket technological dystopianism—for example, Heidegger's outlook, or utopianism—on the other hand, the issue of the relation binding technology and ethics remains open, important, and pressing. Ihde concludes generously with a request: "He [Cohen] owes us, as it were, one more article, directly dealing with how and why we should consider Levinas's importance for the philosophy of technology." Ihde is right; I am honored and I accept.[2] As always, Ihde remains for me a "teacher of philosophy in the best sense."

Bob Gibbs, comrade in Jewish studies, reviewed my second book on Levinas, *Ethics, Exegesis and Philosophy* (2001). He heads his review with an aptly chosen epigram by Joshua ben Perahyah in the Talmudic Tractate *Ethics of the Fathers*: "Provide yourself with a teacher." Perceptively, Gibbs goes to the heart of Levinasian thought, and of my approach, by taking up the peculiarities, the seeming deformities, but more exactly the deformalization, which is too often and wrongly treated as literary stylistics, which accrue from the primacy of ethics over knowledge. This primacy is not a matter of second thoughts about knowledge, taking it as given and then deciding what good it might serve, though such assessments are also worthy. Rather or more profoundly it is a matter of respecting what cannot be shown, explicating what eludes explication, that is, keeping alive the trace of alterity that is ethical importance, significance and not mere signification, through which the meaningful, the intelligible arises: intersubjectivity, the ethics of conversation is not extrinsic to meaning but its source. How to convey this when the very formality of the conveyance—propositions, hypotheses, deductions, references, and the like—bely it? Gibbs is most sensitive precisely here, and therefore attentive and even sympathetic to my efforts to be faithful to the essential elusiveness of the ethical dimension of meaning. "Richard Cohen is a great student of Emmanuel Levinas," he begins his review. "Some of the essays are rich in complex technical philosophical writing, but the point, again and again, is about the importance of being good, and not just thinking about being. This moral style is self-conscious and is obvious. And it dares us to ask ourselves why this more blunt and moral tone is almost embarrassing for philosophers?" It would have been far easier, more conventional and acceptable had Gibbs simply attacked my approach as "moralizing" (as if that were something terrible). But such a cheap shot would have missed everything important about Levinas's thought. Thus, Gibbs recognizes and underscores the necessity of my approach, for an ethics that arises beyond an exclusively epistemological modality, the modality of ethical exigency, of moral and juridical imperative, but at the same time a modality more respectful of knowing than knowing would be if left to its own devices.

More than twenty years later, **Jolanta Saldukaityte**, whom I first met in Vilnius at the centenary conference on Levinas held there in 2006, takes up my article of 2017, "Levinas on Art and Aestheticism: Getting 'Reality and Its Shadow' Right," and reaffirms and deepens Gibbs's earlier meditations on my approach. "Cohen is known to be one of the most, or probably even the most, devoted scholars of Levinas," she writes, and continues: "Cohen opposes the 'postmodern' approach and its striving for originality and creativity by claiming that he himself has nothing original to say but only resays what was already said by Levinas." Nothing original, yes, but ethics must always be resaid and resaid again lest it congeal into mere formality, empty ceremony, dry bones, the "said" oblivious to the "saying." Hence Saldukaityte goes on, bursting with the paradox, enigma, or finesse of ethics: "This position makes Cohen original nonetheless." At once unoriginal and original, not as a contradiction, but bettering it. How? Because, as Saldukaityte's essay goes on to show, my reading of Levinas—especially in the above essay on art—challenges the readings said to be "critical" but only by virtue of misreading, suppression, imposition, turning ethics into a handmaiden, forcing it to serve epistemology or aesthetics, as if Levinas's most fundamental reorientation—the primacy of ethics—can be so simply dismissed and ignored. The "originality" of my approach, as the originality of Levinas's, lies precisely in faithfulness to an always singular and exceptional ethical disruption: the ethical priority of the other person as the source of all intelligibility. Philosophers must learn from ethics again and again the *irresponsibility* of refusing the other person, shattering the alluring kaleidoscopic vistas of their exclusive intellectual redoubts. I applaud the intelligence, diligence, and appreciation—and the faithfulness and originality—which Saldukaityte displays in her contribution, which has the additional merit, allow me to say, of demonstrating an insightful familiarity not with one, two, or even three of my writings but with a truly wide range of my contributions to Levinas studies.

This said, it is appropriate to turn next to **Jean-Michel Salanskis**, whom I also first met at the 2006 Vilnius Levinas centenary conference and whose conference comments and questions, as well as our conversations, have always been enlightening: allowing the title of his contribution, which refers to me, and to himself, "Reading Levinas in a Levinasian Way," indicates why. Salanskis underscores my work's faithfulness to Levinas, declares his own similar allegiance, and criticizes commentators who have deviated by not rising to the same. The paper is rich with insights. I cannot do it justice in a short paragraph. I note his invocation of Frédéric Worms's tri-part periodization of twentieth-century French philosophy—under the headings mind, existence, and structure—to show how it fits and does not fit Levinas. I also note his castigation of commentators who restrict their account of Levinas' concept of the "otherwise than being" to the appearance of this expression in his eponymous book, mistaking—like computer search engines—a phrase for its meaning. Though Salanskis commends the faithfulness of my reading, for which I thank him, his own reading does not follow mine in any particulars because his approach, claiming no less faithfulness, but called "etho-analysis," is elaborated elsewhere in several publications he references. Sympathetic as I am to Salanskis, I cannot say I am convinced by his invocation of the Greek idea of *ethos*, or by his reliance on techniques borrowed from Anglo-American "Analytic" philosophy. Given his probity, profundity, and good will, and our mutual admiration for Levinas, I would ask if it might one day be possible for Salanskis to delineate more sharply the similarities and differences between his "etho-analysis" and my own "ethical exegesis."

Here is a good place to respond to **Edith Wyschogrod**'s review of my first book on Levinas (and Rosenzweig): *Elevations: The Height of the Good in Rosenzweig and Levinas* (1994). I cannot recall when I first met Edith, but in Levinas studies even those of us privileged enough to have begun very early, we were all predated by Edith and grateful for it. Her great understanding of Levinas was matched by her unstinting generosity to younger colleagues, myself included. Her book review appeared in 1996, and is the earliest secondary writing on my work in the present volume. That my first book *Elevations* included several chapters on Rosenzweig, following conversations with Bob Gibbs, came from my effort to unravel the full import of Levinas's declaration, in the preface of *Totality and Infinity*: "We were impressed by the opposition to the idea of totality in Franz Rosenzweig's *Stern der Erlösung*, a work too often present in this book to be cited." Who would not be grateful for such words as Edith Wyschogrod begins her review with: "Richard A. Cohen is an original and exacting interpreter of both Levinas and Rosenzweig." Or those that conclude its second paragraph: "Cohen has evolved a register and tone that convey urgency without sacrificing scholarly rigor." Or the final sentence: "Readings of Levinas and Rosenzweig proliferate. This one is profound and original." I repeat the words with which I dedicated my third book on Levinas, *Levinasian Meditations: Ethics, Philosophy, and Religion* (2010), which appeared not long after Edith Wyschogrod's death in 2009: "In memory of Edith Wyschogrod, first in American Levinas studies, . . . to encourage the 'humanity that adorns the world.'" First in many ways—first dissertation, first book, leading scholar, but always second (and hence first!)—in the best ethical sense, for-the-other.

My debt of gratitude extends further, to **Jack Marsh**, a former student of mine at UNC Charlotte, for his editorial work, certainly, and for his contribution, along with **Christopher L. Southland**, who I do not know, for his survey of "Levinas in North America Today: Richard A. Cohen's Contributions." He distinguishes two broad "schools" of Levinas reception in the English-speaking world: one, including Edith Wyschogrod, Adrian Peperzak, and myself, reads Levinas in a "Levinasian way," to recall Salanskis' felicitous expression, and the other, a "second wave," including Robert Bernasconi and Simon Critchley, reads him in a Derridean way, or more broadly in postmodern ways. (In personal conversation Bernasconi shared with me the fact that he had actually read Levinas before reading Derrida; but the point remains inasmuch as his reading of Levinas, in talks and publications, is by way of Derrida.) In tracing the reception of Levinas in the English-speaking world Marsh and Southland are quite generous regarding the impact and import of my own expositional and scholarly efforts. I do not vouch for the veracity of all the situational details or verbal utterances they claim to record, but the gist of their article does trace the basic contours of Levinas's reception in America.

One of the best decisions I ever made was to "interrupt" my graduate studies at Stony Brook to spend the 1974–75 academic year in Paris. I attended Levinas's classes at the Sorbonne, which at that time meant hearing parts of *Otherwise Than Being or Beyond Essence* from lecture notes. I regret not staying a second year. Twice, however, I was graciously welcomed for conversation and Cointreau at Levinas's apartment in the sixteenth arrondissement. And now for almost fifty years more that conversation has continued, including the interlocutors of the present volume.

I first heard **Masato Goda**'s contribution when he delivered it as a lecture at the Levinas Philosophy Summer Seminar of 2017 held in Berkeley, California, where we first met. At the time it went quite over my head. I knew nothing about rhythm in Levinas's thought, and Goda's presentation did not fill this lacuna. It was only when later I read a late 1950s article by Ilya Ehrenburg on "Lessons of Stendhal" that a bell rang. Here is what Ehrenburg (and Stendhal) writes: "Stendhal attached immense importance to rhythm, both in the development of the narrative and in dialogue. 'When people converse together, you have to show the differences in character by rhythm, and find a rhythm for different feelings.'"[3] There it was, rhythm as expression of character, why not as singularity? Did not Nietzsche, so sensitive to music, insist upon rhythm as no less constitutive of meaning than ideas, indeed as more so, as ur-ideation. Thinking would also flow like dancing! Not, to be sure, an *association* of idea and rhythm, like the simplistic Wagnerian *leitmotifs*, more like an assigned label or brand than an individuating principle. Rather rhythm here works like a symbol, an intimate identity-in-difference—or nonindifference—binding sense and sensibility, what Merleau-Ponty called "style." Goda's sensitive elaboration of rhythm thus provides yet another way to illuminate the singularity of saying and said, signifying and signified, personal and public, and much else in the encounter of singularities in the intersubjectivity of my moral responsibility for-the-other.

Marie-Anne Lescourret—I no longer remember where and how we met, but it is hard to imagine Levinas studies in France without her—honors me with her subtlety and insightfulness, and the generosity of her reading, no less than by the range of her familiarity with my work on Levinas. Her appreciative attention highlights and deepens my own, to the benefit of Levinas. It is a fortunate author who finds such a reader.

My gratefulness, then, is in nowise diminished, or my respect dimmed, when I take exception to the criticism—if it is really that—which she raises on her final pages. "Ethics," she writes, "is not so much a matter of positive good doing than an obeying acknowledgement of the otherwise than being. It is not a matter of care or compassion, but a face-to-face relationship with the inexorable other . . ." It appears that I turn Levinas into a do-gooder, which is certainly not so terrible, one supposes, except insofar as it would misunderstand Levinas by making ethics my activity, an altruist egoism, as it were, thereby losing its deeper sense as *response*, as superlative passivity, indeed the involuntariness ("No one is good voluntarily") of the responsible subject's always untimely and insufficient response to the other's suffering. Certainly such an opposition, and giving primacy to self in it, would be a misreading; but I do not believe this misreading is mine, nor Levinas's, nor Lescourret's. I think in fact that we both see in Levinas's ethics the singular structure of the other-in-me that joins at once alterity and responsibility, trauma and care. In other words, Lescourret is perfectly correct to reject as artificial an *opposition* between the positivity of doing good, on the one hand, and the negativity or "otherwise" of responsiveness, on the other. Indeed, only a few sentences after the above quoted passage, Lescourret writes: "As obliged to you (the other) for calling me into being, my duty is to feed and clothe you." Solicitation and generosity are bound to one another and arise together, albeit as "diachrony" rather than "synchrony." The point is that one does not approach the other with empty hands: this is no doubt because the vulnerability of the other is infinite, and generosity is always inadequate. But that is partly why the most immediate relation between I and other is ethical, an "ought," at once surplus and deficit, a provocation, all the way to "dying for . . ." the other (God forbid!). Of this distinctively ethical intersubjective dialectic in which first is second and second first, let us also recall Levinas's gentler words: "*Après vou.*" Marie-Anne Lescourret knows all this very well, which makes the nuance and depth of her exquisite understanding of my approach to Levinas—and her approach—all the more moving for its modesty and kindness.

Roger Burggraeve, brilliant simpatico early Levinasian scholar. I was privileged to give a keynote talk at the large retirement conference held in his honor at Louvain in 2008. In his chapter he shows us how the seemingly "small" and unsung ethical gestures of ordinary people serve as the true fulcrum of the world's humanity. He shows us Levinas's ethics *avant la lettre* in Vasily Grossman's great anti-Stalinist Russian novel, *Life and Fate* (nearly stifled in manuscript form by the KGB), especially but not exclusively as found in the extraordinary radical "manifesto" of the character Ikonnikov. Despite the world's dark empires of violence, Grossman, Levinas, and Burggraeve do not lose faith in the higher power of human kindness, or its relevance to political justice. Burggraeve does not use my specific formula for the relations uniting ethics and the state, but I do not think he would disagree: morality without justice becomes sentimentality; justice without morality becomes tyranny. The true measure of the state, in other words, contrary to its own tendency, is not power but justice. The justice of its laws and institutions and future, as the true measure of justice—as of persons—is morality, the moral life justice enables and protects, countering egoism, all premised ultimately on the kindness of one toward another. Burggraeve's careful close reading of *Life and Fate* shows us this ethical intersectionality alive even in the hell of Stalinism (and Nazism) brought to life by Grossman's literary genius. Burggraeve, who has in his own life taken this to heart, has lived generously, so to say, rightfully highlights Grossman's expression, "small goodness," the goodness that rests on each person's shoulders, the singular responsibility of each for each, and of each and all for all because nothing, not the entirety of being, is bigger, more precious, or worthier.

Steven Shankman, who I first met many years ago at a major Holocaust conference in Oregon, also appropriates the fundamental deportment or disposition of "senseless kindness," but not as Burggraeve did to analyze its appearance in Grossman's *Life and Fate* but rather now via an exquisite historical-critical exegesis of certain episodes in Cervantes's *Don Quixote*, with special emphasis on Cervantes's critique of the Roman Catholic Church. (In this regard, let us recall the radical scorching words of Ikonnikov's manifesto in *Life and Fate*: "When Christianity clothed it [unqualified kindness] in the teachings of the Church Fathers, it began to fade; its kernel became a husk. . . . Even the teachings of Jesus deprived it of its strength.") Shankman: "My subject is senseless kindness in *Don Quixote*, and how Cervantes often finds this senseless kindness, called mercy (*misericordia*) or charity (*caritas*) in the Christian tradition, betrayed by confessing Catholics during a particularly xenophobic moment in Spanish history that bears an unfortunately uncanny resemblance to our own such perilous moment in Europe and the United States." Shankman's close reading of *Don Quixote* is insightful, suggestive, illuminating, and challenging, but no less, as in his many other wide-ranging writings, it is also a delight to read for being so carefully and beautifully wrought. It was not until early 2017 that I finally read *Don Quixote* cover to cover, but having so recently done so I am especially grateful for Shankman's subtle Levinasian reawakening of its many tales of moral courage and woe.

Appropriately following these chapters devoted to novels, **Rossitsa Varadinova Borkowski**, whom I know from the week-long Levinas Philosophy Summer Seminar held in Rome in 2015, takes up Levinas's account of "art, criticism and ethics" and, she adds, "science." Naturally she invokes Levinas's 1948 article "Reality and Its Shadow," and my 2017 exposition of it, in addition to bringing to bear many additional relevant reflections by Levinas on this topic. It is a difficult, complex, and nuanced topic, to say the least. Her chapter, well-organized, insightful, and illuminating, rises to the occasion and serves as a useful exposition and edification. I would not be surprised if this fine accomplishment also represents a promise of more to come.

With great sensitivity and understanding **Irina Poleshchuk**, who participated in the first Levinas Philosophy Summer Seminar (in Vilnius in 2013), and then attended several subsequent seminars, enters into the rich fields of sensibility—"ethical exegesis and ethical body"—in Levinas's thought. She shows how the body is not at bottom an object or thing, even if it can find origins in both, but more deeply and profoundly a relation to the other, an ethical vulnerability or "passivity" Levinas describes as "maternity"—the other in me. "The first word of any philosophical discussion," she writes, "is not spoken or written but, as Levinas would put it, an address and the signification of sensibility." Considering some of my own writings with Levinas's along such lines, she also includes analyses of relevant contributions by Simon Critchley and John Llewelyn. Poleshchuk attends to deep nonverbal layers of sense, which disrupt Husserl's epistemological template of intentional correlation, invoking Levinas's striking claim: "The relation of proximity . . . is the original language, language without words or propositions, pure communication." Hence her central thesis: "The ethical exegesis is . . . an articulation of sensible embodied self, manifesting in proximity of two interlocutors. My main claim is that ethical exegesis does not stand alone but is tightly bound to the ethical body found at the core of subjectivity." Her exposition is rigorous, intelligent, complex, sensitive, and accordingly greatly rewarding.

Chung-Hsiung Lai, who has been friend and interlocutor since my UNC days, both in Charlotte and in Taiwan (where he invited me to visit), and who attended the first Levinas Philosophy Summer Seminar in Vilnius in 2013, places the ethics of Levinas in dialogue with the "postmodern" *Ethics* (1993) of Pierre Badiou. Knowing my Levinasian reservations regarding Badiou, he does not ignore the divergence of their trajectories, or questions which contest the very possibility of any postmodern ethics. From its early days in France, deconstruction, while making certain technical genuflections to Saussure, succumbed more pervasively to the spell of Heidegger's linguistic turn, which Derrida cast in terms of "writing" or "text" over "speech," *langue* over *parole*, semiotic deferral over ethical responsibility, going to far as to misconstrue the latter as "violence" and "negative theology." Badiou, fellow traveler in postmodernism, but sensitized by its critics to certain of its ethical shortcomings, still takes his cue from Derrida: for example, he appropriates Levinas's ethical *vocabulary* but not his ethics (or any ethics, really), displacing the latter with its simulacrum, hence ideologically. In view of this, Lai's contribution is multiform and important: first, a careful scholarly exposition of Badiou's *Ethics*; second, a pungent critical exposure of its fundamental shortcomings; and finally, product of the contrast with Levinas, a renewed appreciation for Levinas's concepts of adult religion and a responsible humanism—and for what can be salvaged in Badiou—not to mention an openness to further research on the question political ethics.

I first met **James Mclachlan** at UNC Charlotte when he (along with his son) audited my multisemester undergraduate course on *Totality and Infinity*. We were a faithful few (including Jack March). With a second professor of philosophy in the room, the many references I made to Husserl, Heidegger, Bergson, Kant, et al., were at least confirmed, taken seriously, sometimes debated and occasionally supplemented by someone else besides myself. I thank Jim for his friendship, which goes far beyond the classroom. I thank him for the present volume, to which he has contributed and of which he is the lead editor. And not least, I thank Jim for sitting by my side at all our Philosophy Summer Seminars, starting in 2013, in Buffalo, Vilnius, Rome, Paris, New York, and Berkeley, sharing his wide-ranging erudition, his pedagogical skill, his warm humor, his wisdom. May our journey continue together for many years to come.

In his chapter, while cognizant of Sartre's well-known atheism, Mclachlan, ever the contrarian, argues that there is an important sense in which Sartre in *Being and Nothingness* retains religion. The finite human, the "for-itself," though pure negativity, aims to be "in-and-for-itself." McLachlan sees in this "human desire for totality" what classical philosophy spoke of as the desire to be a god. "In relation to Cohen's critiques," Mclachlan writes in his opening paragraph, "I want to show the importance of theology to Sartre's early work, to indicate how what Kate Kirkpatrick calls Sartre's participation in a 'diffuse Augustinianism' is strongly present in the ontological framework of Sartrean existentialism." Having developed such a thesis, Mclachlan still finds it within his wide intellectual compass to acknowledge the validity of the Levinasian critique of Sartrean freedom. Whatever the outcome, Mclachlan makes a strong case that in the interstices of its phenomenologically based studies, Sartre's early thought bears witness to the unacknowledged influence of a dogmatic theological dualism, such as one finds also in Augustine and Neoplatonism. One small disclaimer: regarding my alleged "sympathy for the devil," I admit only to enjoying Mark Twain and William Blake, as well as the eponymous album and song by the Rolling Stones.

I mention only briefly the excellent contribution of **Sandor Goodhart**, which does not refer, as it need not, to my own writings. I cannot remember when I first met Sandy, but I have been happy and grateful to know him for so long, and for his enormous contributions to Levinas studies in America. He is one of the earliest of the American

Levinas scholars, and has the great honor of being the founding figure and the ongoing mentor, the guiding spirit, as it were, of the North American Levinas Society. His chapter is important for its explication of the most radical interpersonal exigency of Levinas's ethics, namely, the singularity of "dying for . . ." the other person, carefully distinguishing it from the ontic-ontological individuation of Heidegger's "being-toward-death."

Scholar and activist **Devorah Wainer** I met in Rome when she attended the 2015 Levinas Philosophy Summer Seminar there; she had traveled from her native Australia to Italy on a higher mission than scholarship. She had come to investigate and bear witness to a refugee crisis, the crisis of suffering endured by the many African and Arab refugees interned on the small Italian island of Lampedusa, east of Tunisia and south of Sicily. Accordingly, she has contributed a deeply moving Levinasian response, an ethical testimony, an outcry, appealing to what in Hebrew is named *chesed*, kindness or compassion, to provoke aid for these and all otherwise silenced victims. (As I write these words, on May 1, 2022, the ranks of the world's refugees have, in two months, been increased by millions of women and children—bombed, shot, tortured, raped, plundered, rendered homeless and hungry by the unprovoked barbaric military-imperialist invasion of Ukraine by Russia.)

Responding to my Spinoza book, **Jacques Rozenberg**, who in 2003 invited me to write a short introduction to the book he edited on ethical issues of the Nuremberg trials, in the present volume presents the reflections of his own abundantly rich intellectual engagement with Spinoza. His chapter is replete with citations from Spinoza's *Ethics* that aptly supplement those found in my own. If I have properly understood the complexity of his outlook, I am grateful and gladdened by the great extent to which our paths through Spinoza reinforce one another.

One of the pleasures—artistic, poetic, intellectual, always personal—of my life was meeting and spending time with **Brunella Antomarini**, of John Cabot University in Rome, where she teaches philosophy, and where I also had the pleasure of teaching four summers and one spring semester from 2002 to 2006. In her chapter she too takes up Spinoza but, in contrast to mine, an alternative Spinoza, more human, warmer, amenable to emotions, even vulnerable, passive, and hence *not* the logicist deterministic all-knowing rationalist whom I and Levinas criticize. To be sure, finding such a Spinoza comes as much from the daring and creative intelligence that is Antomarini's forte as from Spinoza's explicit arguments because in her defense she demands that the *Ethics* be read in reverse, that is, treating Parts III through V, on the emotions and body, as foundational, and Parts I and II, on substance and mind, as secondary if not extraneous. No doubt, for a contemporary thought, such an approach rights Spinoza, stands him on his feet, giving priority to temporality over eternity, embodiment over materiality, and language over idea. It saves Spinoza from himself, that is, poses a new and contemporary existential-phenomenological Spinoza, far more agreeable than the moribund logicist skeletal rationalist Spinoza of old, the one Levinas and I attack. A question remains, however: Is such a makeover correct or desirable, is it beauty or violence, or, as the postmoderns would have it, is its hermeneutic violence sufficiently compensated for by its beautiful results?

Despite the inner coherence of this new and alternative Spinoza, and despite its obvious attraction, its compatibility with contemporary thought, such a better Spinoza—achieved by trumping the first half of the *Ethics* by the second—is in an irrepressible sense no longer Spinoza, or, to say this otherwise, it is Spinoza only if manipulation is fully admitted, which is to say, only if the old bad Spinoza—the rationalist mechanist logicist Spinoza, precisely the Spinoza Levinas and I so severely criticize—is allowed to also have his day. Antomarini's nicer Spinoza certainly has textual grounds, as her chapter carefully has shown, citing from Parts III through V of the *Ethics*, and as such rises head and shoulders above the wholly constructed hermeneutical violence perpetrated by, say, Antonio Negri. Some grounding is better than none, and more is better than less. But if respect for the other, if ethics as Levinas understands it, is to bear its proper weight in the realm of scholarship, then it seems to me that one must go farther. Spinoza contains more than Spinoza admits, true, but this does not entitle him to insights properly developed by Husserl, Heidegger, Merleau-Ponty, Henri, and the like, and does not grant retrofitting him as avatar of contemporary thought. So, creative, brilliant and instructive as is Antomarini's reading, and surely it is all three, let us also let Spinoza be Spinoza, warts and all. All the more does such respect, *critical* respect, enable us to appreciate the abundant profundities—here centrally the primacy of moral responsibility—which he did not.

Richard Sugarman contributes a series of illuminating meditations on Levinas and Judaism, on theodicy, order, Holocaust, and law. First, however, he recalls some congenial moments in our long friendship, over many phone conversations, starting in 1981, joined by our shared love of

Levinas. Because we are likeminded in our understanding and appreciation, let me only comment on what Sugarman calls a "relatively technical issue" of alleged disagreement. Readers familiar with twentieth century thought know well that Levinas "remains," as Sugarman puts it, "completely committed to the phenomenological approach to philosophy from the beginning of his philosophical career to the end." Sugarman suggests that I think otherwise. But this is not so. What I do underscore, however, and perhaps here a misunderstanding has inserted itself, is that Levinas's full commitment to phenomenology, which is to say his full commitment to truth and science, does not preclude but rather demands that all science, objective and transcendental, is subtended and supported—contrary to Husserl's self-understanding of the unsurpassable foundational status of phenomenology—by the irreducible nonobjectifiable and nonintentional transcendence of ethical responsibility. Ethics at once disrupts, and by that very disruption sustains and demands knowing, and hence most certainly also that most rigorous and broadest sense of science which Husserl named phenomenology. So here again Sugarman and I agree. As for the rest of Sugarman's mostly Jewish meditations, they are as usual serious, stimulating, and challenging both intellectually and existentially.

Mark Spencer, a former philosophy graduate student of mine, indeed one of the best at Buffalo, also focuses on religion and phenomenology to raise important and critical epistemological issues. His chapter, "Incarnate Religion," is at once an homage and a critique of Levinas's conception of adult religion, a critique supported, so Spencer argues, by the results of superior and more sensitive phenomenological analyses. Arguing on the basis of more credible phenomenological evidence, Spencer would revise and improve Levinas's conception of religion to no longer exclude (but rather to include) such dimensions as "sacramental life, exclusive universalism, theodicy, or rational theology," such as he believes have found sufficient legitimation via the phenomenological investigations of such Catholic thinkers as Jean-Luc Marion, Max Scheler, and Dietrich von Hildebrand. Much as I greatly respect Spencer, and palpable as is his intelligence and erudition, it seems to me that his thesis and its development are based more on a presupposed and unshakable Catholic theology than on critical dialectical argumentation. As such, it substitutes the rationalization of a deductive apologetics for the presuppositionless phenomenological description to which it would lay claim. Yes, my criticism is strong, but not less so than Spencer's claims.

Spencer believes that by stressing Levinas's adherence to phenomenology Levinas's philosophy must be entirely open to phenomenological criticism. This would be true, of course, if Levinas were only a phenomenologist. But he is not, and not at all because he is irrational or an aesthete. Rather, phenomenology serves his thought for scientific knowledge, and scientific knowledge finds its justification not in more scientific knowledge but outside of knowledge altogether in the transcendence proper to ethics. So what Spencer is really doing in criticizing Levinas is not correcting his phenomenology by better phenomenology but rather subverting Levinas's most central critical stricture, the primacy of ethics, by once again forcing ethics to submit to knowledge. That is to say, by turning phenomenology against Levinas's conception of adult religion, that is, against ethical-religion, Spencer simply replicates and reinforces on the religious plane the very failing to which Levinas's entire philosophy is designed to overcome by overcoming it *ethically*. Theodore de Boer better understood how radical a reorientation Levinas's thought demands when he labeled it a "transcendental ethics," that is, ethics as the irreducible condition of all intelligibility. Ethics is the condition of phenomenology, of science, and hence cannot be overturned by the self-correcting character of all science.

To be sure, ethics is not indifferent to developments in science and technology. I have said so in my comments on Ihde. The phenomenological analyses in Levinas's *Totality and Infinity* that correct earlier phenomenological analyses in Heidegger's *Being and Time*, for instance, are not only better science and offer more perceptive truths, but they also have ethical consequences for these respective philosophers because to say it all too briefly, missing the entire dimension of sensibility Levinas names *jouissance* ("enjoyment") means that Heidegger philosophy has a fundamentally deficient account not only of human embodiment but, accordingly, of suffering, and hence of evil as well. So, too, Heidegger's analyses of *zuhanden*, "ready-to-hand," and *vorhanden*, "present-at-hand," would also and accordingly have to be recontextualized, and this would no doubt alter their ethical sense as well. This is not to say, however, that ethics is a function of phenomenology. Nonetheless, ethics does not arise in some pure vacuum of rationality or spirit, but arises between beings of flesh and blood, a response to vulnerability and suffering. Morality demands the alleviation of suffering. Justice demands that such suffering be understood and treated with the greatest care and precision.

Ethical transcendence, the "idea of infinity," the "face of the other" is not an even more elusive or wondrous version of epistemological *indeterminacy* but more of an imposition, a more immediate imperative, in the exigency of my responsibility to alleviate the neighbor's suffering and the suffering of all. Such exigency and such difficult freedom are not reducible to knowledge even if when extended to all humankind as justice they require knowledge, its universal truths and technology. Adult religion for Levinas is not a deficient knowledge or an obdurate faith, but rather the highest vocation of each: to feed the hungry, clothe the naked, house the refugee, protect and care for "the widow, the orphan, the stranger"—an exigency, a holiness, ever increasing to the measure it is undertaken, all the way to the Most Holy.

Chris Buckman, also a former philosophy graduate student at Buffalo, and co-editor of the present volume, perspicaciously highlights Levinas's conception of a justice unfolding across history by contrasting it with its antipode in Hobbesian and Augustinian politics. "The essential difference in Levinas's view, upending the Augustinian-Hobbesian conception," Buckman writes midway through his essay, "is his conception of the gradual entrance of God's order in history, the temporality of divine justice, in contrast to its eternal permanence." God's genuine incarnation, then, is found neither in miracles nor beyond death, but in the realization of justice in history. Not, as with Hegel, as the unraveling of a preordained truth, not a treat reserved for intellectuals or spiritualists but as goodness, as morality, as responsibility one for another and hence for all humankind. Holy history is political history, the spread of justice here, the kingdom of God *on earth*. Buckman cites Levinas: "The weakness of something that needs time in order to develop must not be regarded abstractly: it points positively here to an order that is greater than the eternity of Platonic Ideas or of Aristotelian forms—an order in which a spirit is in relation with the Other which brings to the spirit more than it is capable of alone." God and religion would no longer offer escapes from the world but the deepest and most serious engagement with it, uplifting the world by more justice. Buckman informs us by way of elaborating Levinas, that Plato, Aristotle, Augustine, Aquinas, as well as Hobbes "fail to grasp the intertwining of the good with the world" and fail to see that "the rightful function of the state is the formation of earthly good." Buckman notes that here Levinas "leans on Maimonides, the great rationalizer, who explains that the Messiah will be known by his efficacy in establishing justice, not by miraculous or supernatural spectacle." Hence, in our unjust world, the primacy of the future, the future of justice, more justice. What can I say but "amen," without the least trace of cynicism. I thank Chris for editing the present volume, I thank him for his thoughtful and inspiring contribution, and I thank him above all for his most valuable and valued friendship, most precious of all.

Some concluding remarks. Just as the exigencies of ethics exceed the centripetal tendencies self-satisfaction, of sameness, bursting these with the surplus, the assignation of responsibility—call it goodness or holiness—so too does ethical philosophy, the thinking of morality and justice, demand a surcharging of thought, an elevation. "The more I answer the more I am responsible," Levinas writes, naming this surplus "glory." To be faithful to this glory—to be responsible as a person, a reader, a scholar—is *to do justice* to Levinas's thought. Ethics, including the struggle for justice, cannot be reduced to numbers or propositions, is not a commodity exchanged from one mind to another. The Jewish tradition uses the term "learning" for this glorious sobriety, charged not only with ideas but with responsibilities, driven by love of neighbor and humanity. Several chapters of the present volume in remaining true to Levinas invoke his conception of "religion for adults." Kant too thought of the ethical inspiration of religion and the teachings of Holy Scripture along these same lines, as he writes in *Religion within the Limits of Reason Alone,* that the latter, Holy Scripture, "should at all times be taught and expounded in the interest of morality . . . that true religion is not to be placed in the knowledge or the profession of what God does or has done for our salvation, but in what we must do to become worthy of it."[4] Can we not read the concluding words of Levinas's preface to *Totality and Infinity* as commentary on the inspiration of the same learning? "It belongs to the very essence of language," states Levinas, "which consists in continually undoing its phrase by the foreword or the exegesis, in unsaying the said, in attempting to restate without ceremonies what has already been ill understood in the inevitable ceremonial in which the said delights."[5]

I thank the editors and all the contributors of the present volume for their share in keeping Levinas's thought alive, by illuminating and challenging it, by shattering again and again the inevitable formal truths, the diverting sophistication, and the perverting ideology by which ethics, morality, and justice lose their edge.

Notes

1. Levinas, *Otherwise Than Being*, transl. Lingis, 159.
2. With the passage of time we now mourn the passing of Don Ihde. One form of that mourning has been making good on my promise to reply to Ihde's criticisms, as an invited paper, given on November 1, 2024, at the Memorial Philosophy Conference held at Stony Brook University (SUNY), entitled "A Handshake with Don Ihde: Postphenomenology and Ethics." It will be published in a collection entitled Memorial to Don Ihde, edited by Jennifer Carter (WordPress, Postphenomenology Series, forthcoming).
3. Ilya Ehrenburg, Chekhov, *Stendhal and Other Essays*, transl. Anna Bostock and Yvonne Kapp (London: MacGibbon & Kee, 1962), 167.
4. Immanuel Kant, *Religion Within the Boundaries of Mere Reason*, in Immanuel Kant, *Religion and Rational Theology*, transl. and ed. Allen W. Wood and George di Giovanni (Cambridge: Cambridge University Press, 1996), 160.
5. Levinas, *Totality and Infinity*, trans. Lingis, 30.

Contributors

Brunella Antomarini (PhD, Gregorian University, Rome) is adjunct assistant professor of philosophy at John Cabot University, Rome. She is the author, editor, and coeditor of twenty books, including *La preistoria acustica della poesia. Per un'antropologia del fenomeno poetico* (Aragno Editore, 2013), *Thinking Through Error* (Lexington Books, 2012), and *La percezione della forma. Trascendenza e finitezza in Hans Urs von Balthasar* (Aesthetica Edizioni, 2004). Prof. Antomarini is also the author and translator of the children's book *Denizens of the Forest* (Poligrapha Ediciones, 1992).

Roger Burggraeve (PhD, Catholic University, Leuven) is emeritus professor of theology at Catholic University, Leuven. He was the cofounder and chair of Leuven's Center for Peace Ethics (1989). He has taught and lectured internationally, in India, Congo, Kenya, Canada, and the United States. Prof. Burggraeve also serves spiritual director at the Holy Spirit College in Leuven. He published hundreds of books, articles, and contributions in English, Dutch, French, Italian, and Japanese, including *An Ethics of Mercy. On the Way to Meaningful Living and Loving* (Peeters, 2016), *The Wisdom of Love in the Service of Love: Emmanuel Levinas on Justice, Peace, and Human Rights* (Marquette University Press, 2002); *Die Ethik der Verantwortlichkeit im Plural. Die Auffassung von Emmanuel Levinas* (Don Bosco Verlag 1997), and *Emmanuel Levinas et la socialité de l'argent. Un philosophe en quête de la réalité journalière. La genèse de 'Socialité et argent' ou l'ambiguïté de l'argent* (Peeters, 1997).

Rossitsa Varadinova Borkowski (PhD, University of Amsterdam) is adjunct professor in humanities and social sciences at Al Akhawayn University, Ifrane, Morocco. She has multiple publications in journals such as *Levinas Studies*, *LiterNet*, and *Sofia Philosophical Review*.

Christopher Buckman (PhD, SUNY Buffalo) is Lecturer of Philosophy, Indiana University Kokomo. He was a participant in the 2016 Levinas Summer Seminar and has published in areas including aesthetics, Kant, ethics, and the practice of teaching philosophy. His current research investigates beauty and ugliness in medieval philosophy.

Richard A. Cohen (PhD, SUNY Stony Brook) is professor of philosophy and Jewish thought at SUNY Buffalo. He was the founder and director of the Jewish Studies programs at University of Alabama, University of North Carolina at Charlotte, and the University of Buffalo. He has taught and lectured widely on various themes in philosophy and Jewish thought both in the USA and internationally, including at University of California, Berkeley; Jewish Theological Seminary in New York City, John Cabot University in Rome, Hebrew University of Jerusalem, Vilnius University, Lithuania; Tel Aviv University, and Meiji University in Tokyo. A Levinas scholar of international reputation, he has translated and introduced numerous Levinas titles, including *New Talmudic Readings* (1999), *Discovering Existence with Husserl* (Northwestern University Press, 1998), *Time and the Other* (Duquesne University Press, 1987), and *Ethics and Infinity* (Duquesne University Press, 1985). He has edited numerous books, including important titles such as *Ricoeur As Another: The Ethics of Subjectivity* (w/James L. Marsh, SUNY Press, 2002), *In Proximity: Emmanuel Levinas and the Eighteenth Century* (with Robert Bernasconi and Melvyn New, Texas Tech University Press, 2001), and *Face to Face with Levinas* (SUNY Press, 1986). Finally, Cohen has authored four well-reviewed monographs: *Elevations: The Height of the Good in Rosenzweig and Levinas* (University of Chicago Press, 1994), *Ethics, Exegesis and Philosophy: Interpretation after Levinas* (Cambridge University Press, 2001), *Levinasian Meditations: Ethics, Philosophy and Religion* (Duquesne University Press, 2010), and *Out of Control: Confrontations between Spinoza and Levinas* (Albany: (SUNY Press, 2016).

Robert Gibbs is a professor of philosophy and religion at the University of Toronto. He was the inaugural director of the Jackman Humanities Institute at the University of Toronto, where he engaged in exploring new horizons for humanities research, supporting leading scholars at all career stages. His research is located on the borderlines of philosophy and religion, with a comparative and historical focus on law and ethics. He has numerous publications in Jewish philosophy and in related fields in

Continental philosophy, including two books, *Correlations in Rosenzweig and Levinas* and *Why Ethics? Signs of Responsibilities*. His current research focuses on higher education, and he has recently completed a book-length manuscript, *Ideas for a Future University*, under contract at UBC Press. In it, he inquires what a research university is for and explores different models of universities by refocusing on the research capacities of students.

Masato Goda (PhD, Tokyo Metropolitan University) is a professor in the Faculty of Letters at Meiji University. He is the Japanese language translator of Levinas's *Totality and Infinity* (Kunishige, 1989), *Otherwise than Being or Beyond Essence* (Asahi, 1990). Professor Goda has published numerous books, including *Levinas: Toward a Revolution of Existence* (Chikuma Shobo, 2000), *Reading Levinas: the Glorious in Everyday Life* (Japan BPA, 1999), and *Levinas's Thought: The Sway of Hope* (Kōbudou, 1988).

Sandor Goodhart (PhD, SUNY Buffalo) is a professor of English and Jewish studies at Purdue University. He served as the director of the Jewish Studies Program (1997–2002), of the Philosophy and Literature Program (2005), and of the Classical Studies Program (2007–2011). He twice served as guest editor for special issues on Emmanuel Levinas for the journal *Shofar* (Summer 2008) and *Modern Fiction Studies* (Spring 2008). He is the author of five books, including *The Prophetic Law: Essays in Judaism* (2014), *Reading Stephen Sondheim* (2000), and *Sacrificing Commentary: Reading the End of Literature* (1996).

Don Ihde (PhD, Boston University) (d. 2024) was Distinguished Professor of Philosophy at SUNY Stony Brook. He was the widely recognized pioneer of philosophy of technology in North America. He authored and edited over twenty books, including *Postphenomenology and Technoscience: The Peking University Lectures* (2009), *Postphenomenology: Essays in the Postmodern Context* (1995), and *Technics and Praxis: A Philosophy of Technology* (1978).

Chung-Hsiung Lai (PhD, University of Nottingham) is Distinguished Professor in the Department of Foreign Languages and Literature at National Cheng Kung University, Taiwan; and former dean of its College of Liberal Arts. His is the author of *Responding to the Other: Revisiting Levinas* (2014) and editor of *Philosophy of the Other* (2009). He has published in numerous journals, such as *Zhongshan Journal of Humanities*, *Levinas Studies*, and *Chinese and Foreign Literature*. Prof. Lai serves as the president of the Philosophy Association of Tainan.

Jack Marsh (PhD, SUNY Binghamton) is a St. Leonard's scholar in the Department of Divinity, University of St. Andrews, Scotland. He is author of *Saying Peace: Levinas, Eurocentrism, Solidarity* (2020) and coeditor of *Normativity, Meaning, and the Promise of Phenomenology* (2019). His work has appeared in many journals, including *Philosophy Today*, *Philosophy and Social Criticism*, and *Levinas Studies*.

James McLachlan (PhD, University of Toronto) is emeritus professor of philosophy and religion at Western Carolina University. He is past co-chair of the Mormon Studies Group at the American Academy of Religion, and organizer of the Personalist Seminar. He has assisted as co-chair of Levinas Philosophy Summer Seminars, in Vilnius, Buffalo, Berkeley, and Rome and was co-director of the NEH Summer Seminar on Levinas at the University at Buffalo in summer 2017 and 2022. His recent publications have dealt with concepts of hell in existentialism, Satan and demonic evil in Boehme, Schelling, and Dostoevsky, and the problem of evil in Mormonism.

Jacques Rozenberg has taught in several French and foreign universities as a full professor. He is an associate researcher at the National Center for Scientific Research. His has a philosophical, scientific, psychoanalytic, and Hebrew background. He is the author and coeditor of fifteen books, as well as numerous articles in French and English, especially regarding Spinoza's philosophy. He was a student of Emmanuel Levinas for two years at Paris 10-Nanterre University.

Jolanta Saldukaitė is Associate Professor and Researcher at Vilnius University, Lithuania. Her research interests include phenomenology, ethics, and the problem of evil. She has published several articles on the philosophy of Emmanuel Levinas. Dr. Saldukaitė is a founding member and co-organizer of the International Levinas Philosophy Summer Seminar (since 2013) and co-editor of several journal issues dedicated to Levinas. Most recently, she has co-edited and contributed to *Morality on the Edge: Modernity and the Holocaust in Lithuania* (Münster: LIT Verlag, 2025). In addition, she is actively engaged in institutionalizing and evaluating philosophical education in Lithuania.

Jean-Michel Salanskis (PhD, University of Paris) is a mathematician and philosopher, and a professor at University of Paris X, Nanterre. A prolific writer, he is the author of many books, including *Lévinas vivant* (2006), *La Gauche et L'égalité* (2009), and *Le constructivisme non standard* (1999).

Steven Shankman (Ph.D., Stanford University) holds the UNESCO Chair in Transcultural Studies, Interreligious Dialogue, and Peace and is co-director of the UNESCO Crossings Institute at the University of Oregon, where he is Distinguished Professor of English and Classics Emeritus. Before coming to Oregon, he taught at Princeton, Columbia, and Harvard.

His work in the Western classical tradition includes *Pope's Iliad: Homer in the Age of Passion* (1983) and *In Search of the Classic: Reconsidering the Classical Tradition, Homer to Valéry and Beyond* (1994). His Penguin edition of Pope's Iliad appeared in 1996. Some of his later work, including *The Siren and the Sage: Knowledge and Wisdom in Ancient Greece and China* (co-authored with Stephen Durrant, 2000) and *Early China/Ancient Greece: Thinking through Comparisons* (co-edited by Stephen Durrant, 2002), compares classical traditions. With Stephen Durrant and four others, he is an editor of *The World of Literature* (1999), an anthology of world literature from a global perspective, which contains some of his own poetic translations from Chinese, Greek, and Latin. He is the author of two books of poems: *Kindred Verses*, a chapbook, appeared in 2000; *Talmudic Verses* was published by Finishing Line Press in 2023. His poetry has appeared in a number of journals including *Tikkun, Sewanee Review, Literary Imagination, Literary Matters,* and *Poetica Magazine. Epics and Other Higher Narratives: An Intercultural Approach*, co-edited by Amiya Dev, appeared in 2010, as did his book *Other Others: Levinas, Literature, Transcultural Studies*. He has been a Guggenheim and an NEH Fellow.

His most recent scholarly book is *Turned Inside-Out: Reading the Russian Novel in Prison* (Northwestern University Press, 2017). He is currently at work on a translation from the French of *Suerte: L'exclusion volontaire*, a semi-autobiographical novel (1995) by Claude Lucas, the so-called "gangster philosopher" who, before writing Suerte, became a devotee of Emmanuel Levinas's first magnum opus, *Totality and Infinity*; and a book of essays on ethics, religion, and literature.

Mark K. Spencer (PhD, SUNY Buffalo) is professor of philosophy at the University of St. Thomas in Minnesota. He is the author of numerous articles and of two books, The Irreducibility of the *Human Person: A Catholic Synthesis (2022)* and *Catholicism and the Problem of God (2023)*.

Richard Sugarman (PhD, Boston University) is professor of philosophy at University of Vermont. He has authored and coedited numerous books, including *Rancor Against Time: The Phenomenology of Ressentiment* (1980), and *Speaking Philosophy: The Posthumous papers of John Wild* (2006). Since 2007 Prof. Sugarman has served as a senior advisor to Vermont senator and US presidential candidate, Bernie Sanders.

Devorah Wainer (PhD, University of Technology) is honorary associate in the Department of Sociology at the University of Sydney. She is a member of the Sydney Asia Pacific Migration Centre. Her research works on developing approaches to human rights through the humanities rather than legal or policy frameworks. She has lectured widely in the United Kingdom, United States, and Australia. She is author of *Beyond the Wire: Levinas vis-à-vis Villawood* (2015) and editor of *Business Feel: Leading Paradigm Shifts in Organizations* (2014).

Edith Wyschogrod (PhD, Columbia University) (d. 2009) was the J. Newton Rayzor Professor Emeritus of Philosophy and Religious Thought at Rice University. She was a member of the American Academy of Arts and Sciences, a Guggenheim Fellow, a fellow of the National Humanities Center, and past president of the American Academy of Religion. Author of five influential books, her *Emmanuel Levinas: The Problem of Ethical Metaphysics* (1974) was the first monograph on Levinas's work to appear in English. Her other notable works include *An Ethics of Remembering: History, Heterology and the Nameless Others* (1998), and *Spirit in Ashes: Hegel, Heidegger and Man Made Mass Death* (1985).

Index

abandonment, 250
absence, 247–252
absolute ethics, 23
absolute freedom, 301
absolute transcendence, 112
absolutism, 203
absurdity, 14–15, 99, 306, 346
Achterhuis, Hans, 55
Adorno, Theodor W., 49
adult religion, 8, 176, 317, 322–330, 372–373, 376, 378–379
The Adventure of French Philosophy (Badiou), 226
adverbial, adverbial modifications and, 7, 16, 257–258, 260–263, 265
aesthetic body, 118
aesthetics, aestheticism and, 48–49, 62–63, 66, 77–87, 90–91, 146–147
affect, 182–183, 189, 195
afterlife, 164
Agamben, Giorgio, 230–231
agency, 26, 339
Ahmed (asylum-seeking refugees), 350–351, 353–354
alienation, 24, 118, 273–274, 279–280, 283
Allison, David, 54, 363
alterity, 12, 18, 65, 73, 295, 318, 365
 in art, 151, 159

clôtural reading and, 113
consciousness and, 109
of the Other, 101, 161, 209, 220–221, 224, 248–249, 279, 302
radicalization of, 150
rhythm and, 97
totality and, 209–210
uncanniness and, 145
vulnerability and, 153
ambivalence, 77–78, 87–91, 158
analytic philosophy, 23, 32, 40, 42nn1–2, 53, 367
Animadversiones (Leibniz), 173
Anissimov, Myriam, 128
annihilation, 185, 195, 299–300, 311
anonymity, 85, 88, 93n41, 98, 148, 176
antebellum South, 201
anthropology, 22–23, 26
Antigone (Greek myth), 144–145
anti-humanism, 216, 226–227
anti-philosophy, 233n36
antipolitics, 209–210
Antomarini, Brunella, 6, 374–375
Aquinas, Thomas, 202, 204
Arbib, Dan, 176
arbitrariness, 3–4, 8n1
Arendt, Hannah, 66, 194
Aristotle, 183–184, 189–190, 204, 207, 261

Aronowicz, Annette, 39
arrhythmia, 95
art, 6, 62–63, 80–90, 152–155, 158, 161–164
  alterity in, 151, 159
  Cohen, R., on, 77–79, 91, 92n17, 156–157, 159–160
  il y a and, 84–85, 87, 91n15
  imitation theory of, 157
  paintings and, 144, 146, 151
  temporality and, 156–159
  uncanniness and, 145, 147–150, 156, 159
assimilation, 137, 139, 170–171
asylum seekers, 201, 338–340, 356nn19–20
asylum-seeking refugees, 340–344, 346–354, 346n33
asymmetry, 4, 11, 301
atheism, 294, 301, 373
Atterton, Peter, 34
Augustine, 294, 297–298, 300, 302, 305, 307
  on political authority, 201, 212n10
  the state and, 201, 203–204, 206–207
Auschwitz, 246, 249, 284, 337, 355n5
Australia, 340–354, 356n20
authenticity, 4, 32, 36, 258–260, 304
authoritarian, 202, 205
authority, 51, 72, 106–107, 204, 212n10
  moral, 202
  political, 174, 201, 203–204
automatons, automatism and, 87, 182

Bachelard, Gaston, 17
Badiou, Pierre, 7, 220, 225–226, 228, 230, 372–373
  on evil, 216–217, 219, 221–224, 231
  on truth, 215–216, 218–219, 221–224, 227, 229, 231, 233n21

Barber, Michael, 41
Barth, Karl, 294–295, 297–298
Bataille, Georges, 18–19
Baudelaire (Sartre), 293, 310
bearing witness, 102, 287, 338–339, 341–344, 346–354, 356n33, 374
Beauvoir, Simone de, 308–309
being, event of, 1–2, 7, 258
being, non-truth of, 78–79
Being and Nothingness (Sartre), 294, 301–302, 305, 309–310, 373
Being and Time (Heidegger), 57–58, 64
being-as-a-victim, 218–219
being-for-being, 301
being-for-death, 218–219, 259
being-for-itself, 262, 302, 305
being-for-the-other, 102, 109, 301, 346, 349–350
being-in-itself, 262, 306, 308
being-in-the-world, 80 91n15, 258, 262
being-to-the-world, 19–21
being-toward-death, 209–210
being-with, 215
ben Perahyah, Joshua, 365
Benjamin, Walter, 49
Bergo, Bettina, 36–37
Bergson, Henri, 3, 8n2, 17–18, 48, 65–66, 118, 209–210
Bernasconi, Robert, 36, 41, 368
Bernini, 156
Bernstein, Richard J., 40
betrayal, 129, 131–133, 139, 152, 222–224
beyond being, 2–3, 5–6, 15, 71
"Beyond Memory" (Levinas), 284–285
the Bible, 57, 59n15, 64, 66, 209, 225
  exegesis and, 110–111
  exlcusion and, 243
  Hobbes interpreting, 204–208
  Sessions interpreting, 201–202
  Spinoza and, 170–171
  theodicy and, 240

The Birth of Tragedy (Nietzsche), 98
Blanchot, Maurice, 18–19, 33
Bloch, Ernst, 49
Bloechl, Jeffrey, 41
Blondel, Charles, 49
Boccaccio, 143–144
body, 8, 82–83, 89, 117, 190, 195–196, 319–325
    ethical, 6, 108, 114, 116–123, 371–372
    language and, 107
    religion and the, 317–318
Boer, Theodore de, 35
Borgmann, Albert, 55–56
Borkowski, Rossitsa Varadinova, 371
Botticelli, 155
Bouckaert, Luk, 35
bourgeois-capitalism, 273
Brave New World (Huxley), 24
breathlessness, 97, 100
Bruhl, Lévy, 80
Brunschvicg, Léon, 17
Buber, Martin, 19, 40, 298, 333n68, 349–350, 355n15
    on collectivity, 339
    Rosenzweig and, 72
    vulnerability and, 261
Buckman, Chris, 378–379
Burggraeve, Roger, 7, 370–371
Burning for the Other (Steven), 41

Calarco, Matthew, 34
capitalism, 216, 273
care, 68, 106, 258–260
Carnets (Levinas), 99–100
Cartesian Meditations (Husserl), 64
Catholic Church, 127–128, 132, 134–136, 371, 376
    Counter-Reformation, 6, 133
    the Inquisition by, 135–136
Cavaillès, Jean, 17
Cavell, Stanley, 41
Céline, Louis-Ferdinand, 96

Cervantes, Miguel de, 131–139, 371
chaos, 3, 86
charity, 100–101, 127, 135, 175, 273, 322
chesed (loving-kindness), 8, 342–344, 374
Childers, William P., 136
Christianity, 6, 11, 19, 203–207, 261, 298–300, 325, 371
    Catholic Church and, 136
    Judaism and, 170–171
    neighborly love and, 68
    political theory of, 201–202
    senseless kindness in, 127
    Shakespeare and, 137–138
classical idealism, 304
classical rationalism, 63
clôtural reading, 113–114
cogito, 309
cognition, 3, 78, 197, 322–323, 326, 328–329, 333n62
Cohen, Hermann, 40, 49
Cohen, Richard, 4–8, 12–13, 47, 50, 52, 61–68, 237–238, 348–349. *See also specific works*
    on art, 77–79, 91, 92n17, 156–157, 159–160
    on Bergson, 209–210
    on bodily life, 322–323, 327
    on ethics, 217
    on the face, 153–154, 157–158
    on genuine religion, 324–325
    on Heidegger, 48–49, 51, 56–58, 73
    on images, 83
    on Judaism, 340
    Levinas studies developed by, 31–36, 38–39
    on Rosenzweig, 38, 71–73
    on Sartre, 293–294, 300–304
    on science, 87–88
    at Stony Brook, 53–55
    on subjectivity, 16
    on suffering, 210, 337–338, 346

Cohen, Richard *(continued)*
　on temporality, 122, 157–158, 210
　on theology, 294–300
　on transcendence, 66, 112
　on vulnerability, 341
collective good, 272–274
collectivity, 24–25, 98, 226, 276, 339
collectivization, general, 272–273
communication
　nonverbal, 115–116, 118, 350, 372
　one-way, 114
　saying-said structure and, 109–112
Communism, 128–131, 272
compassion, 113, 134, 136–137, 175
conatus, 171–172, 176, 183, 185, 187, 189–193, 195–198, 243
conceiving body, 118
consciousness, 93n41, 226, 228, 294, 301, 305–306, 308–310
　alterity and, 109
　images and, 85–86
　Plato on, 83
　proprioception and, 186
　proximity and, 115–116
　self, 64, 300, 361
　split, 67
　universality, 107
Continental philosophy, 32–33, 42nn1–2, 48–51, 59n13, 215–216, 237–240, 251, 363
conversion, religious, 127, 136–137, 139
corporeality, 91, 317, 322–327
correspondence theory, of truth, 62
cosmology, 59n15, 82
Council of Trent, 6, 133
counter-intentionality, 321
Counter-Reformation, Catholic Church, 6, 133
Craig, Megan, 41
criminalization, 338–339, 349

Critchley, Simon, 36–37, 44n17, 109–110, 229, 368, 372
critical anthropology, 26
criticism, aestheticism and philosophical, 77–82
culture of immanence, 89–91, 94n50
cybernetics, 55

Damasio, Antonio, 192
D'Amora, Vladimir, 196
Darwin, Australia, 349
Darwinism, 191
Da-sein, 160, 209–210, 258–260, 263–264
De l'existence à existent (Levinas), 84–85, 88
dead languages, 107
dead philosophy, 32, 35–36
Deane, Herbert A., 206
death, 54, 68, 72, 102, 134, 259, 263–264, 345
deconstruction, 4, 12, 19–20, 36–37, 40, 44n17, 113, 266n18
defamiliarization, 145
deformalization, 86, 337, 365
dehumanization, 345, 352–353
demand, ethical, 23, 25–26, 117, 221
Derrida, Jacques, 4–5, 43n10, 48–49, 220, 230, 238, 266n18, 368
　Cohen, R., on, 51, 73
　on ethics, 35–36, 43n10
　reading of Levinas by, 13–14, 16, 18, 27, 34–35, 38–40, 43n6, 96, 233n15
desacralization, 323–324
Descartes, René, 52, 182, 304, 309–311
desensitization, 149
desire, 139, 171–172, 195, 226, 261–262, 279, 286
　metaphysical, 15–16, 116, 301
　need *vs.*, 249

determinism, 182
Devil, sympathy for the, 310–312
dialogism, 68, 112, 333n68, 339
diaspora, 101, 225–226
difference, 112, 159, 215, 217, 219–221, 369
  irreducible, 68
  ontological, 14
  proximity as, 95
difficult freedom, 251, 301
Difficult Freedom (Levinas), 151, 247, 251–252
digitalization, 216
Dillon, Matt, 261
Dionysus, 98–99
disaster, 222–224
Discovering Existence with Husserl (Levinas), 38, 238
Discovering Levinas (Morgan), 41
disengagement, 160
dis-individuation, 98
disorder, 8n2
divine justice, 207
Don Quixote (Cervantes), 127–128, 131–139, 371
"Don Quixote" (lecture, Levinas), 6, 131
Dostoevsky, Fyodor, 131
Drabinski, John, 38
dualism, 181, 190, 248, 373
duration, 3–4, 156
Durkheim, Emile, 313n13
dying for, 7, 257–264
dystopia, 56–57

egoism, ego and, 93n41, 191, 226, 251, 264–265, 281, 370
egology, 299–300
Egypt, 355n9
Ehrenburg, Ilya, 368–369
Eigentlichkeit (authenticity), 258–259

Elevations (Cohen, R.), 5–6, 38, 71–73, 157–158
emancipation, 170
embodiment, 6, 56, 107, 112–113, 117, 123, 341
  of compassion, 134, 136–137
  ethics and, 88–89
  justice and, 118–119
Emmanuel Levinas (Wyschogrod), 34–35
Emmanuel Levinas's Theory of Language (Lawton), 34–35
empathy, 135, 183–185, 187–189
empiricism, 85
encounters, 17, 21, 122, 153–155, 331n16
end of philosophy, 122
English, 169, 237–238, 342, 354
enjoyment, 24, 148–151
Enlightenment, 324–325
Entre Nous (Levinas), 257–258
epistemology, 64
erotic relation, 119
eschatology, 244–245, 285–287
  failed, 294, 305, 307
essoufflement (breathlessness), 97
eternal, love, 173
eternity, 118, 155–160, 300
ethical body, 6, 108, 114, 116–123, 371–372
ethical demand, 23, 25–26, 117, 221
ethical exegesis, 6, 77, 108–116, 119, 367, 371–372
ethical individualism, 277–282
ethical intrigue, 21, 25
ethical plot, 11, 15
ethical relationship, 115, 173, 176, 319–320, 325, 337
  infinity and, 322–324
  religion and, 298

392 | Index

ethical responsibility, 175, 275, 327, 337, 346, 372, 376
   art and, 146
   Grossman, V., on, 129
   Kantian, 49
   nonverbal communication and, 115
   semantic responsibility vs., 25
   suffering and, 50
ethical sensibility, 340–343
ethical subjectivity, 15, 22, 333n64
ethical-religion, 7–8, 377
ethico-political philosophy, 230–232
ethics, 7, 59n13, 87, 232n1, 281, 361, 365, 379
   absolute, 23
   Derrida on, 35–36, 43n10
   embodied, 88–89
   as first philosophy, 49, 64, 66, 106–108, 122, 209, 362, 364
   Kant on, 106
   kindness and, 5
   knowledge and, 377
   Levinas on, 39, 48–52, 57, 72, 79–80, 88–90, 106–109, 171–172, 215–221, 226–227, 231
   meaning of, 21–22
   of the Other, 219–221, 226–227, 229–230
   religious, 224–225
   of sacrifice, 264
   sense in, 79–80
   Spinoza on, 171–172, 183
   and the state, 370
   technology and, 364–365
Ethics (Badiou), 216–218, 224, 372
Ethics (Spinoza), 171–173, 176, 182, 374–375
Ethics, Exegesis and Philosophy (Cohen), 12–13, 16, 41, 79, 107–108, 240

"Ethics and Cybernetics" (Cohen, R.), 55
Ethics and Infinity (Levinas), 34, 238
Ethics of Deconstruction (Critchley), 36, 113
etho-analysis, 22–27, 367
ethos, 23, 25–27, 367
Études Kierkegaardiennes (Wahl), 295
evil, 207, 273–274, 281, 283, 285, 304, 307–308, 311
   Badiou on, 216–217, 219, 221–224, 231
   Cohen, R., on, 50
   indifference to, 84–85, 87
   justice and, 250
   mercy and, 287
   monstrosity and, 144
   suffering as, 344–346
exclusive universalism, 325, 329
exclusivism, totalizing, 299
exegesis, 48, 50–51, 77–78, 90–91, 93n45, 107
   ethical, 6, 77, 108–116, 119, 367, 371–372
existence, 8n1, 17, 341
Existence and Existents (Levinas), 148, 150
existentialism, 7, 17, 32, 294, 300, 308, 312
exoticism, 85, 87–88, 148–151, 158–159
experience, 17, 21, 107–109, 321–322
   bodily, 327
   as embodiment, 117
   knowledge, 319
   lived, 338, 345–346
   religious, 296, 323, 329
   sensibility of, 111–112
exteriority, 1–3, 89, 150–151
exteriorization, 89
extra-territoriality, 277

the face, 72–73, 119, 131–132, 209, 247–252, 326
  Cohen, R., on, 153–154, 157–158
  impossibility of, 151–155
Face to Face with Levinas (Cohen, R.), 34, 237
face-to-face relations, 4, 7, 176, 245, 294–295, 321–322, 328, 350
  Cohen, R., on, 153–154
  dialogism and, 68
  ethics and, 88, 241–242
  with the Other, 57, 153–155, 172, 220–221, 326
  responsibility and, 271, 276
  technology and, 56
  truth and, 185–186
Fallenbostel, Germany, 344
Fatima (asylum-seeking refugees), 350–351
Feinberg, Chaim, 242, 253n11
feminist philosophy, 32, 42n4
fidelity, 36–37, 150, 174, 221–224, 228–229, 244
Firouz (asylum-seeking refugee), 342
forgetting, 24, 111
forgiveness, 11, 194
for-itself, 294, 301–302, 307–311
Forman, Paul, 58
Foucault, Michel, 33, 145, 233n21
France, 12, 54, 295, 369, 372
  French phenomenology, 17, 318, 321
  French philosophy, 17–20, 26, 226
  Paris, 5, 33, 368
  University of Paris-Sorbonne, 5–6, 33, 131, 169, 368
Frankfurt School, 49
free will, 120, 171–172, 192–193
freedom, 8n1, 20, 296–297, 304, 324, 346–349
  absolute, 301
  belief in, 193–196

  Imperialism and, 302
  moral responsibility and, 169–170
  negative, 193–194
  religious, 170
  responsibility and, 243, 251
  Sartre on, 310–312
  Spinoza on, 176, 185
"Freedom" (Peperzak), 35
Frege, Gottlob, 25
Freud, Sigmund, 145, 160, 163n50
From Existence to Existents (Levinas), 14–15, 22
Fürsorge (solicitude), 12, 258–260, 262, 266n9
future, 211

Gaòn, Se'adyah, 251
gender, 72, 135, 171, 187
generosity, 370
genuine religion, 8, 317, 324–325
German critical theory, 32
German idealism, 63
German phenomenology, 64
Germany, 18, 295, 344
  Nazi, 128–130, 222, 226, 237–238, 272
Gibbs, Robert, 5, 37, 39, 365–367
globalization, 216, 218
glory, 379
"God and Onto-Theo-logy" (lecture, Levinas), 6
Goda, Masato, 6, 368–369
Good, Idea of the, 100–101, 129, 274, 361
Goodhart, Sandor, 7, 150, 373–374
goodness, 7, 27n3, 188, 287, 323, 370–371, 379
  Badiou on, 219
  being for the other and, 3, 27n3
  ethics of, 216, 226–227, 229–232
  evil and, 221–222

goodness *(continued)*
　morality and, 66–67, 378
　responsibility and, 361, 379
　senseless, 128
　small, 7, 67, 271–272, 275–282, 371–372
goodness, primordial, 287
grammar, 61, 64, 130, 245–246
gratuitous gestures, 185–187, 197
Greece, ancient, 57–58, 144–145, 225–226
Greek philosophy, 19, 233n36
Grossman, Edith, 128, 131, 133
Grossman, Vasily, 7, 67, 128–130, 182, 198n2, 271–274, 370–371
Gurwitsch, Aron, 363–364

Habermas, Jürgen, 49
Halbertal, Moshe, 205
Hallward, Peter, 224
Harari, Yuval, 351
Harris, Sam, 351
Harshav, Barbara, 262
Hebrew, 251, 339, 352–353, 374
hedonism, 149
Heelan, Patrick, 53
Hegel, Georg Wilhelm Friedrich, 33
Heidegger, Martin, 4, 7, 61, 91n15, 209–210, 318–319, 377
　anonymous infinity proposed by, 176
　on Antigone, 144–145
　Cohen, R., on, 48–49, 51, 56–58, 73
　cybernetics and, 55
　on *Da-sein*, 160, 209–210, 258–260, 263–264
　on death, 258, 263–264
　on freedom, 304
　on language, 109
　linguistic turn of, 372

　Nazism of, 237–238
　ontological difference and, 14
　Otto and, 295–296
　reading of Levinas by, 12, 14, 18, 21, 27
　technology and, 365
　on uncanniness, 145, 160
Hick, John, 308
hierarchy, 106, 139, 209
Hildebrand, Dietrich von, 318, 321–322, 328
Hill, Patrick, 53
Hitler, Adolf, 222
Hobbes, Thomas, 6–7, 20, 202–211, 212n10, 378
holiness, the "Holy" and, 260, 295–298, 313nn12–13, 338
　compassion, 113
　the face and, 152
　the sacred *vs.*, 243
Holmes, Stephen, 205
the Holocaust (the Shoah), 50, 69n11, 240, 242–245, 249–250, 293–294, 337, 345, 355n2, 355n5
homeostasis, 192
hubris, 39, 57
Hughes, Brendan, 261
human psyche, 4, 183
human rights, 218, 276–277, 356n20
humanism, 50–51, 195, 216, 226–227, 231, 271, 304
humanity, 26–27, 218, 226, 230, 250, 338, 345–346
humanization, 271, 275–277, 287
humanness, 260–261
humiliation, 182–183
Husserl, Edmund, 18, 61, 318–319, 321–322, 363–364, 372, 376
　Heidegger and, 238, 295–296
　on intersubjectivity, 64
　Levinas on, 241
　on sensible intuition, 115

Huxley, Aldous, 24
hypermasculinity, 187

ICT. *See* information and communications technology
The Idea of the Holy (Otto), 295–296
idealism, 308–309
   classical, 304
   German, 63
ideality word, 24–25
identity, 26, 153–154, 219–220, 258, 369
The Idiot (Dostoevsky), 131
idolatry, 146, 158, 204, 206, 274
Ihde, Don, 5, 33, 55, 362–365, 380n2
il y a (there is), 3, 14–15, 19, 227–228, 234n40, 248, 297
   anonymity of, 93n41, 148
   art and, 84–85, 87, 91n15
   as nonsense, 93n42, 99–101
   rhythm and, 95
Illeity, 248–249
images, 82–84, 92n35, 146, 149–151
   consciousness and, 85–86
imagination, 183–184, 189, 192, 195–198
imitation theory, of art, 157
immanence, 119, 171–172, 181–182, 227, 231
   culture of, 89–91, 94n50
immigration, 201. *See also* asylum seekers
immortality, 82–83, 218–219, 227, 229, 283
Imperialism, 274–275, 302
importance, of importance, 361
imprisonment, detention and, 338–354
In Search of Lost Time (Proust), 101
inanimate objects, 159
incarcerated persons, 340–352
indifference, 148, 257, 338, 343–344
   to evil, 84–85, 87

individuality, individualism and, 112, 187, 190
   ethical, 277–282
individuation, 98
indivisibility, 192
inertia, 191–193, 195
infinity, infinite and, 2–3, 16, 249, 297, 327, 330, 333n66
   anonymous, 176
   demand of ethics, 172
   ethical relation and the, 322–324
   material, 228
   responsibility and, 102, 243, 258, 265, 323–324
   time and, 173, 251
   totality and, 248
   unspeakability, 110
information and communications technology (ICT), 56
inhumanity, 181
in-itself, 294, 305–310
in-itself-for-itself, 294, 305
innocence, suffering and, 250–251
the Inquisition, 135–136
instability, 148, 187–191
instrumental functionalism, 364
intelligibility, 102, 220, 361, 364–366, 377
intentional acts, 318–319, 322, 327, 329–330
intentionality, intention and, 115, 120–121, 330
interhumanity, 122
interiority, 2, 85–87, 89–90, 93n41, 152–153
internalization, 89
international law, 240, 338, 343–344, 356n20
interruption, 79, 82–84, 113
intersubjectivity, 64, 67, 122, 148, 173–174, 365, 370
   language and, 109

intervals, 156–157
interwar philosophy, 295
Introna, Lucas, 56
Iran, 341
irrationality, 84
irresponsibility, 366
"Is Ontology Fundamental" (Levinas), 151
Islam, 127, 136–139
Israel, 204, 206, 239, 246, 284
Italy, 374

James, William, 240
Jefferson, Thomas, 202
Jentsch, Ernst, 145
Jewish studies, 38–39, 170, 239, 365
Jim Crow laws, 202
jouissance ("enjoyment"), 377
Journey to the End of the Night (Céline), 96
Judaism, Jewish thought and, 6–7, 19, 101–102, 222, 296, 340. *See also* the Bible; the Torah
  Hebrew and, 251, 339, 352–353, 374
  the Holocaust and, 50, 240, 242–245, 249–250
  Levinas and, 33, 37–40, 49–50, 63–66, 69n6, 72–73, 225–226, 237–254
  mysticism and, 72–73, 174
  postmodern, 337
  prisoners of war and, 344–345
  secular, 170
  Shakespeare and, 138
  Spain and, 127, 136
  Spinoza and, 170
  suffering and, 337–338
  the Talmud in, 50, 57, 63, 66, 114, 203, 206, 243–249, 251–252

justice, 12, 100–101, 276–277, 340, 361–362, 377–379
  divine, 207
  embodiment as, 118–119
  evil and, 250
  without morality, 370
  ressentiment and, 241
  the state, 174–176

Kabbalah, 174
Kafka, Franz, 254
Kant, Immanuel, 2, 49, 85–86, 106, 197, 218–219, 362, 379
Kavan (asylum-seeking refugee), 341–342
Kearney, Richard, 302
Kidman, Nicole, 261
Kierkegaard, Søren, 251, 295
Kierkegaard and the Existential Philosophy (Shestov), 295
kindness, 5
  chesed and, 8, 342–344, 374
  senseless, 127–129, 131–135, 139, 182, 198n2
King, Martin Luther, Jr., 202
Kirkpatrick, Kate, 294
Korsgaard, Christine, 41
kosher food, 353–354

Lacan, Jacques, 28n6
Lagrée, Jacqueline, 174
Lai, Chung-Hsiung, 7, 372–373
language, 1–3, 71, 223, 245, 350, 356n31, 379. *See also specific languages*
  analytic philosophy and, 32
  dead, 107
  ethical exegesis and, 108–116
  maternity and, 120
  Nietzsche on, 98
  ontological, 99, 109–112, 223n15

original, 116, 372
and the Other, 116
theological, 298
transcendence and, 110
translation and, 6, 33–35, 38, 50, 95, 133, 169, 224, 262, 342
written forms, 106–107
Latin, 133
Lawton, Phillip, 34–35
Leibniz, Gottfried Wilhelm, 173, 240
Lescourret, Marie-Anne, 5, 11, 369–370
Levinas (Malka), 95–96
Levinas, Emmanuel. *See specific topics*
Levinas, His Life, and Legacy (Nemo), 225
Levinas and James (Craig), 41
"Levinas on Art and Aestheticism" (Cohen, R.), 80
Levinas Studies, 31, 34–42
Levinas Studies (journal), 41
Levinasian Meditations (Cohen, R.), 41, 108, 111, 113, 153, 217, 224, 293–294
Lévy-Bruhl, Lucien, 91n15, 98
Life and Fate (Grossman, V.), 7, 67, 128–130, 271–272, 277–282, 370
lifeless life, 159
Lingis, Alphonso, 5, 32–34, 54, 362–363
linguistics, 61, 107
linguistic turn, 63, 340, 372
listening, 107, 114
Lithuania, 345
living philosophy, 32, 35–36
Llewelyn, John, 114, 372
Locke, John, 202
logical positivist movement, 32
loneliness, 250
"Loss of Breath" (Poe), 96–97, 103n7

love, 24, 67, 143–144, 172–173, 189, 286–287, 325
of neighbors, 68, 72, 174
Lovecraft, Howard Phillips, 145
loving-kindness (*chesed*), 8, 342–344, 374
Lyotard, Jean-François, 18

Maimonides, 378–379
Malka, Salomon, 95–96
Marion, Jean-Luc, 318, 321, 328–329
Marsh, Jack, 5, 368
martyrdom, 101–102
Marxism, 23, 273, 293
materialism, materiality and, 11, 149–150, 152, 190, 323–324
maternity, 28n4, 108, 116–123, 372
mathematics, 228
McDonagh, Martin, 160–161
McLachlan, James, 373
meaning, 2–3, 21–22, 111, 122, 296, 318–319, 365
birth of, 117
ethics and, 88, 147, 286–287
limits of, 35
of order, 245–247
sense and, 107, 116
transcendence and, 153
meaningless suffering, 325–326, 337–338, 340, 341–346
Meditations (Descartes), 309
memory, 160–161, 248, 283, 338, 345
Mendel, Menachem, 242
Merchant of Venice (Shakespeare), 137–139
mercy, 67, 127–128, 131–134, 138, 175, 287
Merleau-Ponty, Maurice, 21, 58, 97, 118, 151, 237, 369
messianism, 208, 225, 230–231, 261, 272, 285–287

metaphysical desire, 15–16, 116, 301
metaphysics, 3, 174, 244–245, 249, 308–309
  desire and, 15–16, 116, 301
  ethical, 57, 77–78, 80, 87, 146, 246
Micah (prophet), 343
Michelangelo, 156, 163n50
midrash, midrashim and, 8, 57, 339–354, 355n12, 355n14
misogyny, 171
Miteinandersein, 258–259
monarchies, 204–205, 209
monism, 172
monotheism, 65, 202–204, 206–208
monstrosities, monsters and, 6, 144, 147, 156–157, 160–161, 161n2
Mopsik, Charles, 174
moral authority, 202
moral body, 117
moral relativism, 240
moral responsibility, 161, 317, 338, 364, 369, 375
  aesthetics and, 147
  ethical body and, 118
  freedom and, 169–170
moral terrorism, 216, 218
morality, 6–7, 47–48, 66–67, 203, 240, 340, 361, 377
  the holy and, 243, 296
  humanity and, 250
  without justice, 370
  monsters and, 145
  religion and, 174–175, 203–204
  science and, 106
  Spinoza on, 175
  totality and, 244–245
Morgan, Michael, 41
mortality, 118–119, 218–219, 261
Moses, Robert, 56
Moyn, Samuel, 295
multiplicity, 249
musicality, 95

Muslims, 127, 136–139
mysticism, Jewish, 72–73, 174

Naess, Arne, 173
Nancy, Jean-Luc, 230
naturalism, 204
Nausea (Sartre), 310
Nazi Germany, Nazism and, 128–130, 222, 226, 237–238, 272
Neely, Sol, 41
Nefesh Ha-Hayym (Volozhin), 174
negation, 305–307, 310–311
negative freedom, 193–194
Negri, Antonio, 176, 375
neighbors, love of, 68, 72, 174
Nemo, Philippe, 225
neuter, 19
neutrality, 55–57, 340, 364
New, Melvyn, 41
New Talmudic Readings (Levinas), 38
Nicomachean Ethics (Aristotle), 183
Nietzsche, Friedrich, 72, 98–99, 188, 240–241, 245, 369
nihilism, 99, 219, 224, 230–231, 240
Ninety-five Poems and Hymns by Judah Halevi (Rosenzweig), 41
non-adult religion, 324, 327–330
nonindifference, 112, 369
nonneutrality, technological, 55–57
nonsense, 81, 84–85, 87, 90–91, 93n42, 99–101
non-truth of being, 78–79
nonverbal communication, 115–116, 118, 350, 372
non-violent violence, 275
North America, Levinas in, 31–42
Notebooks During Captivity (Levinas), 101–102
nothingness, 8n2, 92n30, 101, 228, 234n40, 306, 311–312
noumena-phenomen relations, 86

obedience, 114, 175, 191
objective order, 1, 110
objectivity, 86, 306
objects, 21–22, 85–86, 159, 318–319
Of God Who Comes to Mind (Levinas), 13, 16, 242–243
On Escape (Levinas), 1, 5, 14, 22
On God Who Comes to Mind (Levinas), 22
"On Maurice Blanchot" (Levinas), 146
one-for-the-other, 15, 23–24, 119–120, 257, 285, 287
one-way communication, 114
ontological event, 1–2, 4, 78, 81–83
ontologism, 1–2, 14–15
"Ontology and Ethics" (Bouckaert), 35
order, 86, 209, 211, 212n10
  meaning and, 245–247
  moral, 207–208
  sociopolitical, 271–277, 282
The Origin of the Other (Moyn), 295
original language, 116, 372
the Other, 2–4, 27n3, 207, 234n40, 300–304, 331n16, 349–350
  alterity of, 101, 161, 209, 220–221, 224, 248–249, 279, 302
  Badiou on, 216–217, 225
  breaking of rhythm by, 98
  Buber and, 339
  as divine, 242
  ethics of the, 219–221, 226–227, 229–230
  face of the, 73, 152–154, 326
  freedom and, 176
  otherness of the, 295
  proximity to, 115
  Spinoza on, 182
other-in-the-same, 119–121
otherwise than being, 1, 13–17, 21, 67–68, 117, 245, 367, 369
  enjoyment and, 24

  ethical commitment and, 26–27
  rhythm and, 99
Otherwise Than Being or Beyond Essence (Levinas), 5, 8n2, 13, 33–35, 95, 298, 362, 368
  Cohen, R., 65
  ethical subjectivity in, 22
  exegesis in, 114
  on exoticism of art, 88
  il y a in, 93n42
  language in, 107–108
  maternity in, 119
  subjectivity in, 15
Otto, Rudolf, 295, 313n12
Out of Control (Cohen, R.), 42, 128, 169–176, 182, 238
"Oval Portrait" (Poe), 156–157
Ovid, 159

paganism, 325
paintings, 144, 146, 151
Paradiso-Michau, Michael, 41
Paris, France, 5, 33, 368
Parmenides, 61, 307–308
participation, 80, 84–85, 91n15
Pascal, Blaise, 311
pastness, 210, 265
Penn State, 5, 32–34, 53–54, 362–363
Peperzak, Adriaan, 35
persistence, 193–195
pessimism, 276
la petite bonté (small goodness), 7, 67, 271–272, 275–282, 371–372
phenomenology, 4, 7–8, 12, 22, 238m 63, 363, 376–377
  "being-to-the-world," 19–21
  exegesis and, 107–108
  existential, 35
  French, 17, 318, 321
  German, 64
  Levinas and, 35–39, 57, 65, 115, 147, 238–240

phenomenology *(continued)*
  linguistic, 345
  realist, 318, 321–322
  of Sartre, 302–303
  of Spinoza, 185, 193
  transcendence and, 317–322
Philip III (King), 127
"Philosophical Determination of Culture" (Levinas), 88–89
philosophy. *See specific topics*
The Philosophy of Spinoza (Wolfson), 170
Pickering, Andrew, 55
The Picture of Dorian Gray (Wilde), 159
pietà, 136–137
The Pillowman (play), 160–161
pity, 175, 183–184, 187–189
Plato, 67, 84, 91n15, 112, 146, 206–208, 238
  on consciousness, 83
  Timaeus by, 79, 82–84
  on truth, 62, 110
Plotinus, 300, 307
Poe, Edgar Allan, 95–97, 103n7, 145, 156–157
poetry, 89, 95–97, 109, 342
Poleshchuk, Irina, 371–372
Political Treatise (Spinoza), 171
politics, 56, 59n13, 201–202, 212n10, 229–230
positivism, 32
post-Holocaust theology, 7
postmodernity, postmodernism and, 215, 230–231, 232n1, 366, 368, 372
  Cohen, R., opposing, 146
  suffering and, 337
  values and, 261–262
postphenomenology, 58
post-postmodernism, 215–217, 229–232

poststructuralism, 18, 32, 36–39
post-traumatic stress disorder (PTSD), 345
postwar philosophy, 32
pragmatism, 32
Praxiteles, 159
The Primitive Soul (Lévy-Bruhl), 98
primordial event, 2
prisoners-of-war, 344–345
prisons, "Supermax" maximum security, 341–342
promise, 248–249
pronunciation, 115
Proper Names (Levinas), 88, 93, 146
proprioception, 186
Proust, Marcel, 96, 101
providence, 249–250
proximity, 108–116, 118, 120
  consciousness and, 115–116
psyche, 121
PTSD. *See* post-traumatic stress disorder
pure communication, 116
Pushkin, Alexander, 149
Putnam, Hillary, 40

Quakerism, 299

racism, 68
radical responsibility, 105, 273
Rakover, Yosel, 247
Rami (asylum-seeking refugee), 344, 346–348
rational theology, 314n26, 317, 326, 376
rationalism, 6, 63, 85, 170, 182–187, 193, 275
rationality, 57, 61, 65, 83, 105–106, 251, 326
Rawls, John, 23
ready-to-hand *(Zu-handenheit)*, 258, 377

real transcendence, 317–318, 320–323, 325, 327–330
realism, 20, 231, 272
realist phenomenology, 318, 321–322
"Reality and Its Shadow" (Levinas), 77–81, 87–88, 90, 92n35, 146–147, 371
reason, 79–82, 84, 87–88, 108, 197, 225, 241, 245
reciprocity, 11, 85
Refugee Convention (1951), 340, 356n20
refugees, refugee crisis and, 8, 338–344, 346–354, 355n9, 356nn19–20, 374
refusal, 350
relativism, moral, 240
religion, 4, 6–7, 237–238, 332n49, 353. *See also specific religions*
  adult, 8, 176, 317, 322, 325–330, 372–373, 376, 378–379
  conversion and, 127, 136–137, 139
  ethical relation and, 298
  ethics and, 224–225
  freedom of, 170
  genuine, 8, 317, 324–325
  morality and, 174–175, 203–204
  non-adult, 324, 327–330
  paganism and, 325
  politics and, 201–202
Religion within the Limits of Reason Alone (Kant), 379
religiosity, 327
representation, 119, 145
responsibility, 243–245, 265, 301, 319–321, 361–362, 370–371, 379
  ethical, 25, 50, 146, 175, 275, 327, 337, 346, 372, 376
  etymological origin of, 185
  face-to-face, 271, 276
  for-the-other, 89, 106, 130, 172, 257, 259–260, 263, 273

freedom and, 243, 251
individual, 193
infinite, 102, 243, 258, 265, 323–324
legal, 338
mercy and, 133
moral, 118, 147, 161, 169, 317, 338, 364, 369, 375
Spinozist, 172
responsible humanism, 372–373
responsiveness, 107, 121, 230–231, 343, 369–370
ressentiment, 241
Rey, Jean-François, 176
rhythm, 6, 84–85, 95–102, 369
Ricœur, Paul, 18, 338 59
Ricoeur As Another (Cohen, R.), 41
rights, of man, 22, 216, 218–219
Robbins, Jill, 39
romanticism, 56–57, 65, 184
Rosenzweig, Franz, 19, 40, 239, 261, 295, 298, 367
  Cohen, R., 38, 71–73
  on time, 264
Rozenberg, Jacques, 6, 374

sacralization, 274–275
sacrament, 317, 323, 327–328, 333n64
the sacred, 243, 295–297, 308–309, 313n13, 323–324, 327–328
sacrifice, 257, 260–261, 263–264
Saint Genet (Sartre), 310
Salanskis, Jean-Michel, 4–5, 366–367
Saldukaityte, Jolanta, 6, 366
sameness, 243, 302, 318, 379
Santos, Fernanda, 338–339
Sarafian, Deran, 261
Sartre, Jean-Paul, 7–8, 8n1, 92n35, 97, 373
  Augustinian ontology of, 305
  Cohen, R., on, 293–294, 300–304
  on freedom, 310–312

Satan, 293, 310–312
Saussure, Ferdinand de, 372
saying-said, structure, 109–112
Scheler, Max, 318, 321–322, 328
Schelling, F. W. J., 145
Scholem, Gershom, 19, 69n6
science, 55–58, 78–79, 82–84, 87–91, 106
secular ethics, 324
secular Judaism, 170
security technology, 342
segregation, 345
Sein, 12
Sein und Zeit (Heidegger), 258–260, 262, 265
self-alienation, 118
self-consciousness, 64, 300, 361
self-enclosure, 148, 150, 160
selfhood, 296
selfish, 298–299
self-love, 325
self-satisfaction, 148, 162n16, 379
self-sensing, 186, 190–191, 319, 321, 327, 330
self-separation, 189–190
self-sufficiency, 14
Selinger, Evan, 55
semantic responsibility, 25
sensance, 25
senseless kindness, 127–129, 131–135, 139, 182, 198n2
senses, 25, 79–80, 82, 85–91, 99–100, 372
　meaning and, 107, 116
　totality and, 189–190
sensibility, 116–123, 188
　bodily, 319, 321, 326
　ethical, 340–343
　of experience, 111–112
　of listening, 107
　maternal, 119–124
sentimentality, 370

separation, 15, 109–110, 172, 186–190
Sessions, Jeff, 201–202, 208, 211
Shabbat, 351–354
Shakespeare, William, 137–139
shame, 149, 303–304
Shankman, Steven, 6, 371
Shestov, Lev, 295
the Shoah. *See* the Holocaust
signification, 2–3, 102, 111–112, 119, 122
simulacrum, 150–151, 222, 224, 231
sin, 207–208, 293, 305, 310
singularity, 152–153, 346
small goodness (*la petite bonté*), 7, 67, 271–272, 275–282, 371–372
Smith, Michael, 262
socialist realism, 272
sociopolitical order, 271–277, 282
Socrates, 146, 362
solicitators, 24–26
the Sorbonne (University of Paris-Sorbonne), 5–6, 33, 131, 169, 368
soul, 82–83, 286, 338
Southland, Christopher L., 368
sovereignty, 175, 202–203, 205–210
Spain, 19, 127–128, 131–136, 371
Spencer, Mark, 8, 376–378
Spinoza, Baruch, 6–7, 238, 240, 374–375
　on *conatus*, 171–172, 176, 183, 185, 187, 189–193, 195–198, 243
　on ethics, 171–172, 183
　on freedom, 176, 185
　Levinas and, 169–176, 181–198
spiritualism, spirituality and, 17, 287, 323, 338
split consciousness, 67
stability, 155–156, 187–192
Stalinism, 7, 271–276, 282–284
Stambaugh, Joan, 262

the state, 136, 174–176, 201–211, 276–277, 370
Stern der Erlösung (Rosenzweig), 367
Steven, Richard, 41
Stony Brook, 5, 33, 53–55, 358, 363
structuralism, 17, 32, 44n17
subjectivity, 4, 12, 14–16, 281–282, 333n64, 372
  art and, 86–87
  embodied, 117–118
  liberation from, 109
  maternal, 119–121
  of the Other, 304
  Sartre and, 306
  truth and, 223
subject-language, 223–224
suffering, 102, 293, 307, 361, 374, 377
  aestheticism and, 84
  Cohen, R., on, 210, 337–338, 346
  compassion and, 113
  embodiment and, 117
  ethical responsibility and, 50
  as evil, 344–346
  humiliation and, 182–183
  images of, 149
  innocence and, 250–251
  Judaism and, 337–338
  meaningless, 325–326, 337–338, 340, 341–346
  of others, 186
  preventing, 210
  righteousness and, 246–247
  Stalinism and, 272
  the state and, 211
  theodicy and, 240, 329–330
  useless, 241
  vulnerability and, 191
Sugarman, Richard, 7, 375–376
SUNY Buffalo, 41, 239
supernatural, 323
surveillance, 346, 348
survival, 68

survivor guilt, 345
Syria, 355n9

tactility, 115
the Talmud, 63, 66, 114, 203, 206, 243–249, 251–252
  interpretative tradition of, 50, 57
Taylor, Charles, 41
technology, 342
  ethics and, 364–365
  as nonneutral, 55–57
  philosophy of, 5, 55–58, 363–365
"Technology" (Cohen, R.), 55
Teitelbaum, Joel, 241
temptation, 149–150
terrorism, moral, 216, 218
theodicy, 7, 50, 293–294, 297–298, 325
  Auschwitz as the end of, 284
  coined by Leibnitz, 240
  evil and, 307
  suffering and, 240, 329–330
theological turn, 318, 321
theology, 7–8, 11, 20, 242–243, 249–250, 329
  Cohen, R., on, 294–300
  rational, 314n26, 317, 326, 376
  of Sartre, 293–294, 305–312
The Theory of Intuition in Husserl's Phenomenology (Levinas), 38, 92n17, 241
there is. See *il y a*
third person, 12
Tillich, Paul, 294
Timaeus (Plato), 79, 82–84
time, temporality and, 261, 265, 347, 352–353, 356n31
  art and, 156–159
  Cohen, R., on, 122, 157–158, 210
  embodiment and, 118
  of ethics, 122
  infinite, 173, 251, 287

time, temporality and *(continued)*
    intervals and, 156–157
    the Other and, 73
    promises and, 248–249
    rhythm and, 95, 100–101
    Rosenzweig on, 264
    the trace and, 247–248
Time and the Other (Levinas), 34, 248
Time in the Philosophy of Emmanuel Levinas (Cohen, R.), 35
The Time of the Nations (Levinas), 107
To Die For (1989 film), 261
To Die For (1995 film), 261–262
togetherness, 230
the Torah, 238, 243–244, 284, 324, 339–340, 343, 355nn12–13
    laws of, 251
    Levinas on, 206, 247
total war, 272
totalitarianism, 55, 229, 274, 276, 279–280
totality, 7, 67, 116, 294, 297–298, 300, 305
    alterity and, 209–210
    of being, 3, 210, 229, 299, 303
    morality and, 244–245
    sense and, 189–190
    Spinozist, 176, 186–187, 192
    violence of, 229
Totality and Infinity (Levinas), 1–2, 6, 13–16, 95–96, 229, 244, 367, 377
    English translation of, 34–35
    enjoyment in, 148
    ethical exegesis in, 111–113
    ethical subjectivity in, 22
    Grossman, V., and, 279
    Nietzsche and, 240
    rhythm in, 98–99
totalizing exclusivism, 299
touch, 115–116
the trace, 100, 247–249

Tractatus Theologico-Politicus (Spinoza), 174–176
transcendence, 1–3, 27n3, 240–242, 249–252, 307
    absolute, 112
    Cohen, R., on, 66, 112
    ethical exegesis and, 116
    immanence *vs.*, 227
    of intentionality, 120
    liberation of, 190
    maternity and, 119
    meaning and, 153
    the Other and, 216, 229
    rationalism and, 63
    real, 317–318, 320–323, 325, 327–330
    Spinoza and, 171–172
    the trace and, 100, 247–248
"The Transcendence of Words" (Levinas), 146
translation, 6, 50, 169, 224, 262, 342
    English, 33–35, 38
    Japanese, 95
    Latin in, 133
trauma, 344–345, 351–352
Trump, Donald, 201
truth, 24, 63, 67, 82–84, 88, 297, 307–308
    Badiou on, 215–216, 218–219, 221–224, 227, 229, 231, 233n21
    Plato on, 62, 110
    proximity and, 116
    science and, 106
Tsevi, Sabbatai, 170–171
Turkle, Sherry, 56
tyranny, 370

ulteriority, 193
uncanny, 6, 156–157, 161, 164n65
    art and the, 145, 147–150, 156, 159
understanding, 21, 107

universalism, exclusive, 325, 329
universality, 107, 277
University of Vermont, 239
unknowability, 89
unlimited forgiveness, 55
unspeakability, infinite, 110
utilitarianism, 172
utopia, 56–57, 273

values, 20, 171–172, 175, 182, 208, 261–262, 322, 340
vampires, 261
Van Sant, Gus, 261
the Vatican, 346–347
Venus, 155
verbal discourse, 115
verbs, 96–97, 128
Villawood Detention Centre, Sydney, 344, 346–348, 351–353
"Violence and Metaphysics" (Derrida), 5, 13
visa applications, 346–348
the void, 228, 231, 234n40
Volozhin, Rav Hayym de, 174
vorhanden ("present-at-hand"), 377
vulnerability, 117, 120, 123, 261, 273–274, 276–277, 341
 alterity and, 153
 empathy and, 183–184
 humanism and, 181
 language and, 107
 negative freedom and, 195

Nietzsche on, 188–189
 rationalism and, 182
 self-sensing and, 186
 suffering and, 191

Wahl, Jean, 295
Wainer, Devorah, 374
Walzer, Michael, 209
Washington Post, 201
water, 192–193
waves (imagery), 95–96, 150, 162n25
Weil, Simone, 17
Whitehead, Alfred North, 299
Wiener, Norbert, 55
Wild, John D., 237
Wilde, Oscar, 159
Winner, Langdon, 56
witness, bearing, 102, 287, 338–339, 341–344, 346–354, 356n33, 374
Wittgenstein, Ludwig, 61–63, 66, 69n4
Wolfson, Harry A., 170
World War II, 99–102, 128–129, 344–345
Worms, Frédéric, 17–18, 367
Wyschogrod, Edith, 34–35, 38–39, 44n20, 151, 367–368

xenophobia, 127, 371

Zionism, 203, 241
Zu-handenheit (ready-to-hand), 258, 377

www.ingramcontent.com/pod-product-compliance
Lightning Source LLC
Chambersburg PA
CBHW020120240426
43673CB00038B/537